PUZZLED

A memoir of growing up with OCD

Pan Cooke

Rocky Pond Books

Please note that this book contains content about disordered eating.

ROCKY POND BOOKS
An imprint of Penguin Random House LLC, New York

First published in the United States of America by Rocky Pond Books, an imprint of Penguin Random House LLC, 2024

Visit us online at PenguinRandomHouse.com.

Library of Congress Cataloging-in-Publication Data is available.

ISBN 9780593615621 (pbk) 10 9 8 7 6 5 4 3 2 1

ISBN 9780593615614 (hc) 10 9 8 7 6 5 4 3 2 1

Manufactured in China

TOPL

Design by Cerise Steel
Text set in Hynings Handwriting

This is a work of nonfiction. Some names and identifying details have been changed.

To Erica

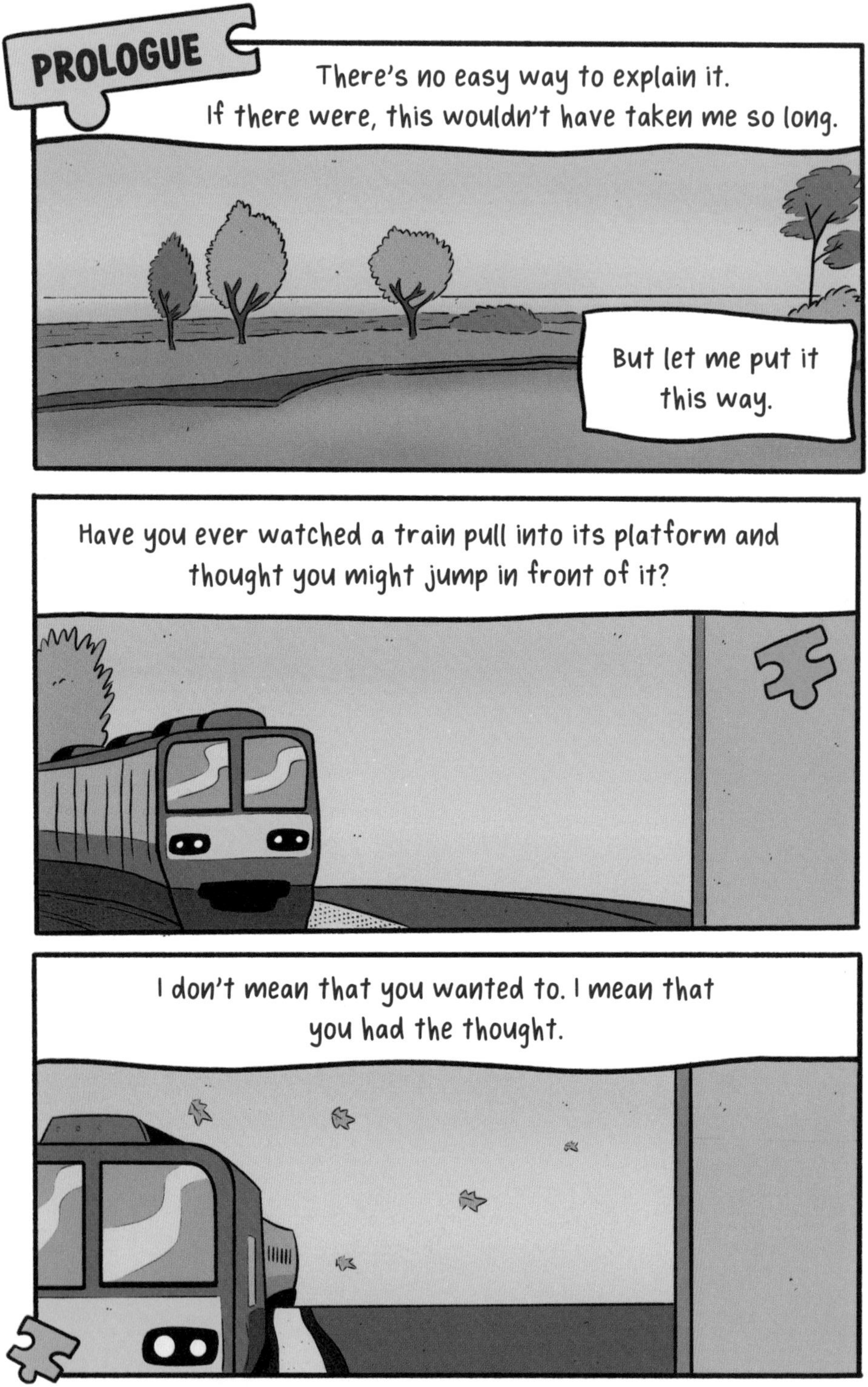
PROLOGUE
There's no easy way to explain it.
If there were, this wouldn't have taken me so long.
But let me put it this way.
Have you ever watched a train pull into its platform and thought you might jump in front of it?
I don't mean that you wanted to. I mean that you had the thought.

Or how about, have you ever knocked on wood to prevent something bad from happening?

Admit it. Odds are, you probably have.

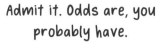

Stuff like that is surprisingly normal.

Until it's not.

But I'm getting ahead of myself. I should probably start at the beginning.

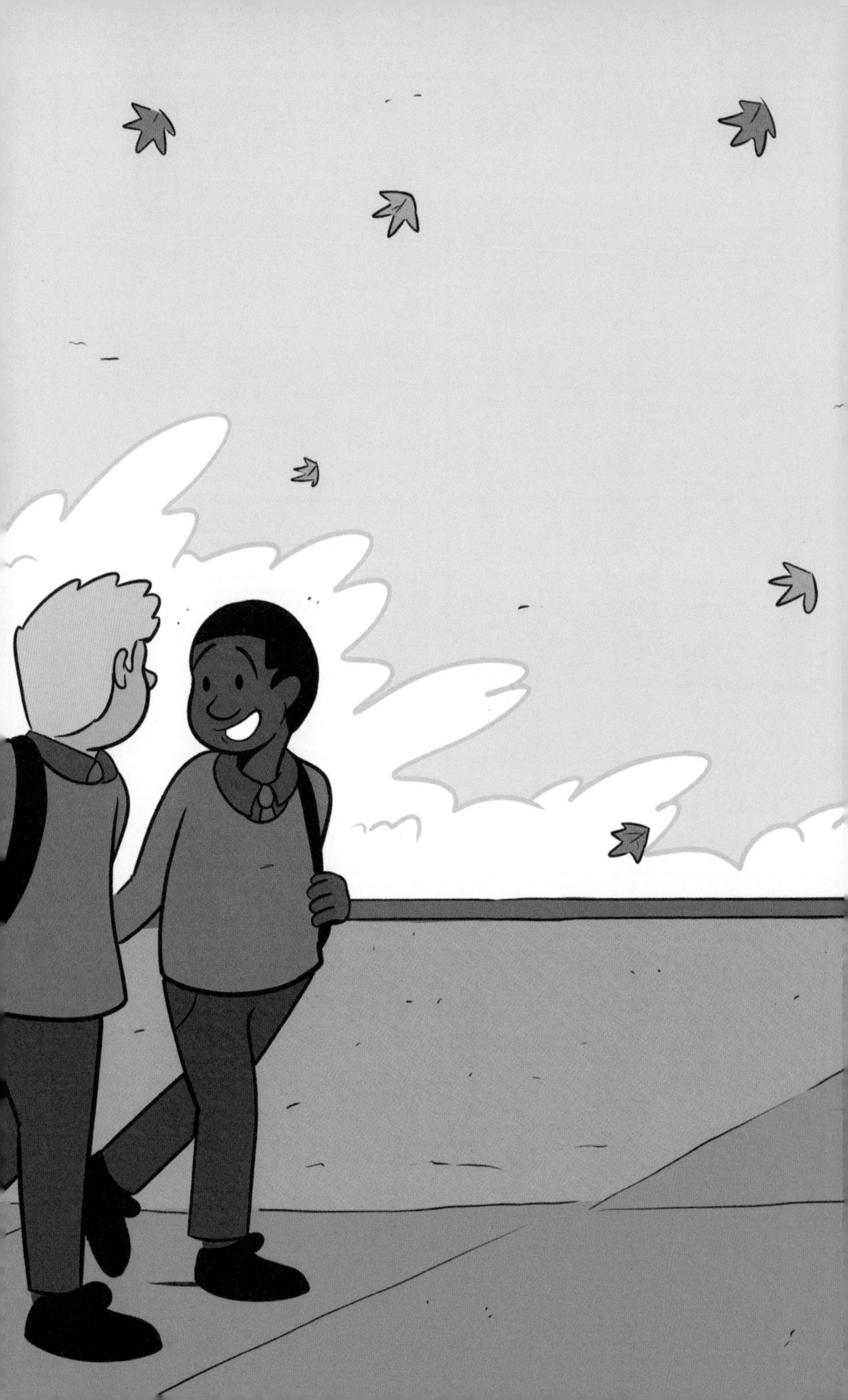

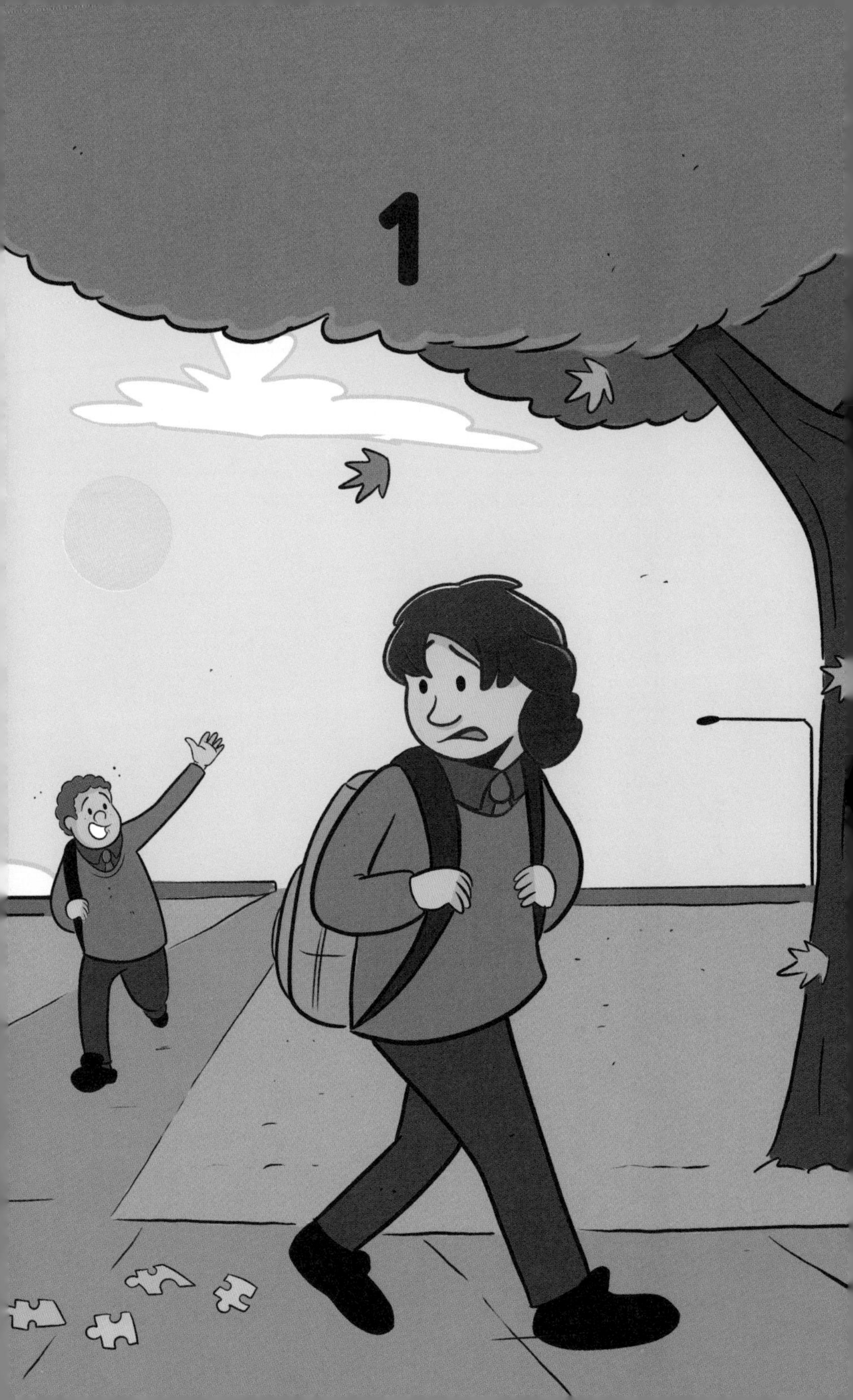
1

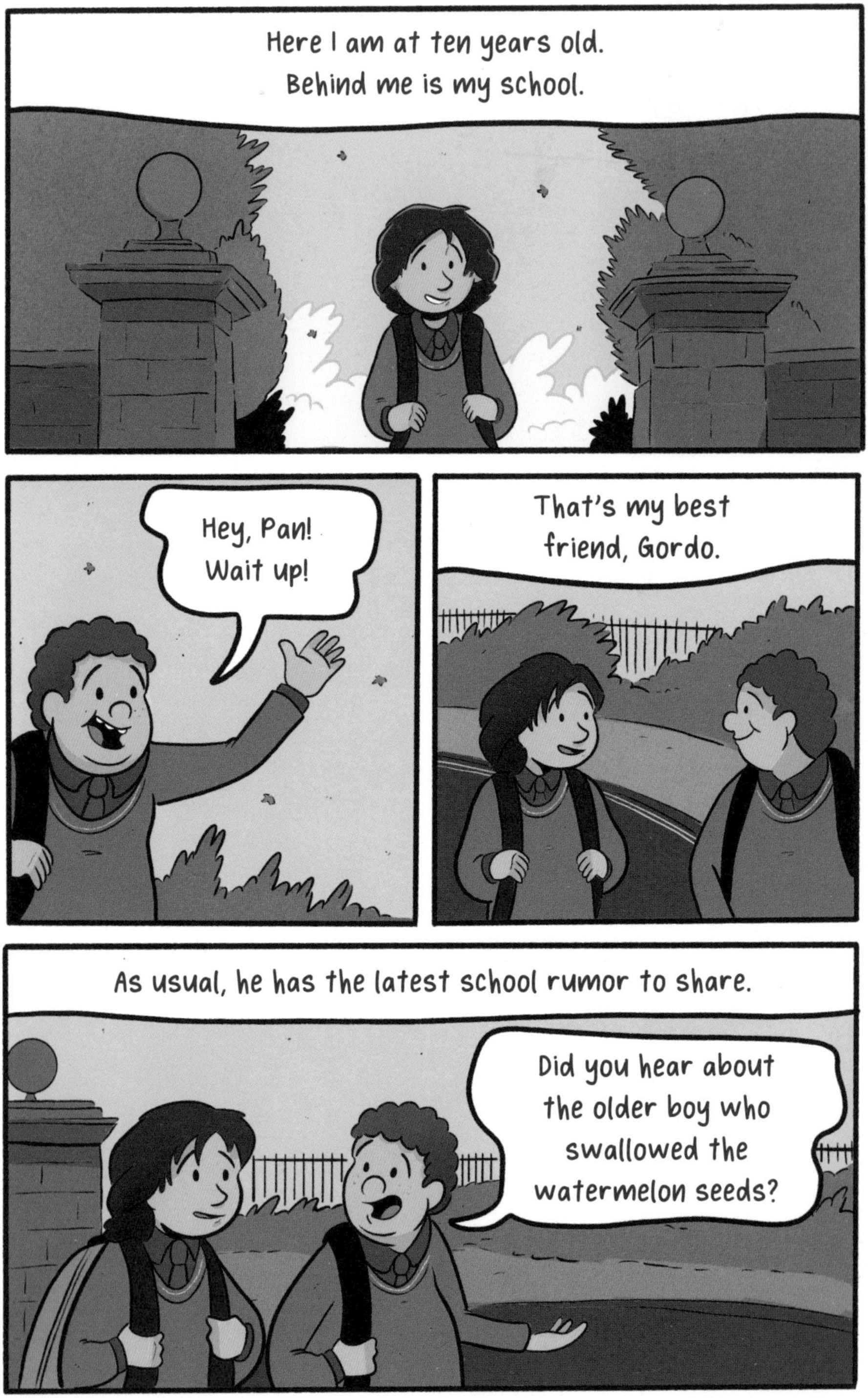
Here I am at ten years old.
Behind me is my school.
Hey, Pan!
Wait up!
That's my best
friend, Gordo.
As usual, he has the latest school rumor to share.
Did you hear about
the older boy who
swallowed the
watermelon seeds?

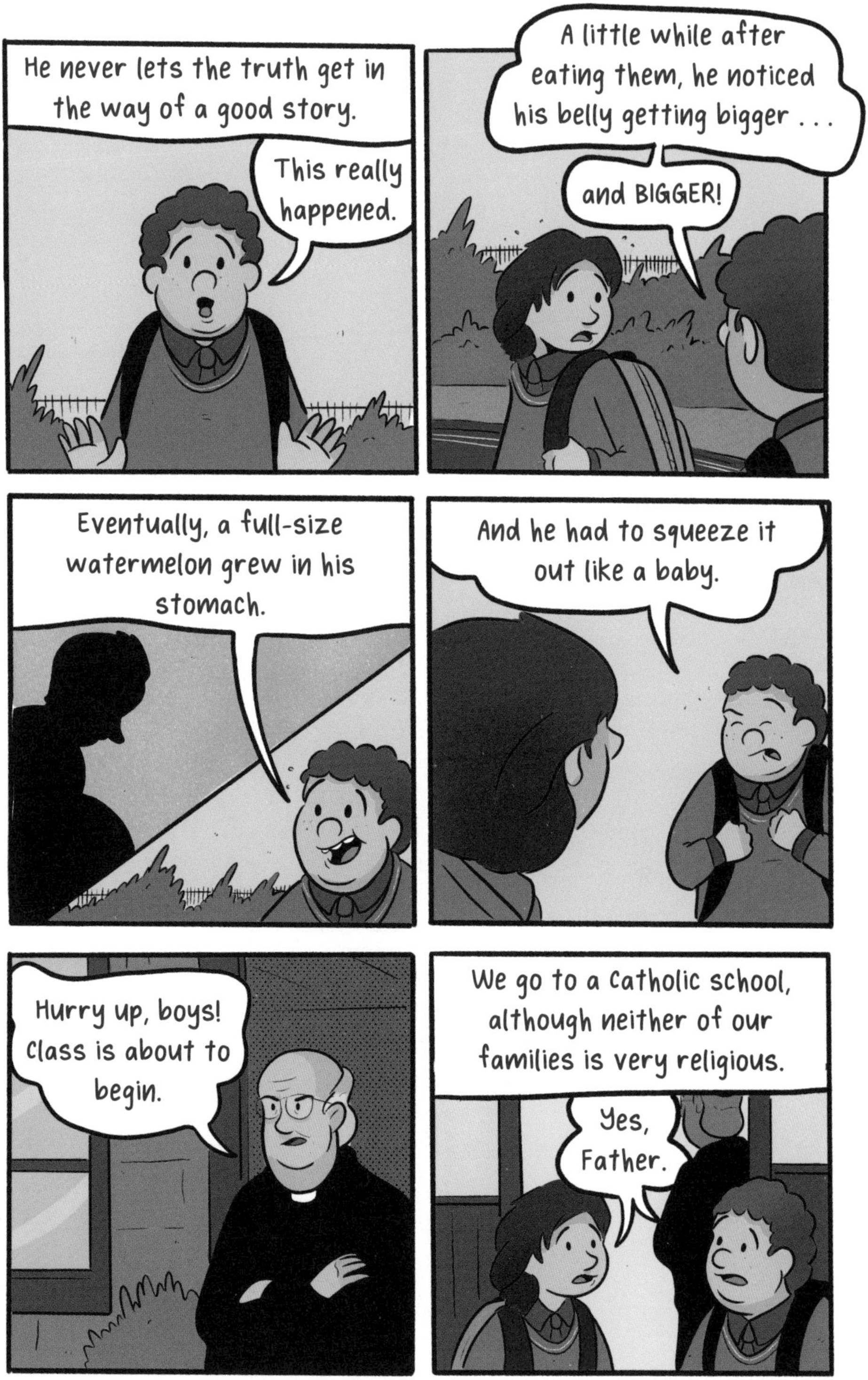
He never lets the truth get in the way of a good story.
This really happened.
A little while after eating them, he noticed his belly getting bigger . . .
and BIGGER!
Eventually, a full-size watermelon grew in his stomach.
And he had to squeeze it out like a baby.
Hurry up, boys! Class is about to begin.
We go to a Catholic school, although neither of our families is very religious.
Yes, Father.

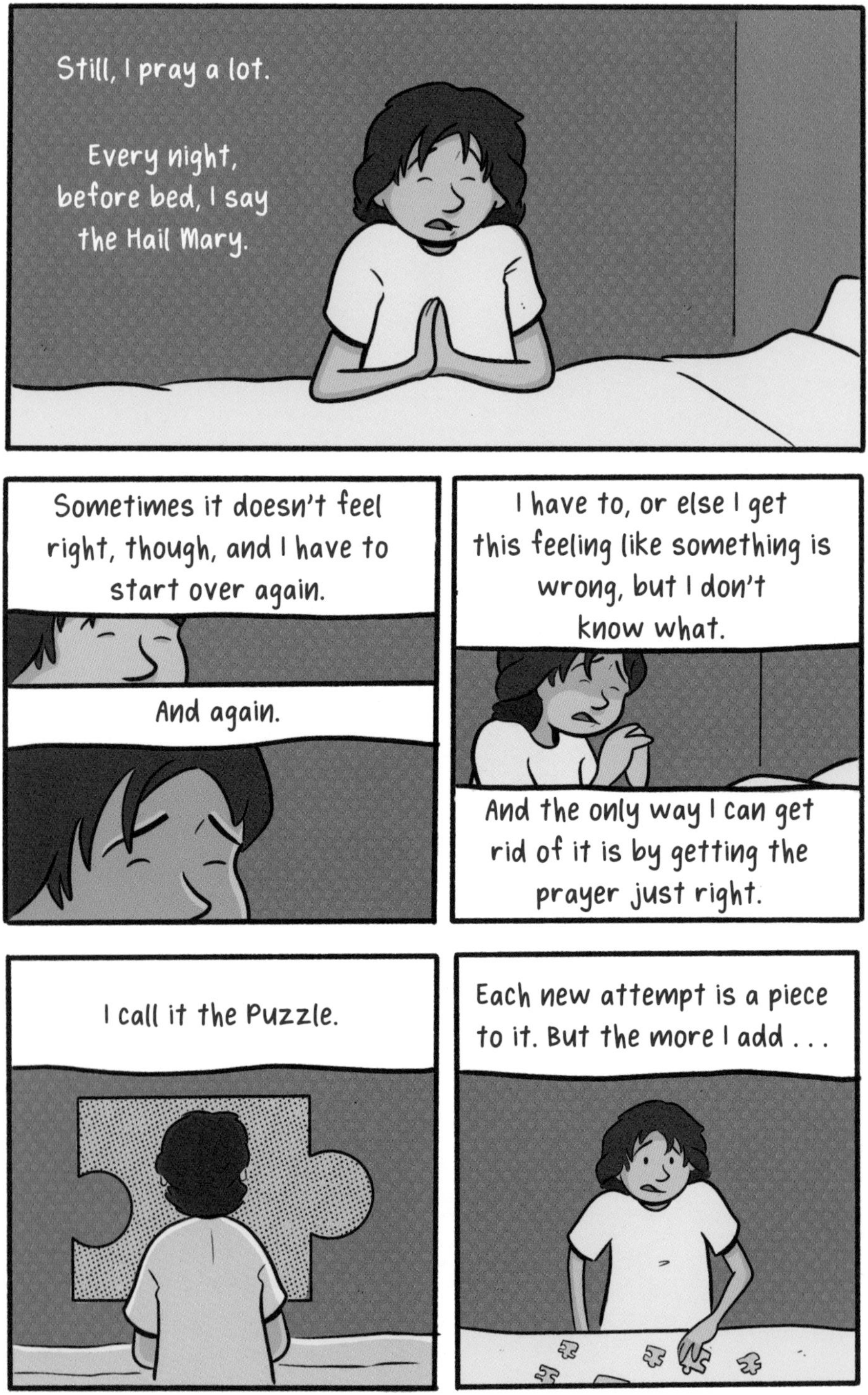
Still, I pray a lot.
Every night, before bed, I say the Hail Mary.
Sometimes it doesn't feel right, though, and I have to start over again.
And again.
I have to, or else I get this feeling like something is wrong, but I don't know what.
And the only way I can get rid of it is by getting the prayer just right.
I call it the Puzzle.
Each new attempt is a piece to it. But the more I add . . .

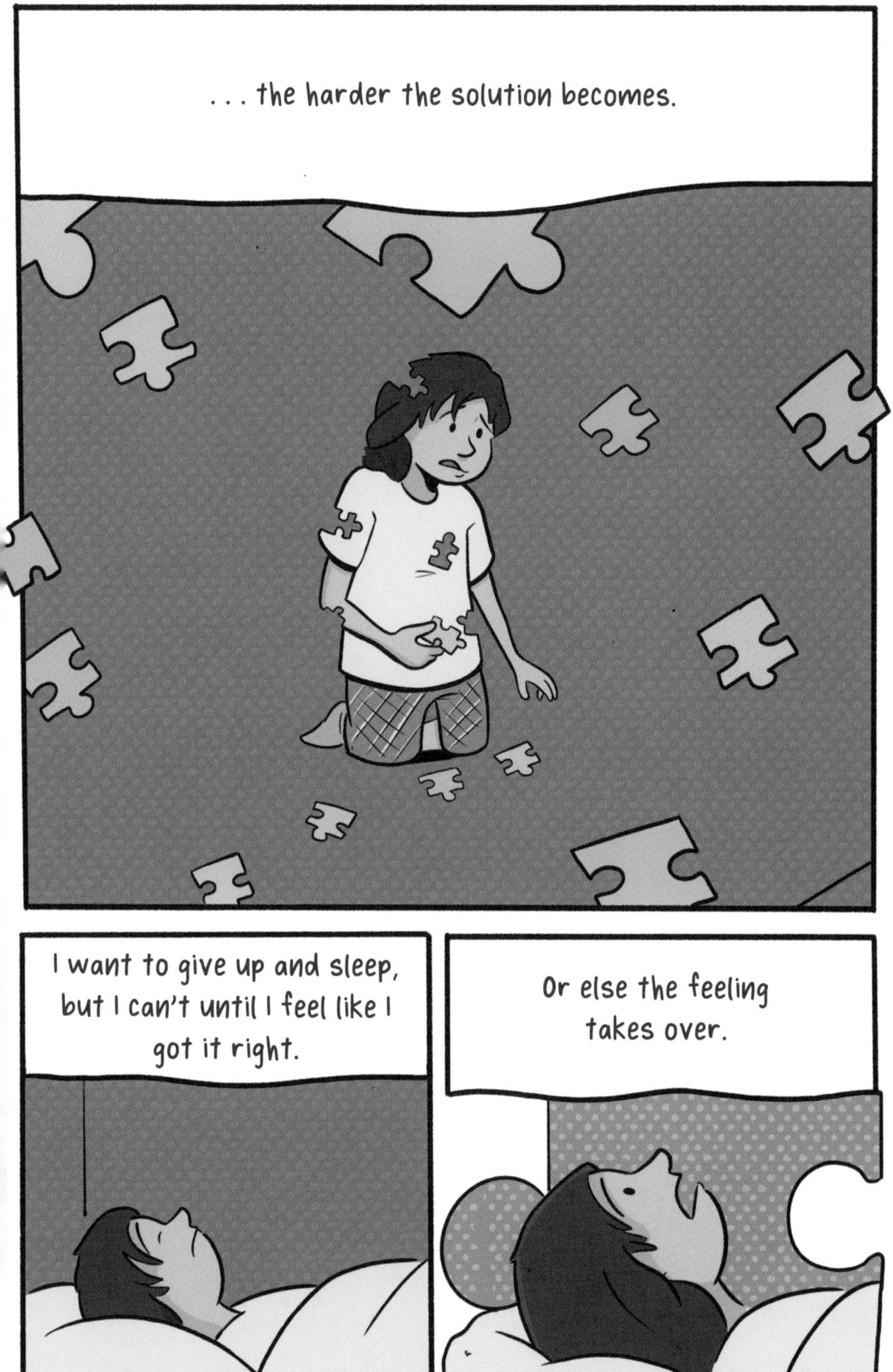
. . . the harder the solution becomes.
I want to give up and sleep, but I can't until I feel like I got it right.
Or else the feeling takes over.

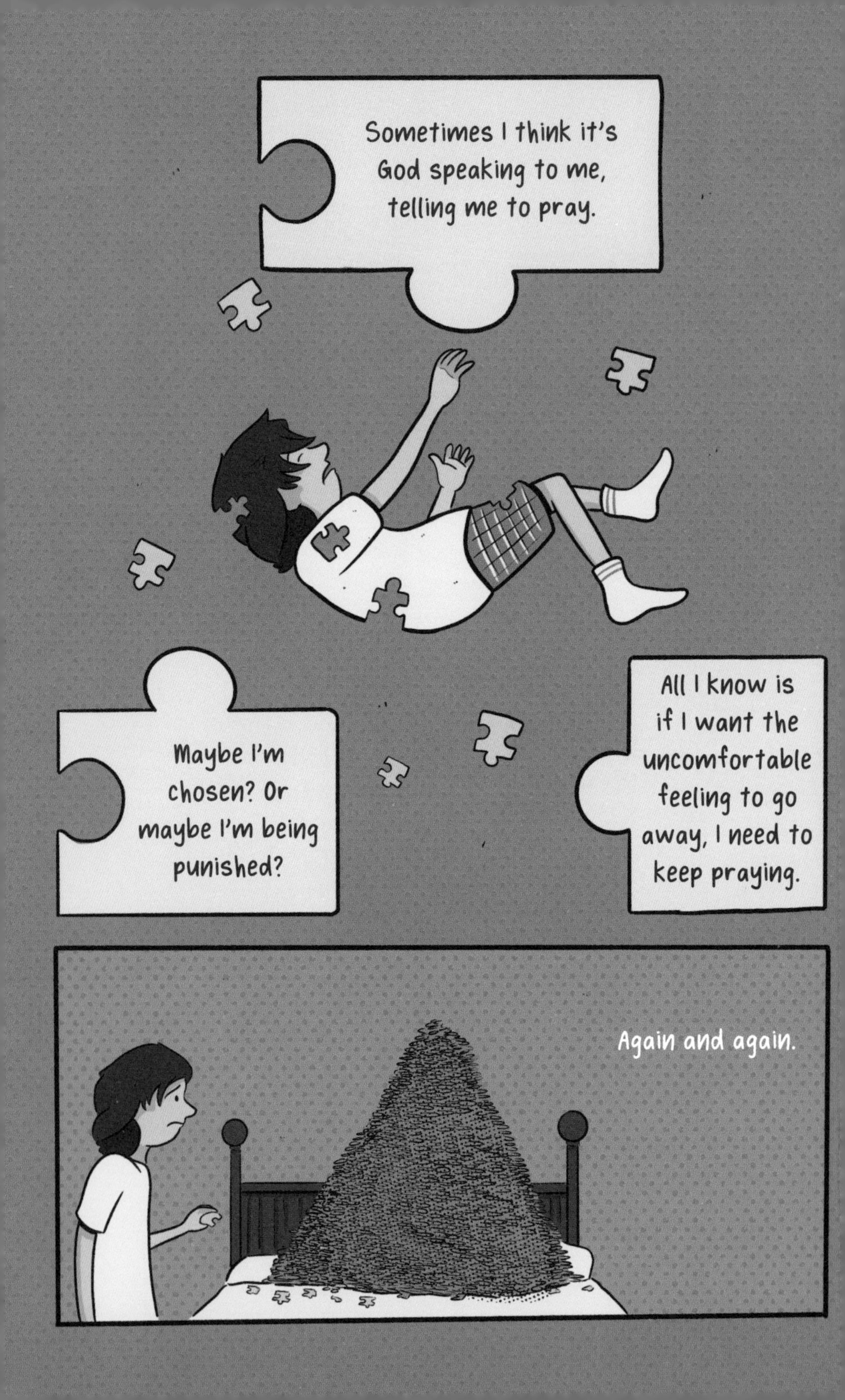
Sometimes I think it's God speaking to me, telling me to pray.
Maybe I'm chosen? Or maybe I'm being punished?
All I know is if I want the uncomfortable feeling to go away, I need to keep praying.
Again and again.

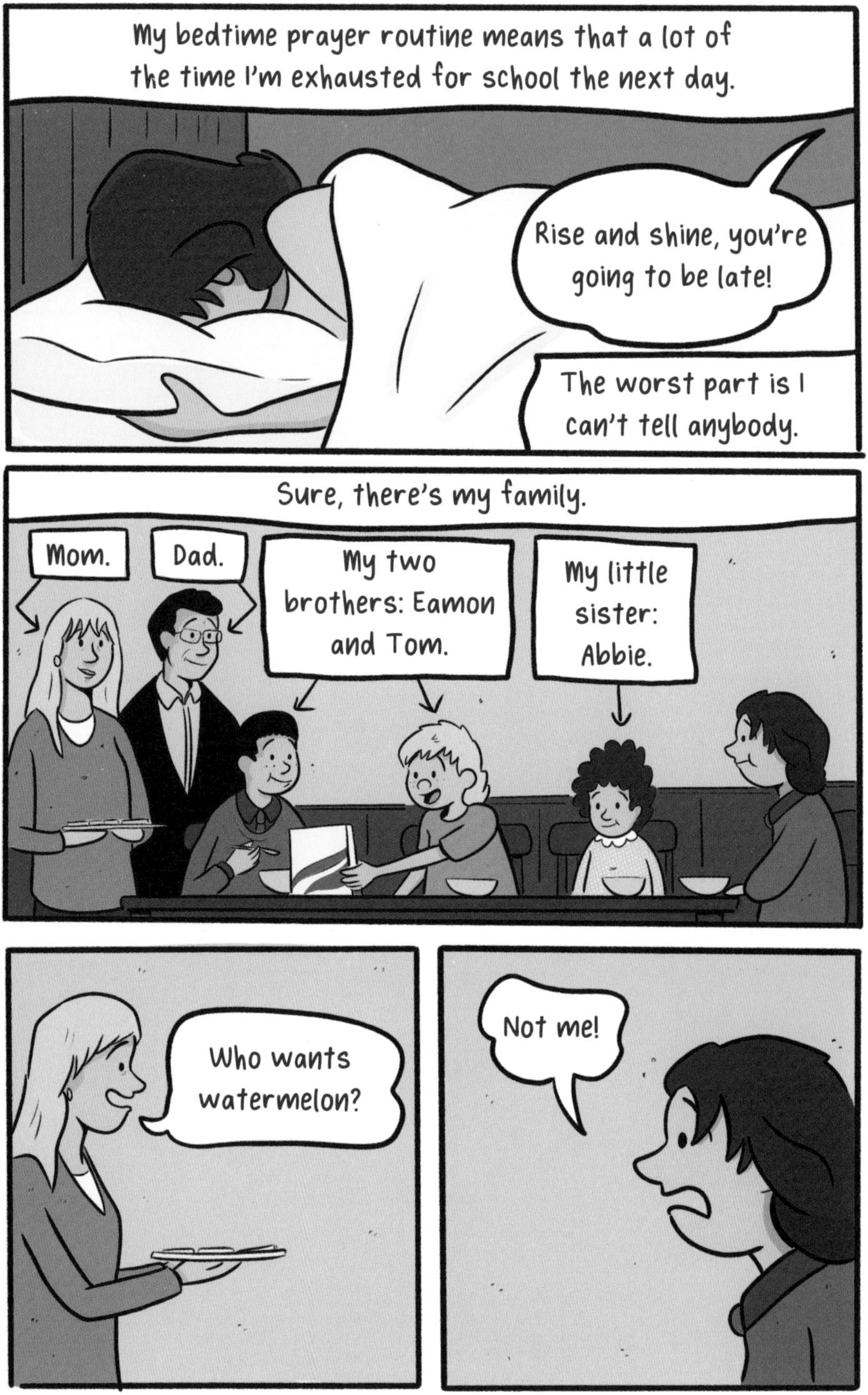
My bedtime prayer routine means that a lot of the time I'm exhausted for school the next day.
Rise and shine, you're going to be late!
The worst part is I can't tell anybody.
Sure, there's my family.
Mom.
Dad.
My two brothers: Eamon and Tom.
My little sister: Abbie.
Who wants watermelon?
Not me!

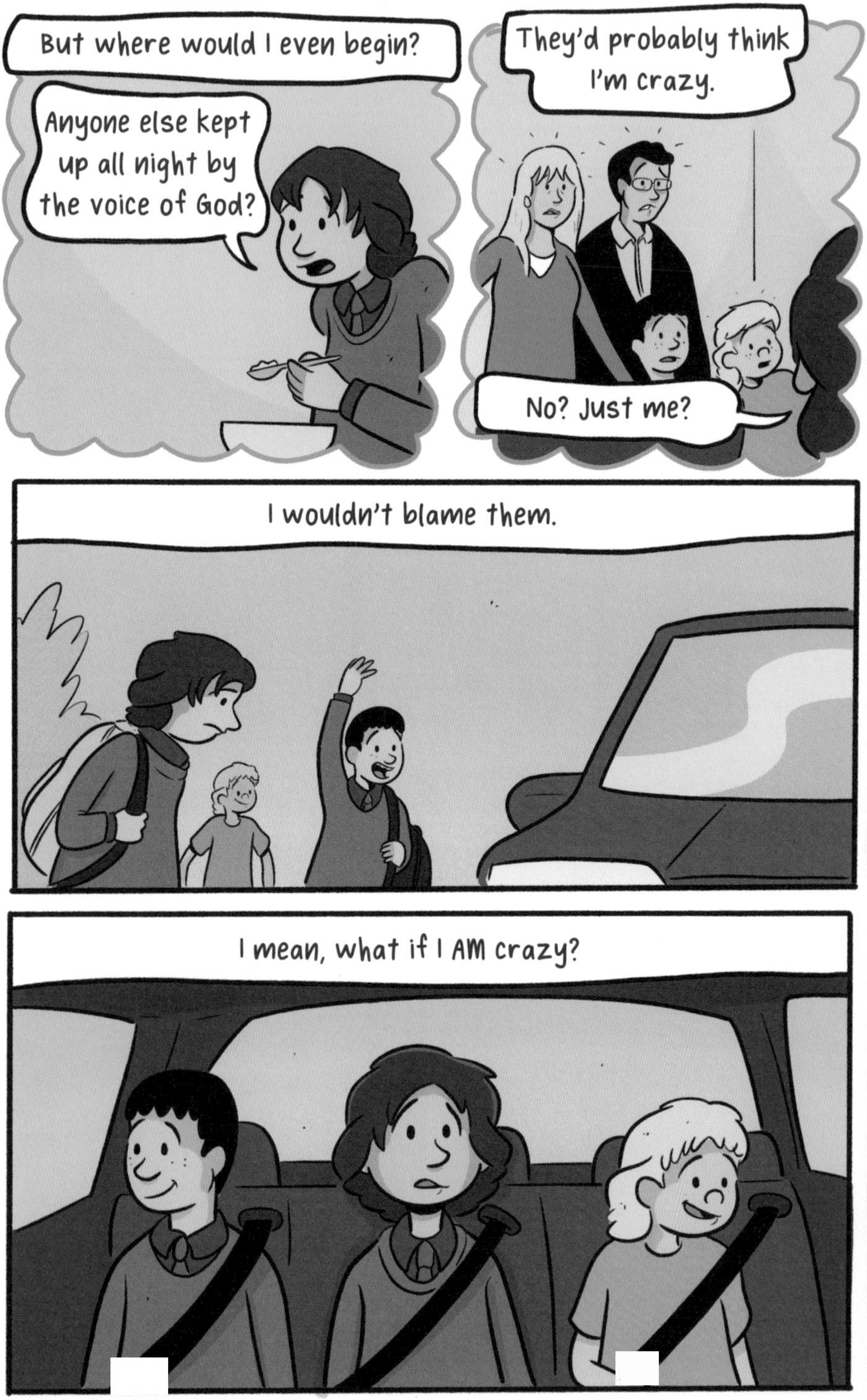
But where would I even begin?
Anyone else kept up all night by the voice of God?
They'd probably think I'm crazy.
No? Just me?
I wouldn't blame them.
I mean, what if I AM crazy?

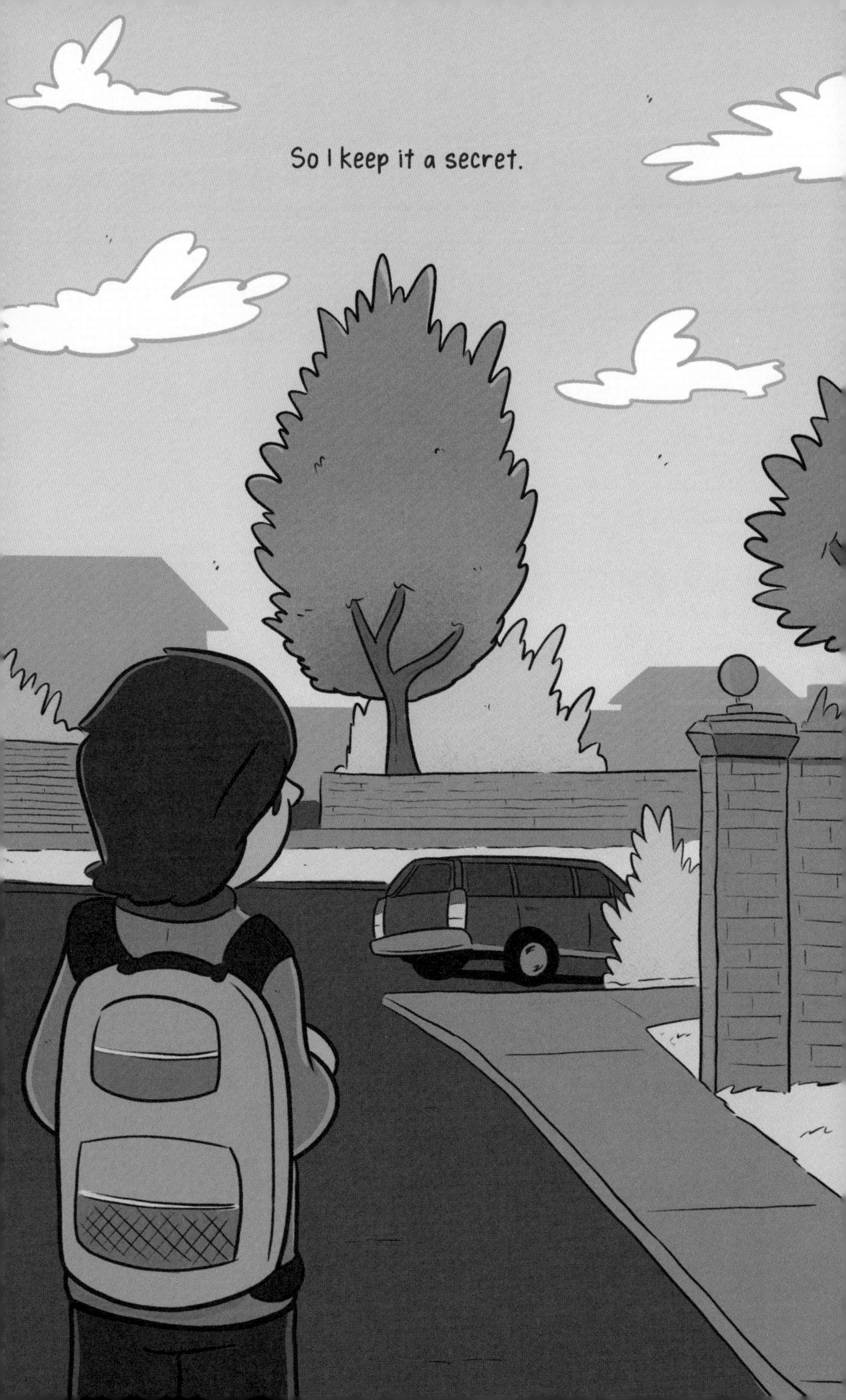
So I keep it a secret.

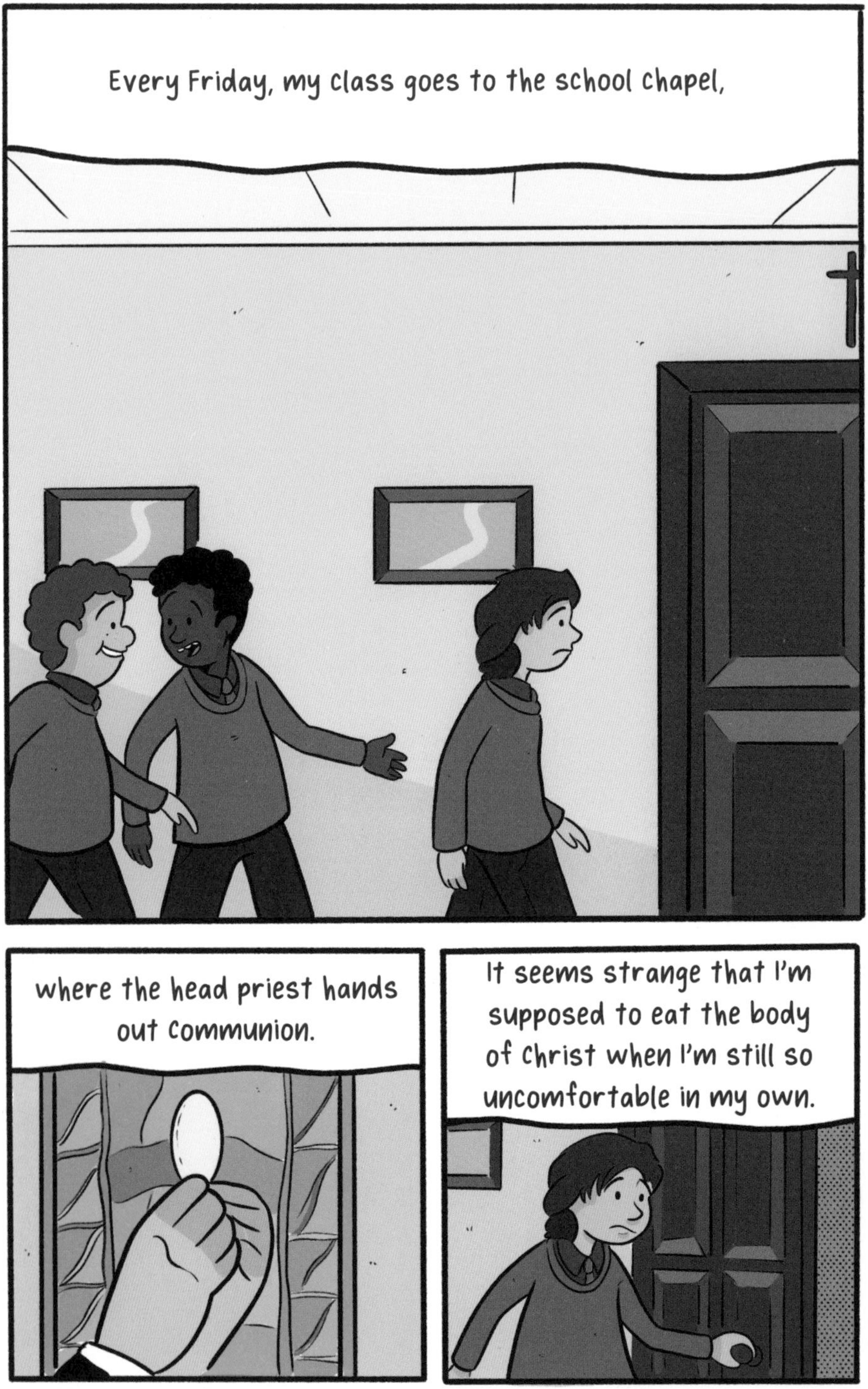
Every Friday, my class goes to the school chapel,
where the head priest hands out communion.
It seems strange that I'm supposed to eat the body of Christ when I'm still so uncomfortable in my own.

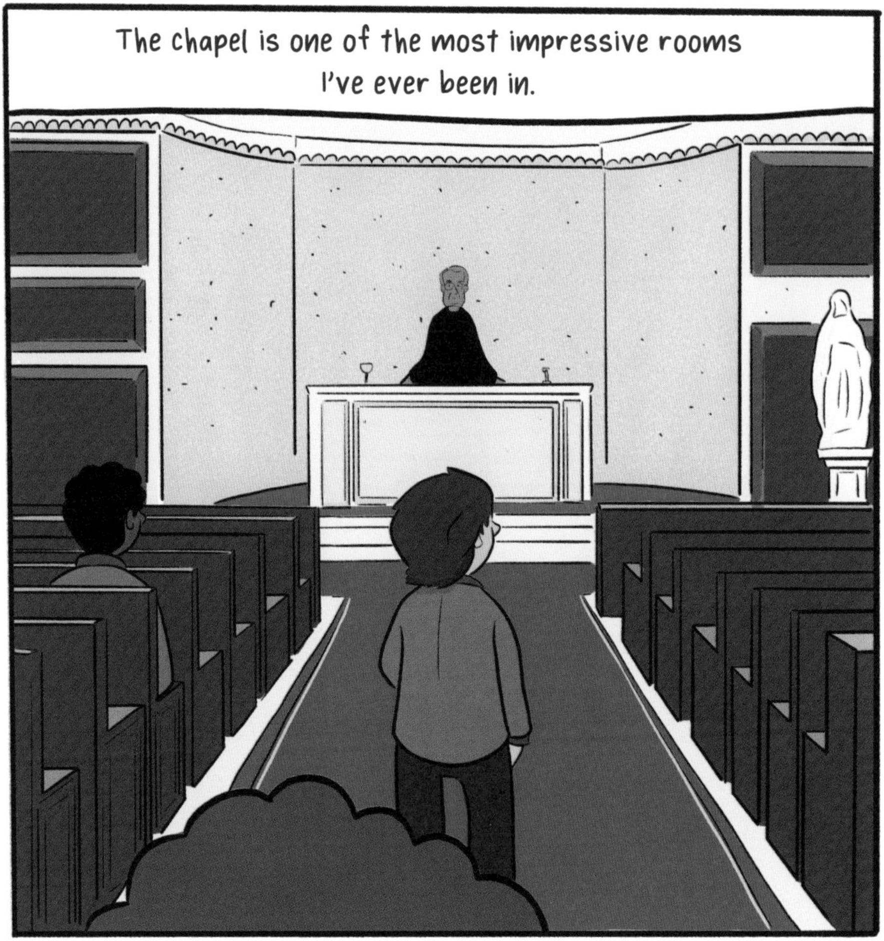
The chapel is one of the most impressive rooms I've ever been in.

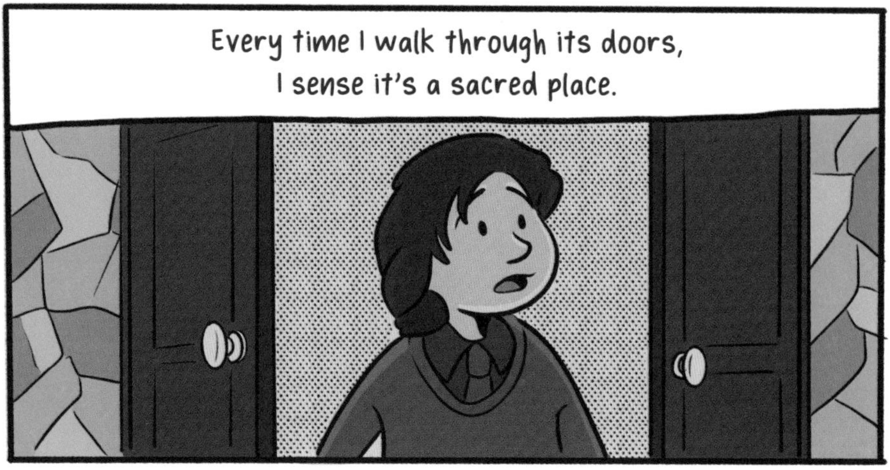
Every time I walk through its doors, I sense it's a sacred place.

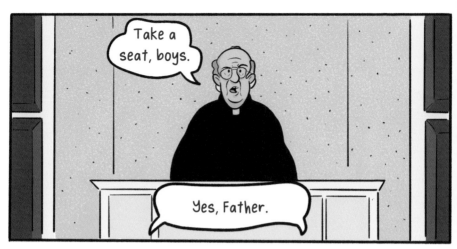

Take a seat, boys.

Yes, Father.

It's a daily thing, but I still feel weird calling priests *Father*.

One day I asked my dad . . .

Does it bother you that I call the priests at school *Father*?

And he said . . .

No, just don't call them *Dad*.

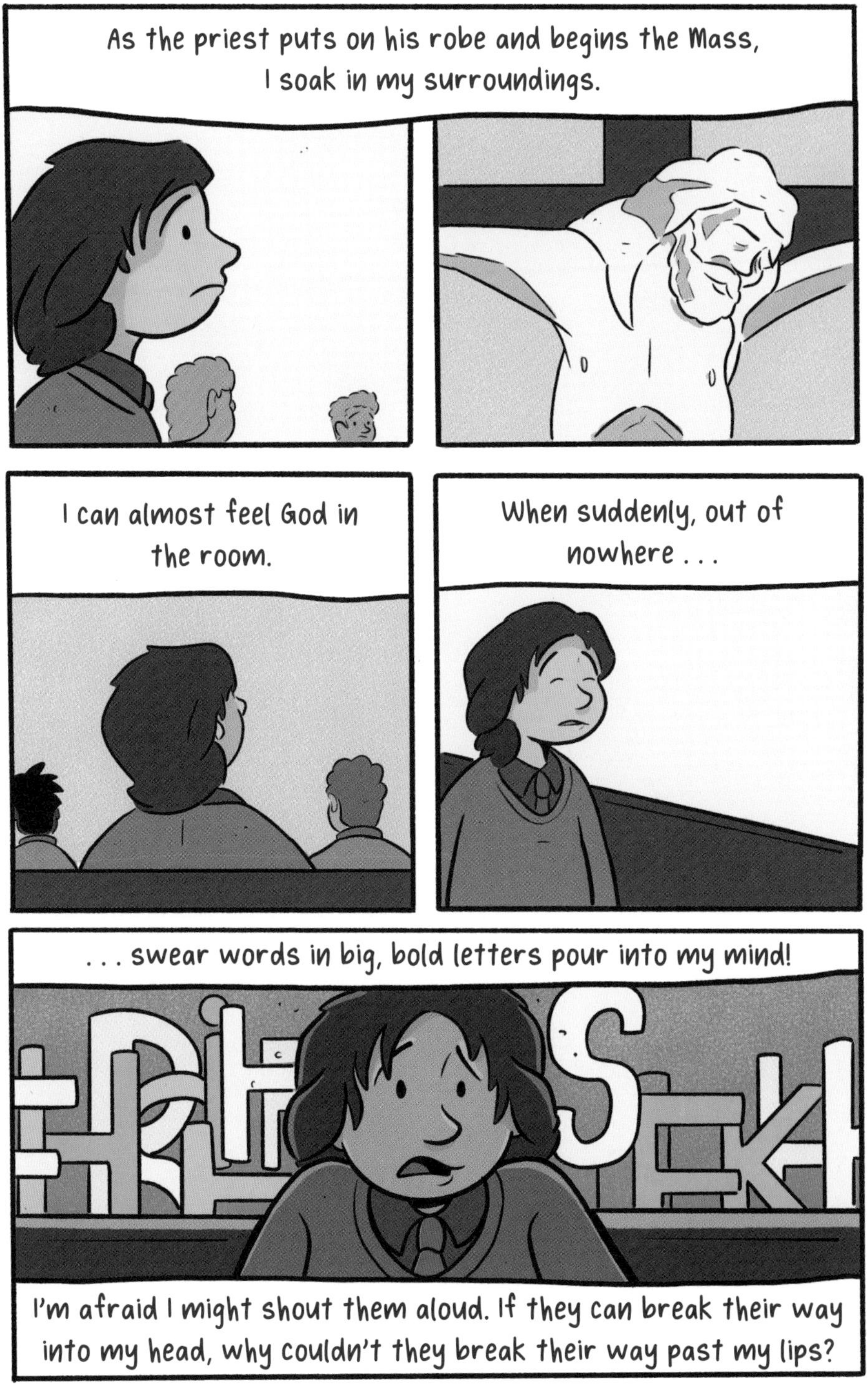
As the priest puts on his robe and begins the Mass, I soak in my surroundings.
I can almost feel God in the room.
When suddenly, out of nowhere . . .
. . . swear words in big, bold letters pour into my mind!
I'm afraid I might shout them aloud. If they can break their way into my head, why couldn't they break their way past my lips?

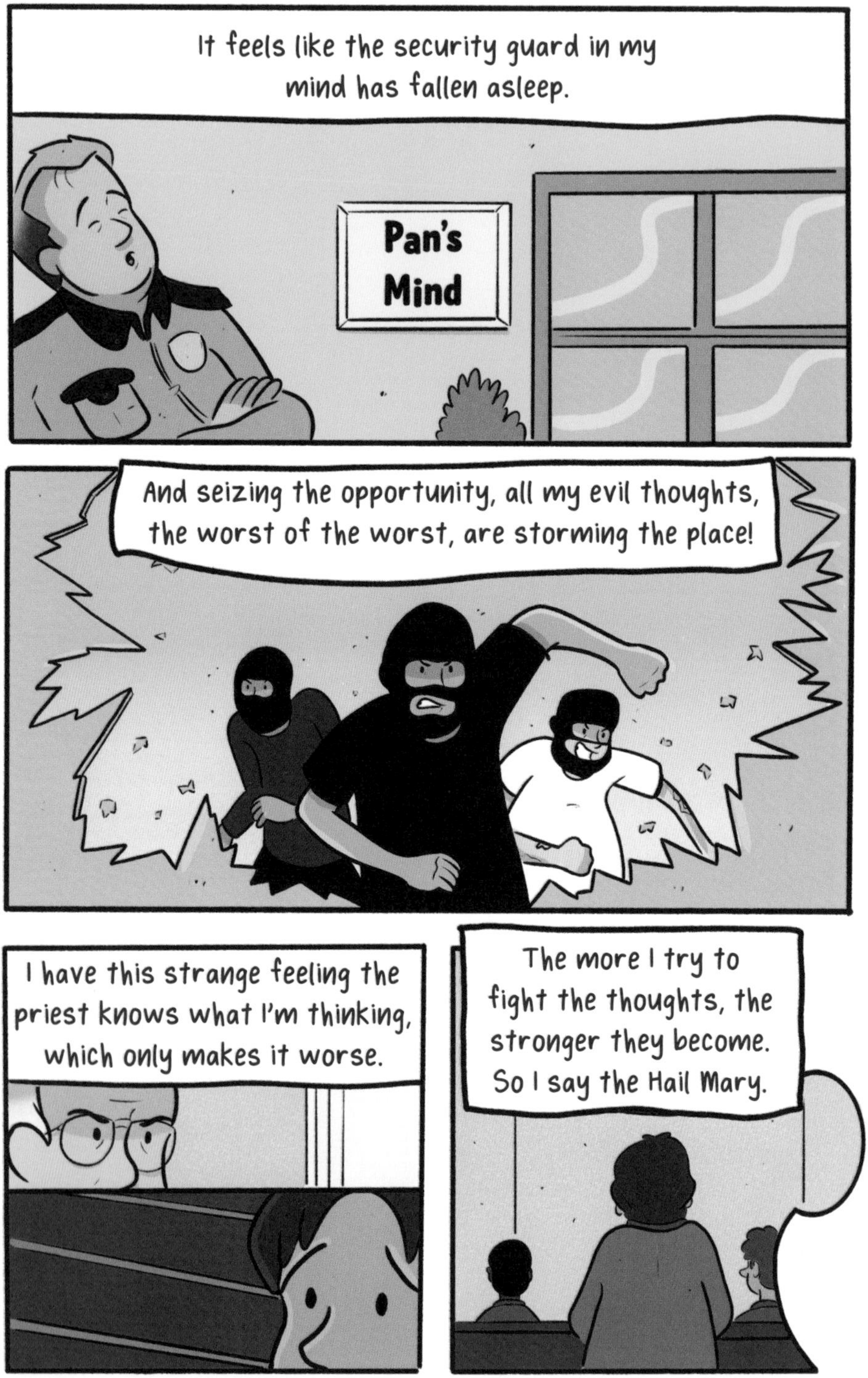
It feels like the security guard in my mind has fallen asleep.
Pan's Mind
And seizing the opportunity, all my evil thoughts, the worst of the worst, are storming the place!
I have this strange feeling the priest knows what I'm thinking, which only makes it worse.
The more I try to fight the thoughts, the stronger they become. So I say the Hail Mary.

Over and over again.

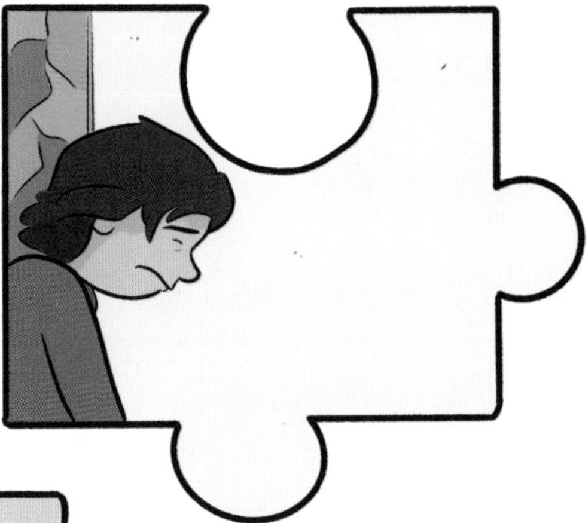

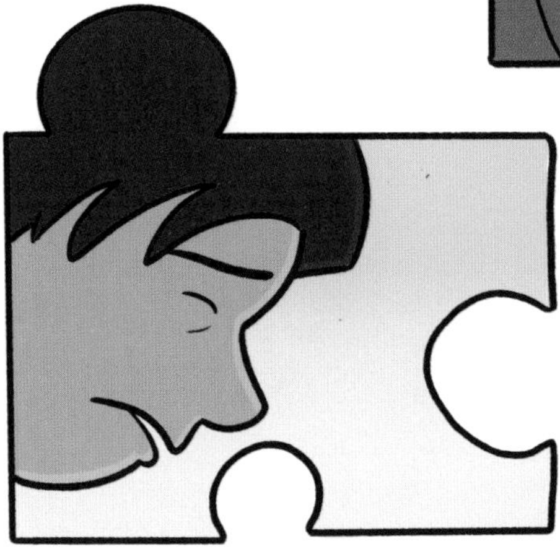

I squeeze my eyes shut and follow the same pattern, piece by piece.

By piece.

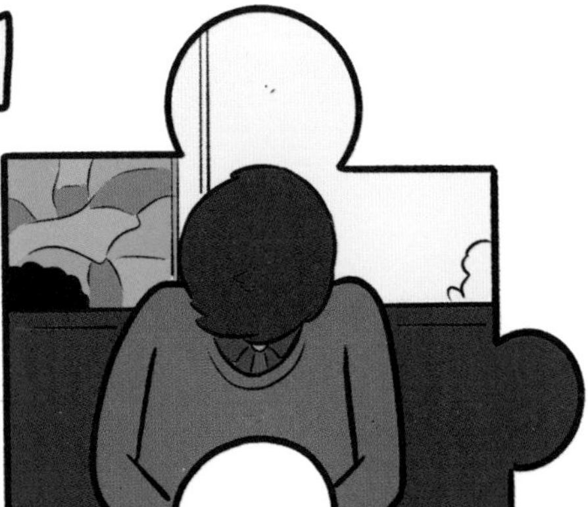

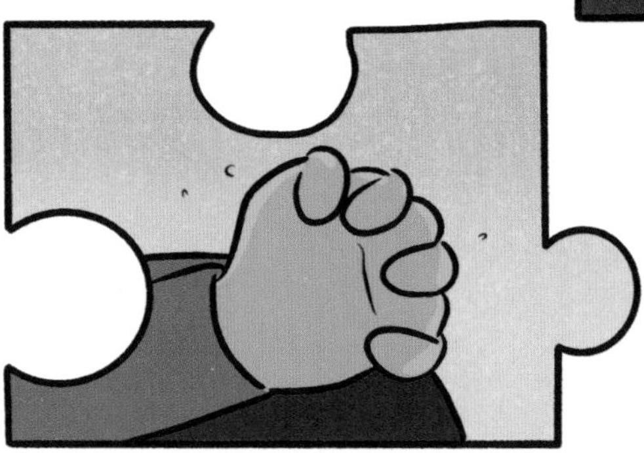

By piece.

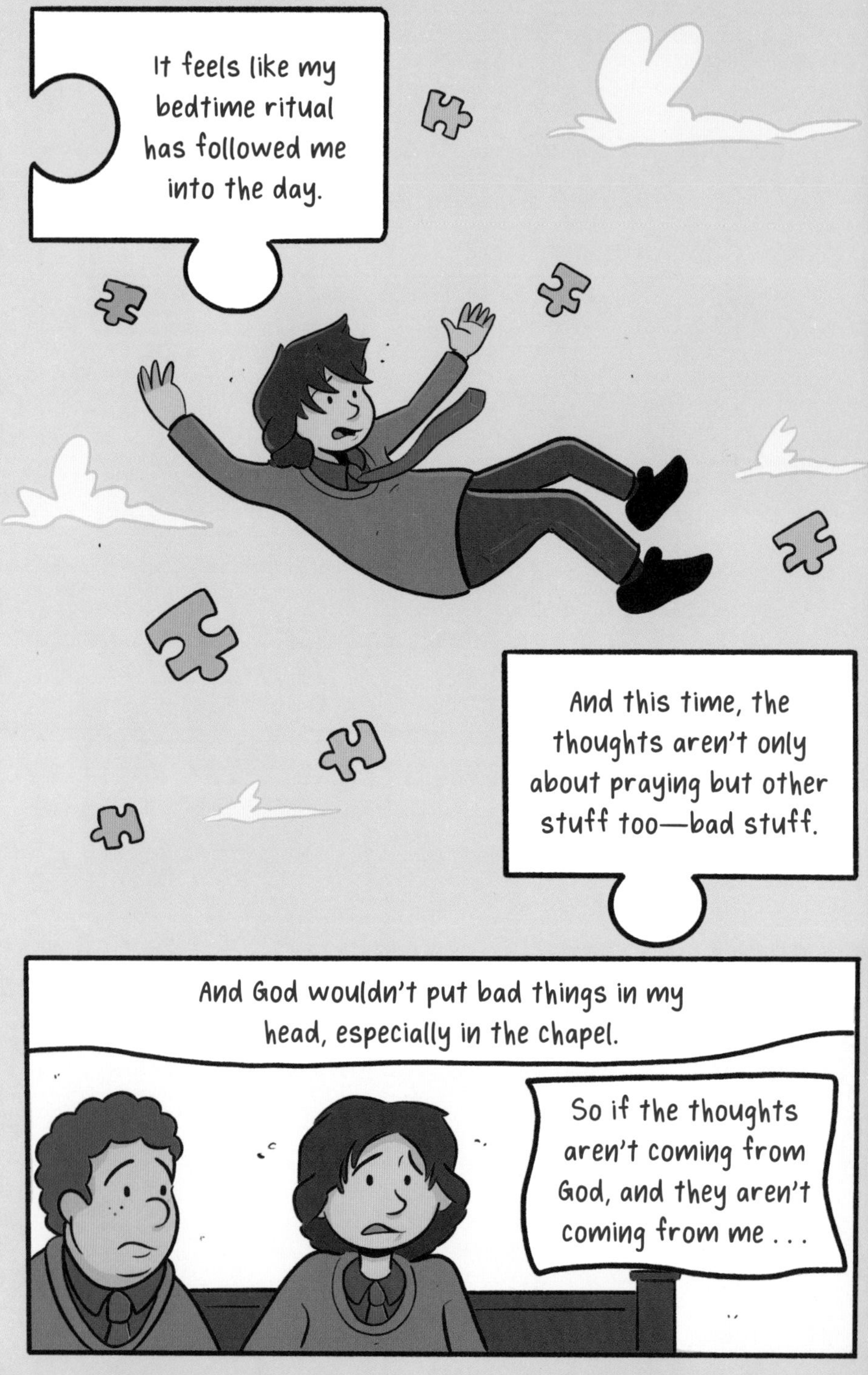
It feels like my bedtime ritual has followed me into the day.
And this time, the thoughts aren't only about praying but other stuff too—bad stuff.
And God wouldn't put bad things in my head, especially in the chapel.
So if the thoughts aren't coming from God, and they aren't coming from me . . .

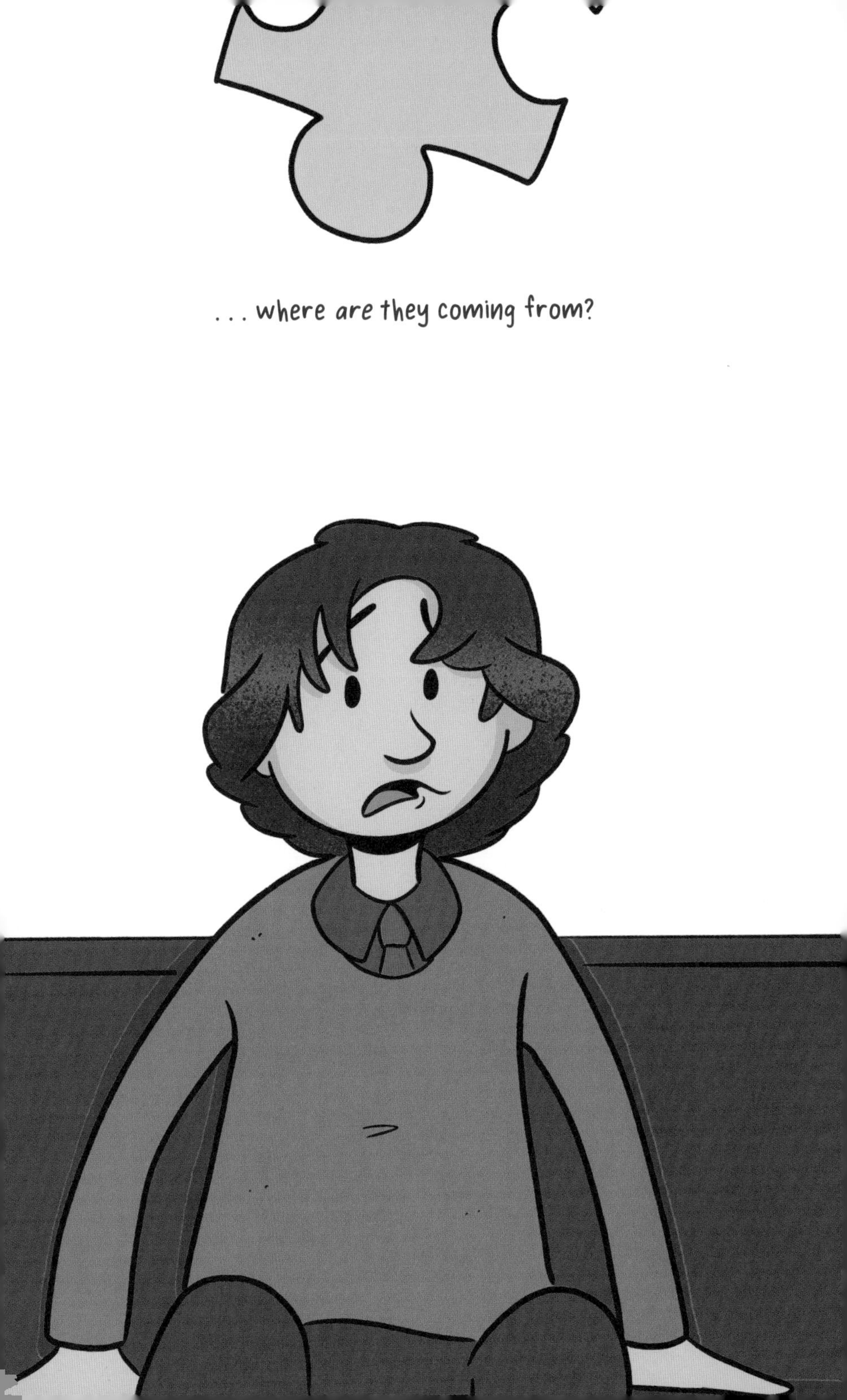
. . . where are they coming from?

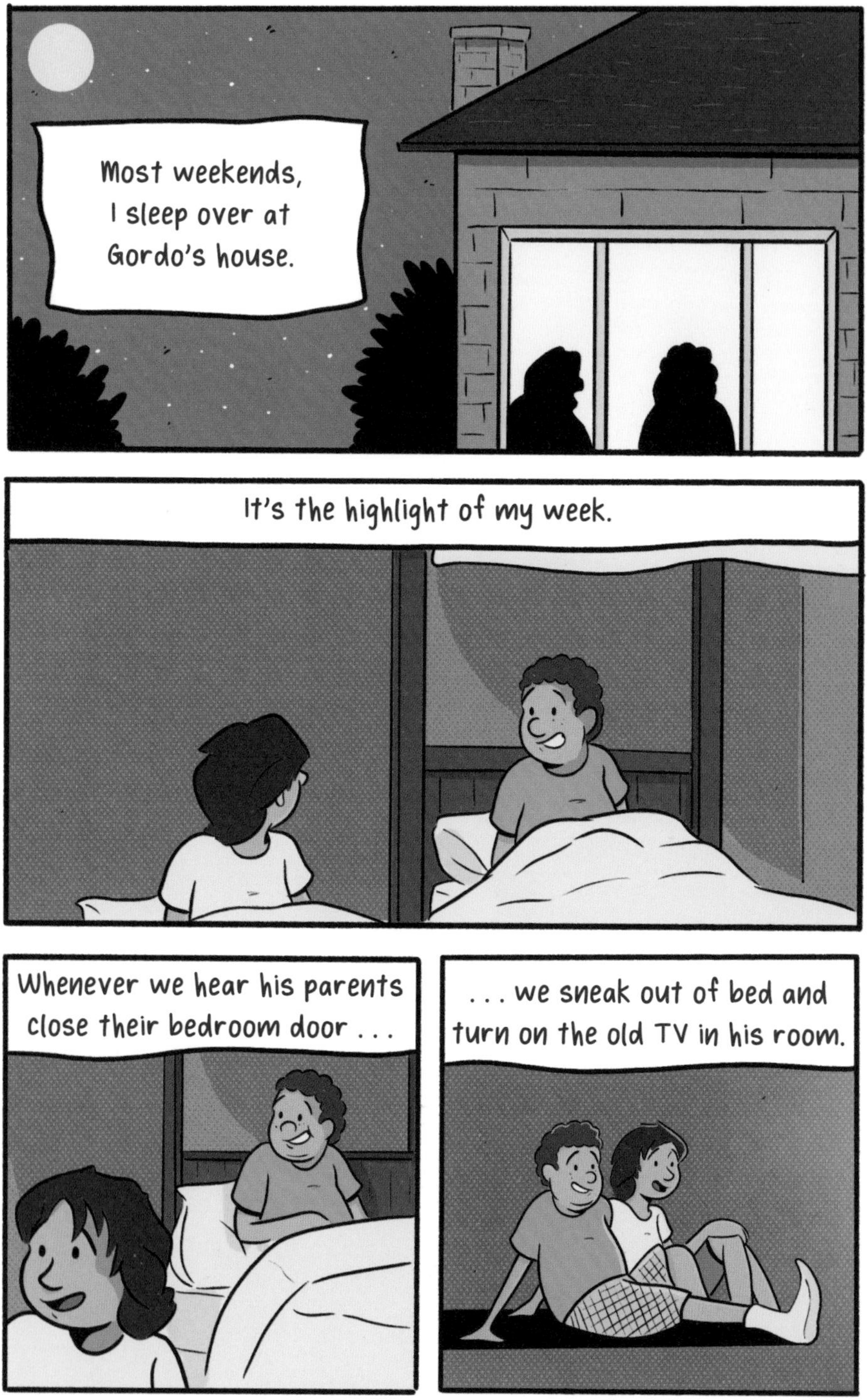
Most weekends, I sleep over at Gordo's house.
It's the highlight of my week.
Whenever we hear his parents close their bedroom door . . .
. . . we sneak out of bed and turn on the old TV in his room.

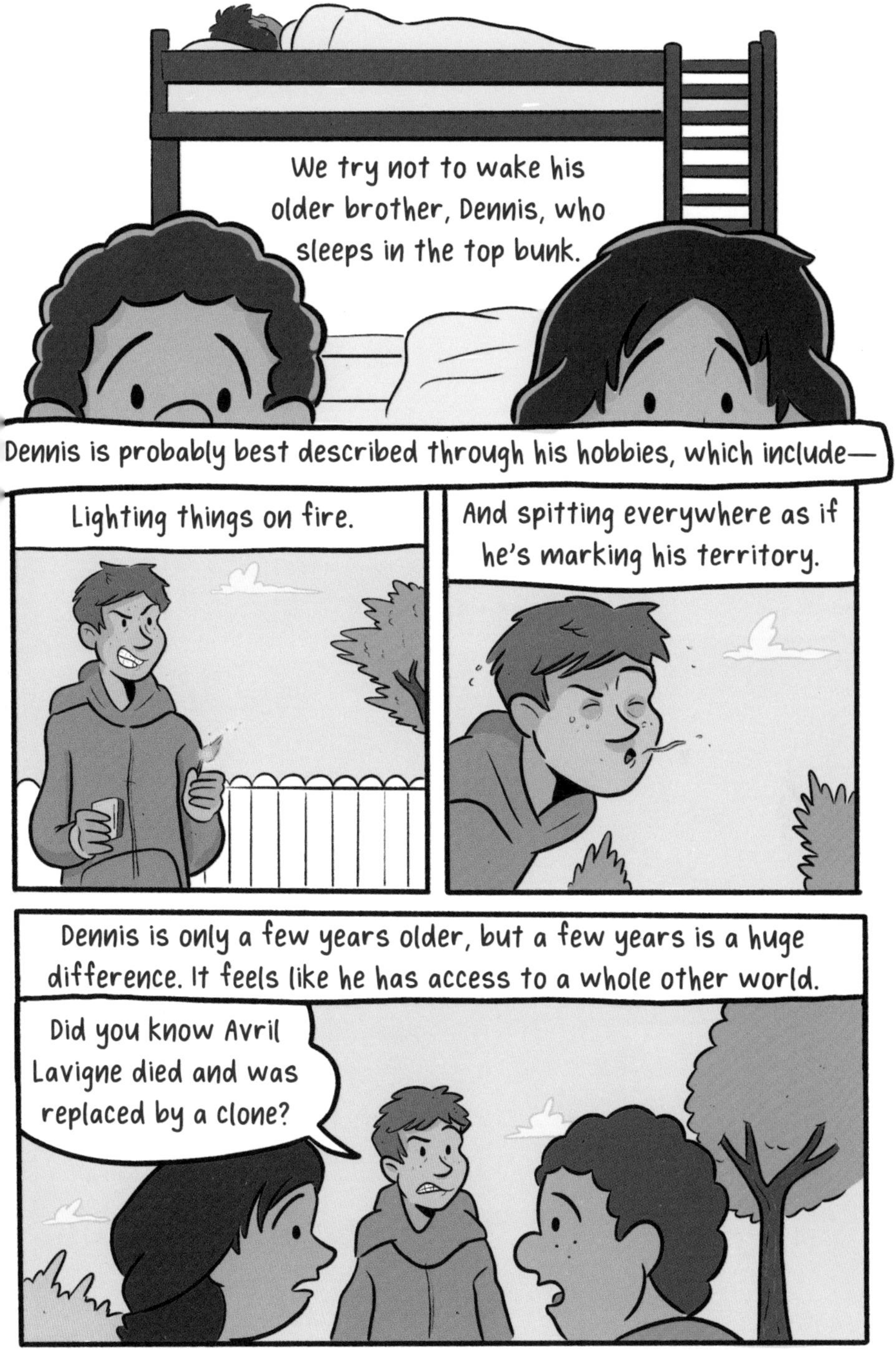
We try not to wake his older brother, Dennis, who sleeps in the top bunk.
Dennis is probably best described through his hobbies, which include—
Lighting things on fire.
And spitting everywhere as if he's marking his territory.
Dennis is only a few years older, but a few years is a huge difference. It feels like he has access to a whole other world.
Did you know Avril Lavigne died and was replaced by a clone?

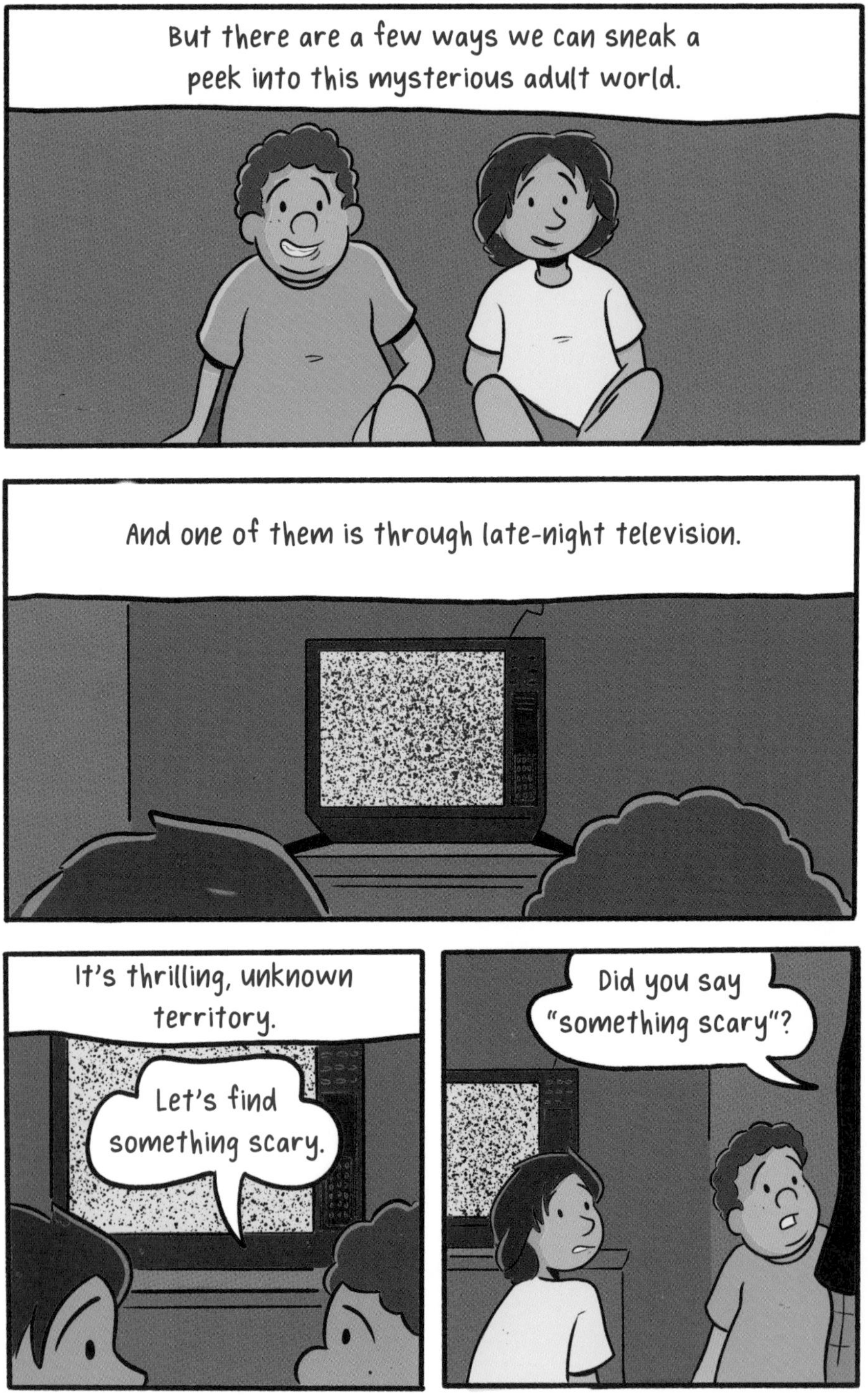
But there are a few ways we can sneak a peek into this mysterious adult world.
And one of them is through late-night television.
It's thrilling, unknown territory.
Let's find something scary.
Did you say "something scary"?

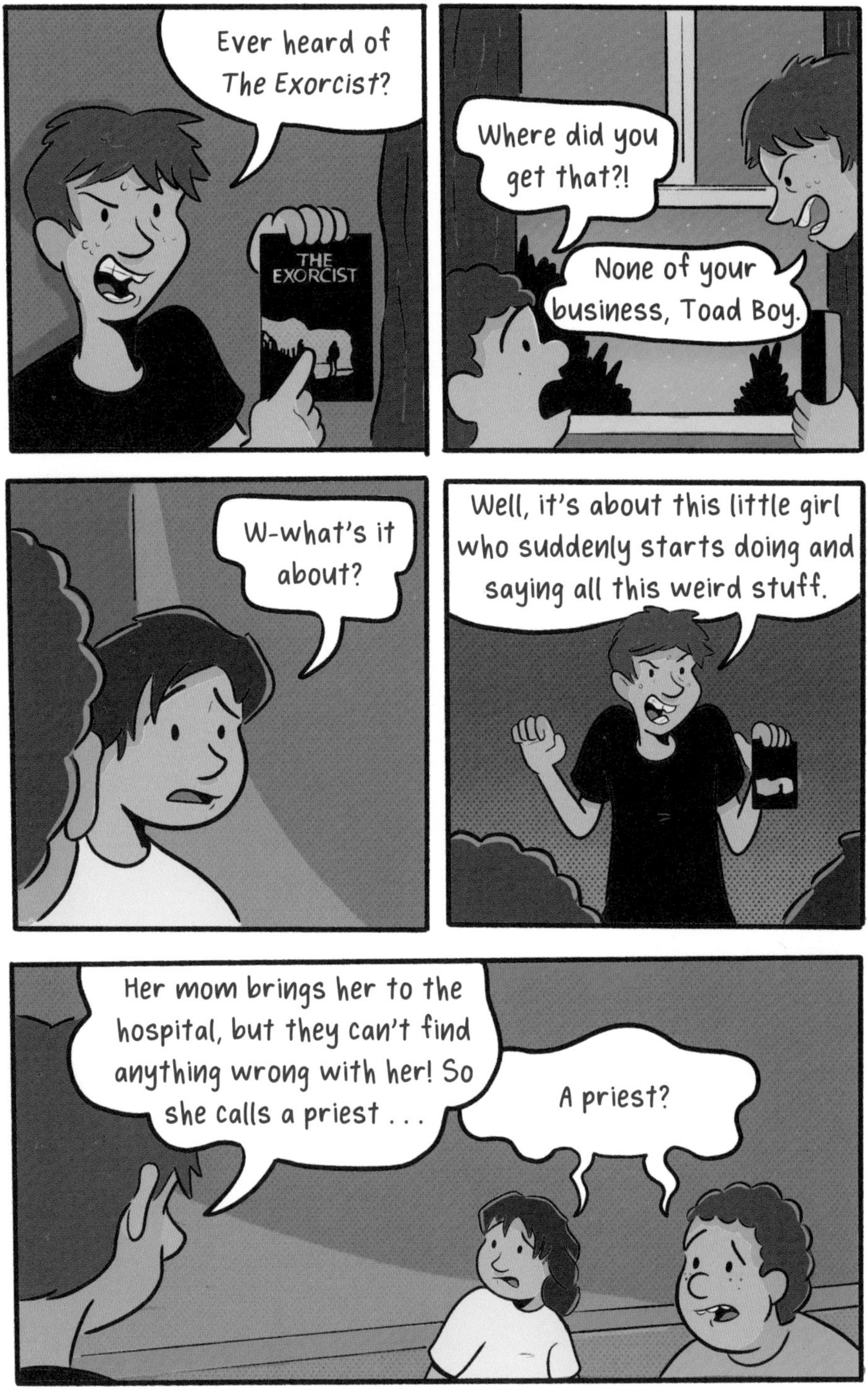
Ever heard of The Exorcist?
THE EXORCIST
Where did you get that?!
None of your business, Toad Boy.
W-what's it about?
Well, it's about this little girl who suddenly starts doing and saying all this weird stuff.
Her mom brings her to the hospital, but they can't find anything wrong with her! So she calls a priest . . .
A priest?

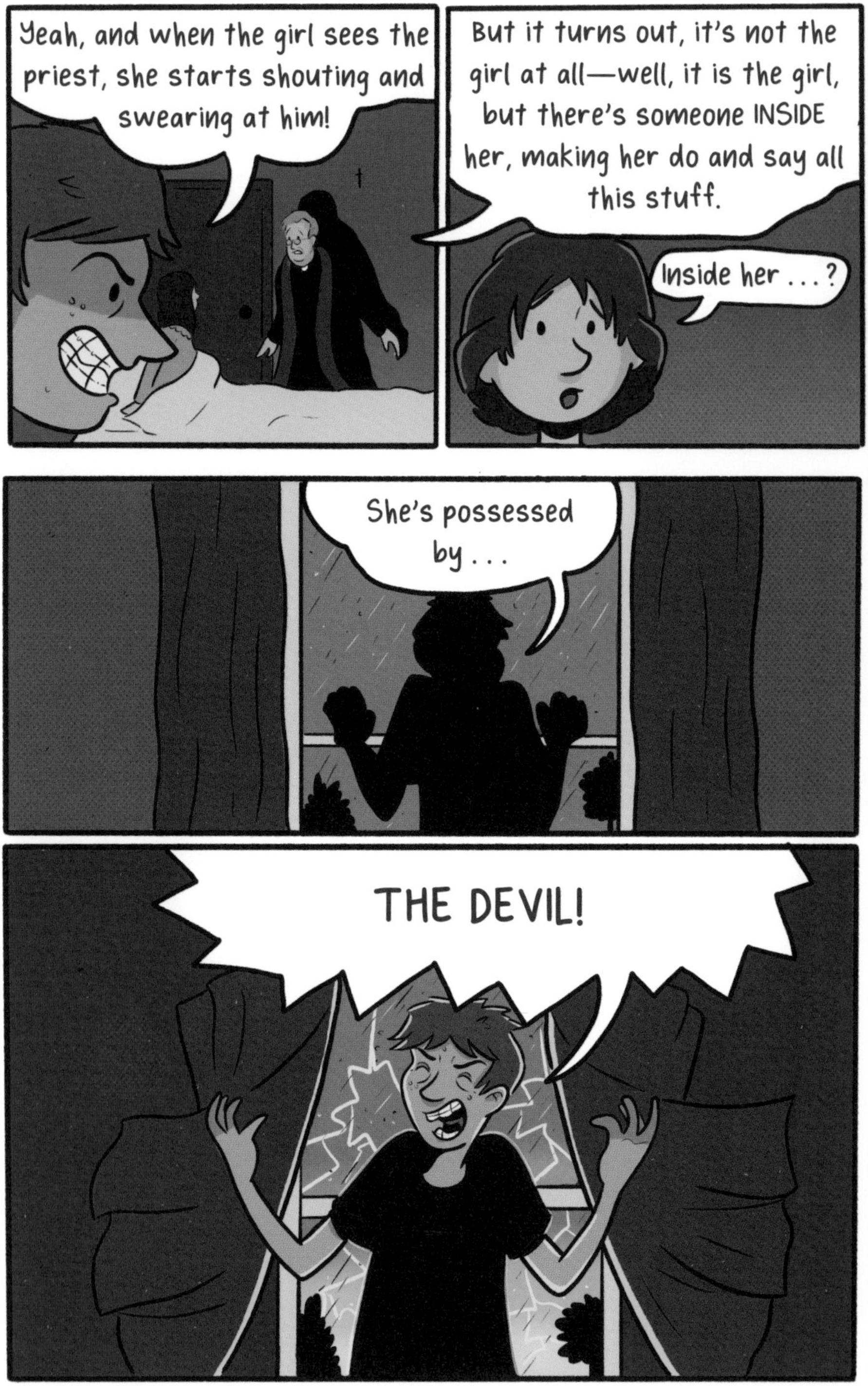

Yeah, and when the girl sees the priest, she starts shouting and swearing at him!
But it turns out, it's not the girl at all—well, it is the girl, but there's someone INSIDE her, making her do and say all this stuff.
Inside her . . . ?
She's possessed by . . .
THE DEVIL!

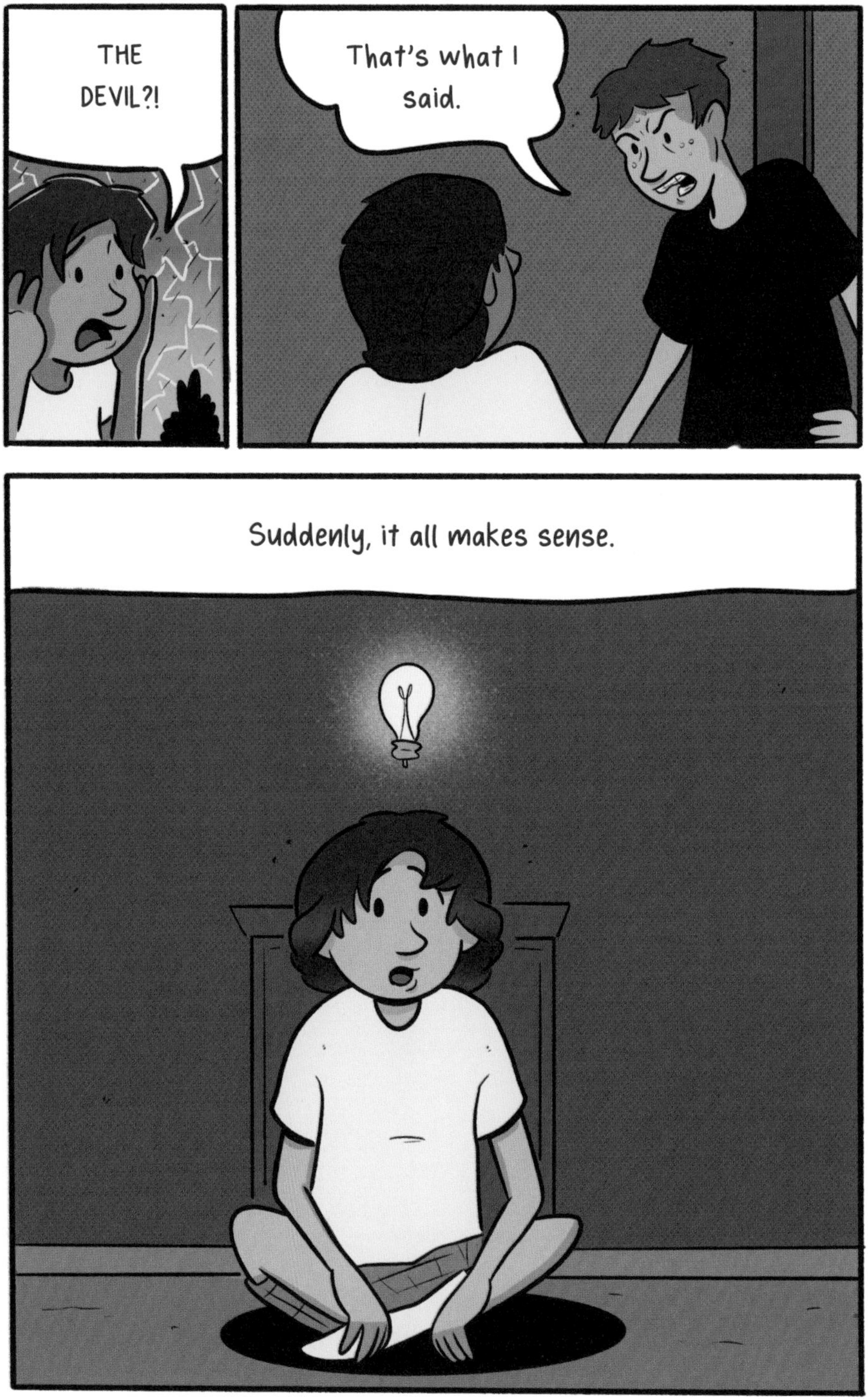
THE DEVIL?!
That's what I said.
Suddenly, it all makes sense.

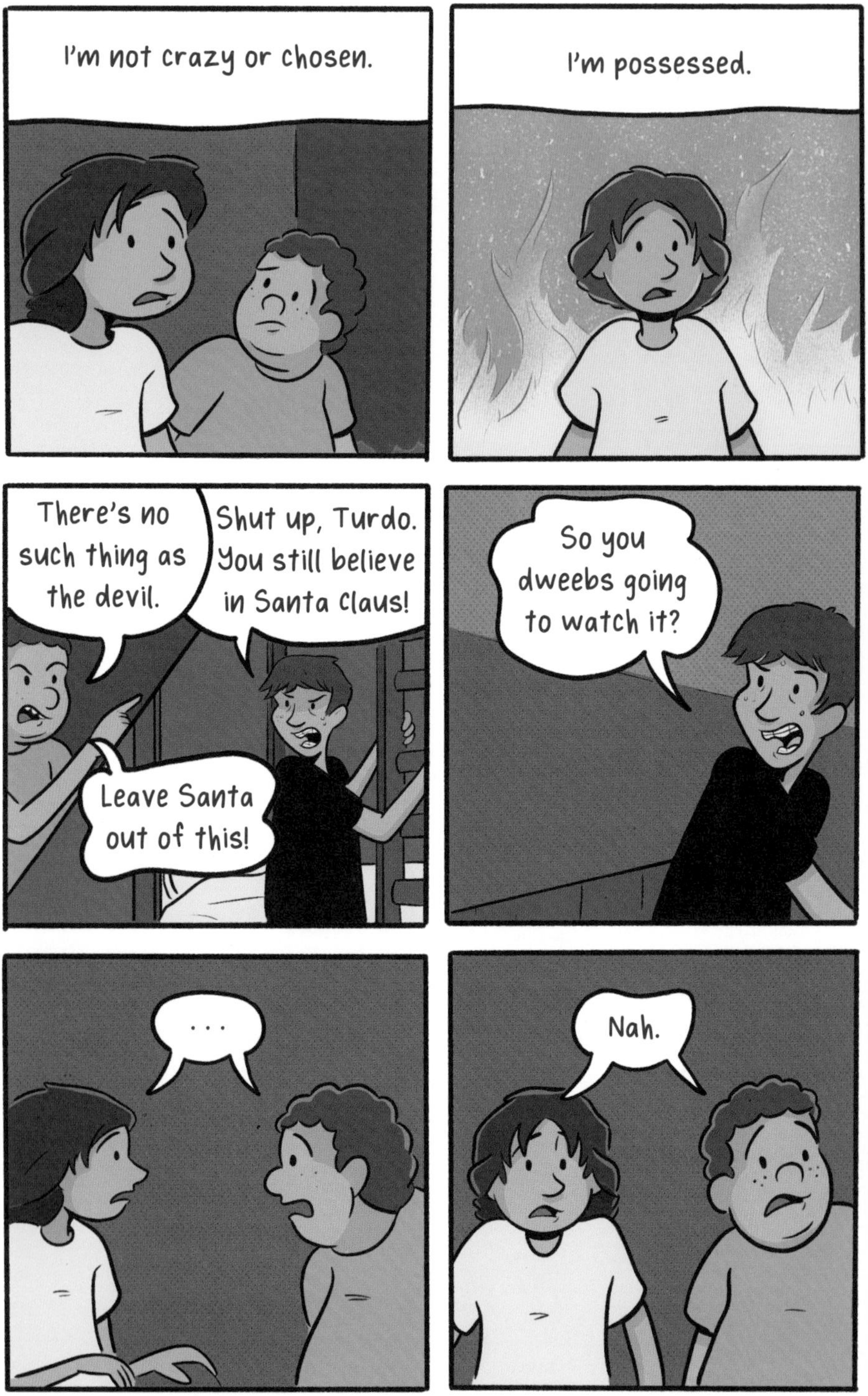
I'm not crazy or chosen.
I'm possessed.
There's no such thing as the devil.
Shut up, Turdo. You still believe in Santa Claus!
Leave Santa out of this!
So you dweebs going to watch it?
. . .
Nah.

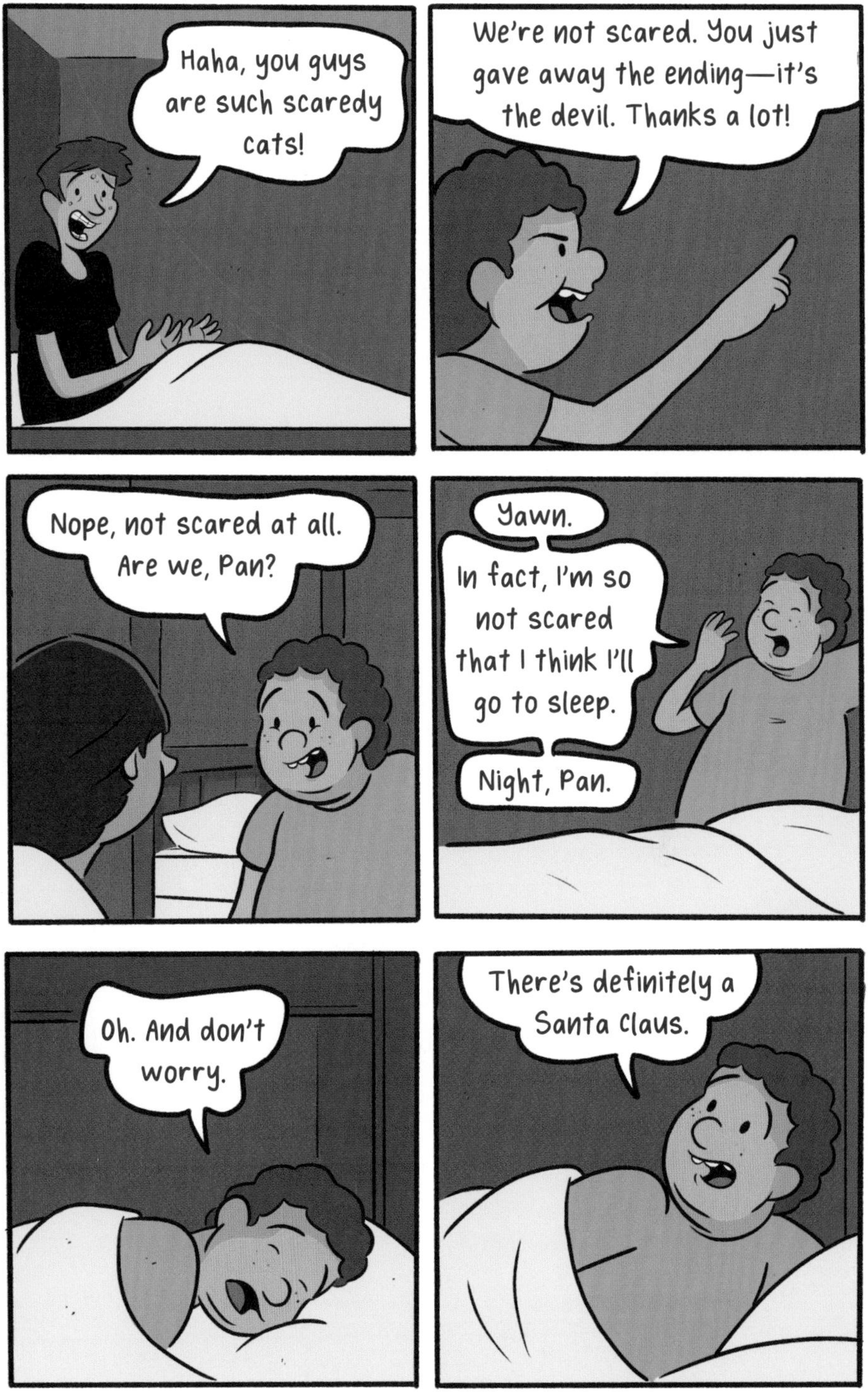
Haha, you guys are such scaredy cats!
We're not scared. You just gave away the ending—it's the devil. Thanks a lot!
Nope, not scared at all. Are we, Pan?
Yawn.
In fact, I'm so not scared that I think I'll go to sleep.
Night, Pan.
Oh. And don't worry.
There's definitely a Santa Claus.

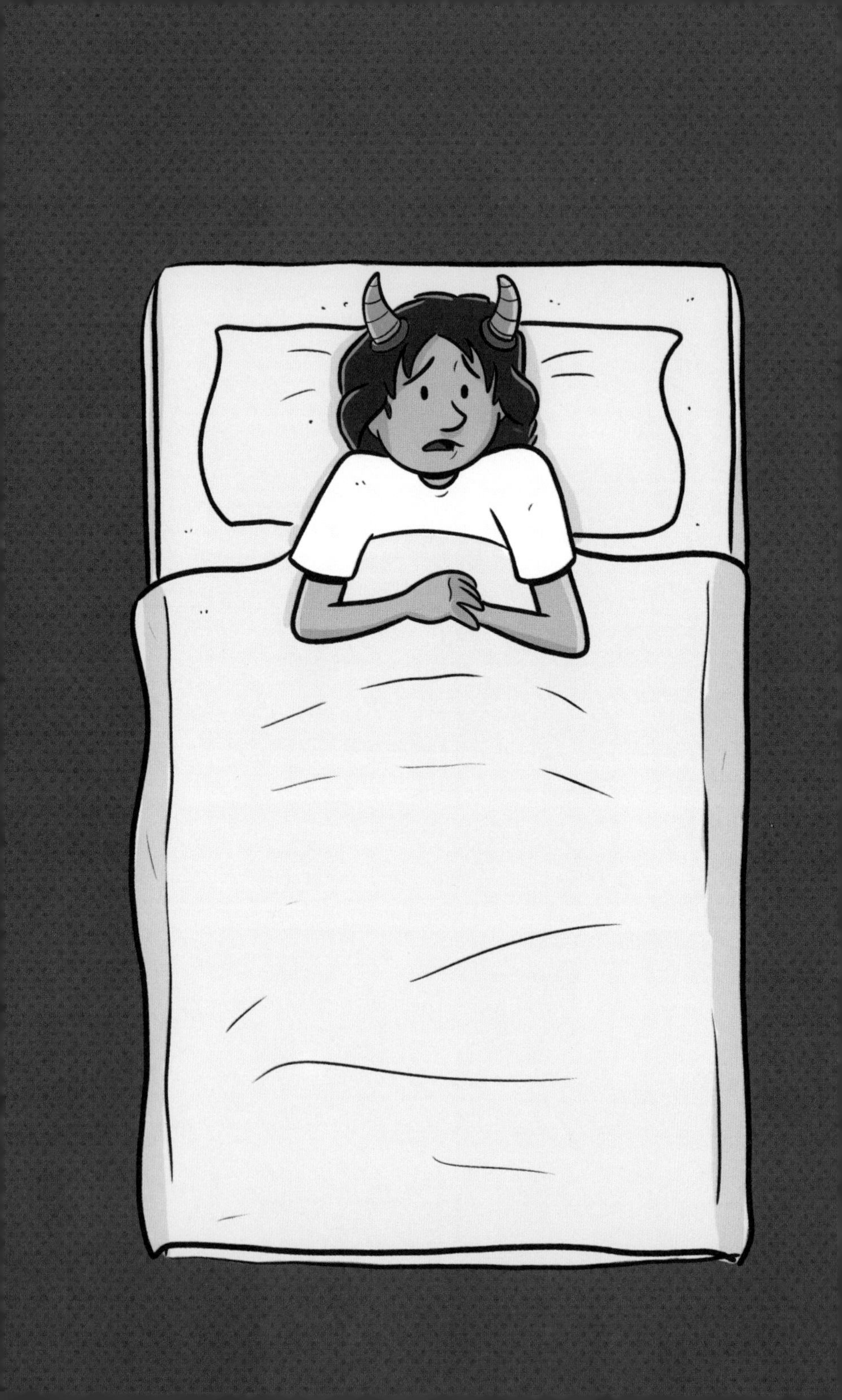

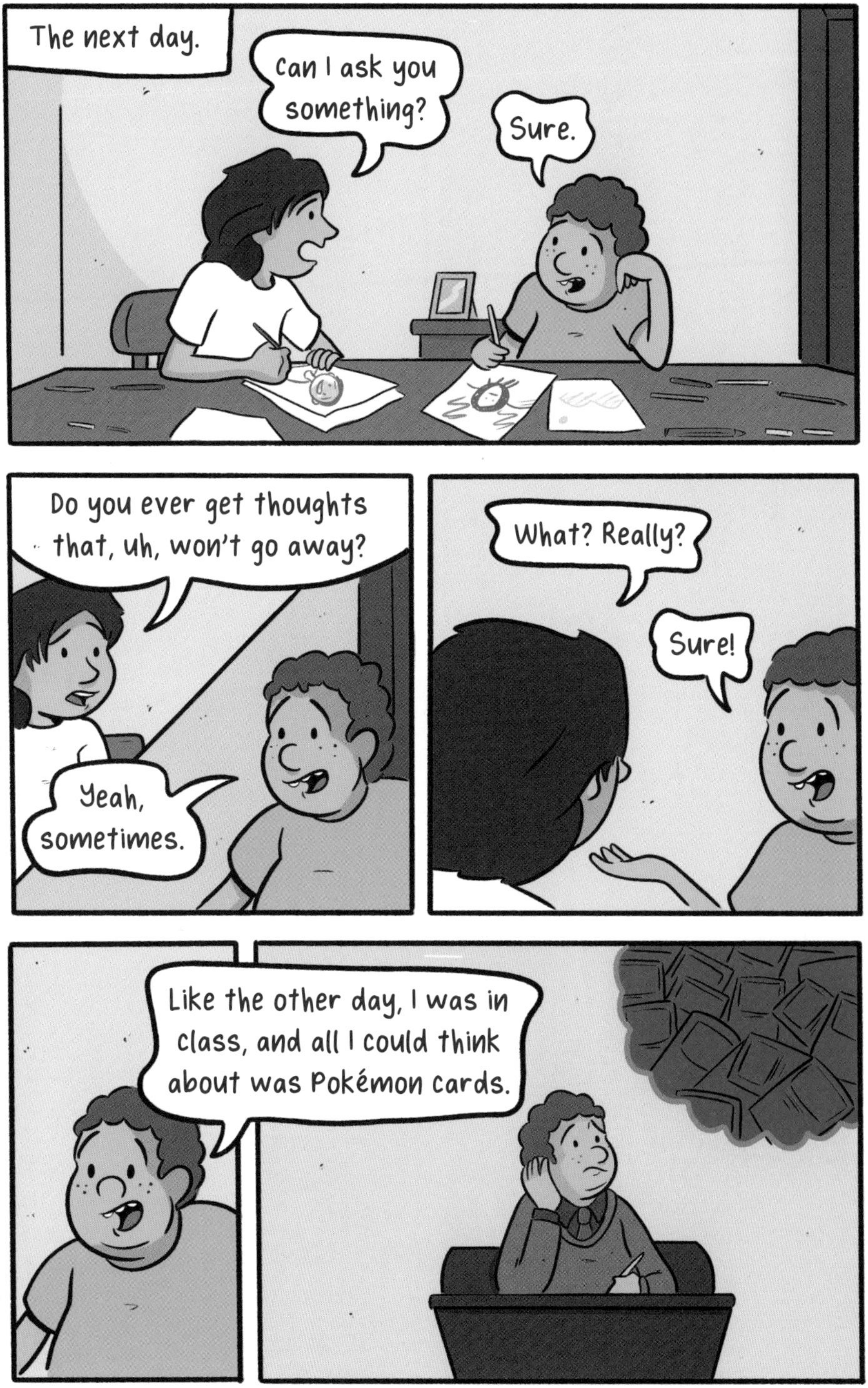
The next day.
Can I ask you something?
Sure.
Do you ever get thoughts that, uh, won't go away?
Yeah, sometimes.
What? Really?
Sure!
Like the other day, I was in class, and all I could think about was Pokémon cards.

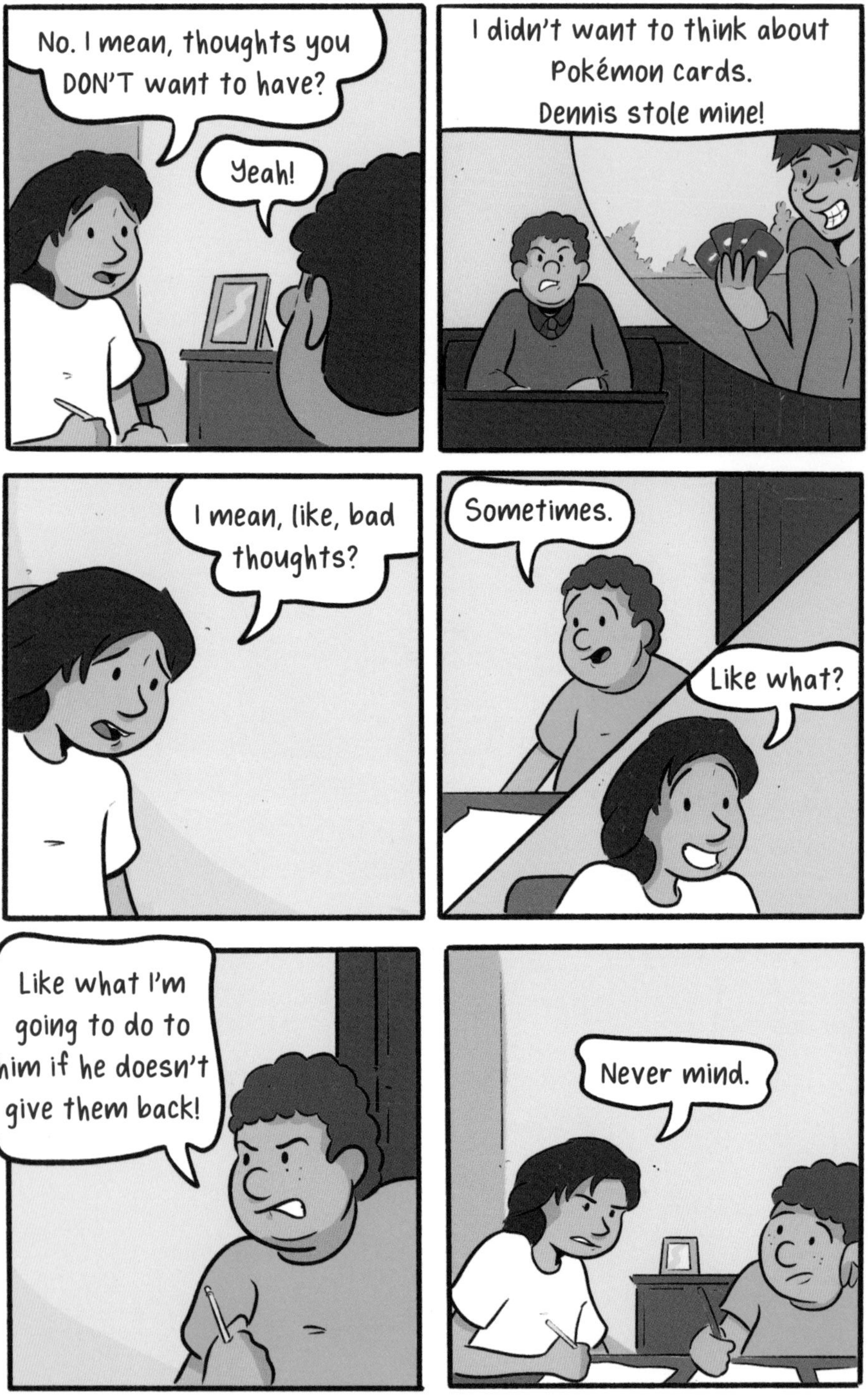
No. I mean, thoughts you DON'T want to have?
Yeah!
I didn't want to think about Pokémon cards. Dennis stole mine!
I mean, like, bad thoughts?
Sometimes.
Like what?
Like what I'm going to do to him if he doesn't give them back!
Never mind.

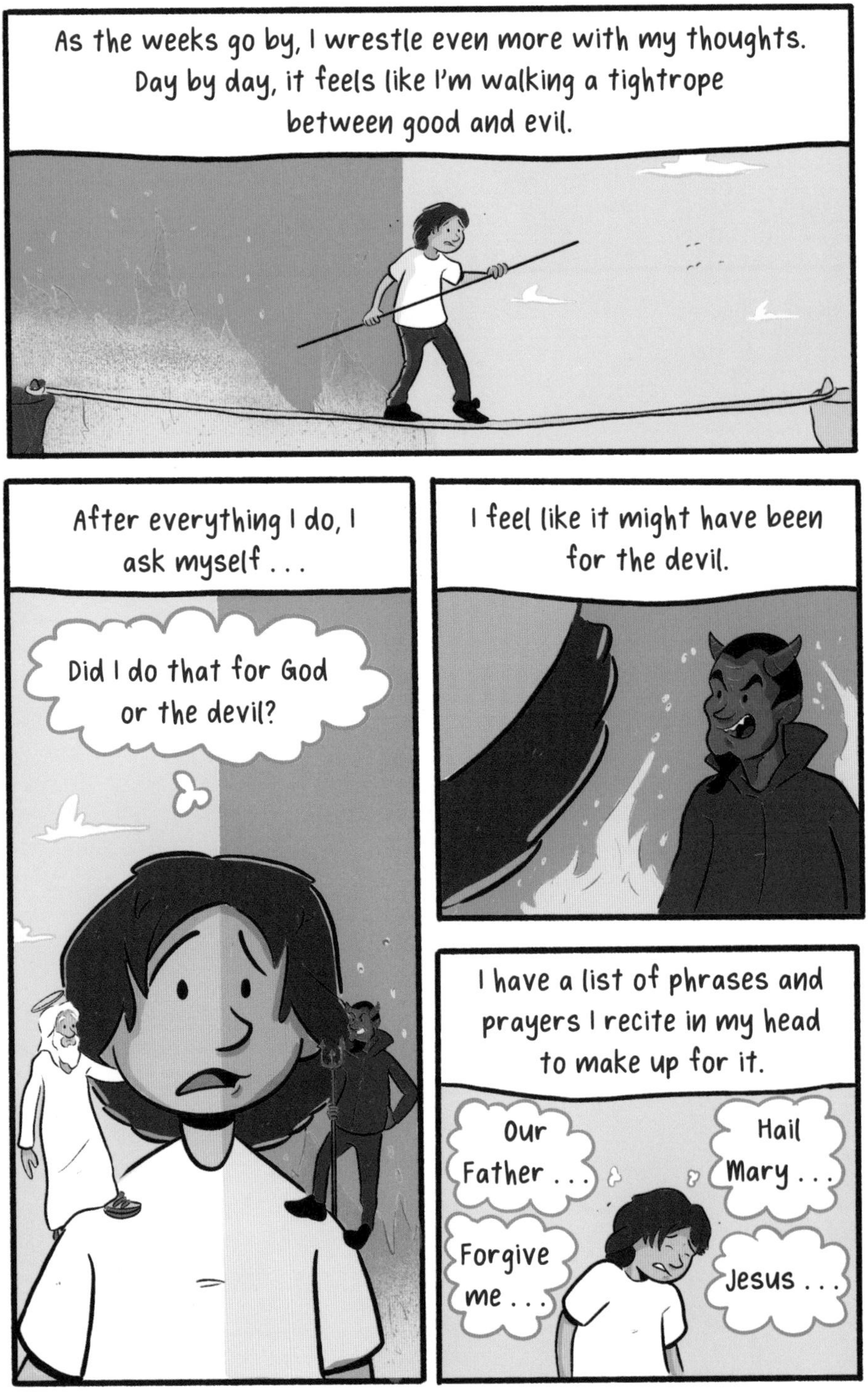
As the weeks go by, I wrestle even more with my thoughts. Day by day, it feels like I'm walking a tightrope between good and evil.
After everything I do, I ask myself . . .
Did I do that for God or the devil?
I feel like it might have been for the devil.
I have a list of phrases and prayers I recite in my head to make up for it.
Our Father . . .
Hail Mary . . .
Forgive me . . .
Jesus . . .

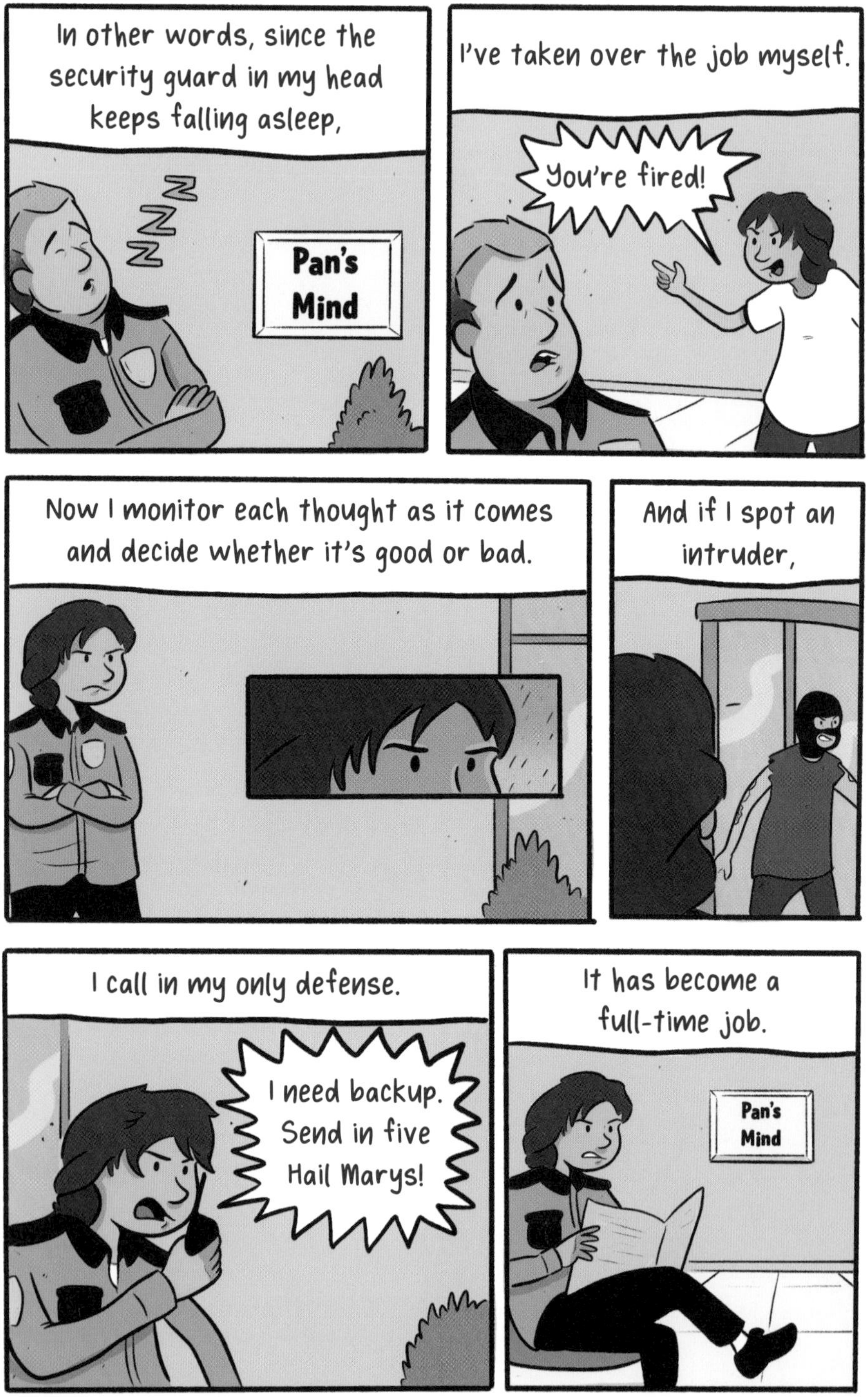
In other words, since the security guard in my head keeps falling asleep,
Pan's Mind
I've taken over the job myself.
You're fired!
Now I monitor each thought as it comes and decide whether it's good or bad.
And if I spot an intruder,
I call in my only defense.
I need backup. Send in five Hail Marys!
It has become a full-time job.
Pan's Mind

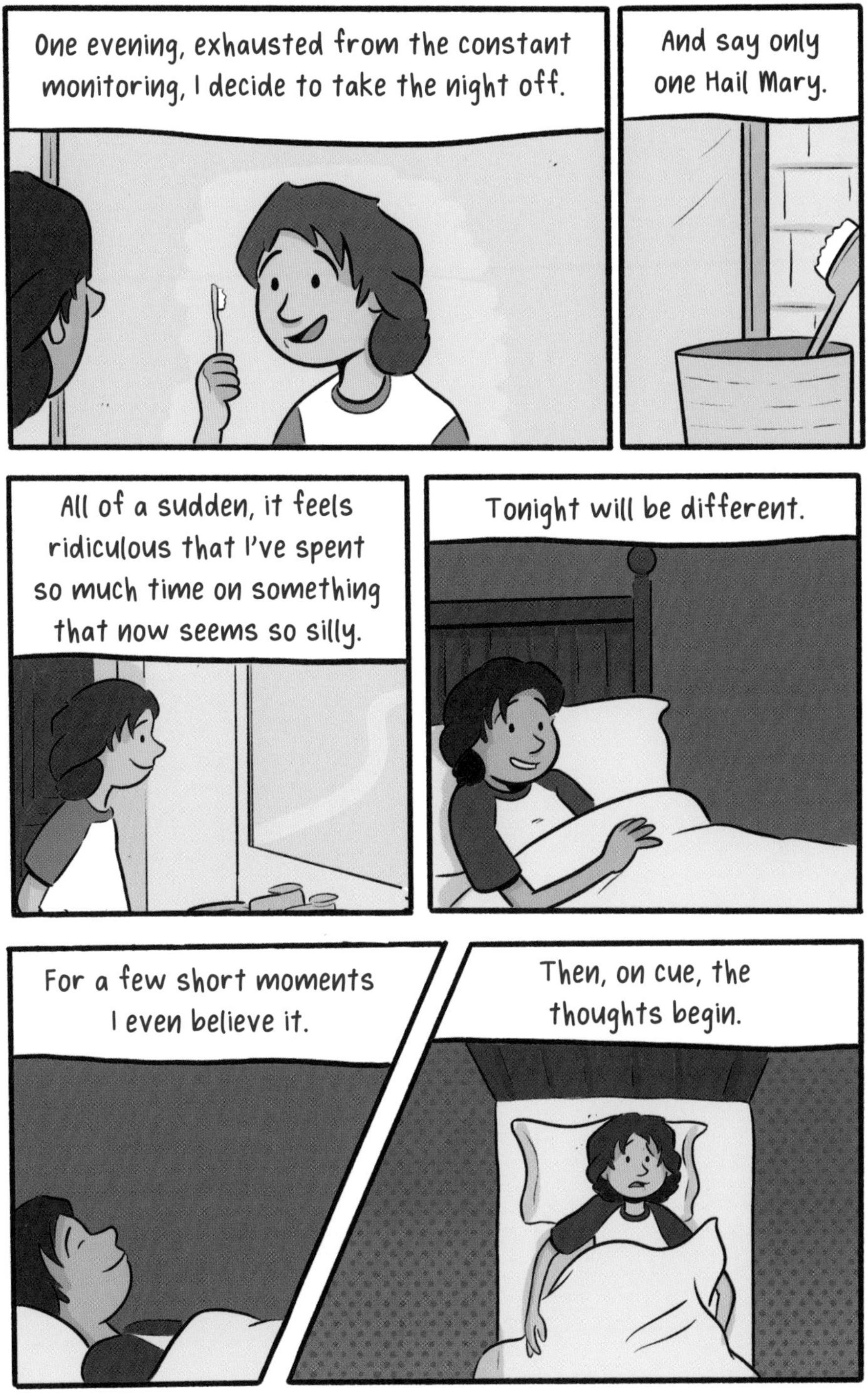
One evening, exhausted from the constant monitoring, I decide to take the night off.
And say only one Hail Mary.
All of a sudden, it feels ridiculous that I've spent so much time on something that now seems so silly.
Tonight will be different.
For a few short moments I even believe it.
Then, on cue, the thoughts begin.

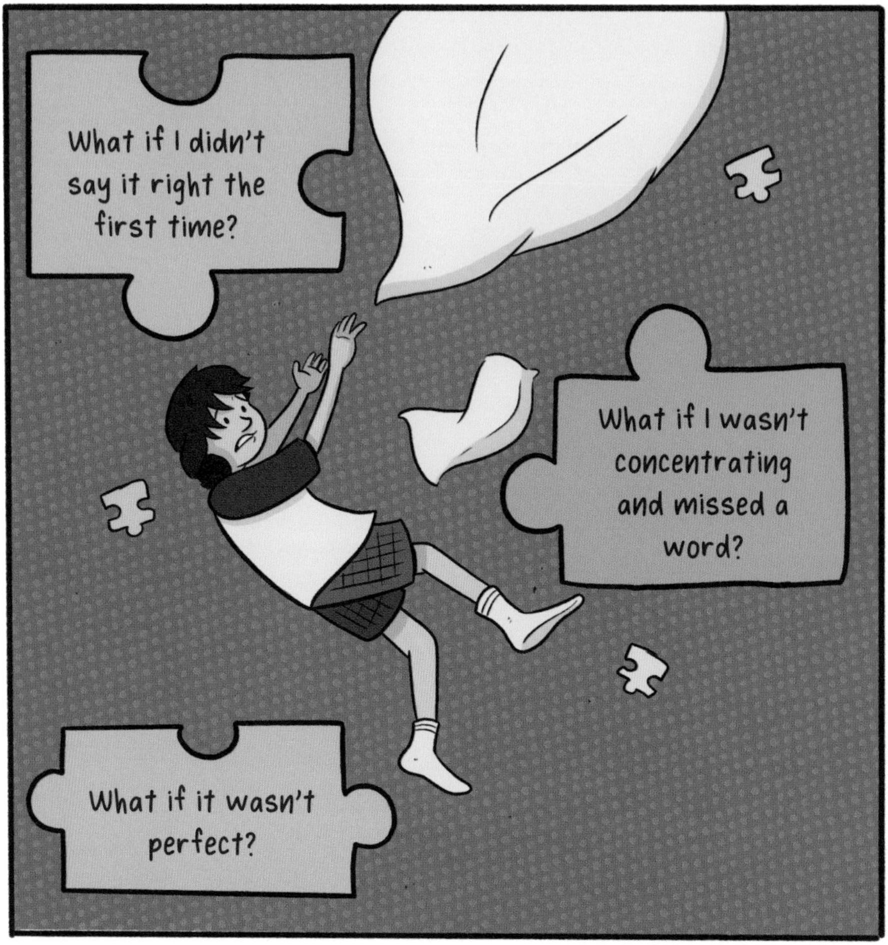
What if I didn't say it right the first time?
What if I wasn't concentrating and missed a word?
What if it wasn't perfect?

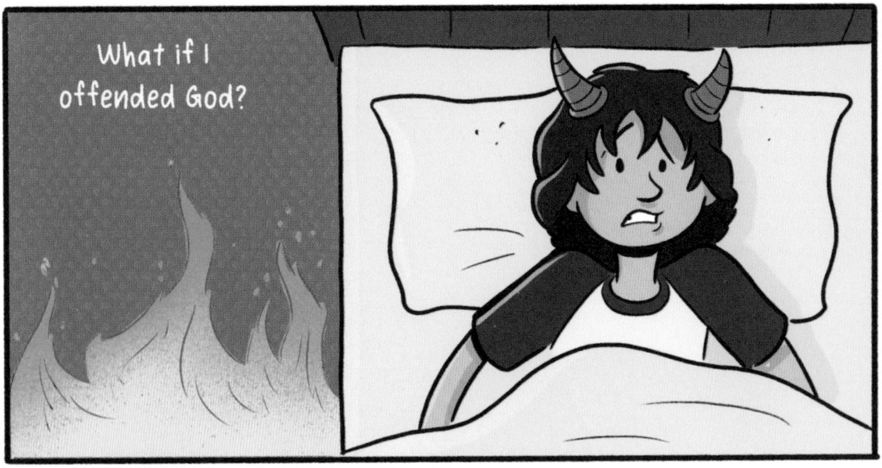
What if I offended God?

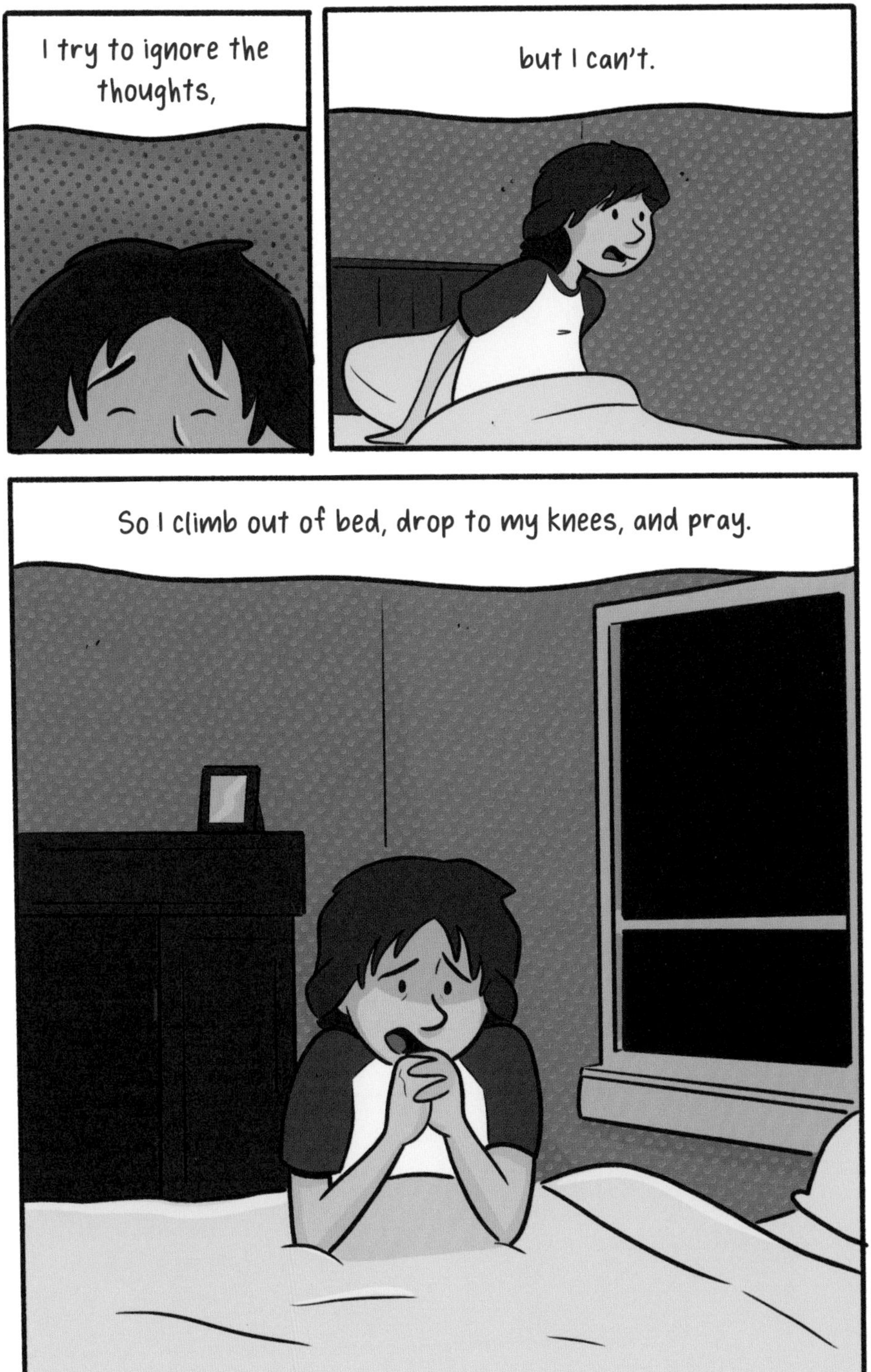
I try to ignore the thoughts,
but I can't.
So I climb out of bed, drop to my knees, and pray.

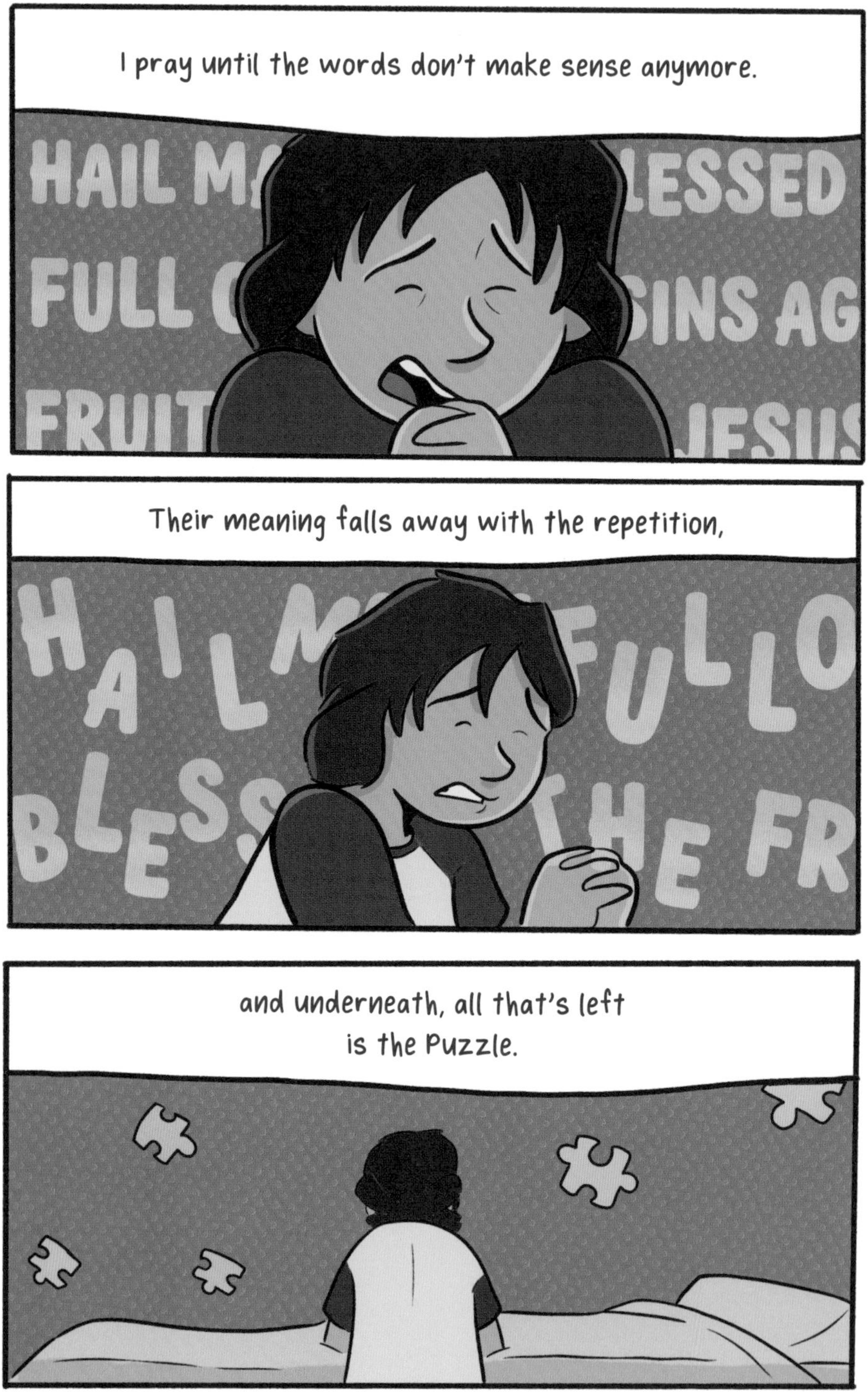
I pray until the words don't make sense anymore.
Their meaning falls away with the repetition,
and underneath, all that's left is the Puzzle.

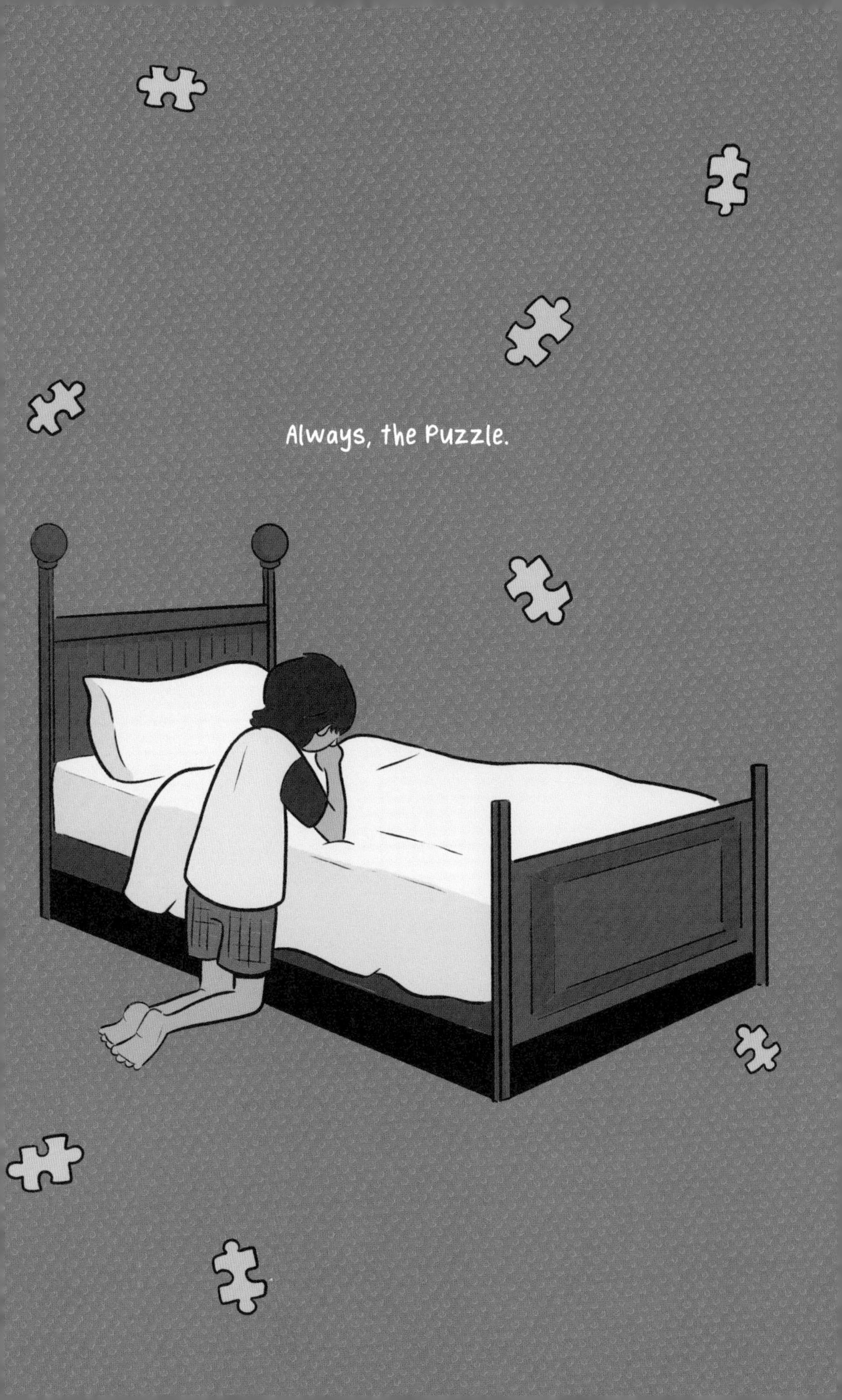
Always, the Puzzle.

2

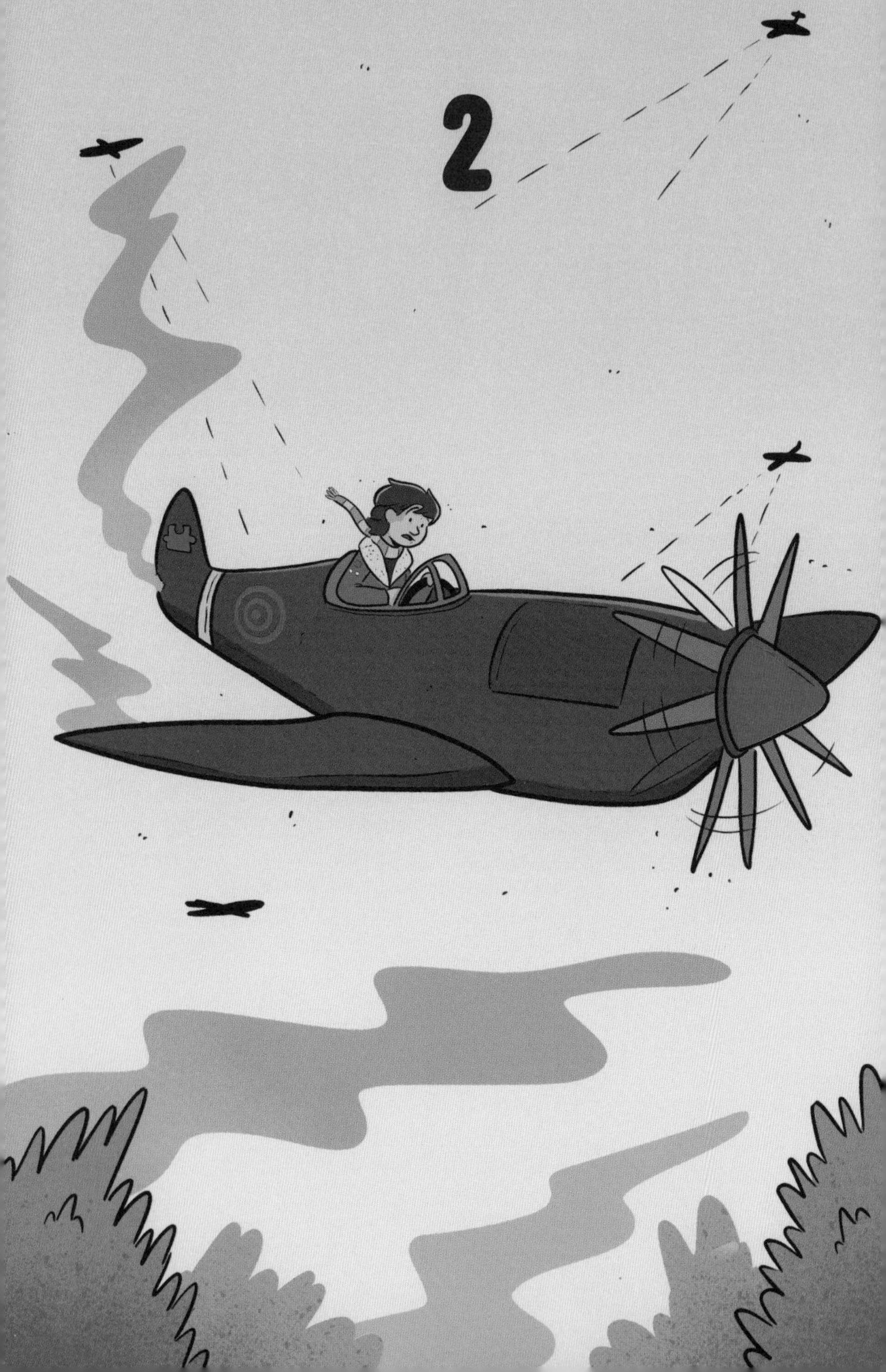

I'm twelve now, and the good news is I don't feel the need to pray anymore. I'm not sure why. The ritual sort of faded away as I got older. I'm not complaining.

The bad news is it's no longer in question; I'm definitely crazy.

Basically, the puzzle is still around. The thing that has changed is how I solve it.

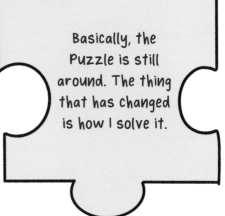

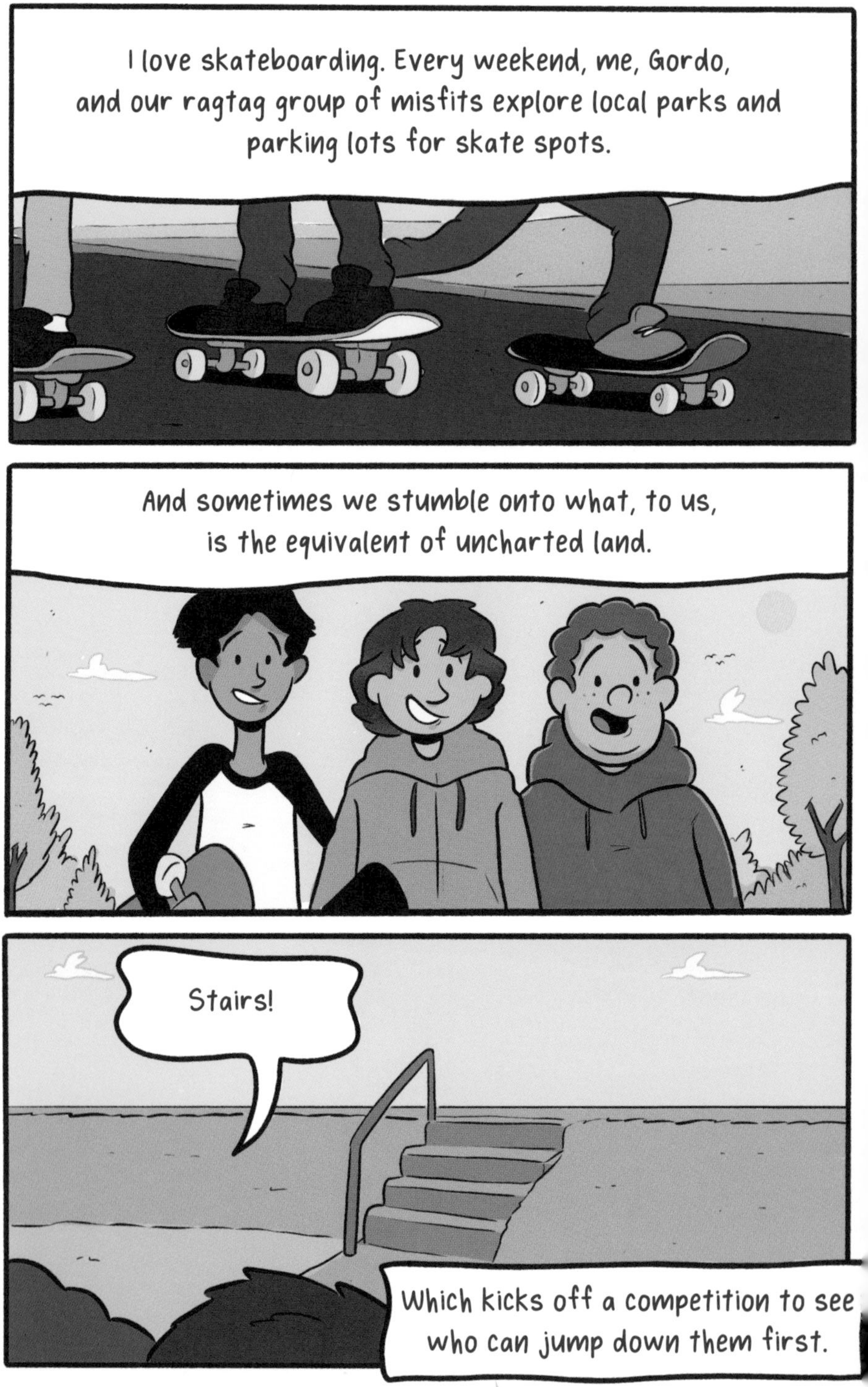
I love skateboarding. Every weekend, me, Gordo, and our ragtag group of misfits explore local parks and parking lots for skate spots.
And sometimes we stumble onto what, to us, is the equivalent of uncharted land.
Stairs!
Which kicks off a competition to see who can jump down them first.

I roll up to the edge, then jump off my board at the last second.

It clacks down step by step by step.

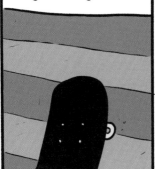

The adrenaline pumps through my body as I speed up for each new attempt.

I've learned the best thing to do is not think and just jump.

It's also important to commit. You're more likely to get hurt if you back out while in midair.

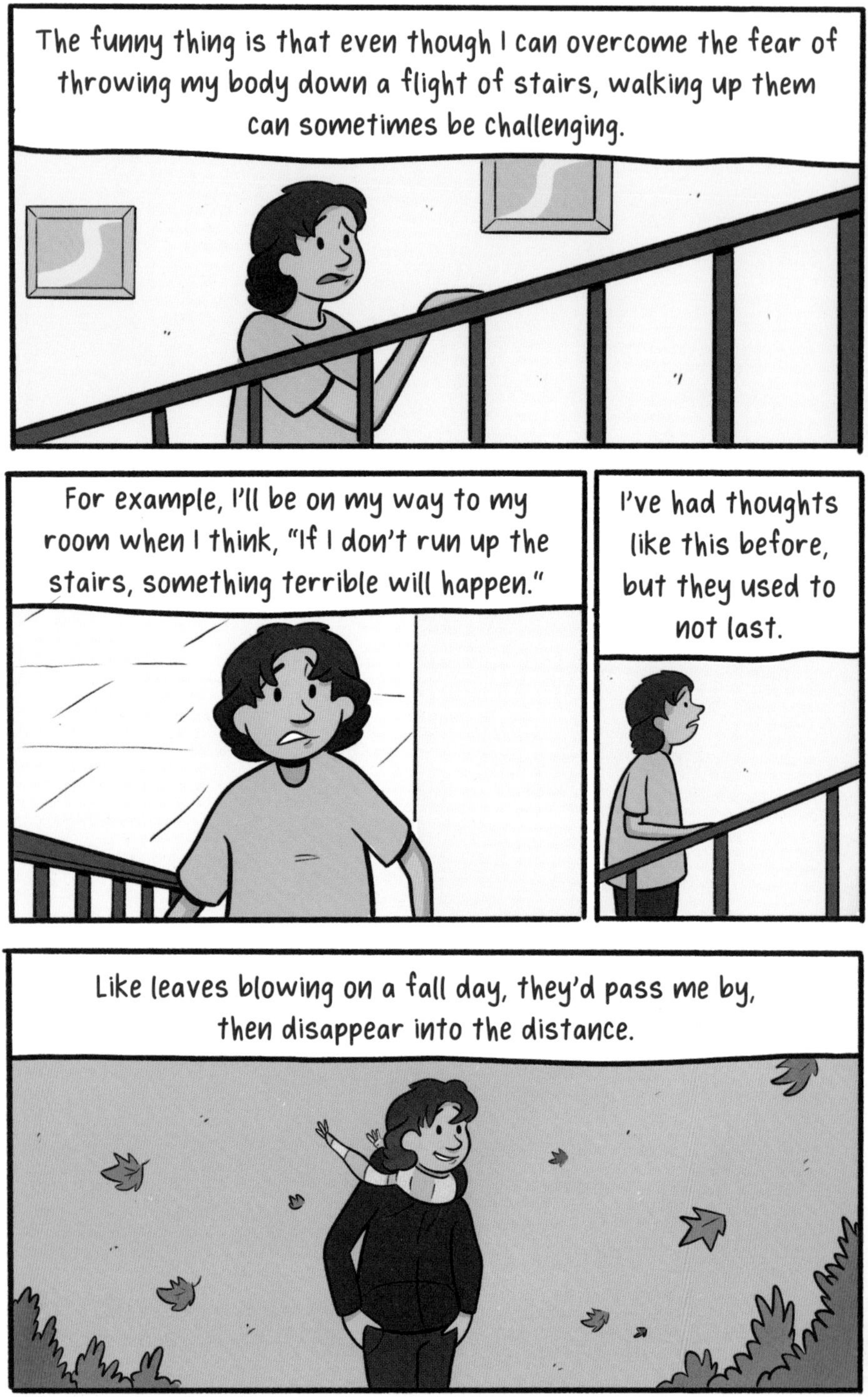
The funny thing is that even though I can overcome the fear of throwing my body down a flight of stairs, walking up them can sometimes be challenging.
For example, I'll be on my way to my room when I think, "If I don't run up the stairs, something terrible will happen."
I've had thoughts like this before, but they used to not last.
Like leaves blowing on a fall day, they'd pass me by, then disappear into the distance.

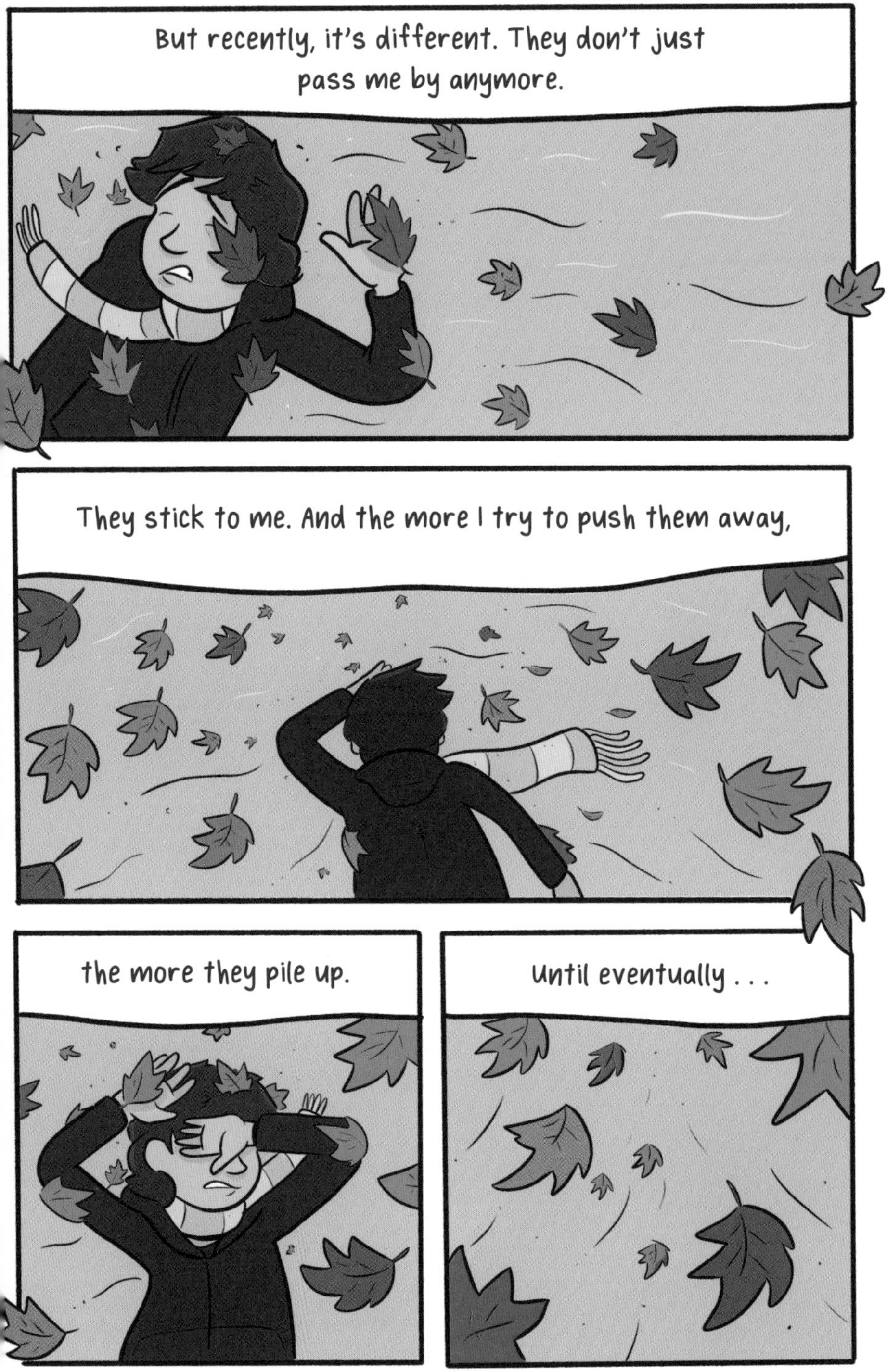
But recently, it's different. They don't just pass me by anymore.
They stick to me. And the more I try to push them away,
the more they pile up.
Until eventually . . .

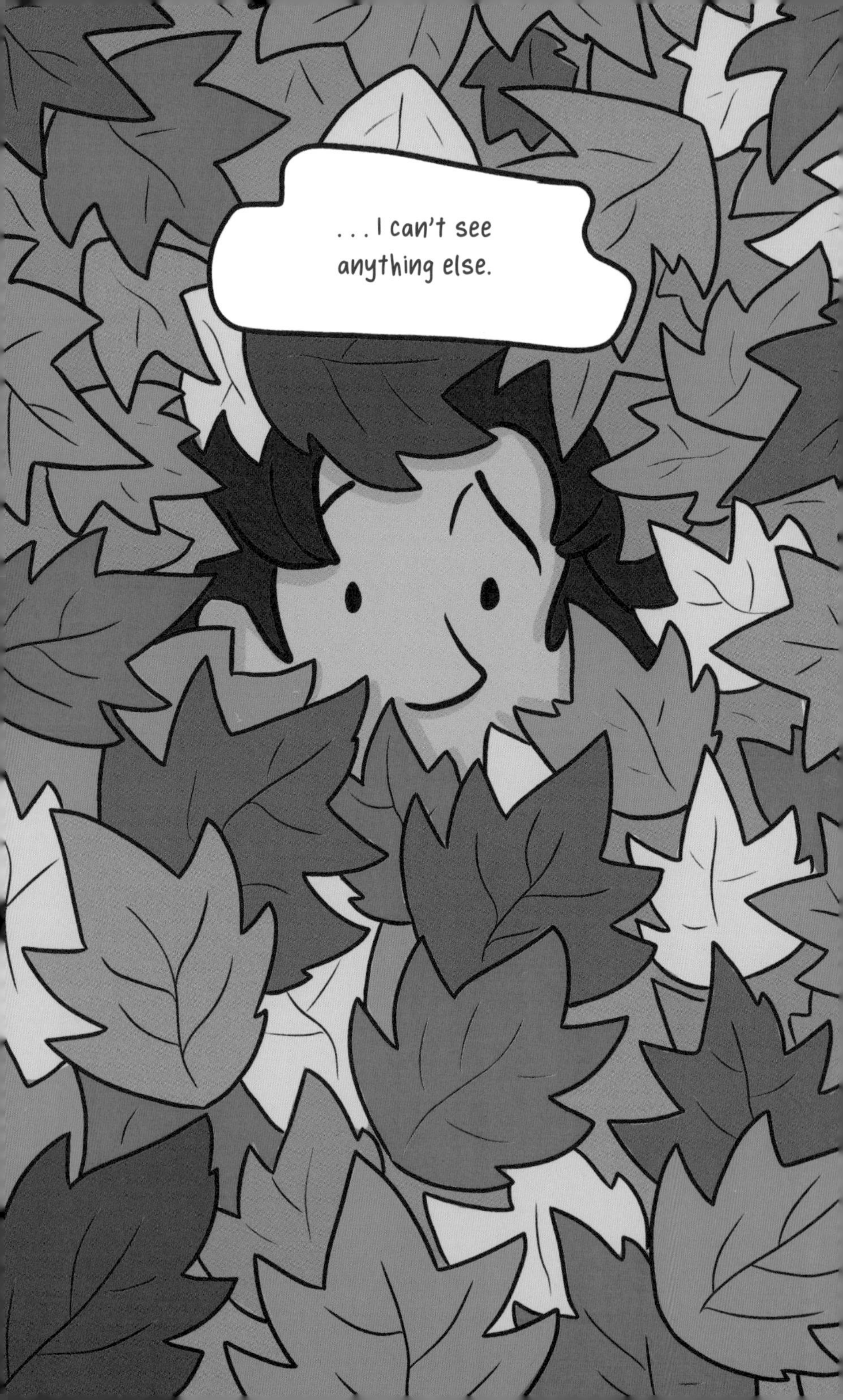
. . . I can't see anything else.

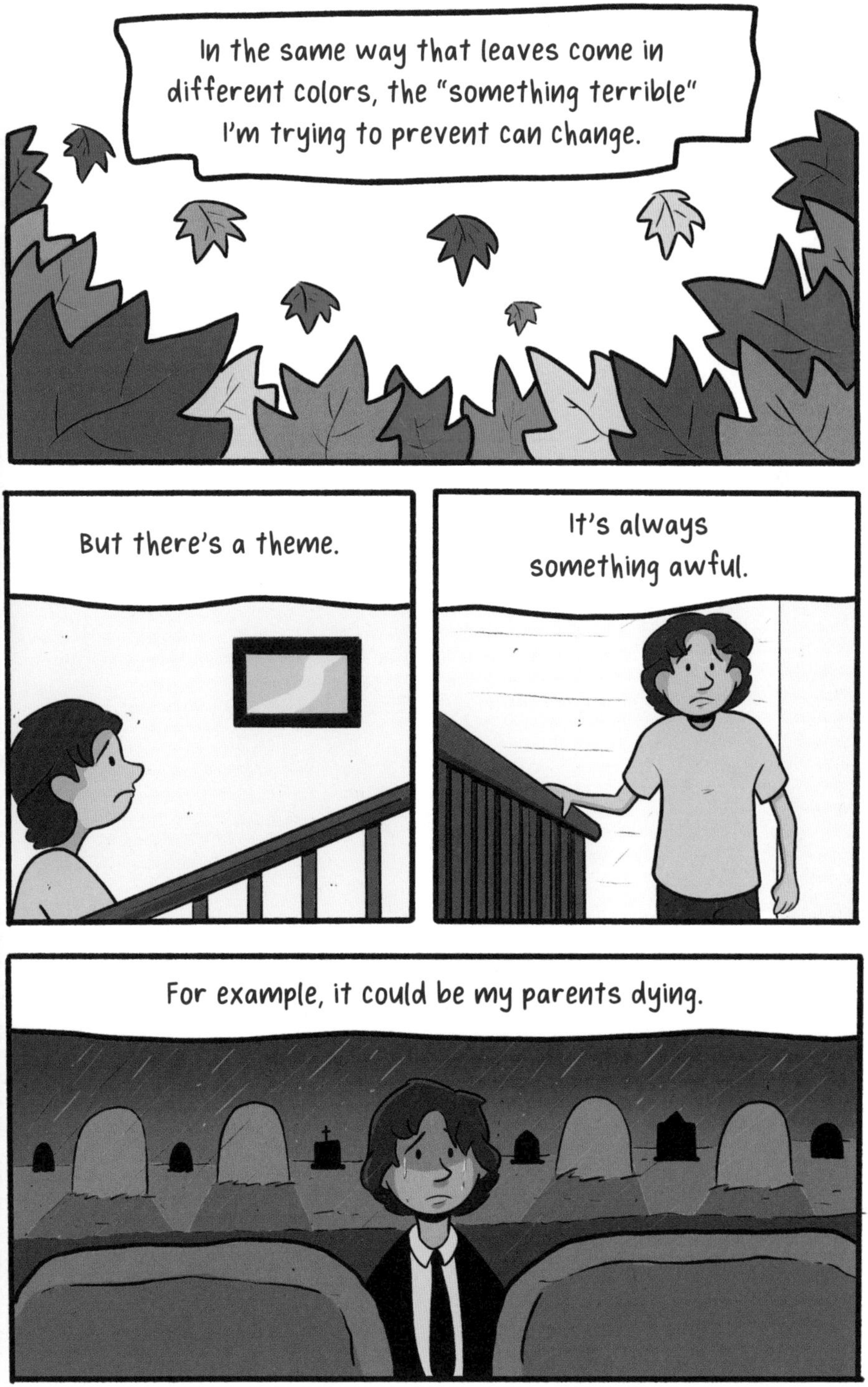
In the same way that leaves come in different colors, the "something terrible" I'm trying to prevent can change.
But there's a theme.
It's always something awful.
For example, it could be my parents dying.

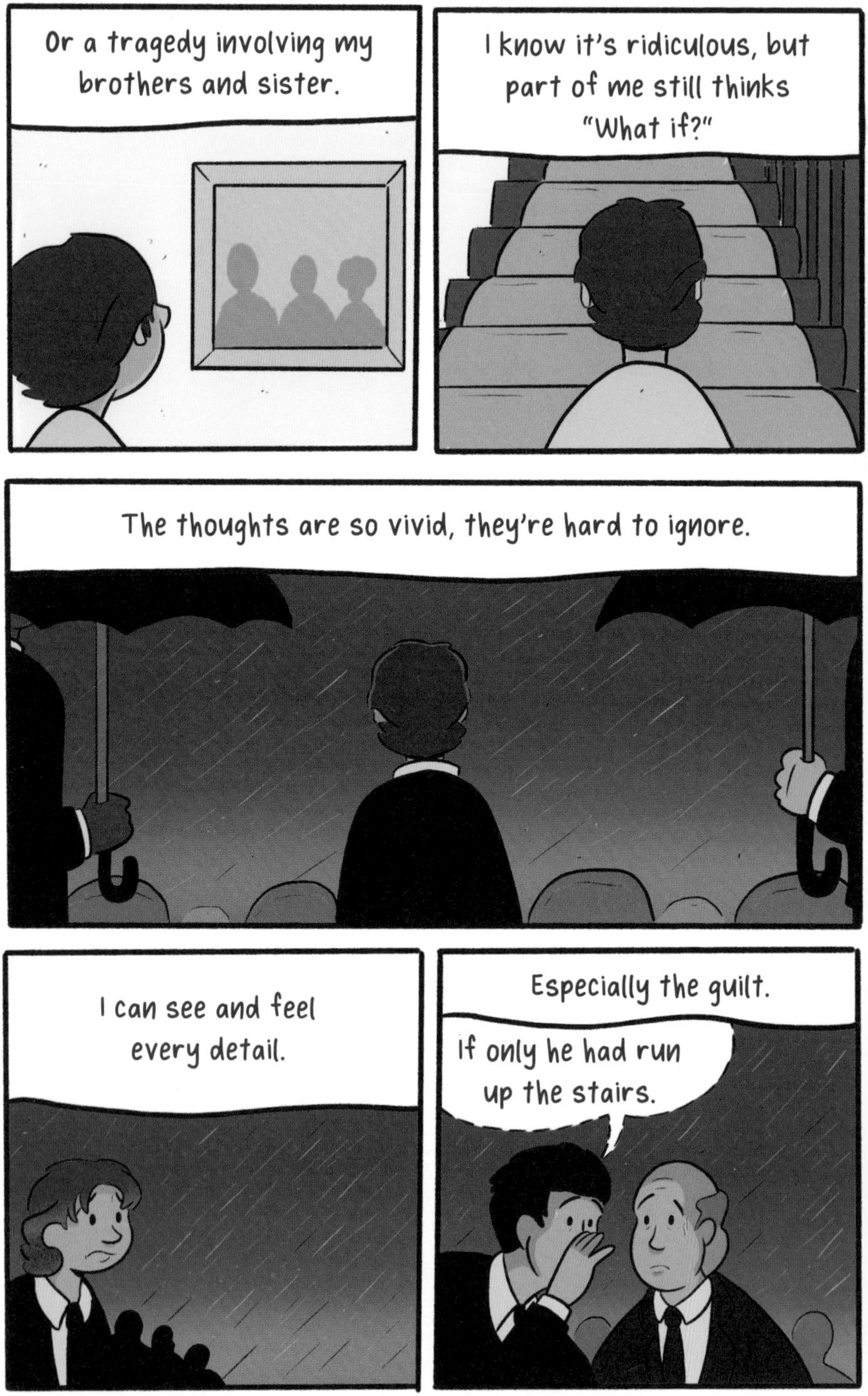

Or a tragedy involving my brothers and sister.
I know it's ridiculous, but part of me still thinks "What if?"
The thoughts are so vivid, they're hard to ignore.
I can see and feel every detail.
Especially the guilt.
If only he had run up the stairs.

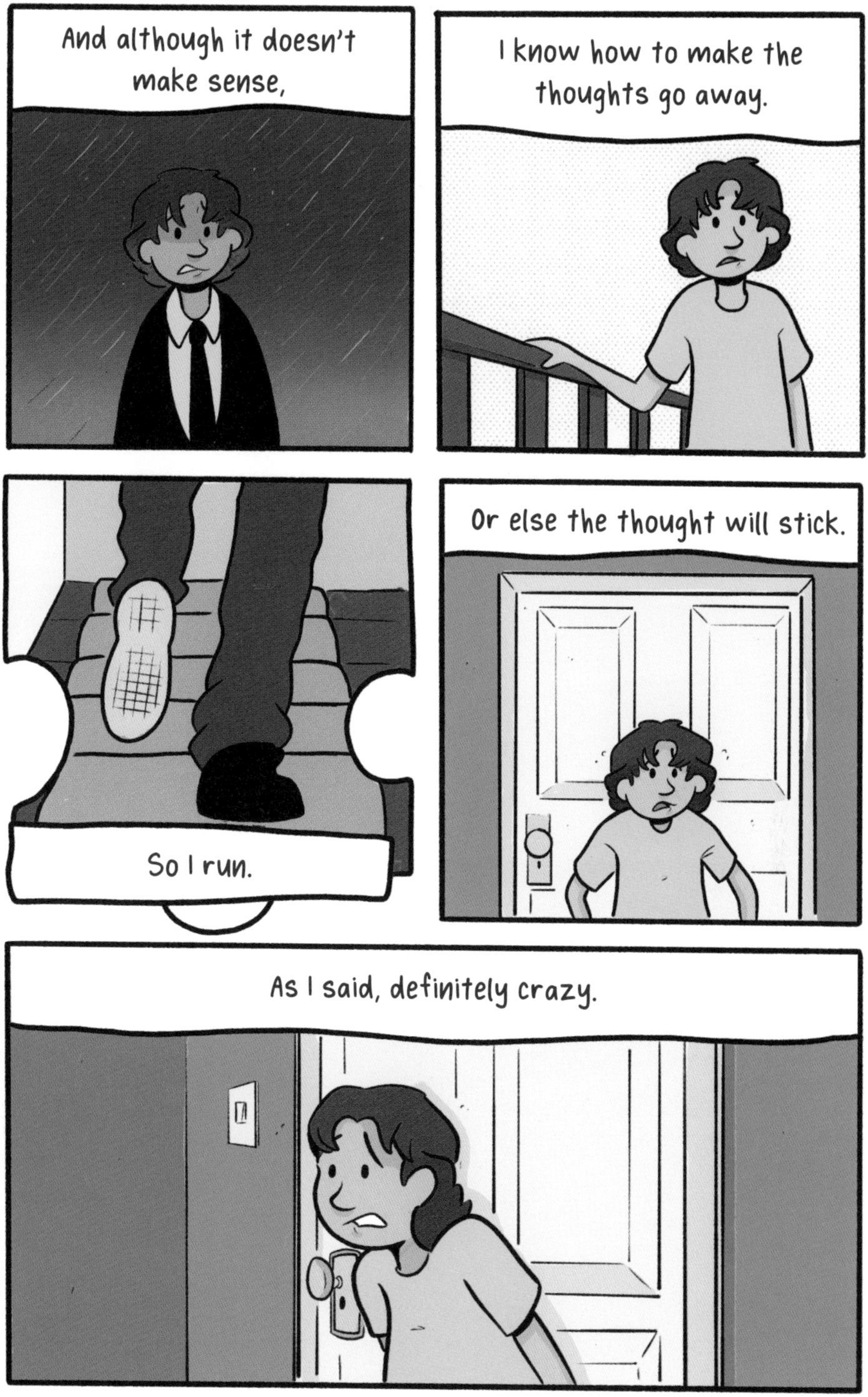
And although it doesn't make sense,
I know how to make the thoughts go away.
So I run.
Or else the thought will stick.
As I said, definitely crazy.

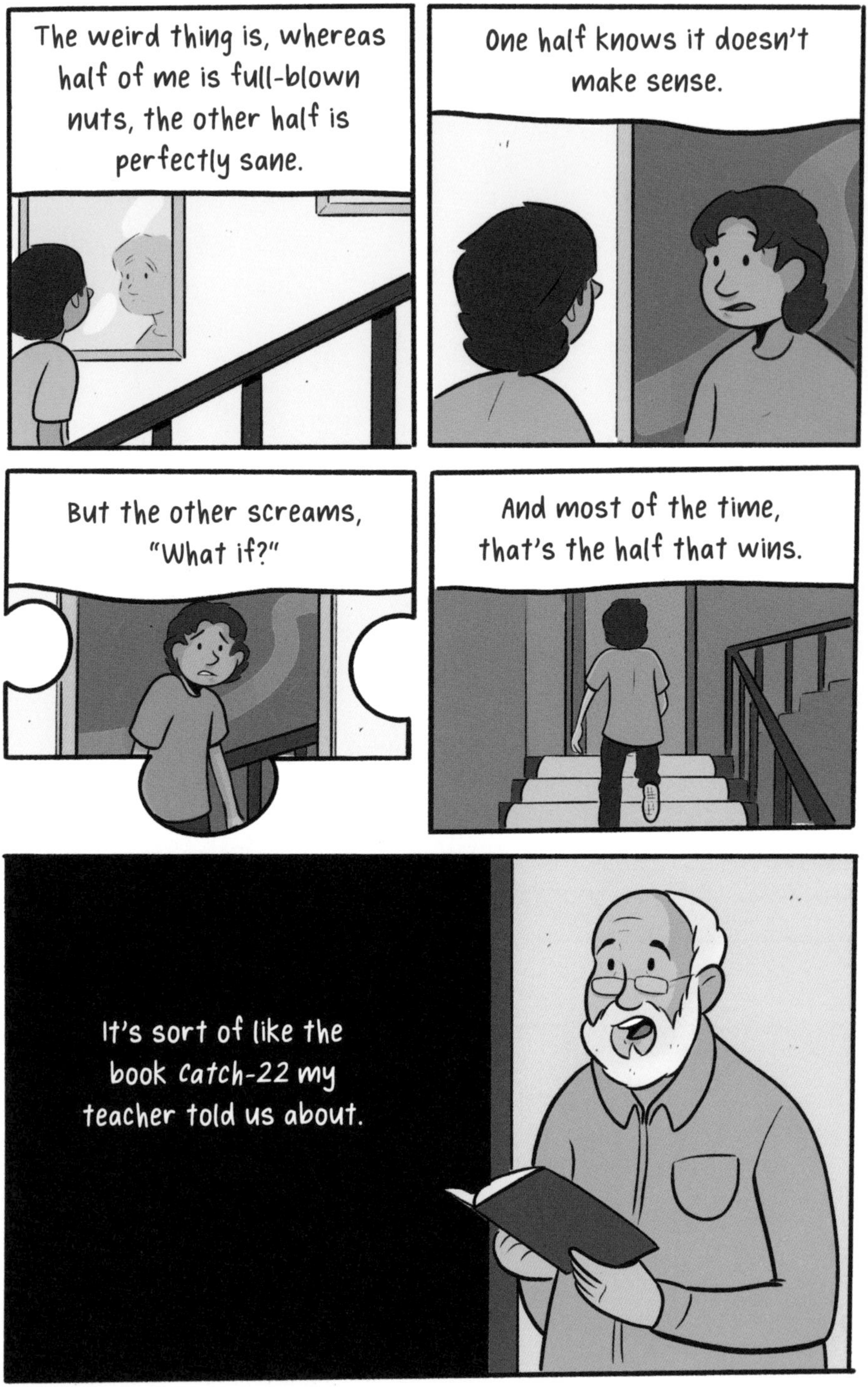
The weird thing is, whereas half of me is full-blown nuts, the other half is perfectly sane.
One half knows it doesn't make sense.
But the other screams, "What if?"
And most of the time, that's the half that wins.
It's sort of like the book *Catch-22* my teacher told us about.

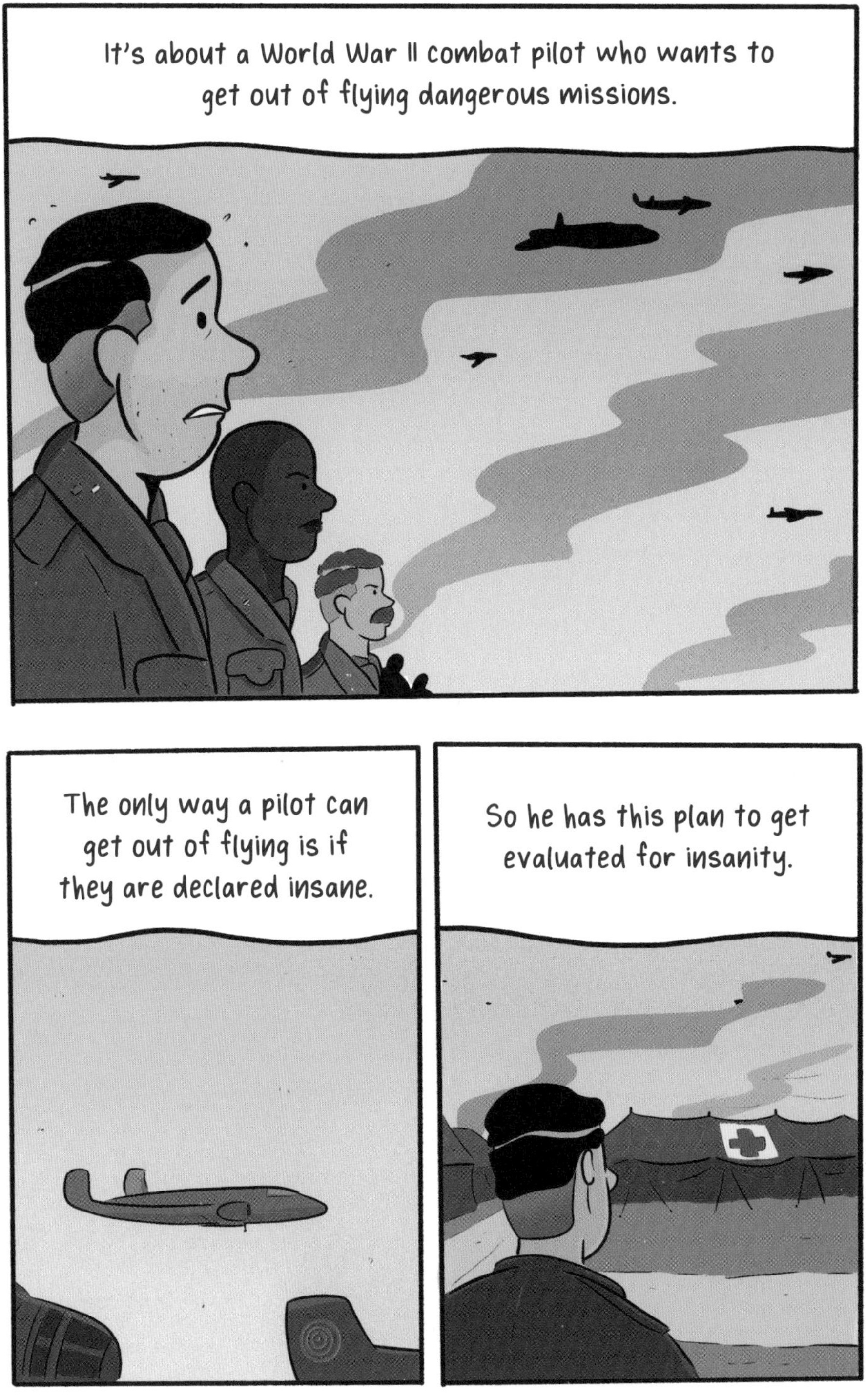
It's about a World War II combat pilot who wants to get out of flying dangerous missions.
The only way a pilot can get out of flying is if they are declared insane.
So he has this plan to get evaluated for insanity.

But the thing is, the doctor tells him anyone applying to be found insane must understand the dangers.

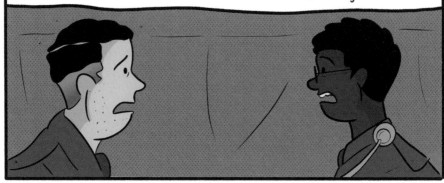

And therefore be sane!

So he has to fly!

I know running up the stairs to save my family's lives is insane, but I still have to do it.

So I guess I'm a bit like that combat pilot. Or at least I like to think so.

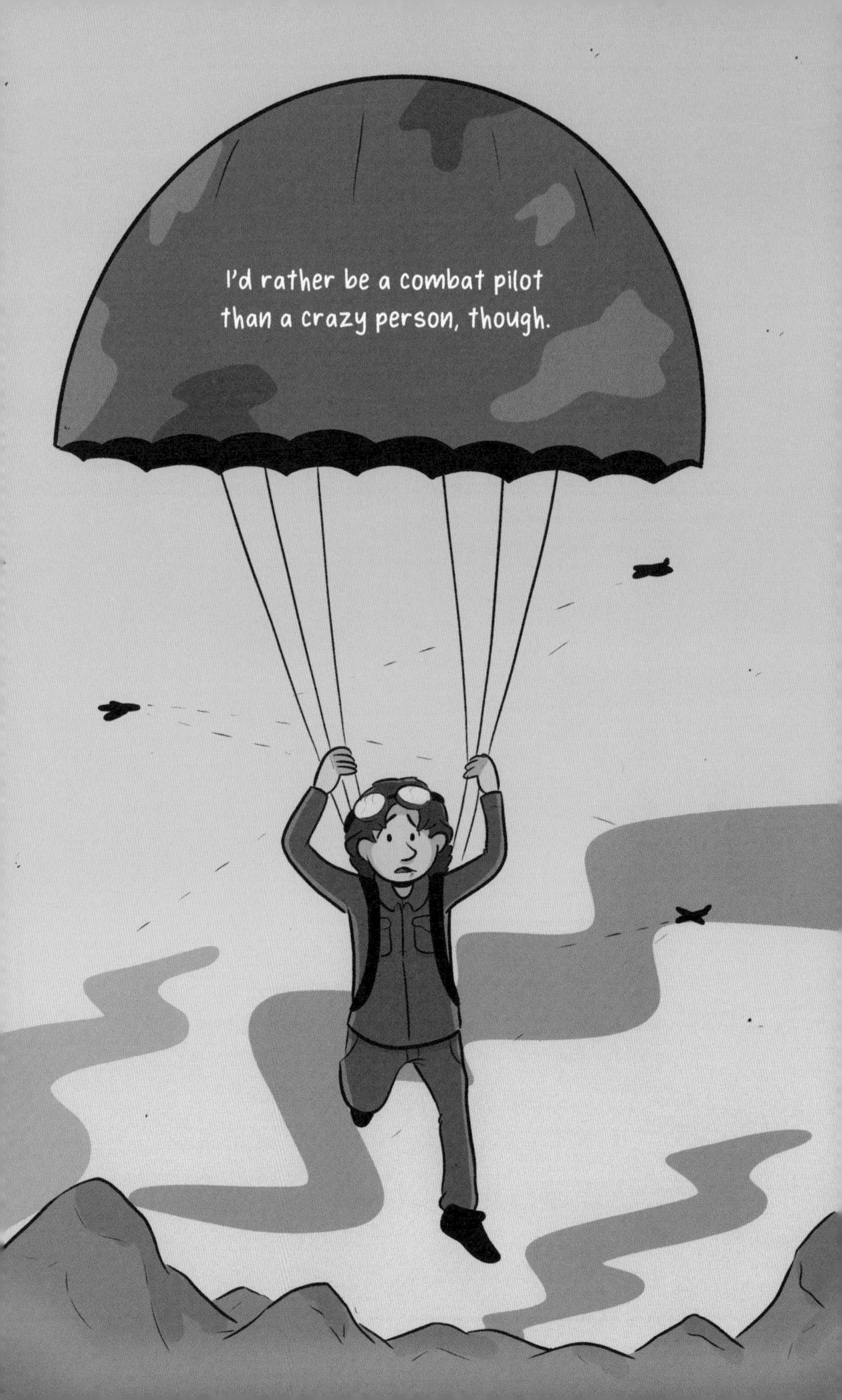
I'd rather be a combat pilot
than a crazy person, though.

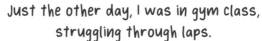

Just the other day, I was in gym class,
struggling through laps.

Running doesn't make sense
to me. I can only think of two
reasons why anybody
would run.

To get somewhere

or to escape.

Circling the field, I'm not getting anywhere.
And because gym class is mandatory—I can't escape.

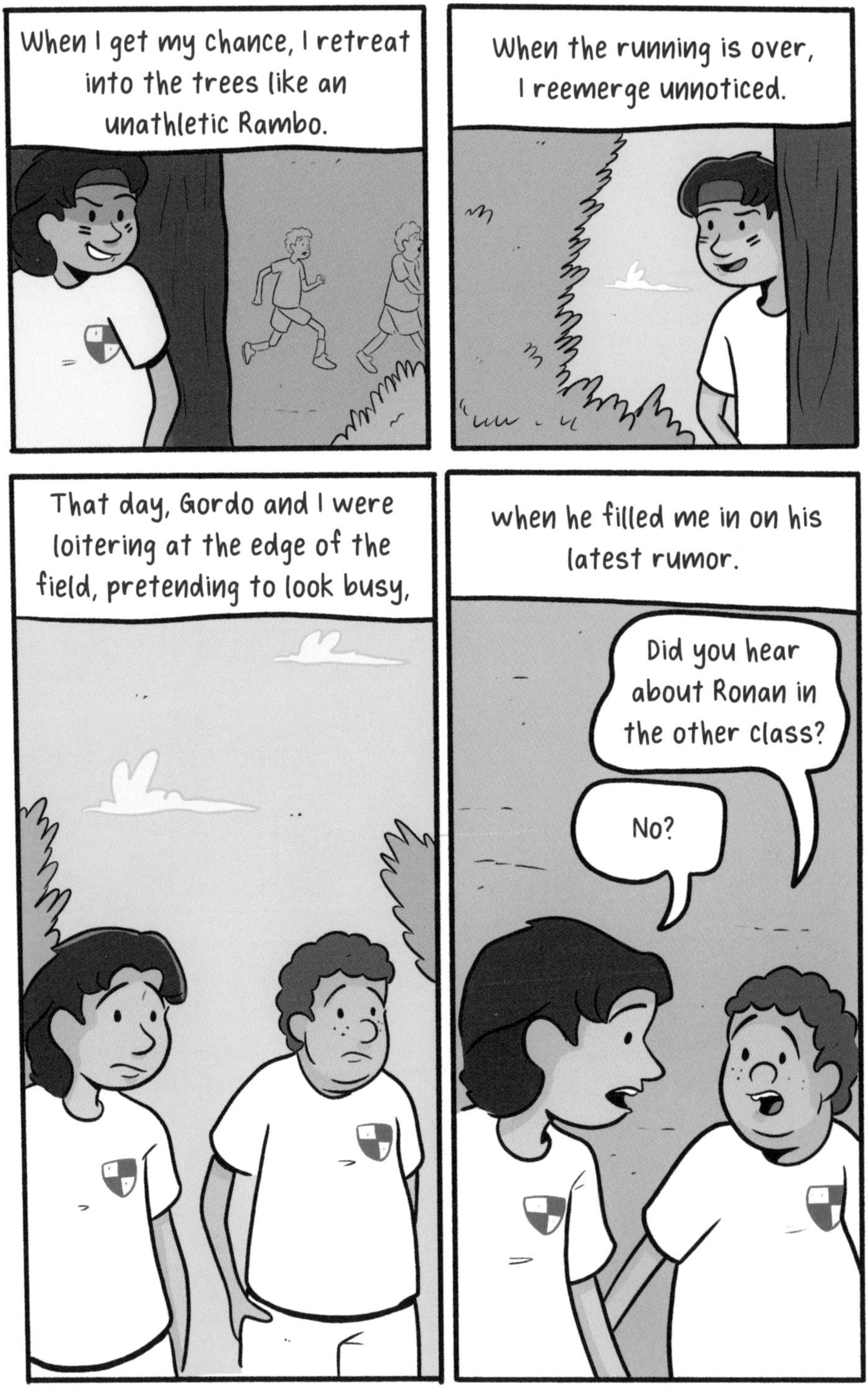
When I get my chance, I retreat into the trees like an unathletic Rambo.
When the running is over, I reemerge unnoticed.
That day, Gordo and I were loitering at the edge of the field, pretending to look busy,
when he filled me in on his latest rumor.
Did you hear about Ronan in the other class?
No?

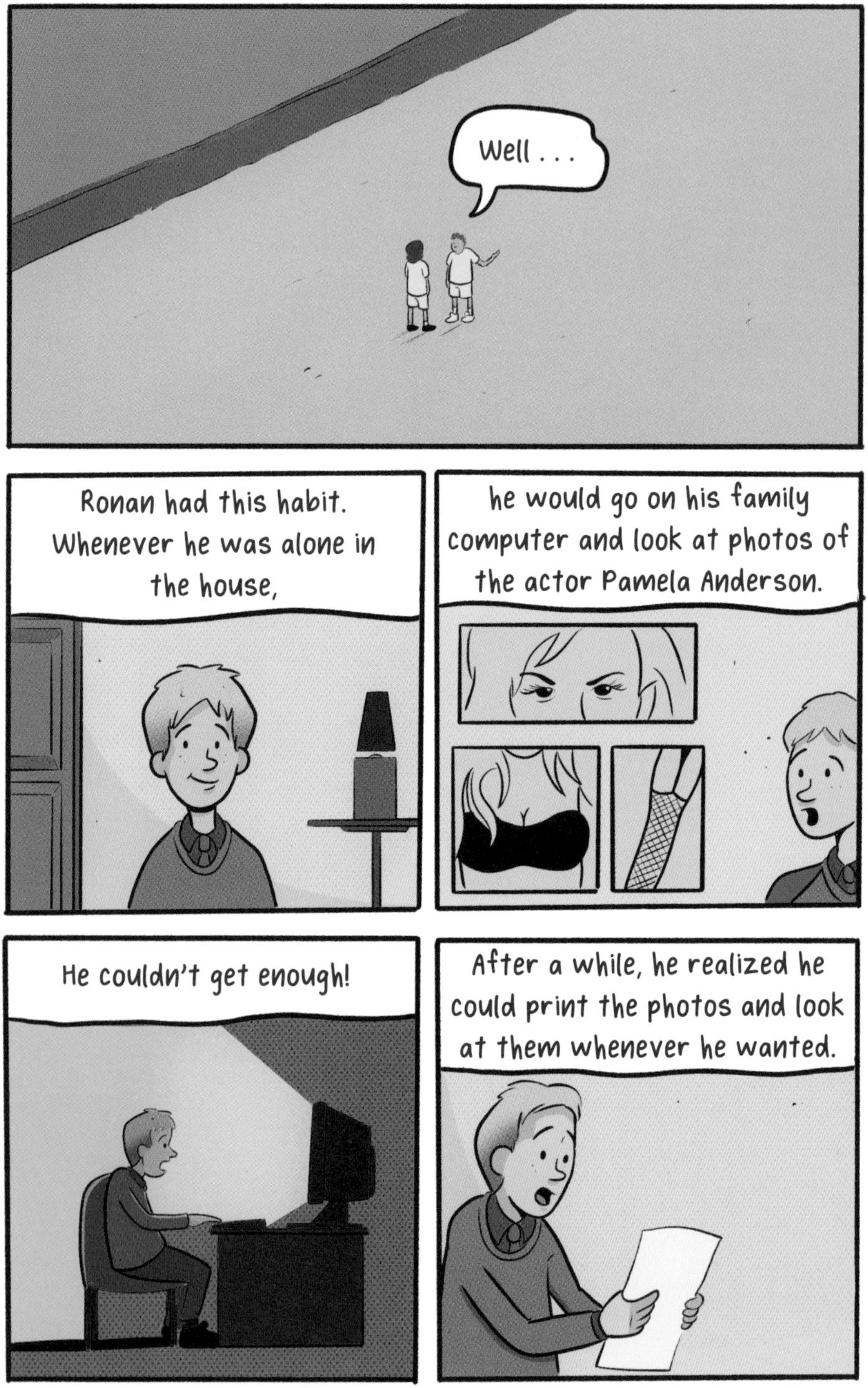

Well . . .
Ronan had this habit. Whenever he was alone in the house,
he would go on his family computer and look at photos of the actor Pamela Anderson.
He couldn't get enough!
After a while, he realized he could print the photos and look at them whenever he wanted.

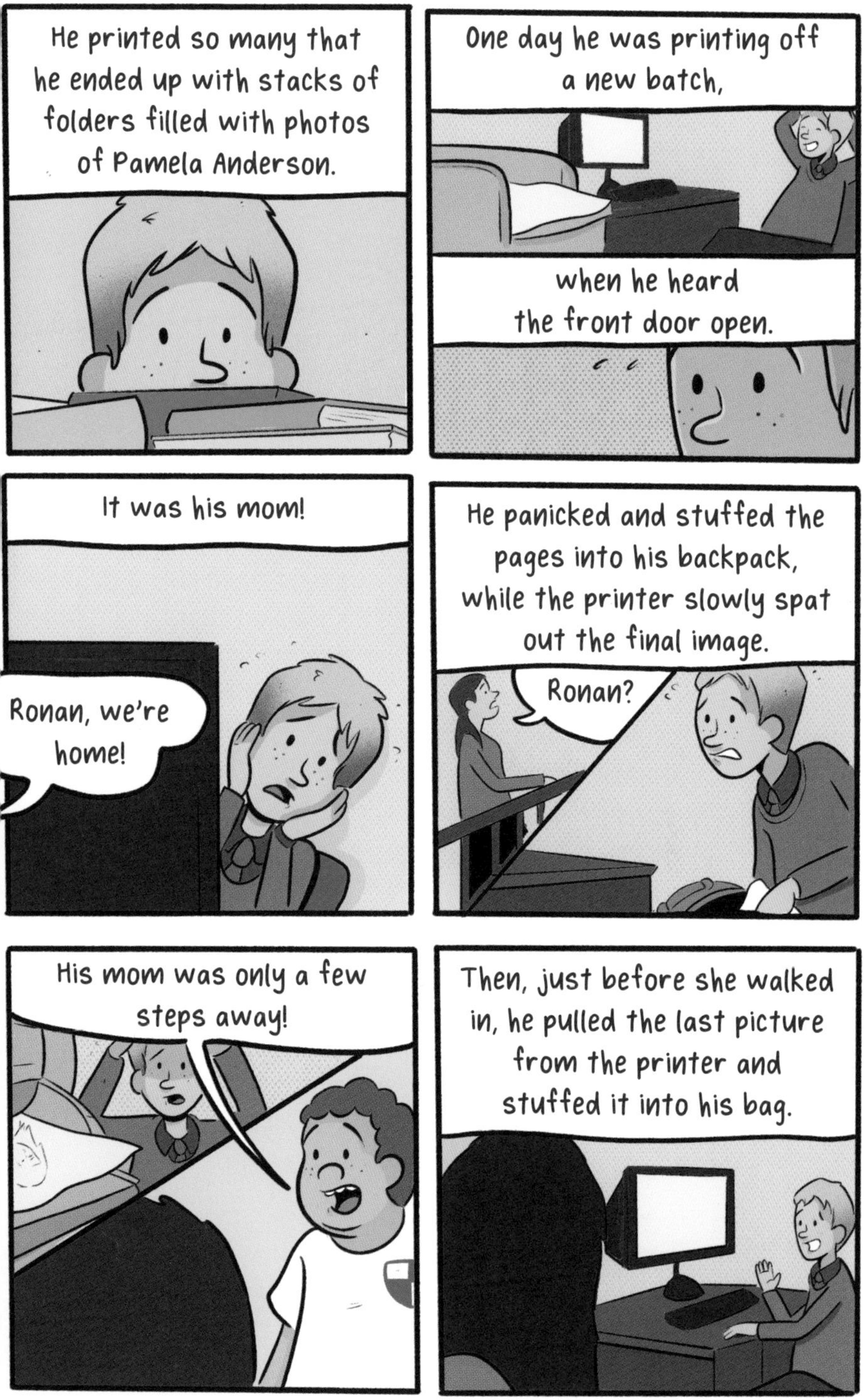
He printed so many that he ended up with stacks of folders filled with photos of Pamela Anderson.
One day he was printing off a new batch,
when he heard the front door open.
It was his mom!
Ronan, we're home!
He panicked and stuffed the pages into his backpack, while the printer slowly spat out the final image.
Ronan?
His mom was only a few steps away!
Then, just before she walked in, he pulled the last picture from the printer and stuffed it into his bag.

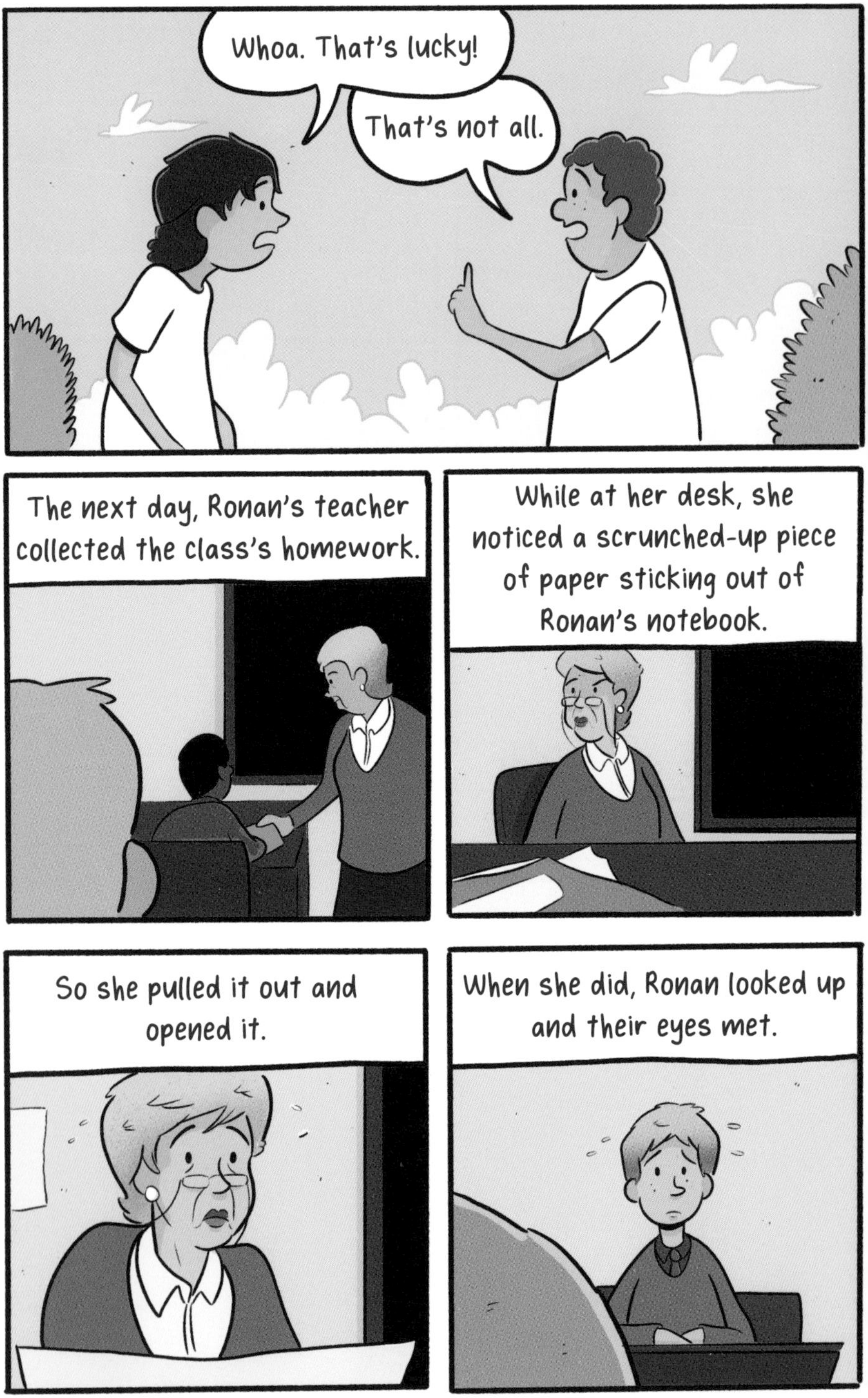
Whoa. That's lucky!
That's not all.
The next day, Ronan's teacher collected the class's homework.
While at her desk, she noticed a scrunched-up piece of paper sticking out of Ronan's notebook.
So she pulled it out and opened it.
When she did, Ronan looked up and their eyes met.

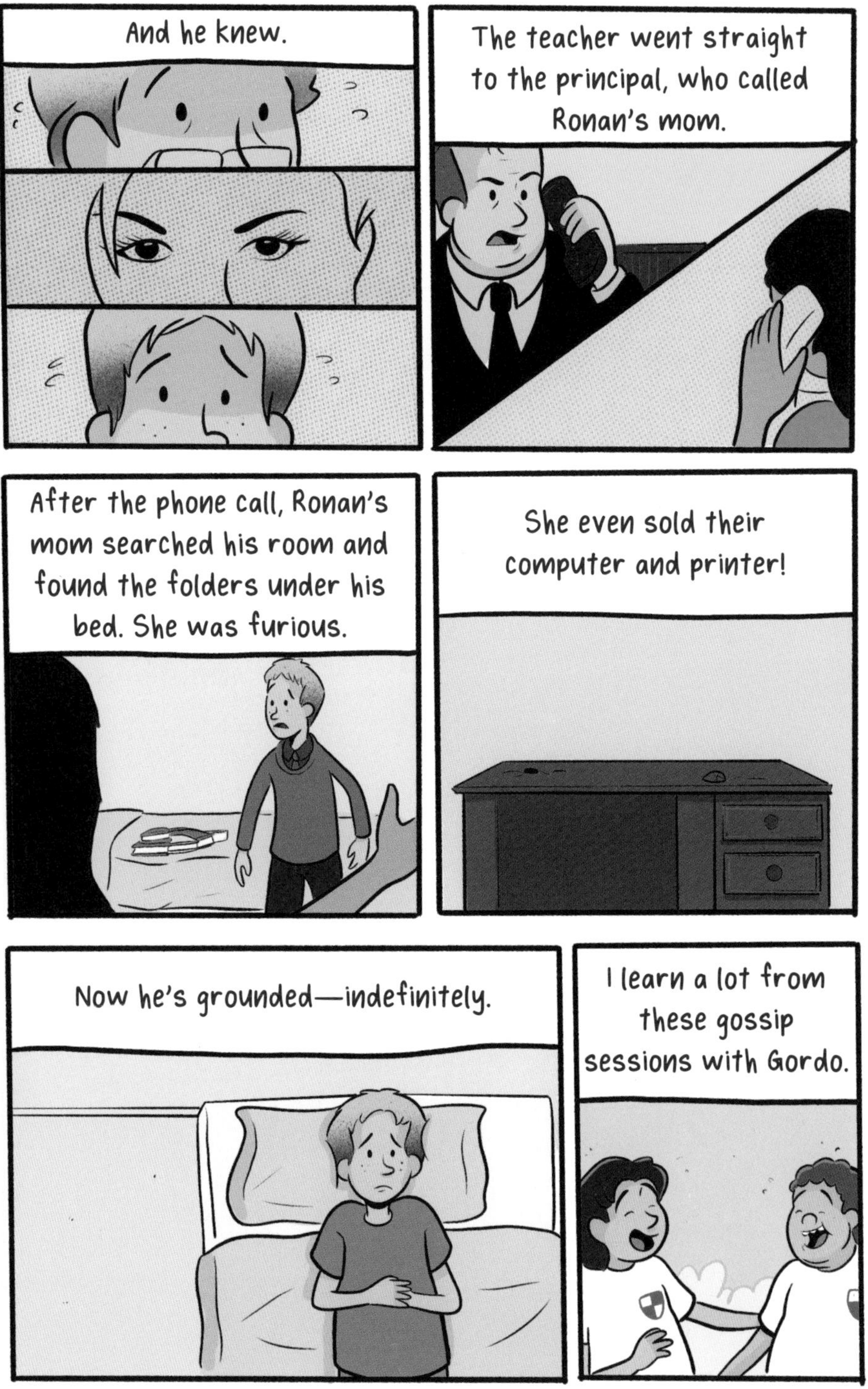
And he knew.
The teacher went straight to the principal, who called Ronan's mom.
After the phone call, Ronan's mom searched his room and found the folders under his bed. She was furious.
She even sold their computer and printer!
Now he's grounded—indefinitely.
I learn a lot from these gossip sessions with Gordo.

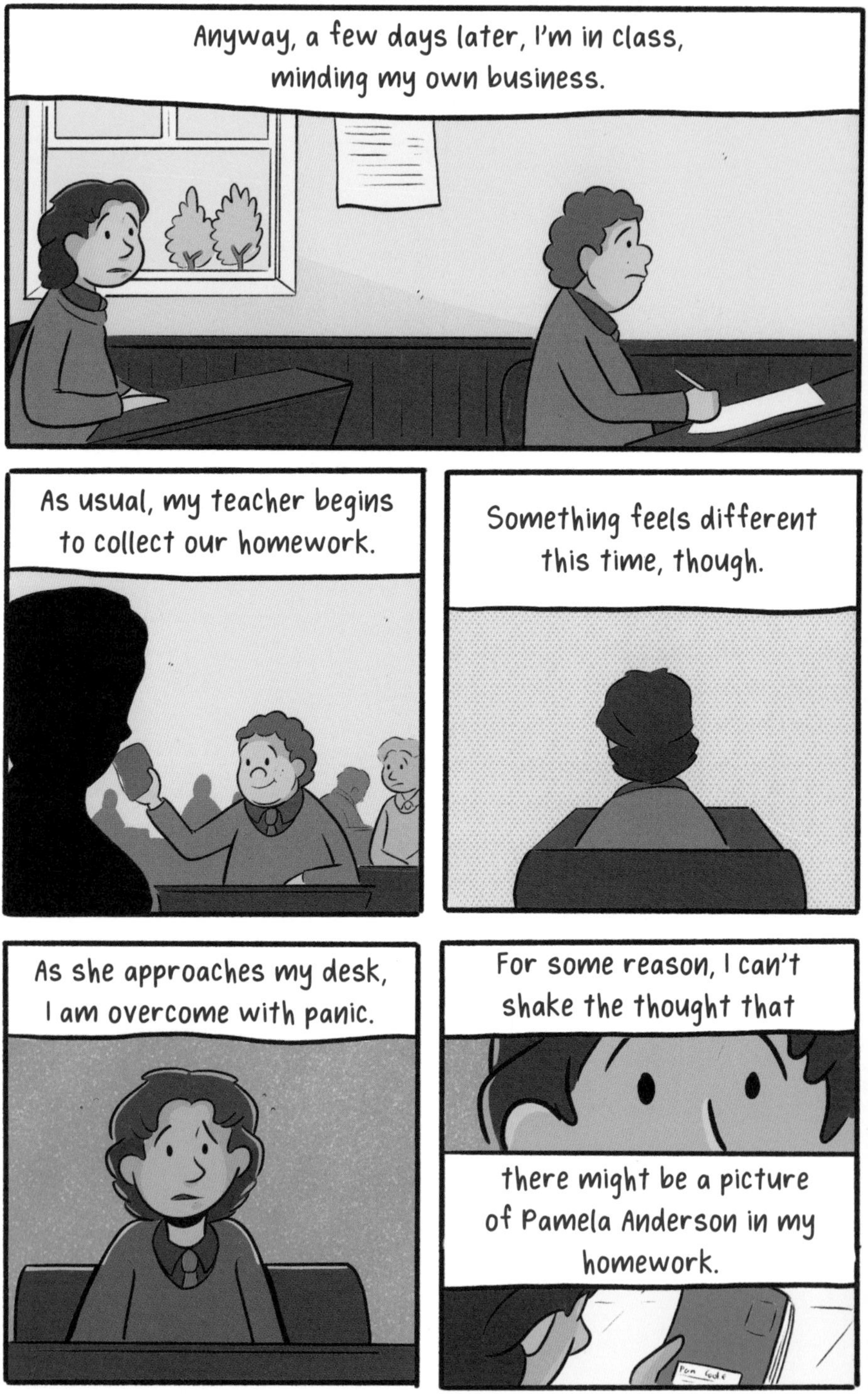

Anyway, a few days later, I'm in class, minding my own business.
As usual, my teacher begins to collect our homework.
Something feels different this time, though.
As she approaches my desk, I am overcome with panic.
For some reason, I can't shake the thought that
there might be a picture of Pamela Anderson in my homework.

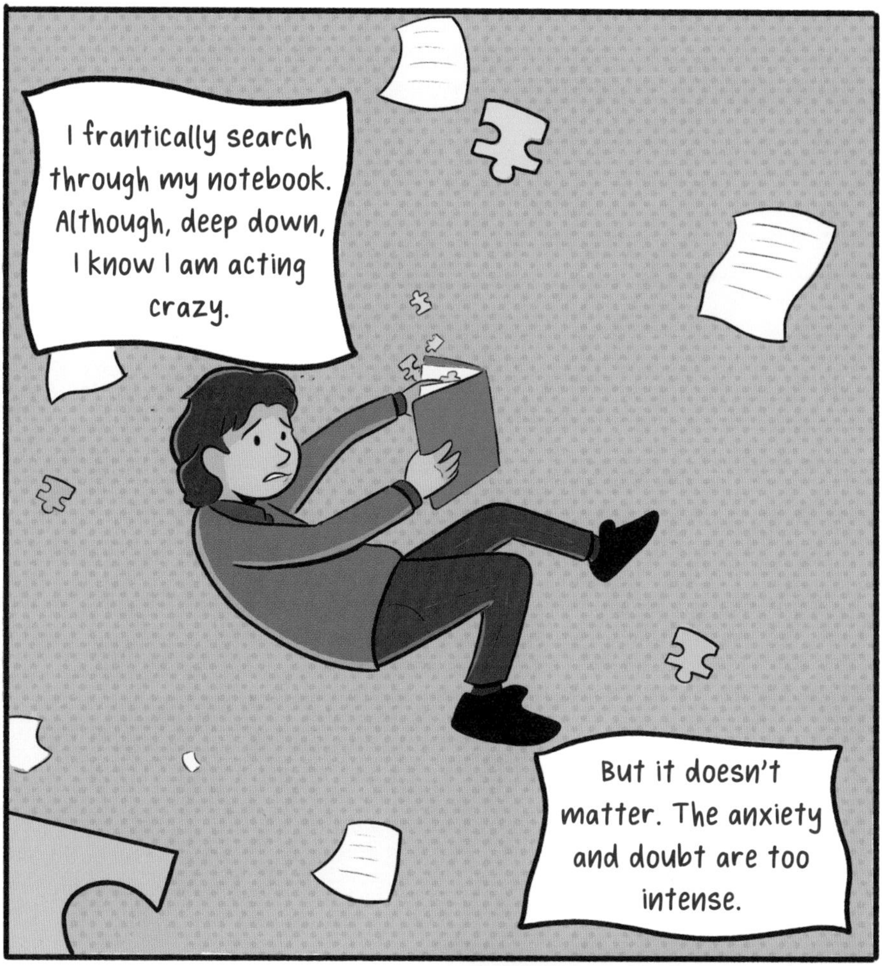
I frantically search through my notebook. Although, deep down, I know I am acting crazy.
But it doesn't matter. The anxiety and doubt are too intense.

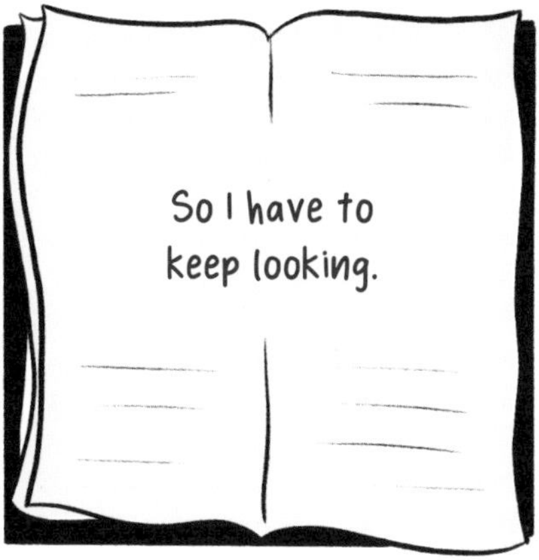
So I have to keep looking.

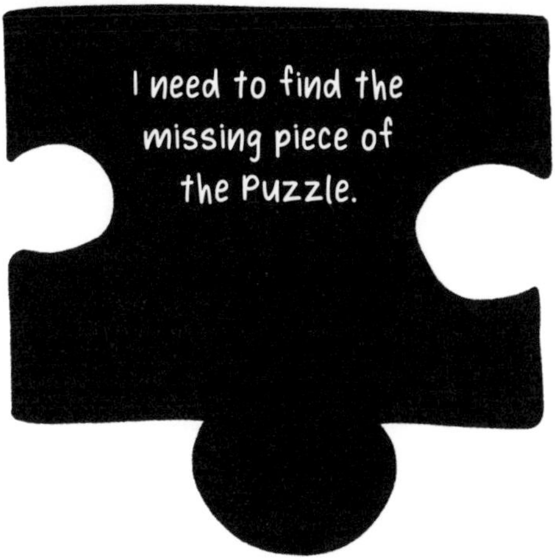
I need to find the missing piece of the puzzle.

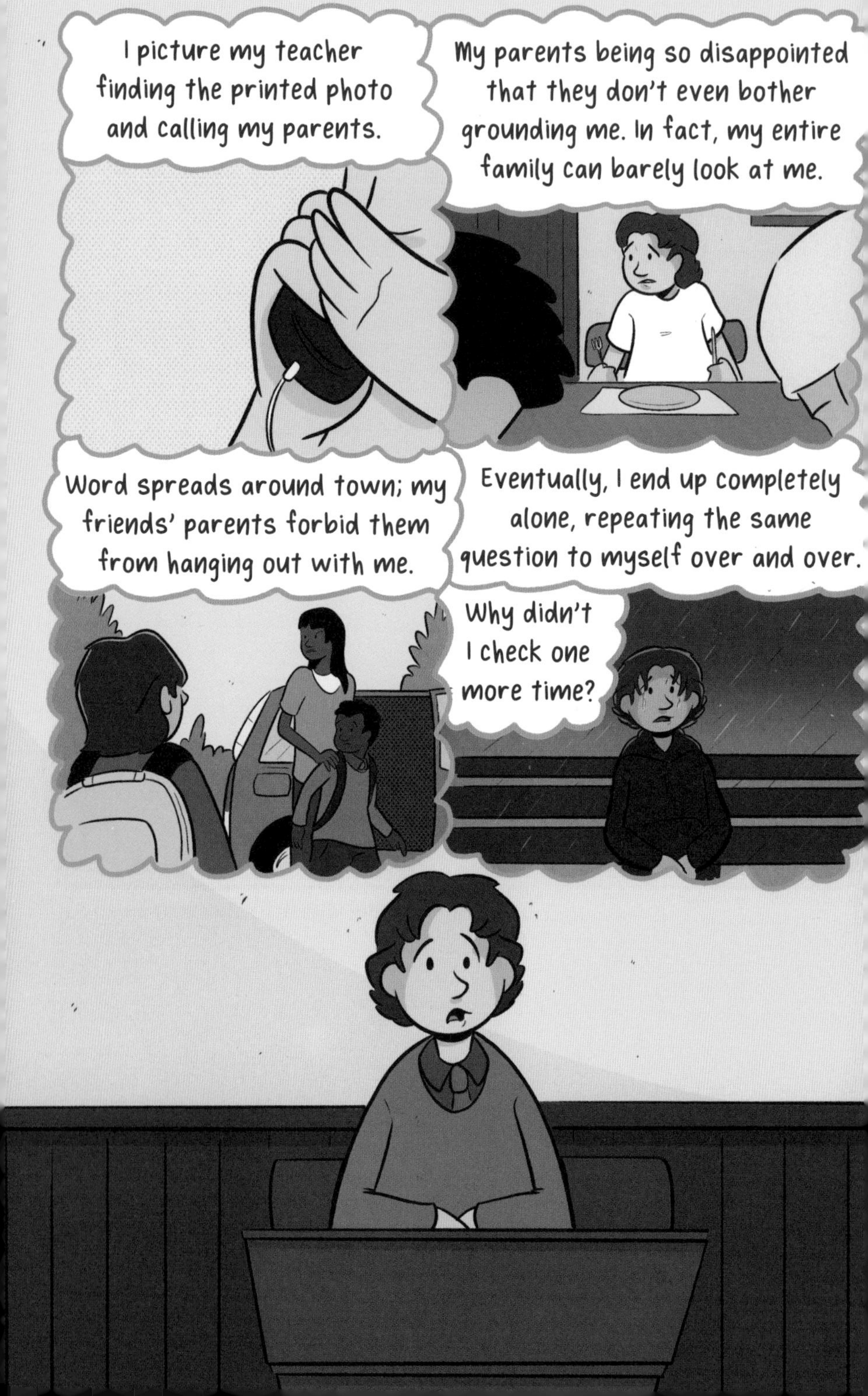
I picture my teacher finding the printed photo and calling my parents.
My parents being so disappointed that they don't even bother grounding me. In fact, my entire family can barely look at me.
Word spreads around town; my friends' parents forbid them from hanging out with me.
Eventually, I end up completely alone, repeating the same question to myself over and over.
Why didn't I check one more time?

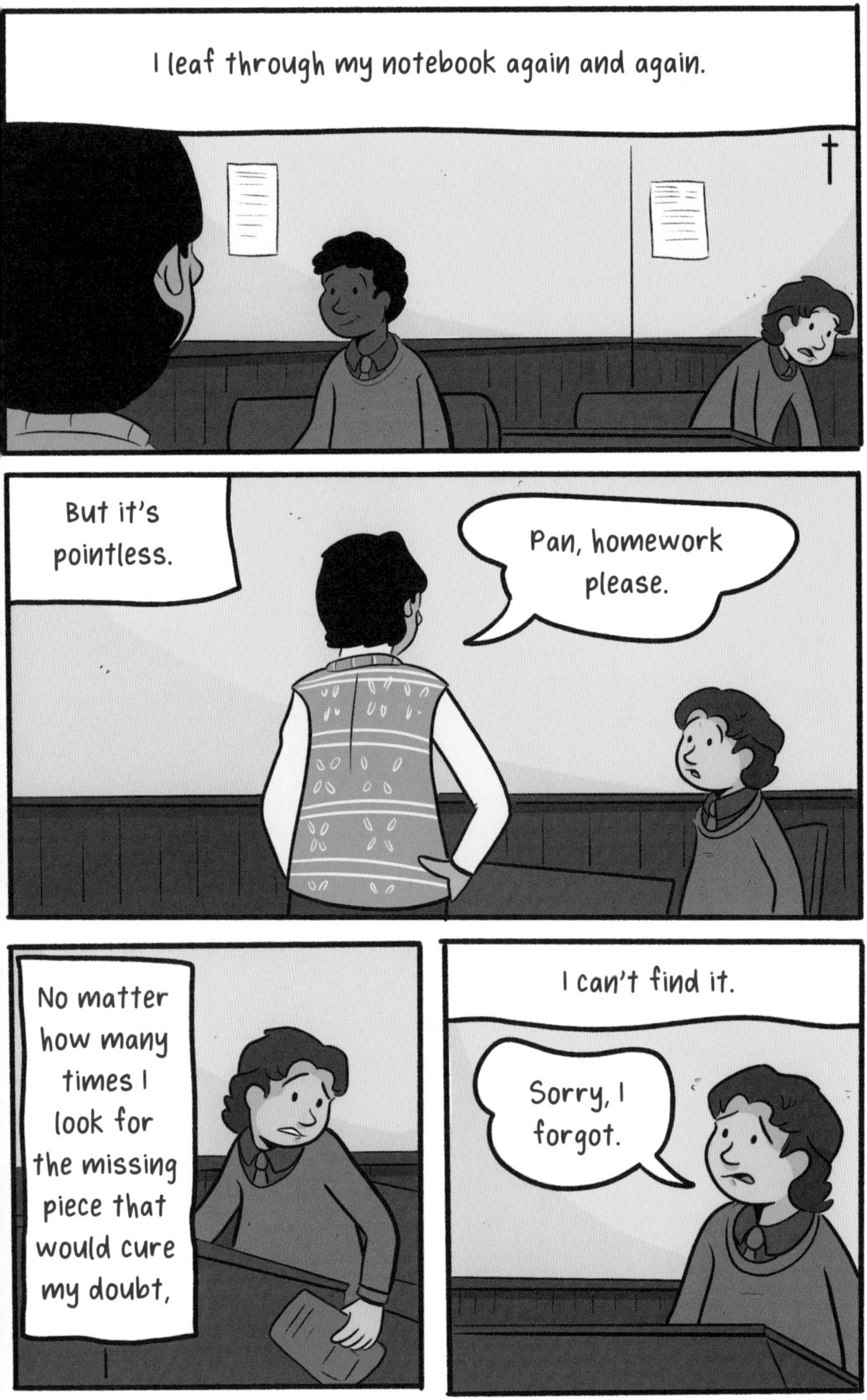
I leaf through my notebook again and again.
But it's pointless.
Pan, homework please.
No matter how many times I look for the missing piece that would cure my doubt,
I can't find it.
Sorry, I forgot.

I never do.

3

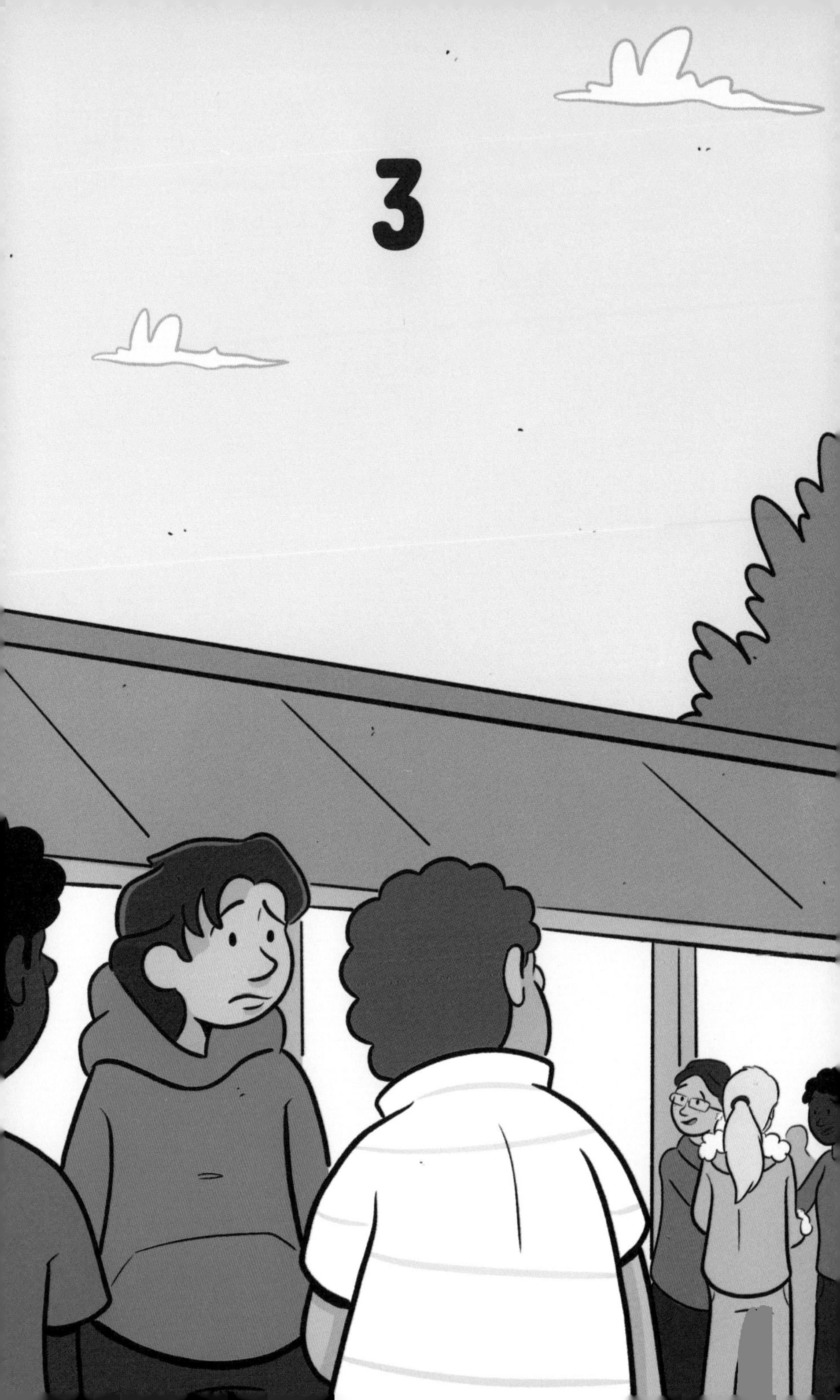

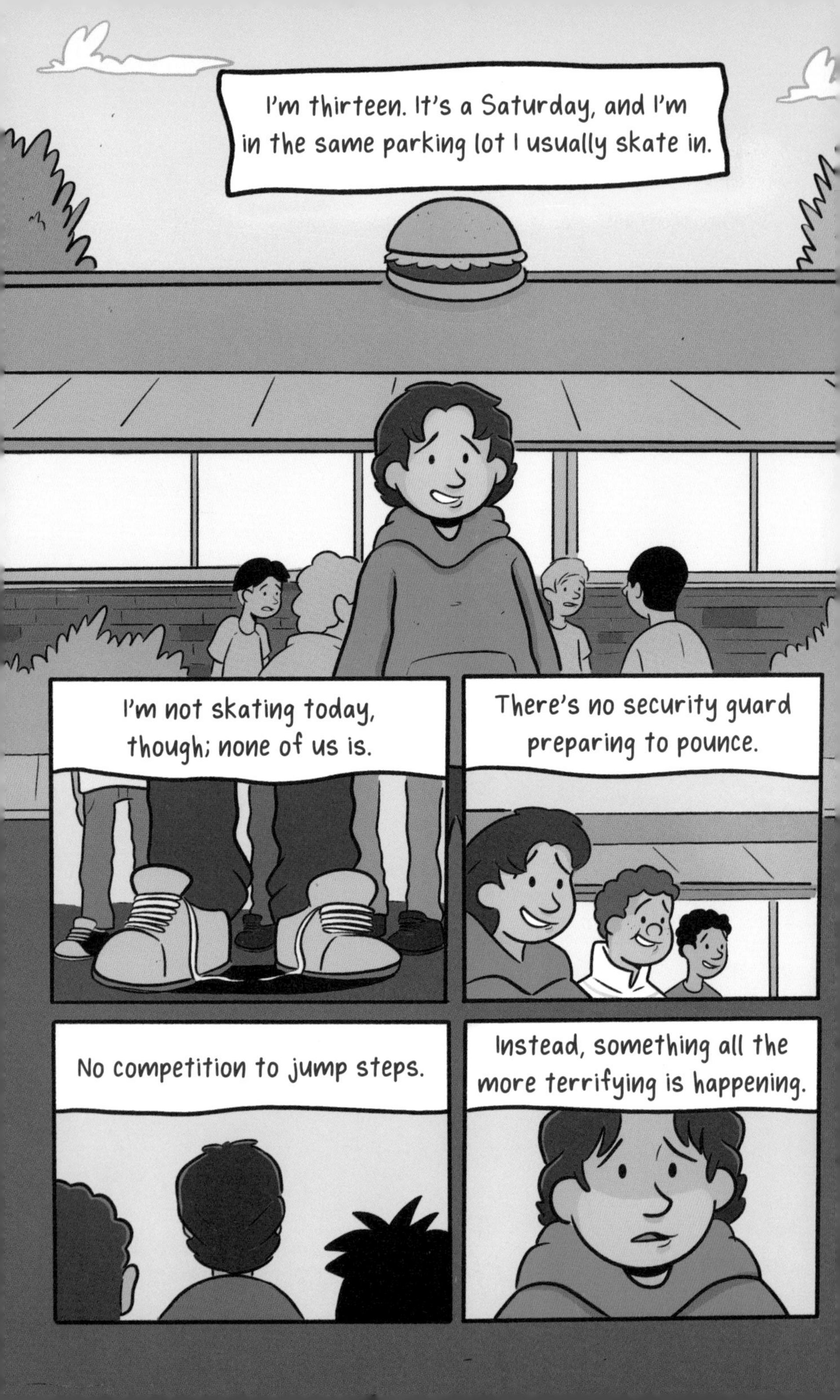
I'm thirteen. It's a Saturday, and I'm in the same parking lot I usually skate in.
I'm not skating today, though; none of us is.
There's no security guard preparing to pounce.
No competition to jump steps.
Instead, something all the more terrifying is happening.

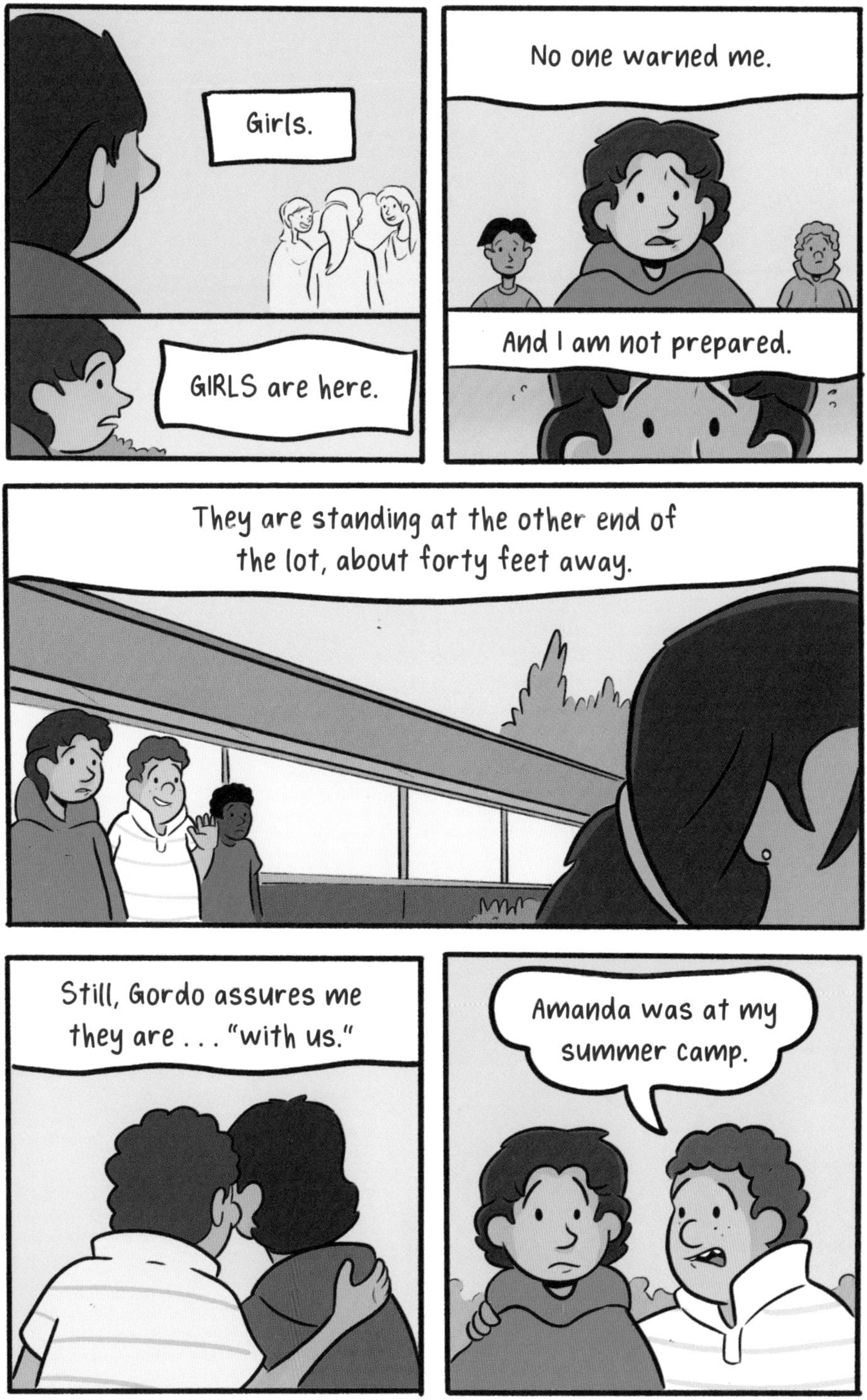
Girls.
GIRLS are here.
No one warned me.
And I am not prepared.
They are standing at the other end of the lot, about forty feet away.
Still, Gordo assures me they are . . . "with us."
Amanda was at my summer camp.

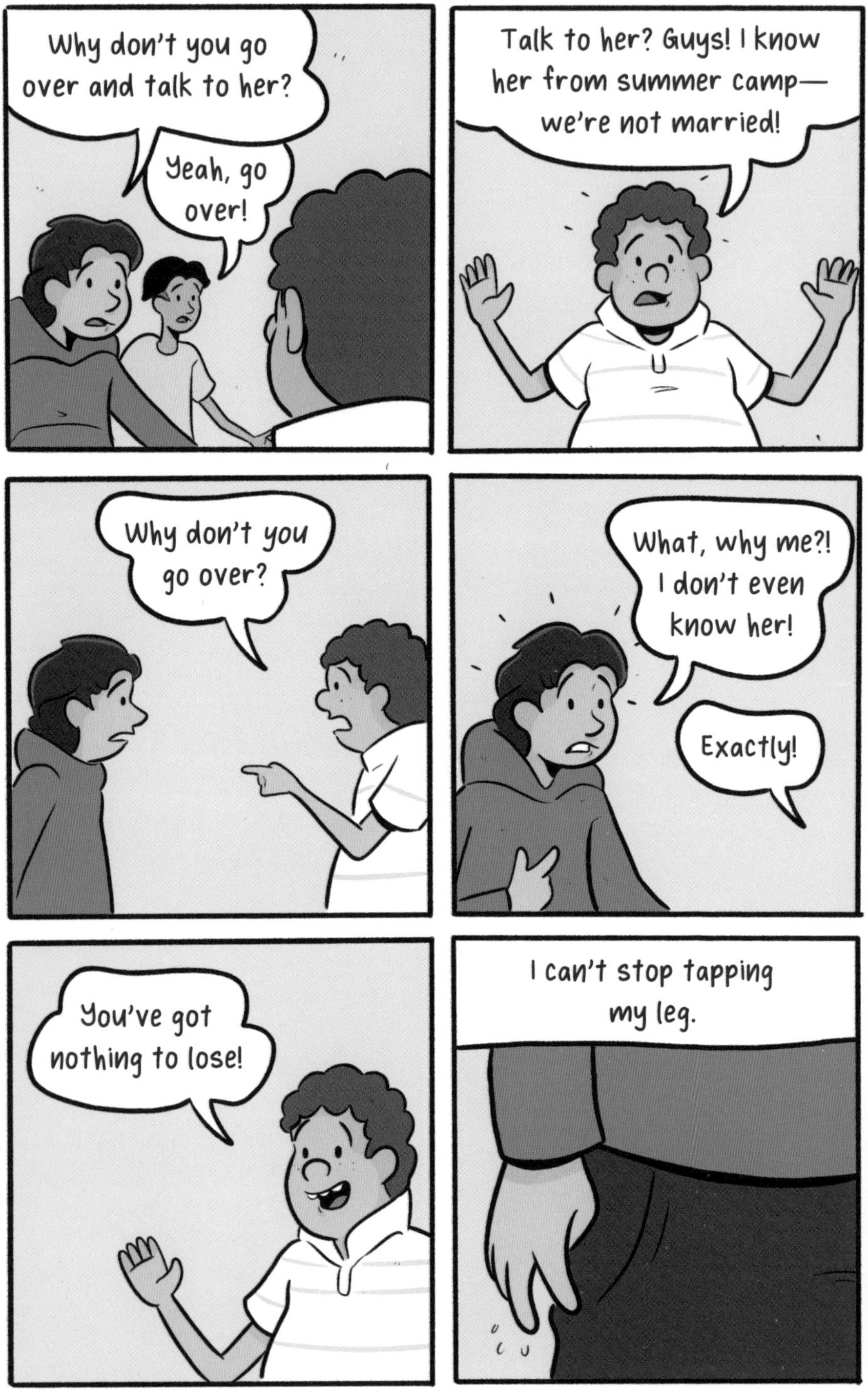
Why don't you go over and talk to her?
Yeah, go over!
Talk to her? Guys! I know her from summer camp—we're not married!
Why don't you go over?
What, why me?! I don't even know her!
Exactly!
You've got nothing to lose!
I can't stop tapping my leg.

It's like I'm sending myself reassuring messages in Morse code.

Stay calm. Just count and breathe.

1,2,3 . . .

1,2,3 . . .

1,2,3 . . .

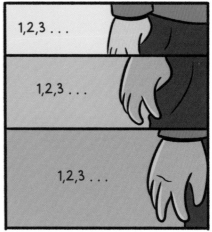

I have this thing with counting, especially at night.

It all starts while brushing my teeth.

At first, everything's normal. But then the feeling that something is wrong arrives, followed by the counting.

1,2,3 . . .

1,2,3 . . .

And before I know it, I'm caught up trying to solve the Puzzle again.

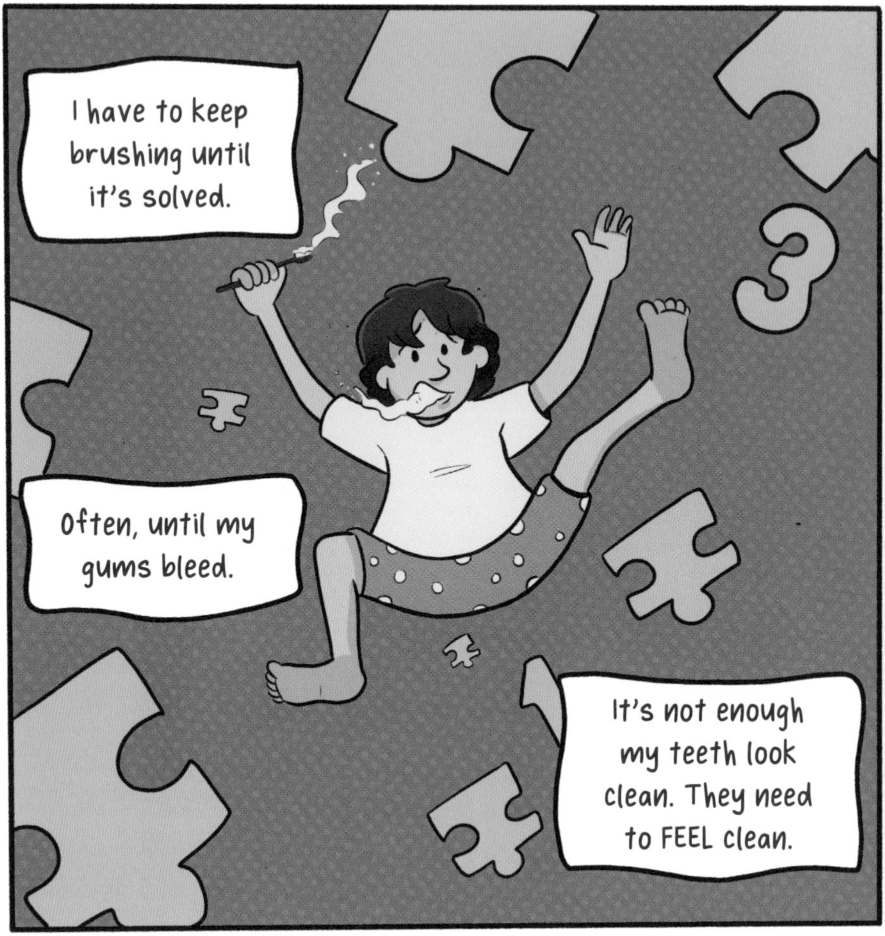
I have to keep brushing until it's solved.
Often, until my gums bleed.
It's not enough my teeth look clean. They need to FEEL clean.

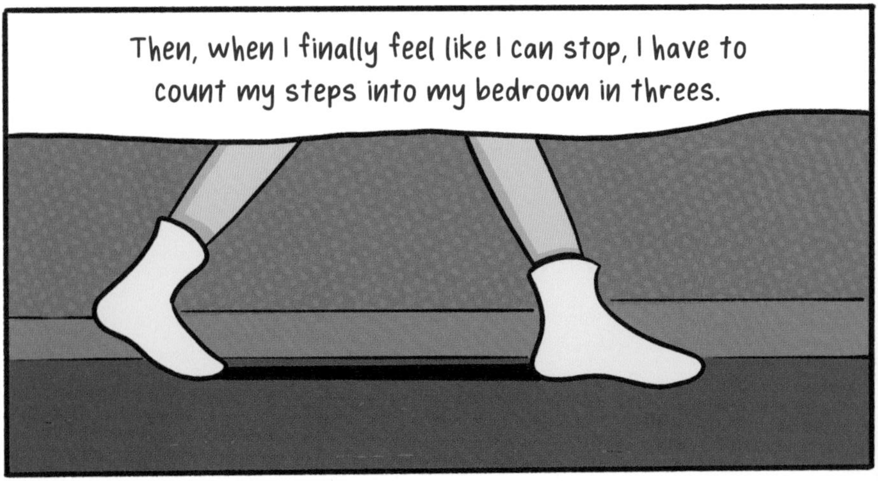
Then, when I finally feel like I can stop, I have to count my steps into my bedroom in threes.

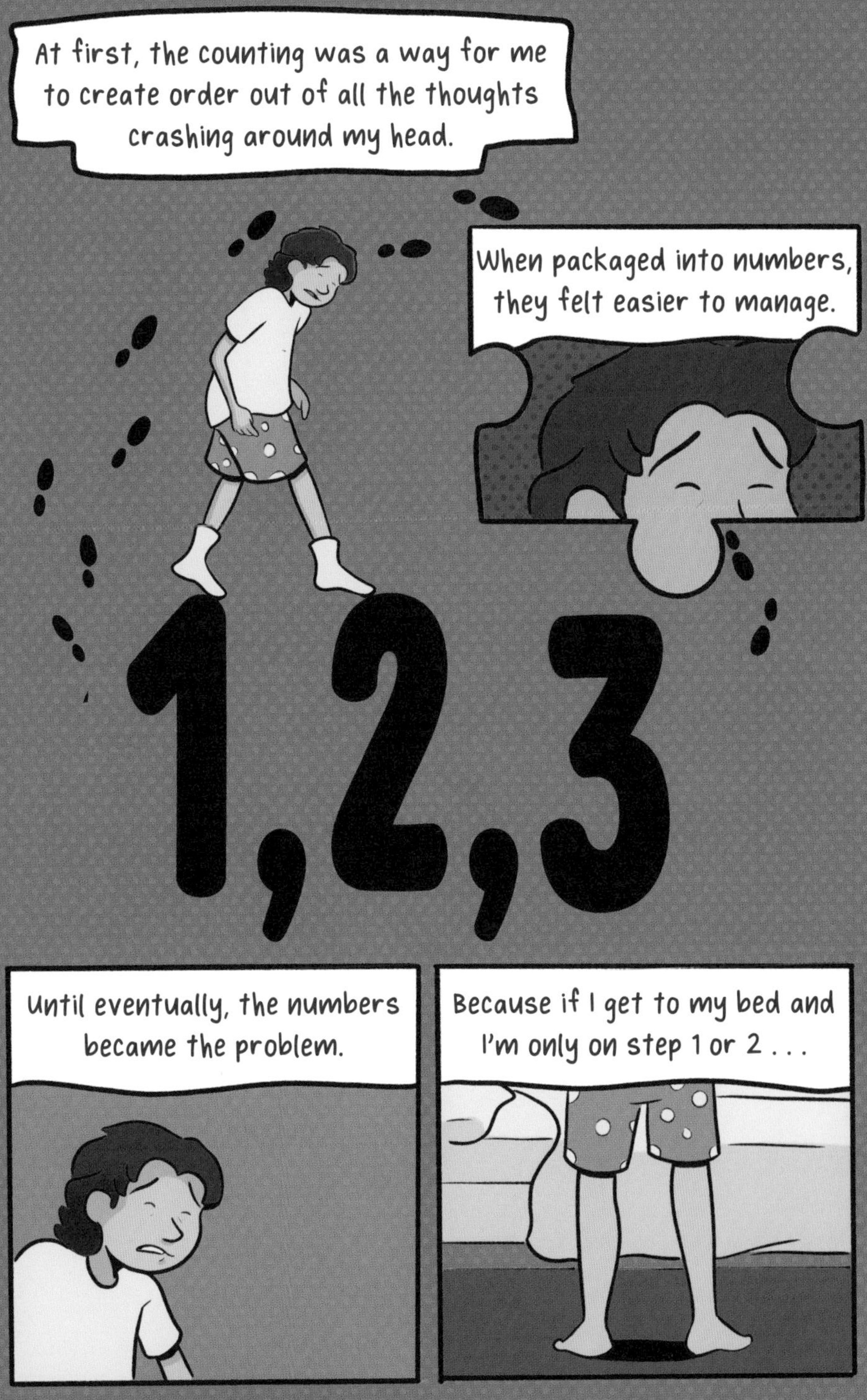
At first, the counting was a way for me to create order out of all the thoughts crashing around my head.
When packaged into numbers, they felt easier to manage.
1,2,3
Until eventually, the numbers became the problem.
Because if I get to my bed and I'm only on step 1 or 2 . . .

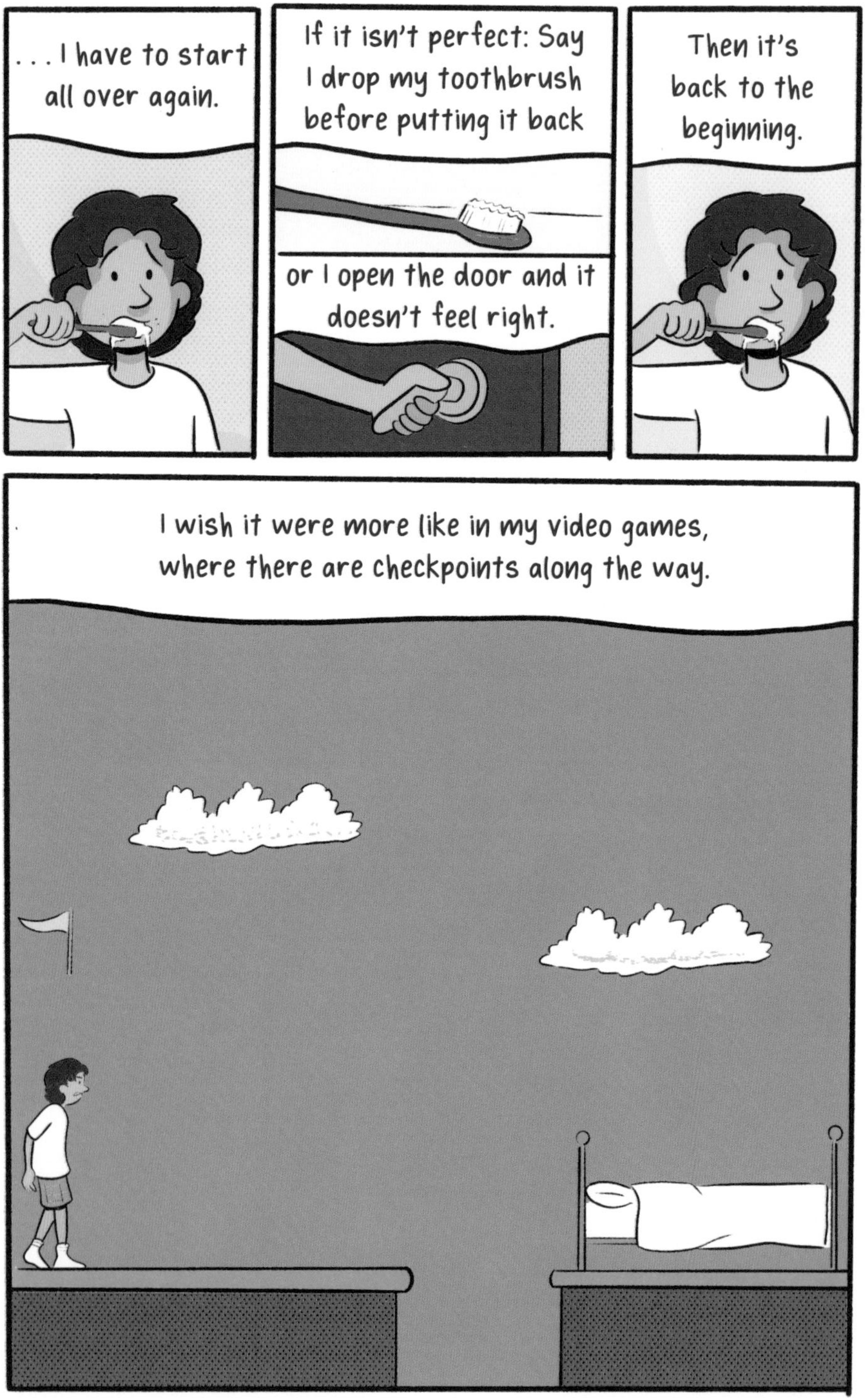
. . . I have to start all over again.
If it isn't perfect: Say I drop my toothbrush before putting it back
or I open the door and it doesn't feel right.
Then it's back to the beginning.
I wish it were more like in my video games, where there are checkpoints along the way.

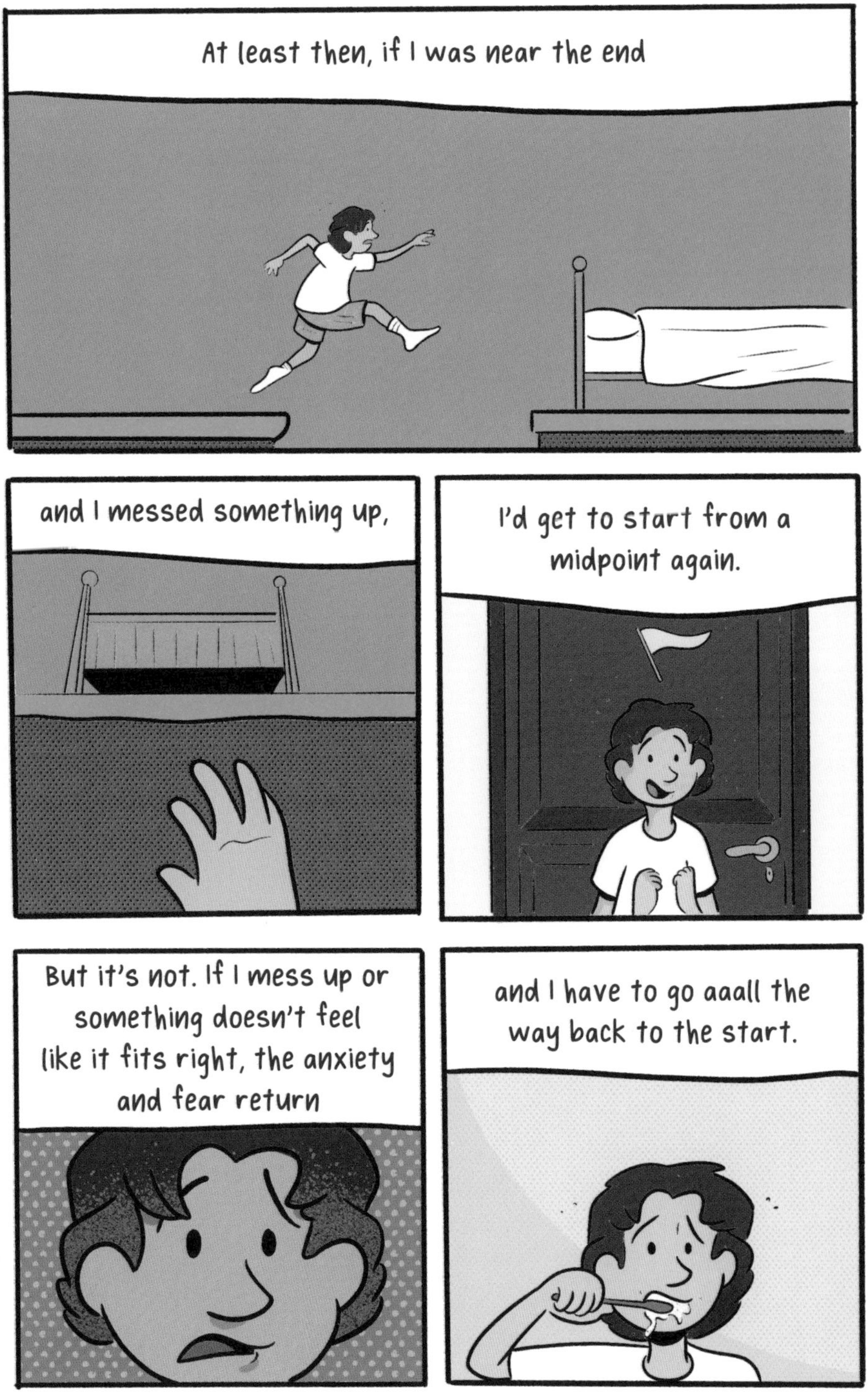
At least then, if I was near the end
and I messed something up,
I'd get to start from a midpoint again.
But it's not. If I mess up or something doesn't feel like it fits right, the anxiety and fear return
and I have to go aaall the way back to the start.

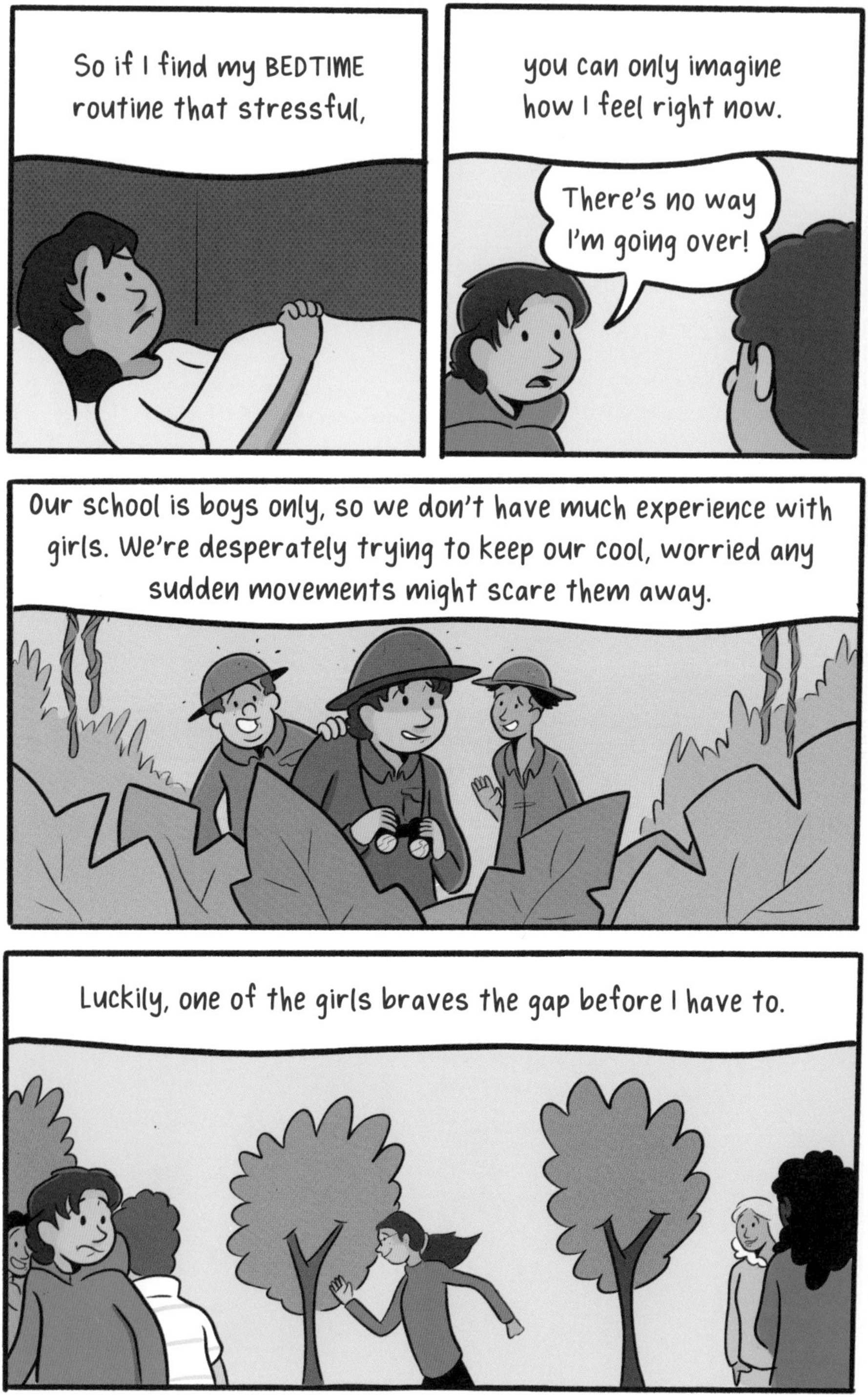

So if I find my BEDTIME routine that stressful,
you can only imagine how I feel right now.
There's no way I'm going over!
Our school is boys only, so we don't have much experience with girls. We're desperately trying to keep our cool, worried any sudden movements might scare them away.
Luckily, one of the girls braves the gap before I have to.

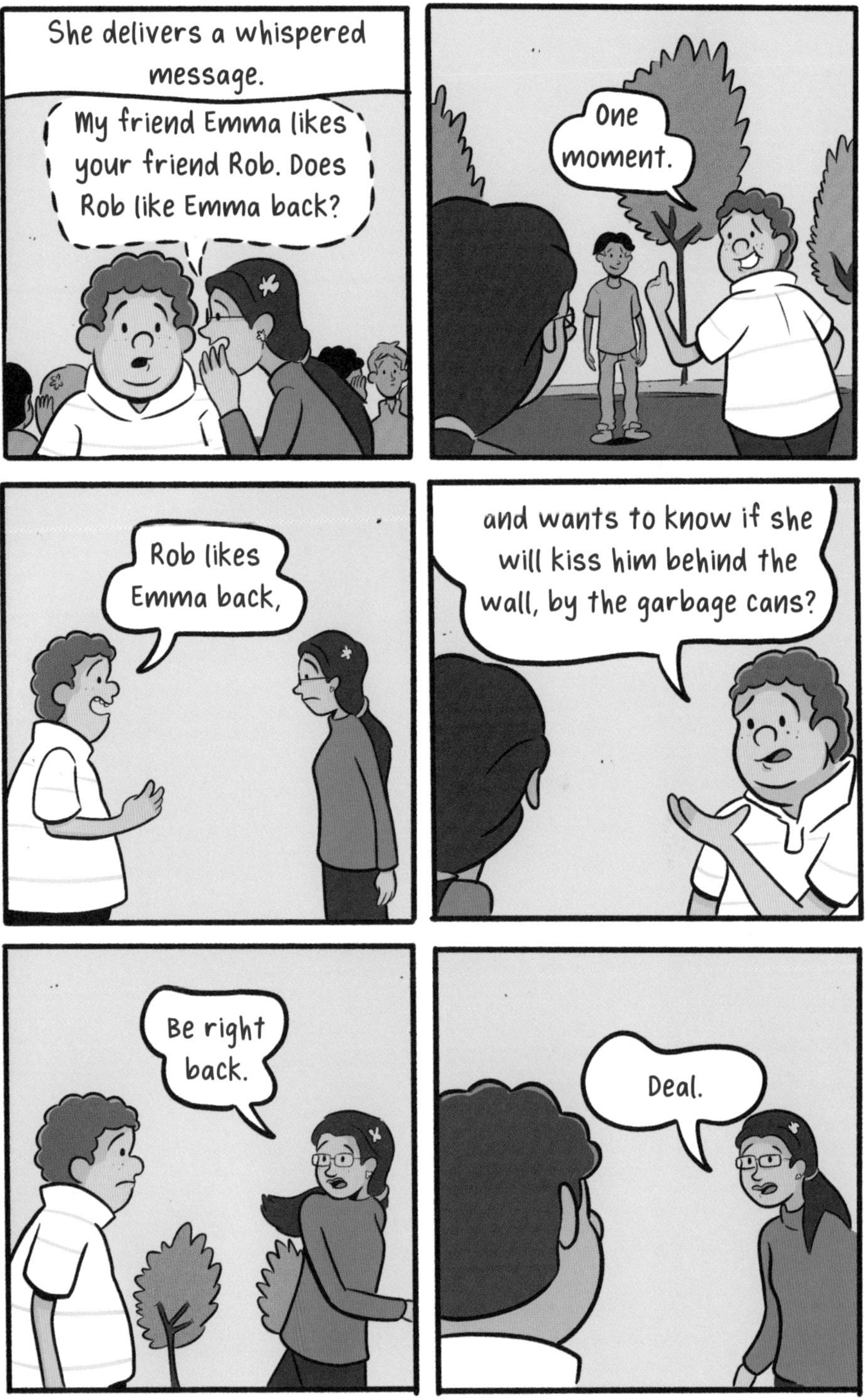
She delivers a whispered message.
My friend Emma likes your friend Rob. Does Rob like Emma back?
One moment.
Rob likes Emma back,
and wants to know if she will kiss him behind the wall, by the garbage cans?
Be right back.
Deal.

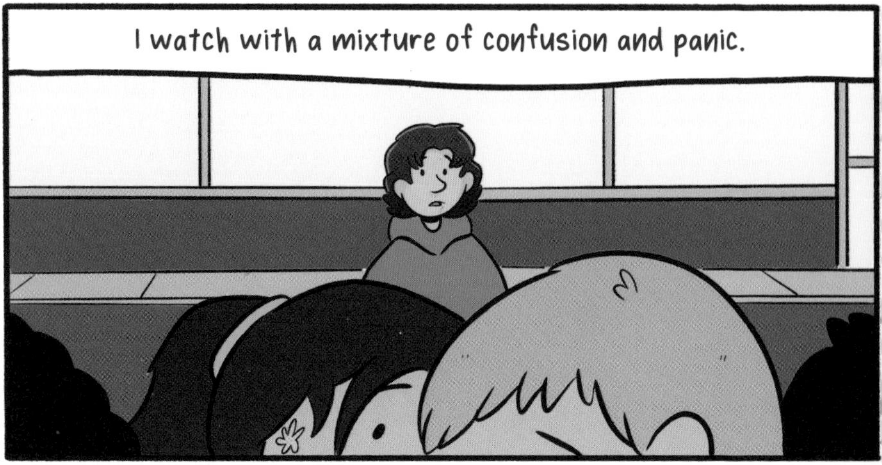
I watch with a mixture of confusion and panic.

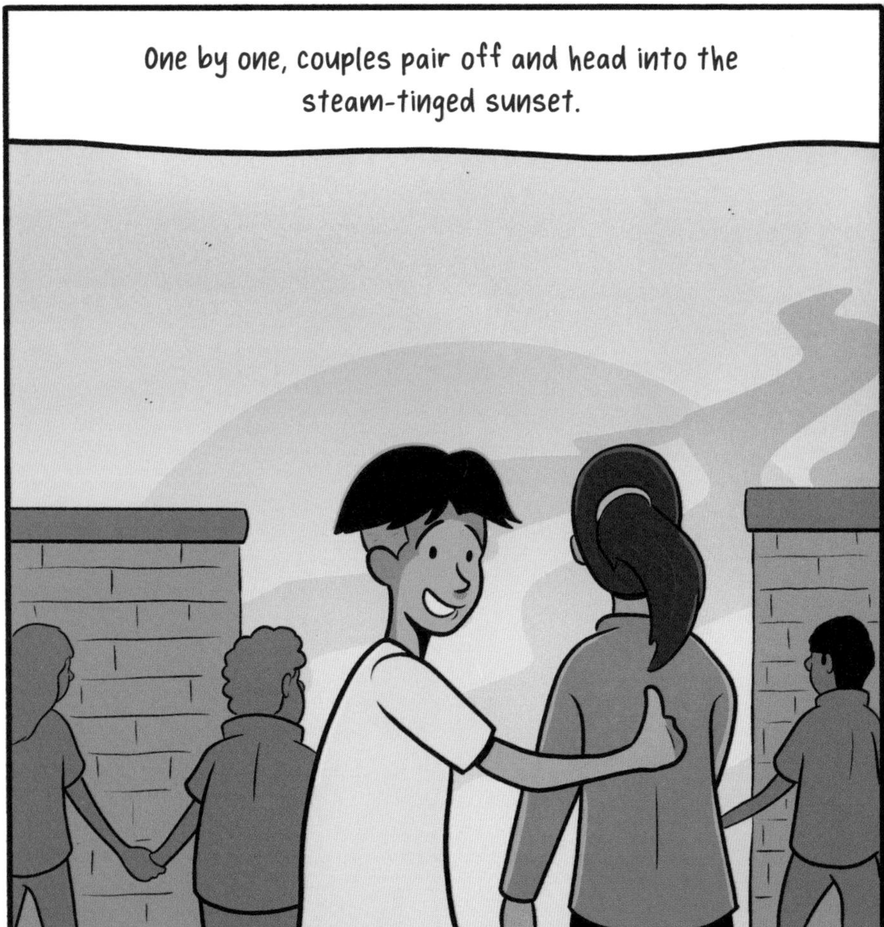
One by one, couples pair off and head into the steam-tinged sunset.

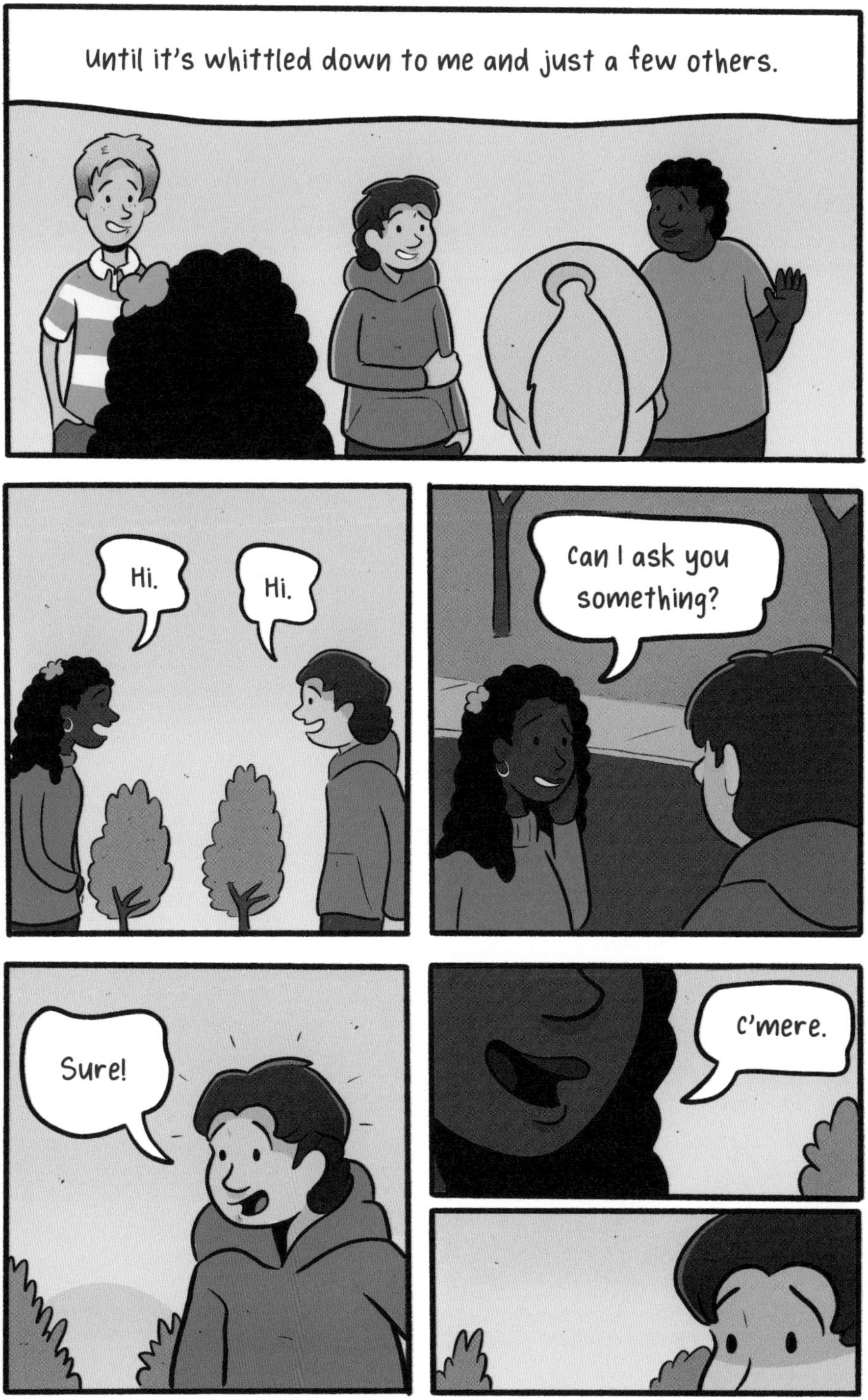
Until it's whittled down to me and just a few others.
Hi.
Hi.
Can I ask you something?
Sure!
C'mere.

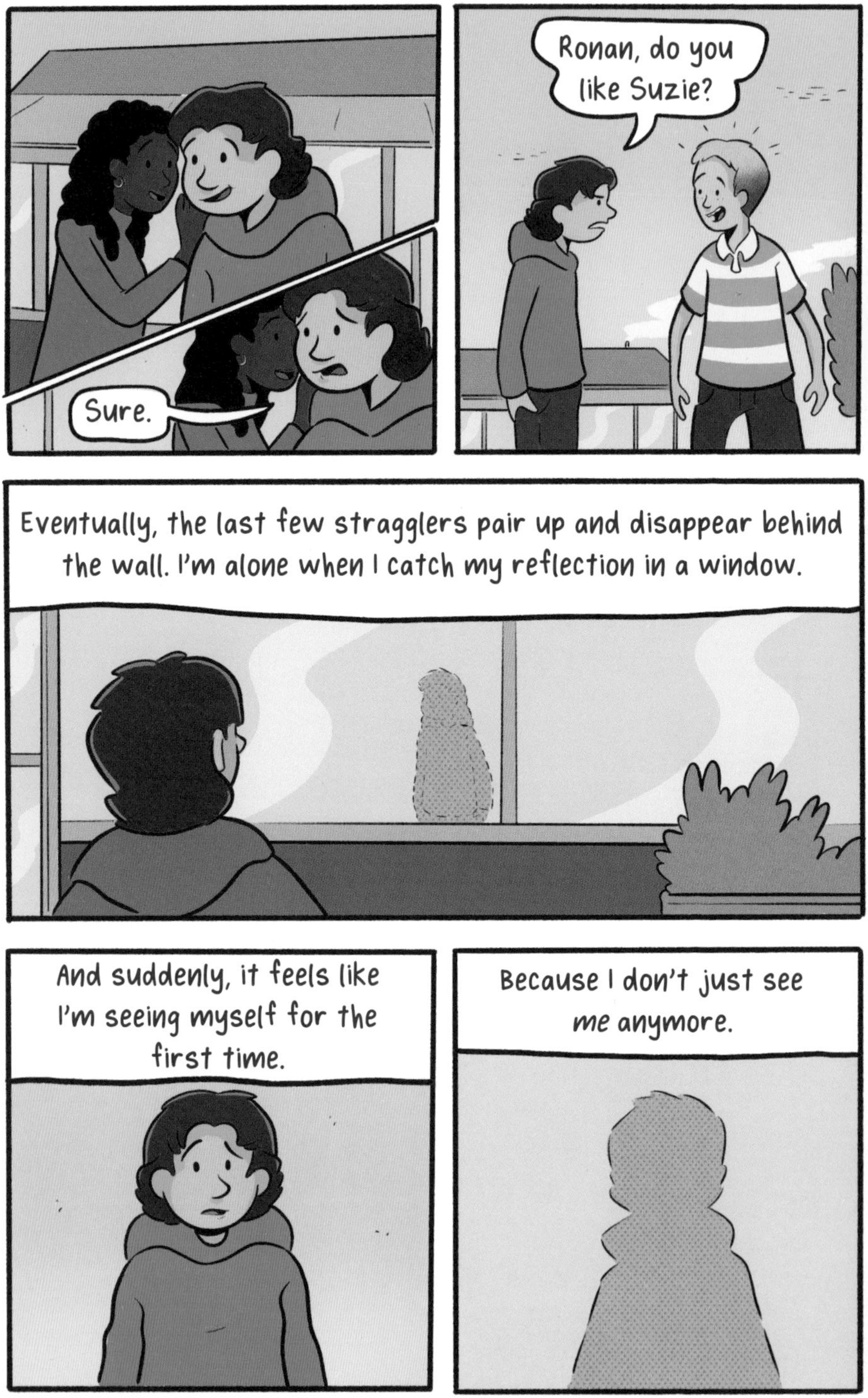
Sure.
Ronan, do you like Suzie?
Eventually, the last few stragglers pair up and disappear behind the wall. I'm alone when I catch my reflection in a window.
And suddenly, it feels like I'm seeing myself for the first time.
Because I don't just see *me* anymore.

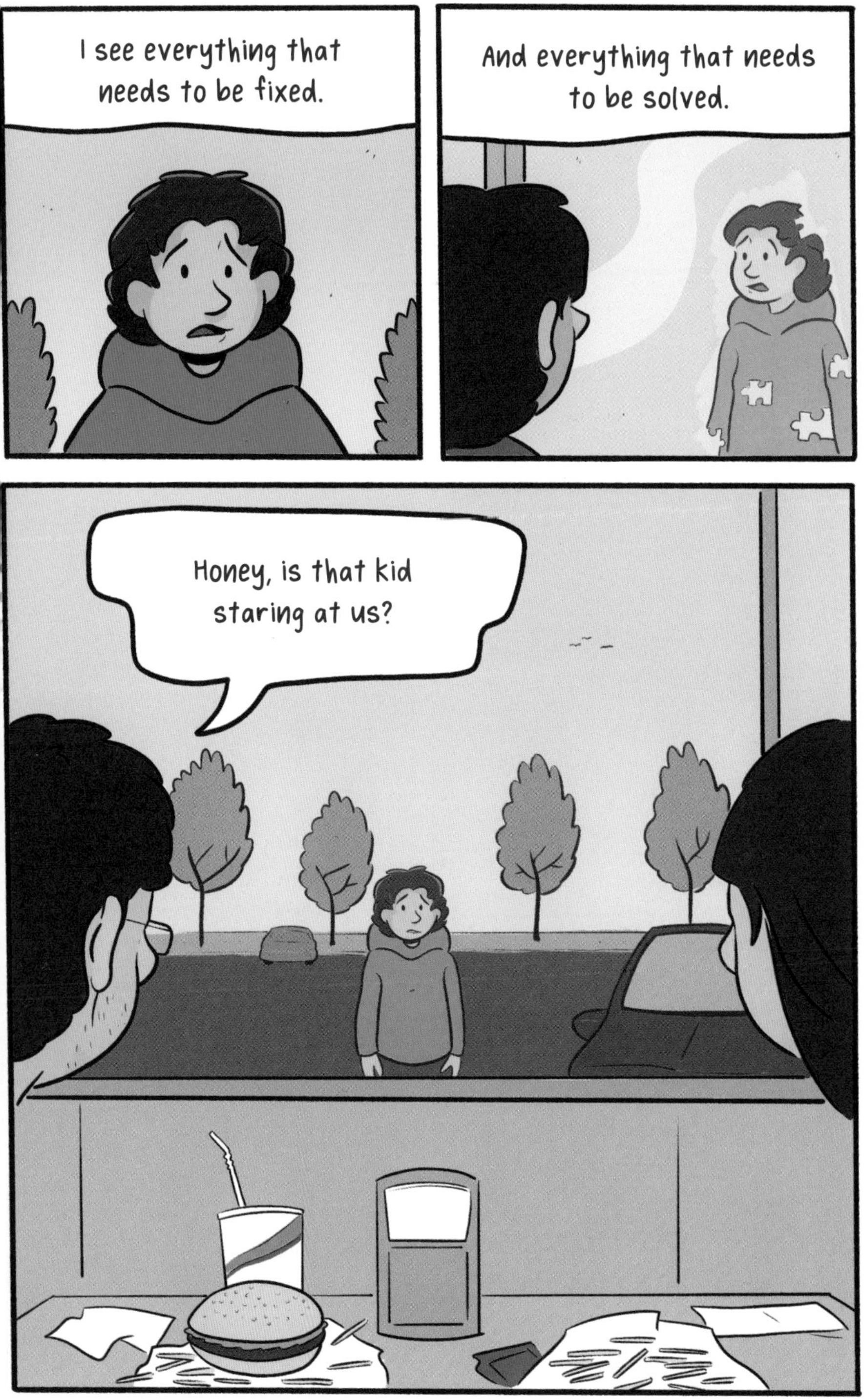
I see everything that needs to be fixed.
And everything that needs to be solved.
Honey, is that kid staring at us?

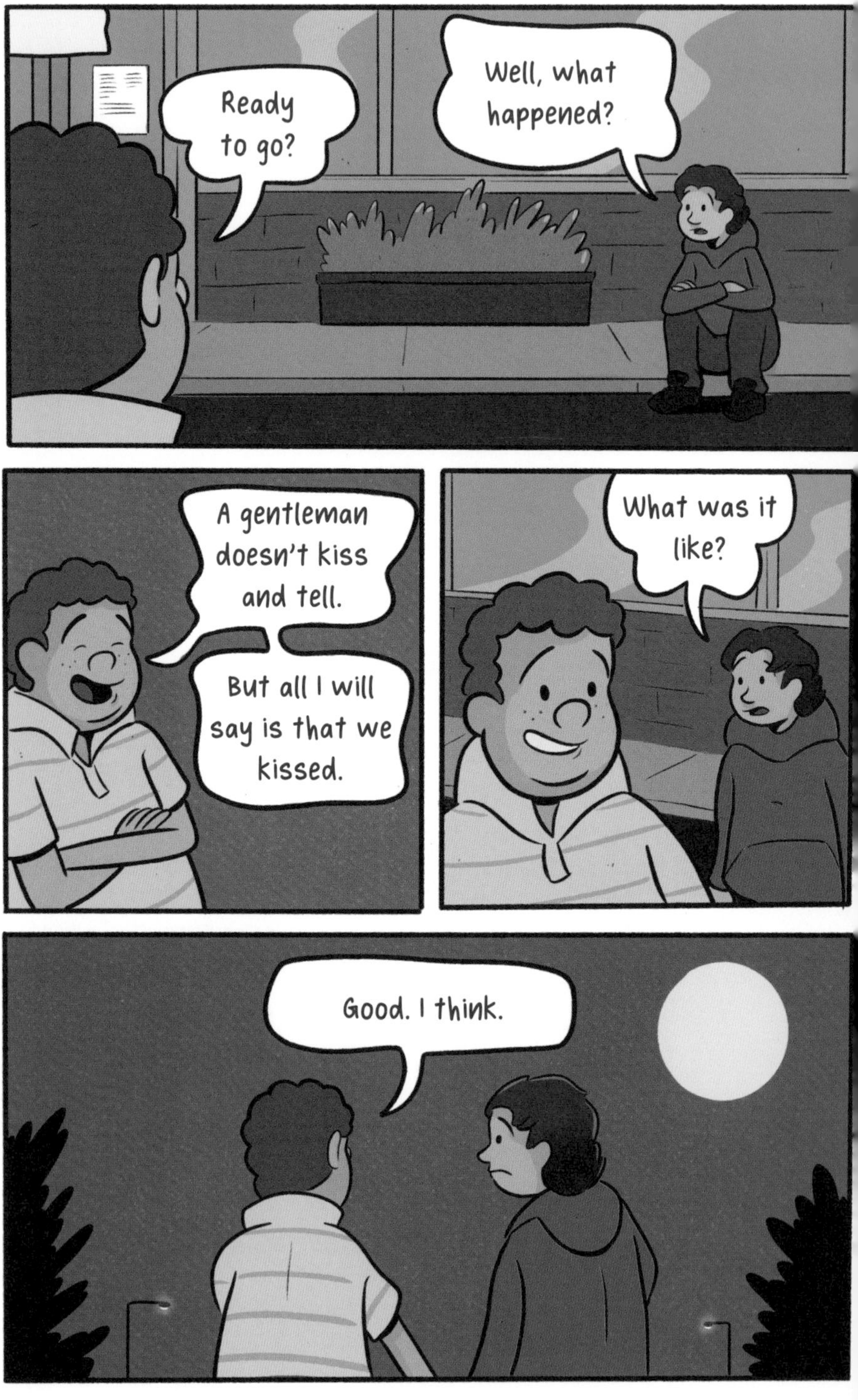
Ready to go?
Well, what happened?
A gentleman doesn't kiss and tell.
But all I will say is that we kissed.
What was it like?
Good. I think.

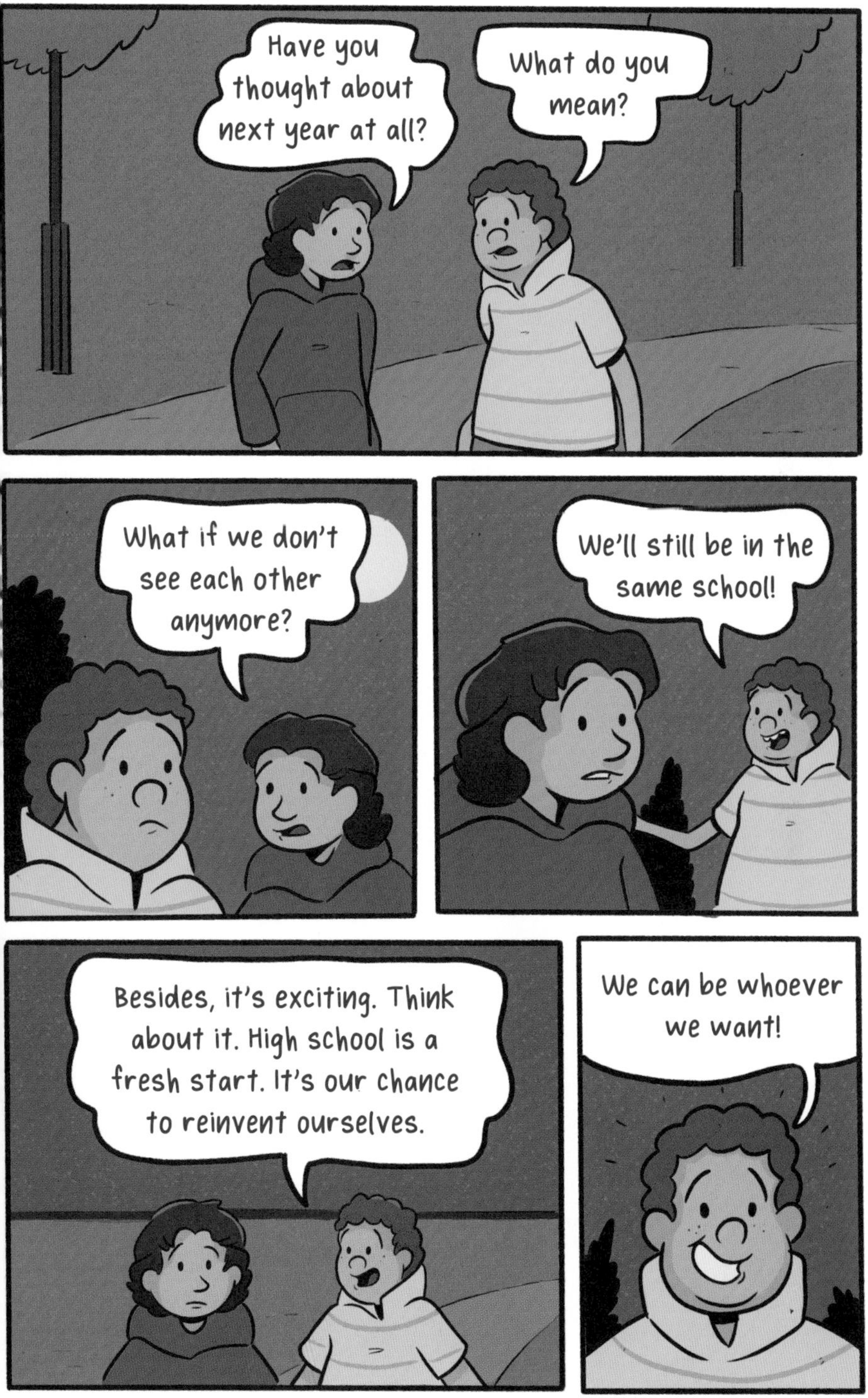
Have you thought about next year at all?
What do you mean?
What if we don't see each other anymore?
We'll still be in the same school!
Besides, it's exciting. Think about it. High school is a fresh start. It's our chance to reinvent ourselves.
We can be whoever we want!

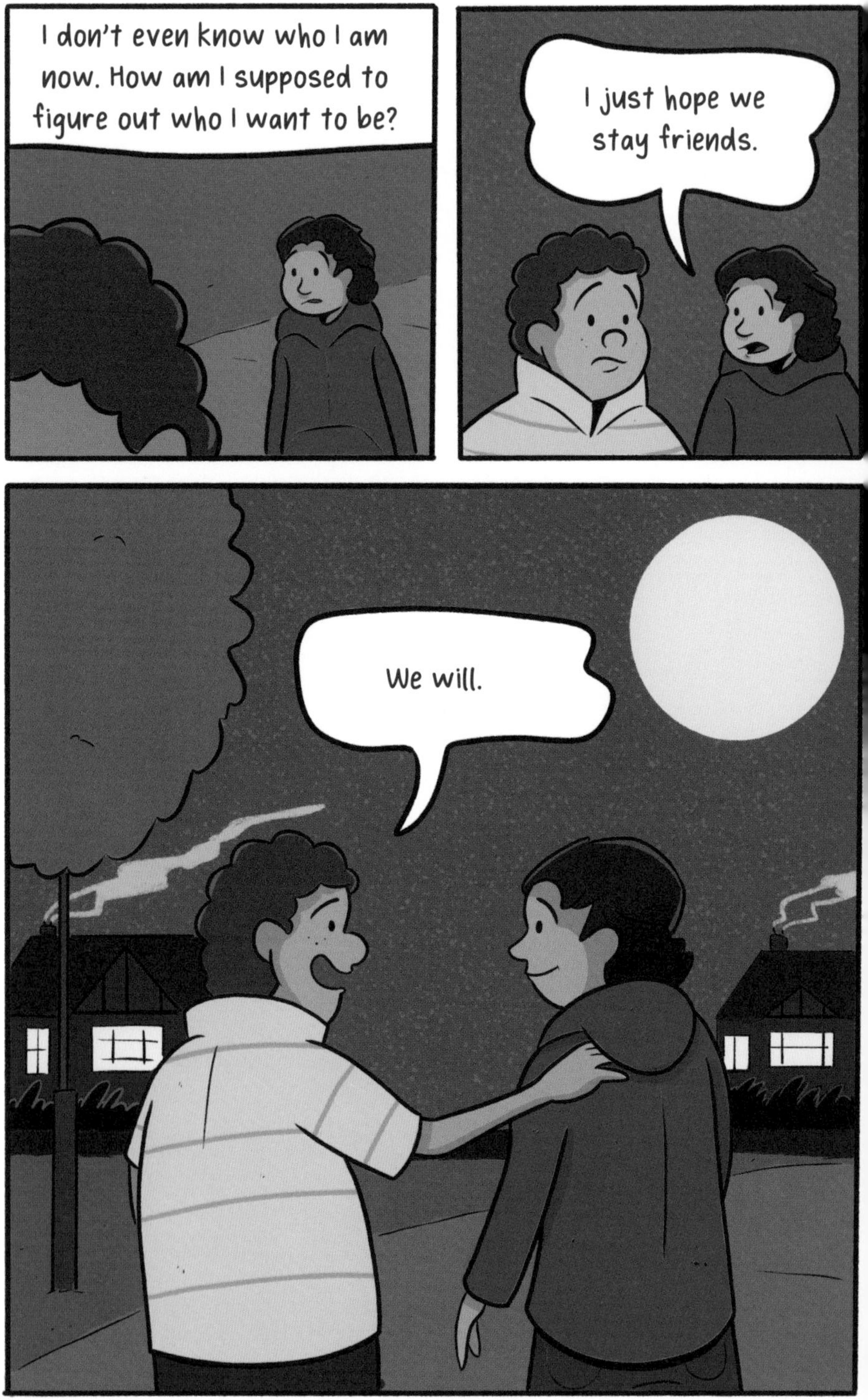
I don't even know who I am now. How am I supposed to figure out who I want to be?
I just hope we stay friends.
We will.

4

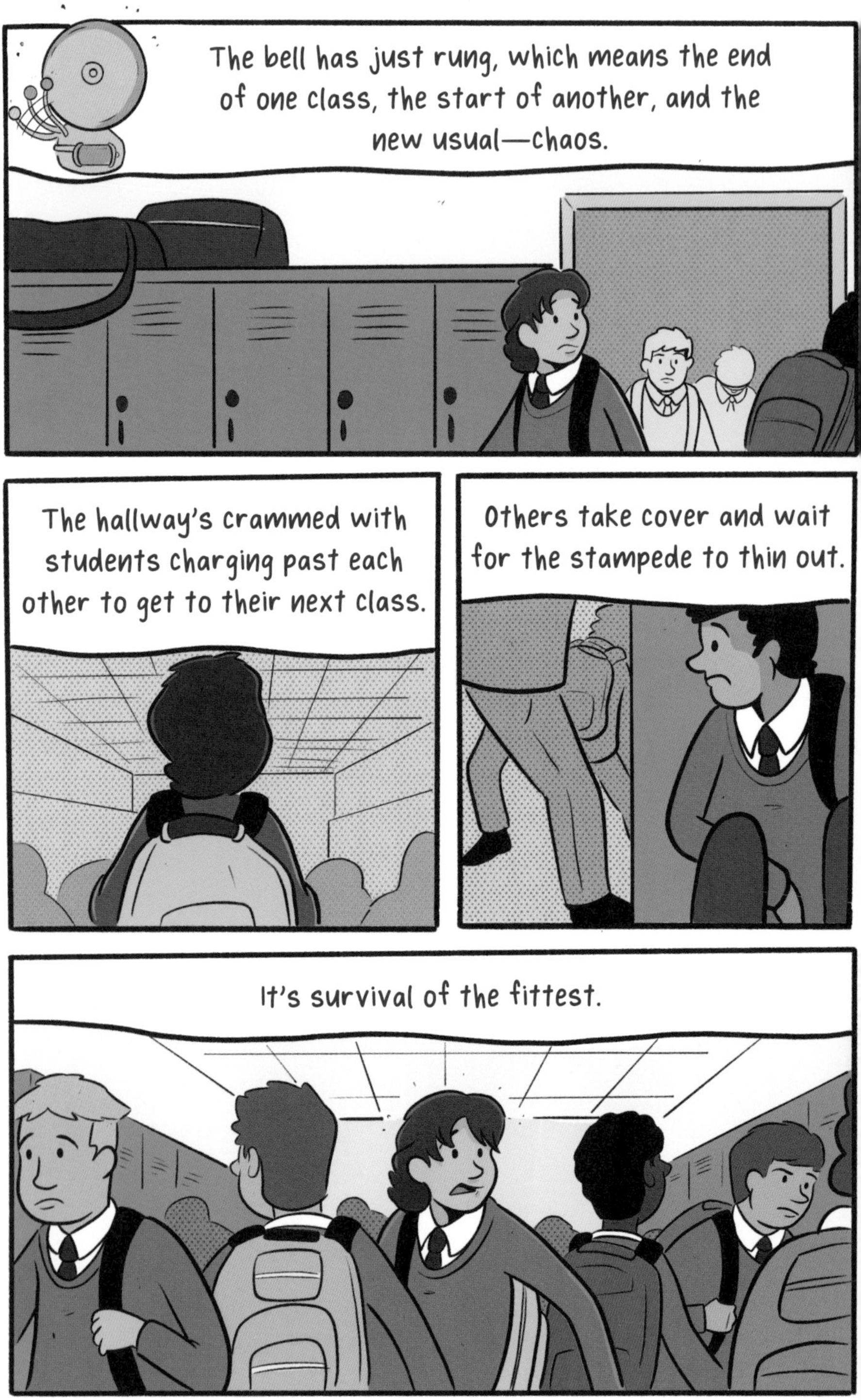
The bell has just rung, which means the end of one class, the start of another, and the new usual—chaos.
The hallway's crammed with students charging past each other to get to their next class.
Others take cover and wait for the stampede to thin out.
It's survival of the fittest.

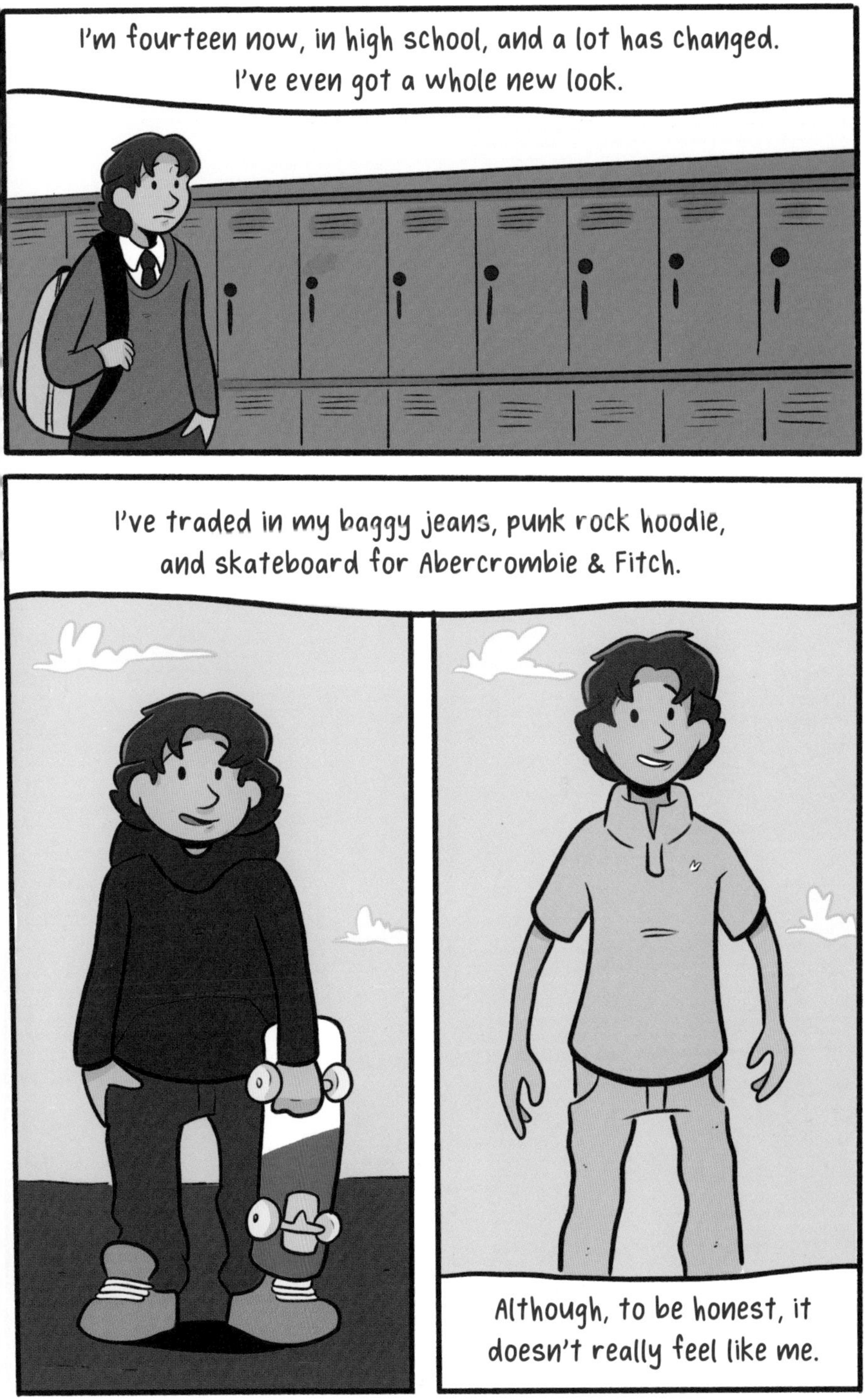
I'm fourteen now, in high school, and a lot has changed. I've even got a whole new look.
I've traded in my baggy jeans, punk rock hoodie, and skateboard for Abercrombie & Fitch.
Although, to be honest, it doesn't really feel like me.

But I'd dress as a hot dog
if everyone else were.

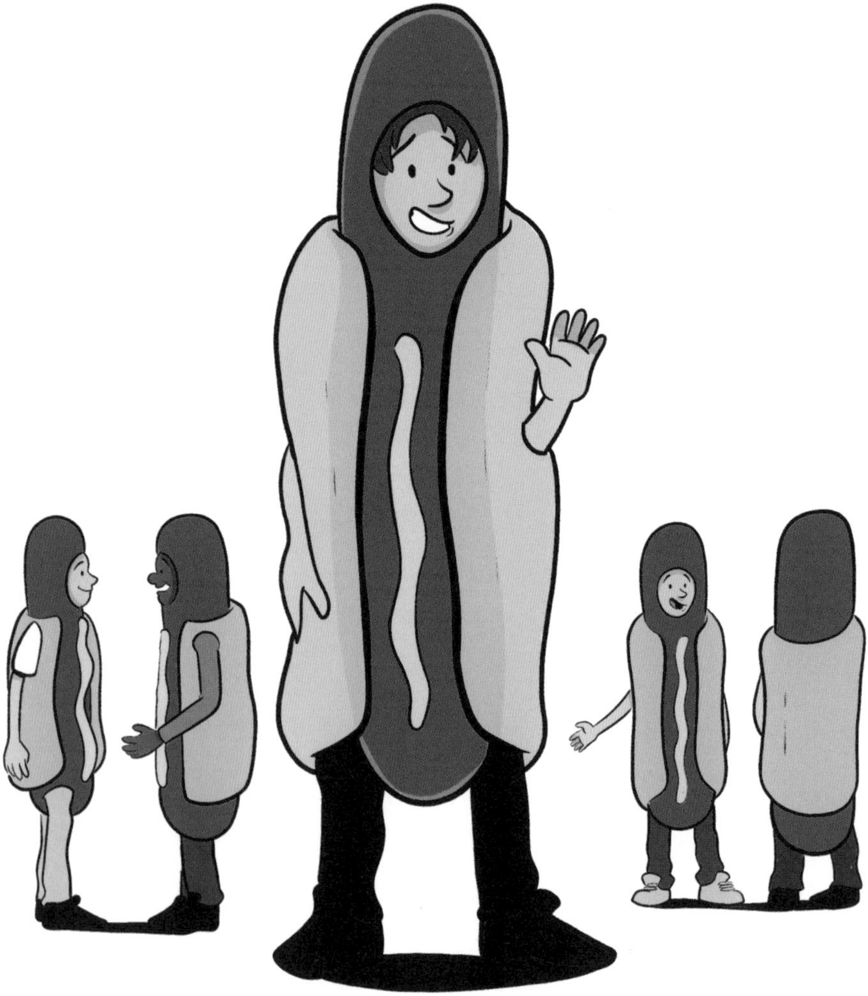

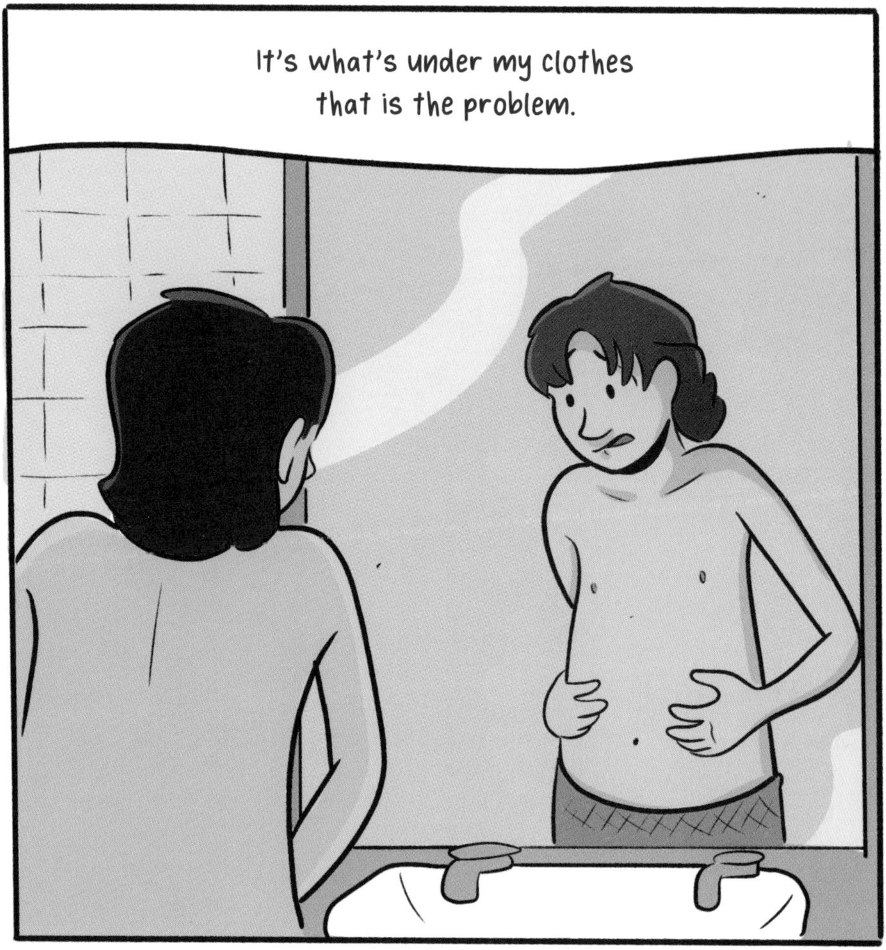
It's what's under my clothes
that is the problem.

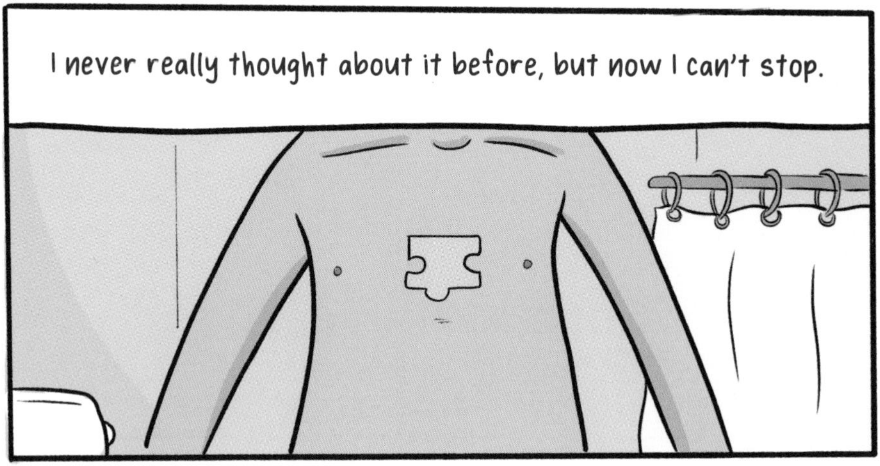
I never really thought about it before, but now I can't stop.

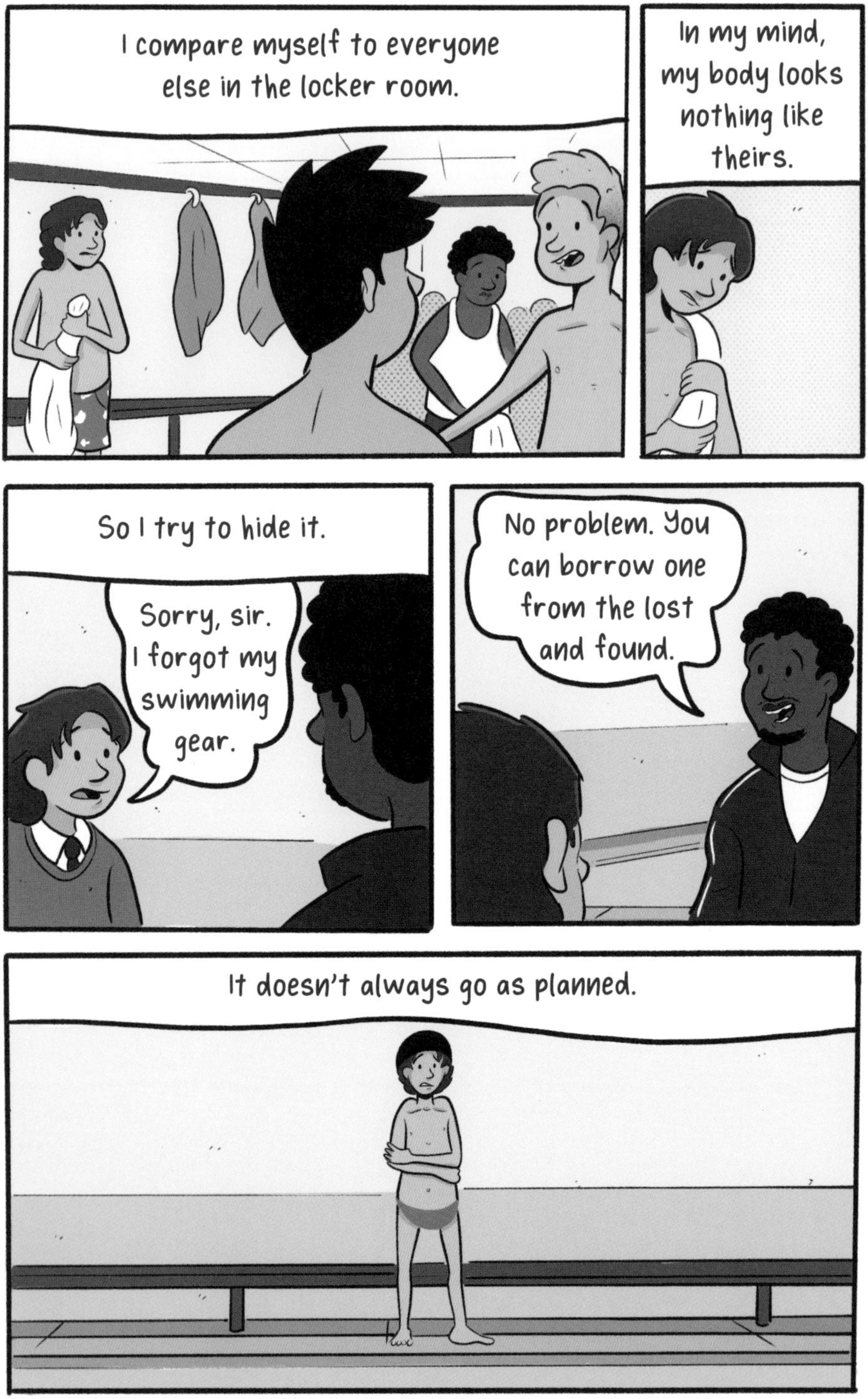
I compare myself to everyone else in the locker room.
In my mind, my body looks nothing like theirs.
So I try to hide it.
Sorry, sir. I forgot my swimming gear.
No problem. You can borrow one from the lost and found.
It doesn't always go as planned.

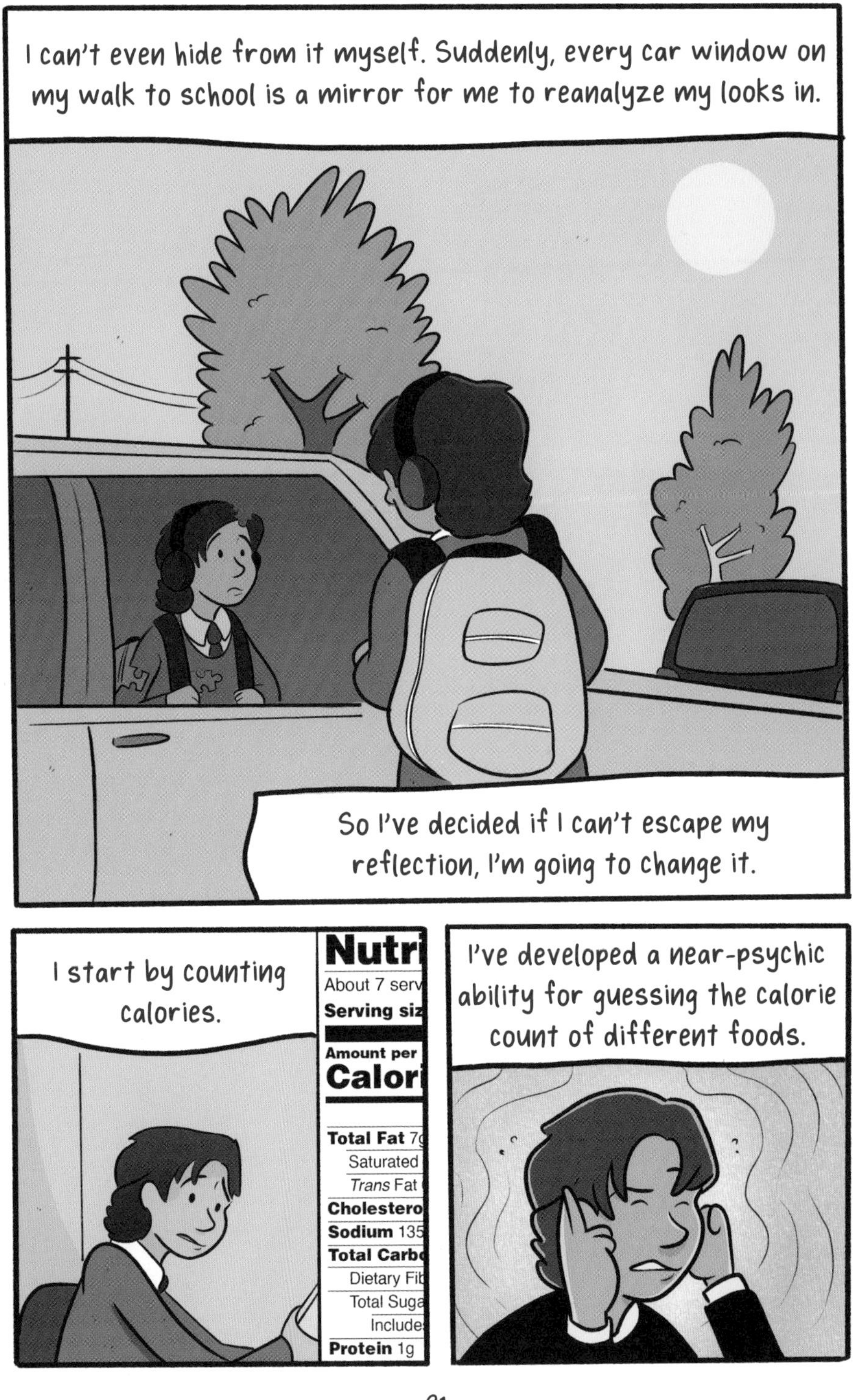

I can't even hide from it myself. Suddenly, every car window on my walk to school is a mirror for me to reanalyze my looks in.
So I've decided if I can't escape my reflection, I'm going to change it.
I start by counting calories.
Nutri
About 7 serv
Serving siz
Amount per
Calori
Total Fat 7g
Saturated
Trans Fat
Cholestero
Sodium 135
Total Carbo
Dietary Fib
Total Suga
Include
Protein 1g
I've developed a near-psychic ability for guessing the calorie count of different foods.

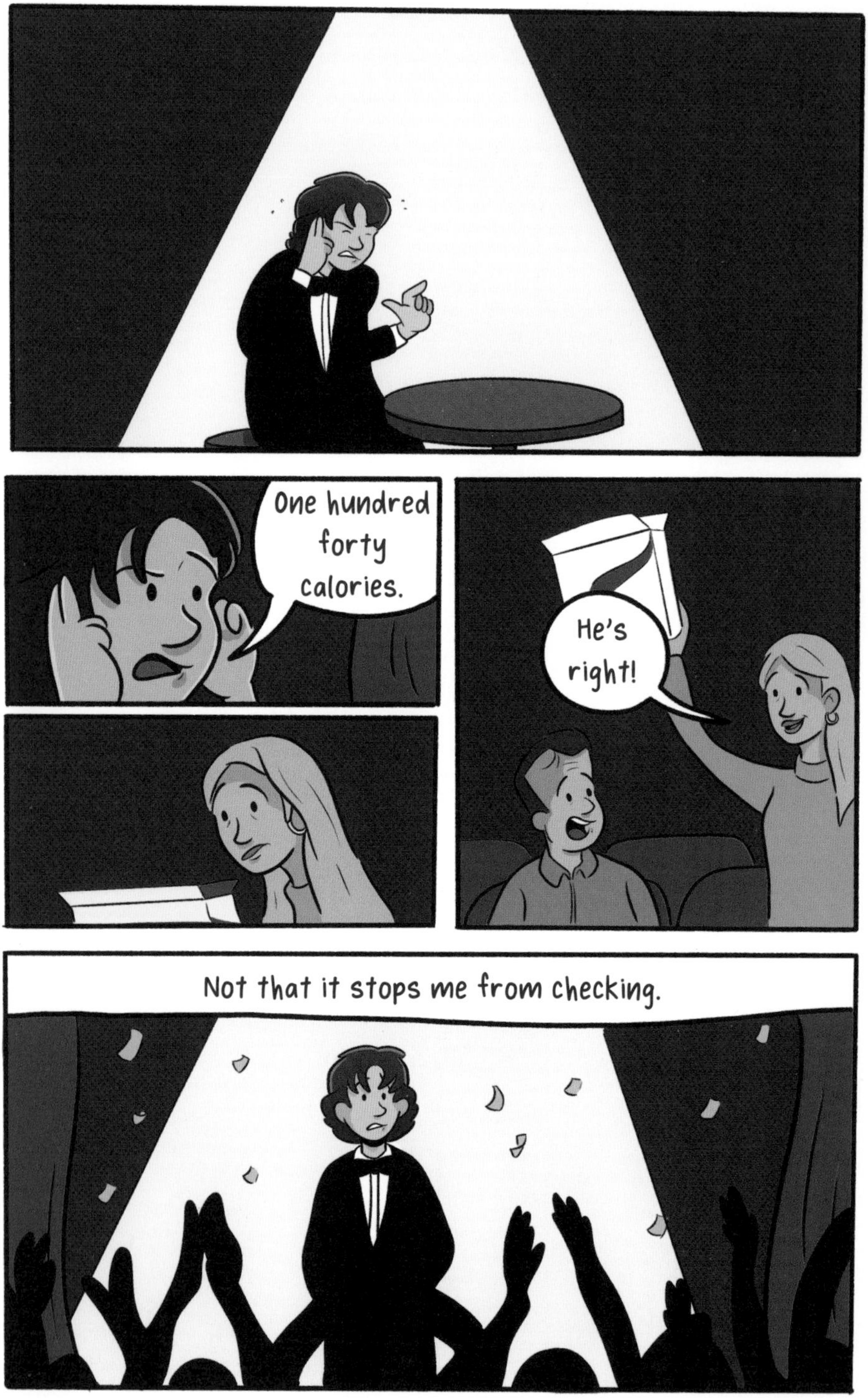
One hundred forty calories.
He's right!
Not that it stops me from checking.

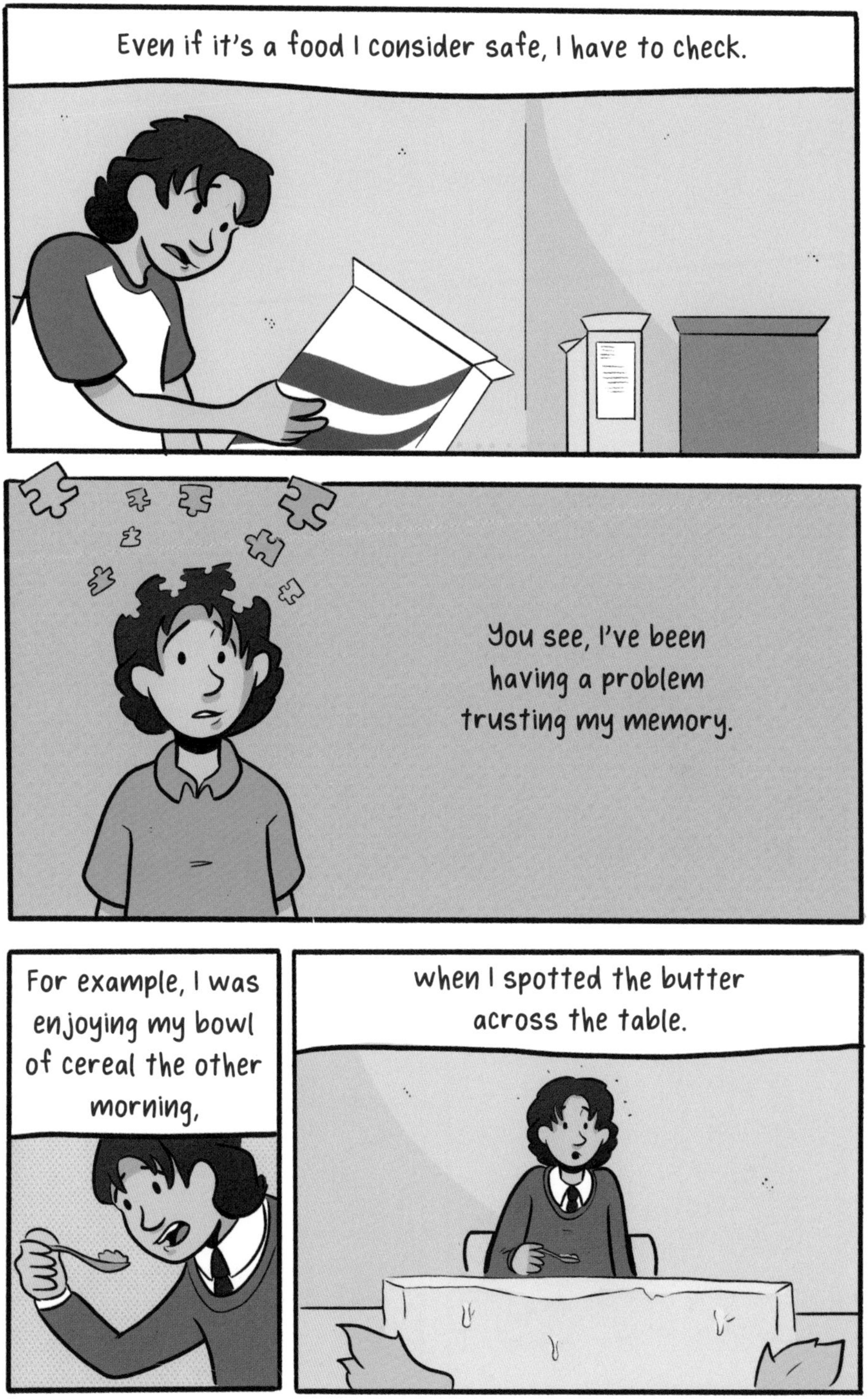

Even if it's a food I consider safe, I have to check.
You see, I've been having a problem trusting my memory.
For example, I was enjoying my bowl of cereal the other morning,
when I spotted the butter across the table.

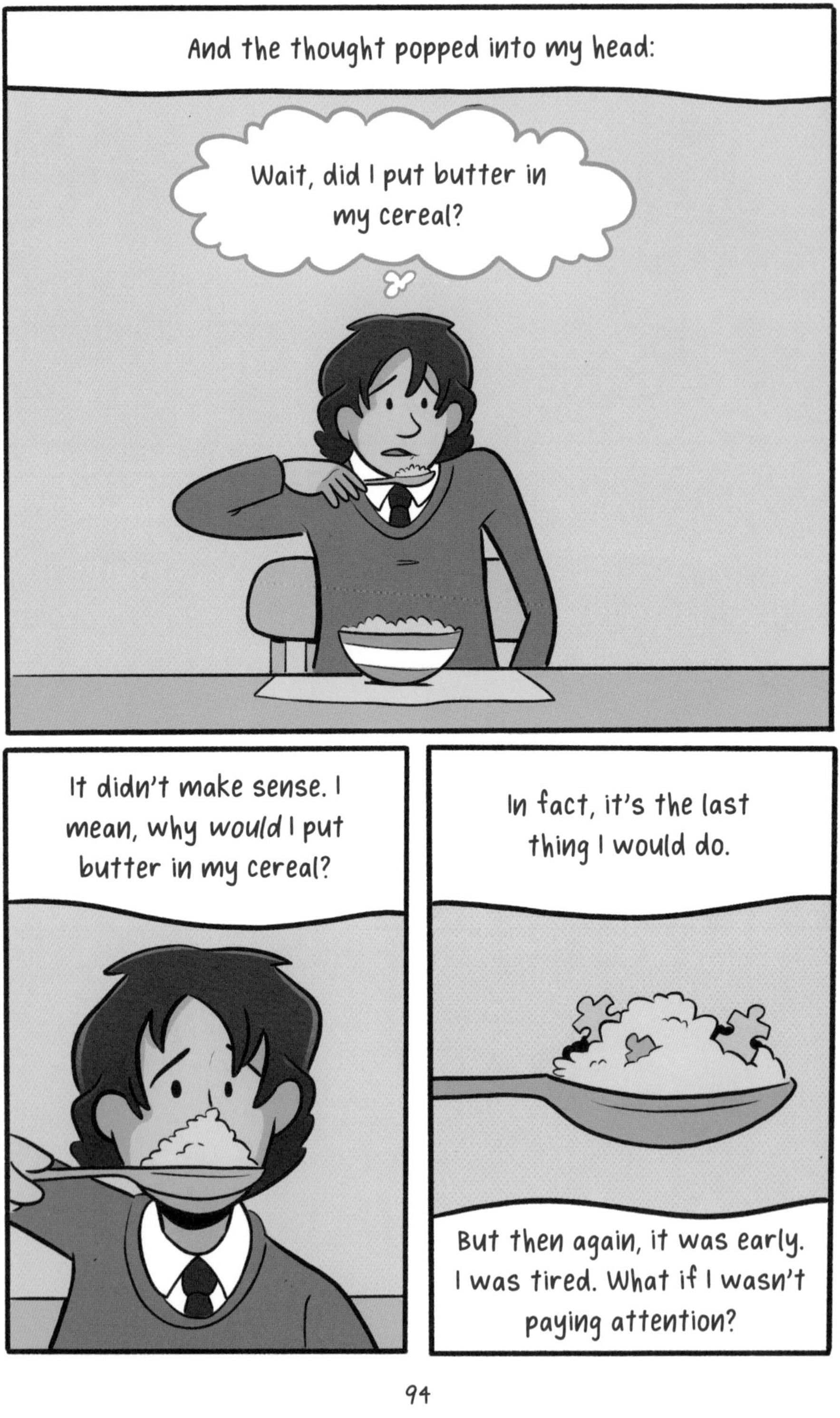
And the thought popped into my head:
Wait, did I put butter in my cereal?
It didn't make sense. I mean, why *would* I put butter in my cereal?
In fact, it's the last thing I would do.
But then again, it was early. I was tired. What if I wasn't paying attention?

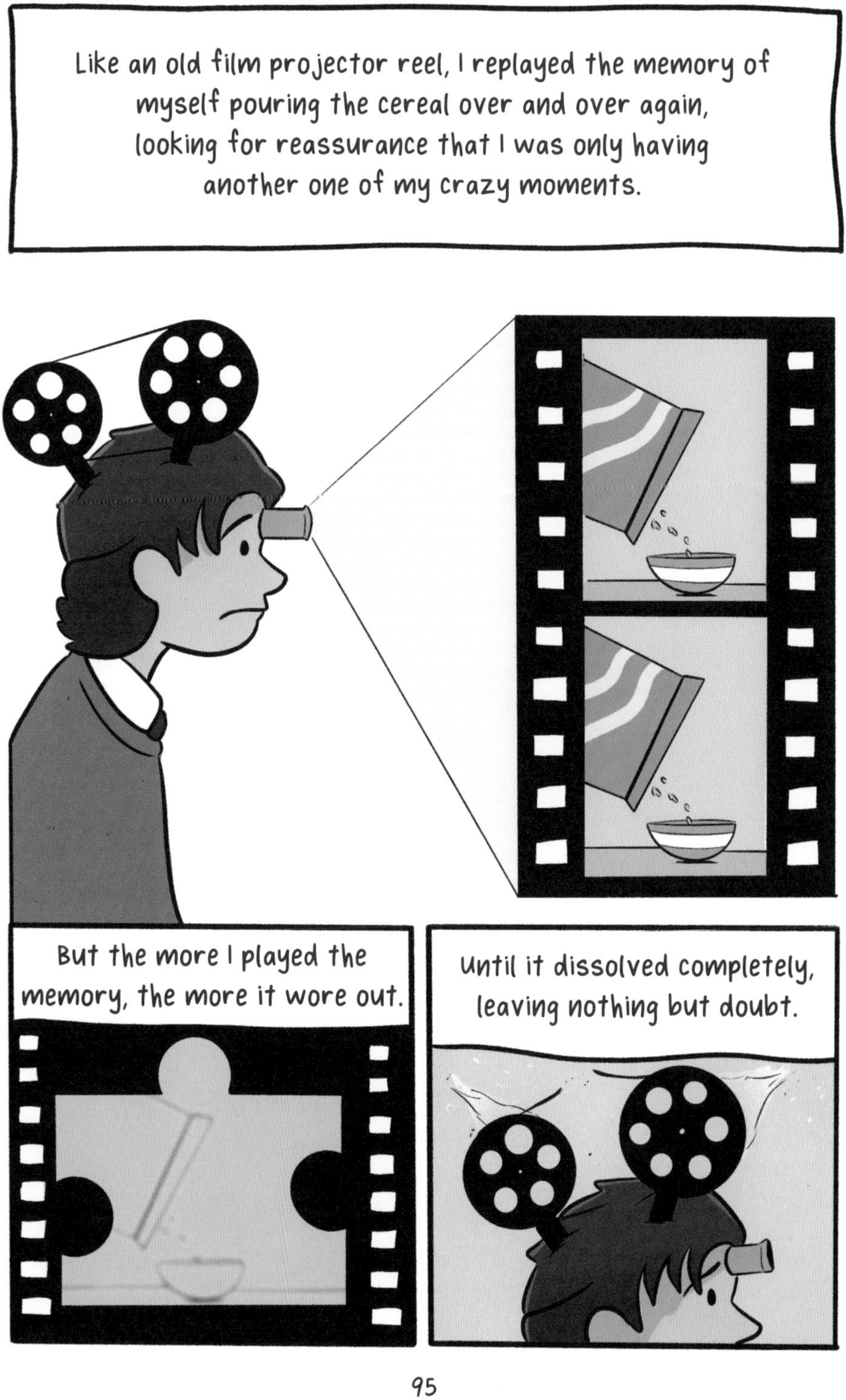
Like an old film projector reel, I replayed the memory of myself pouring the cereal over and over again, looking for reassurance that I was only having another one of my crazy moments.
But the more I played the memory, the more it wore out.
Until it dissolved completely, leaving nothing but doubt.

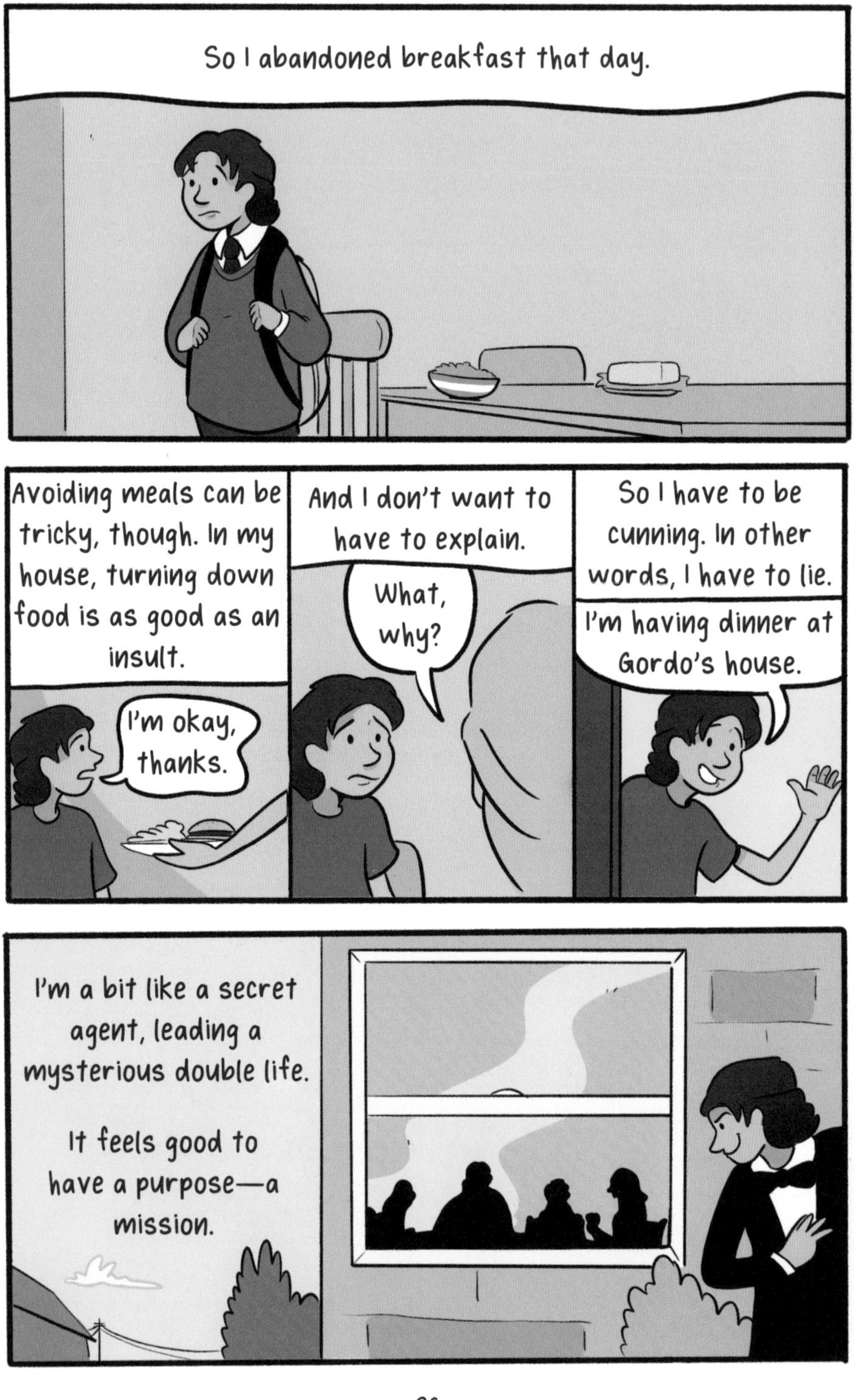

So I abandoned breakfast that day.
Avoiding meals can be tricky, though. In my house, turning down food is as good as an insult.
I'm okay, thanks.
And I don't want to have to explain.
What, why?
So I have to be cunning. In other words, I have to lie.
I'm having dinner at Gordo's house.
I'm a bit like a secret agent, leading a mysterious double life.
It feels good to have a purpose—a mission.

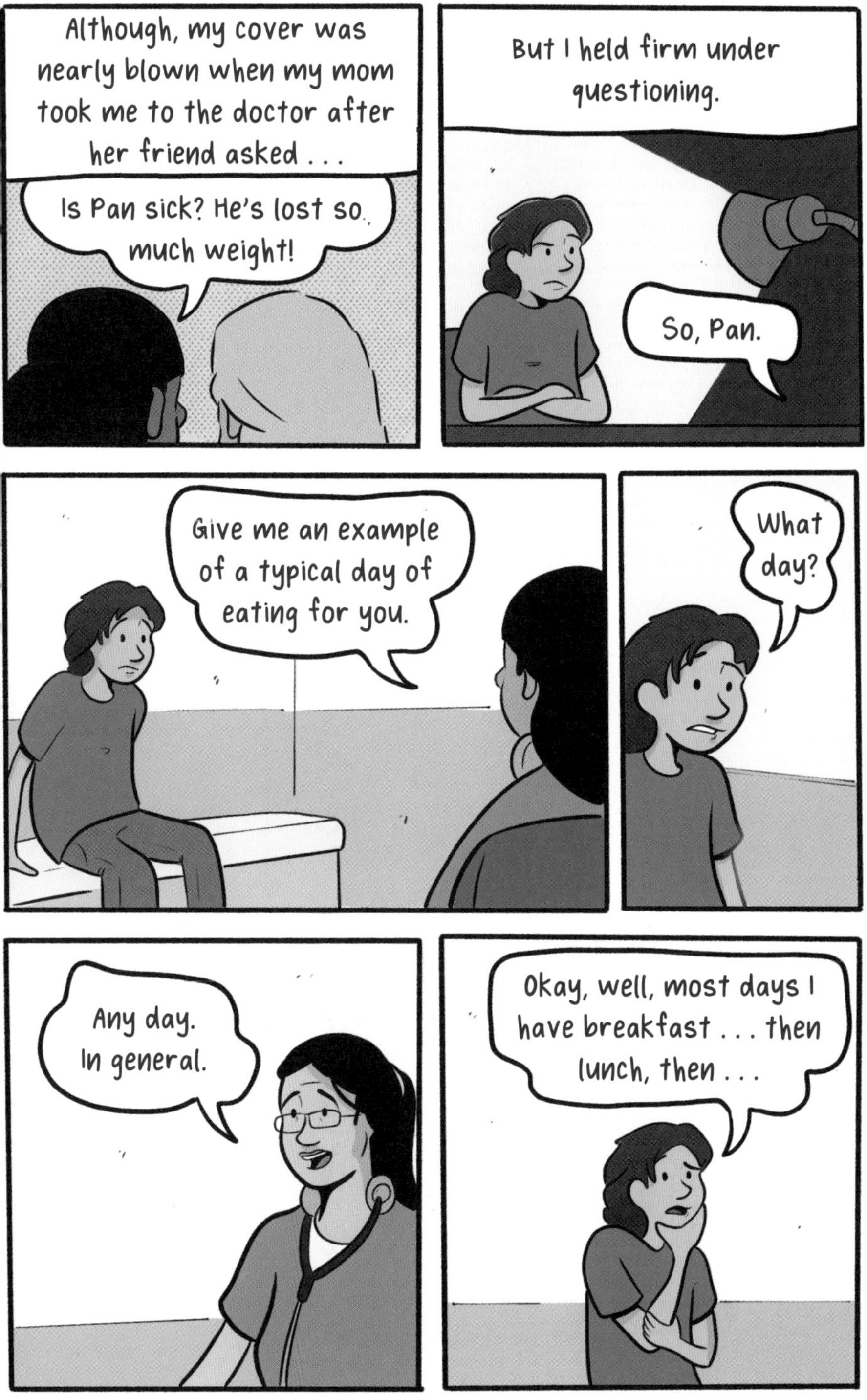
Although, my cover was nearly blown when my mom took me to the doctor after her friend asked . . .
Is Pan sick? He's lost so much weight!
But I held firm under questioning.
So, Pan.
Give me an example of a typical day of eating for you.
What day?
Any day. In general.
Okay, well, most days I have breakfast . . . then lunch, then . . .

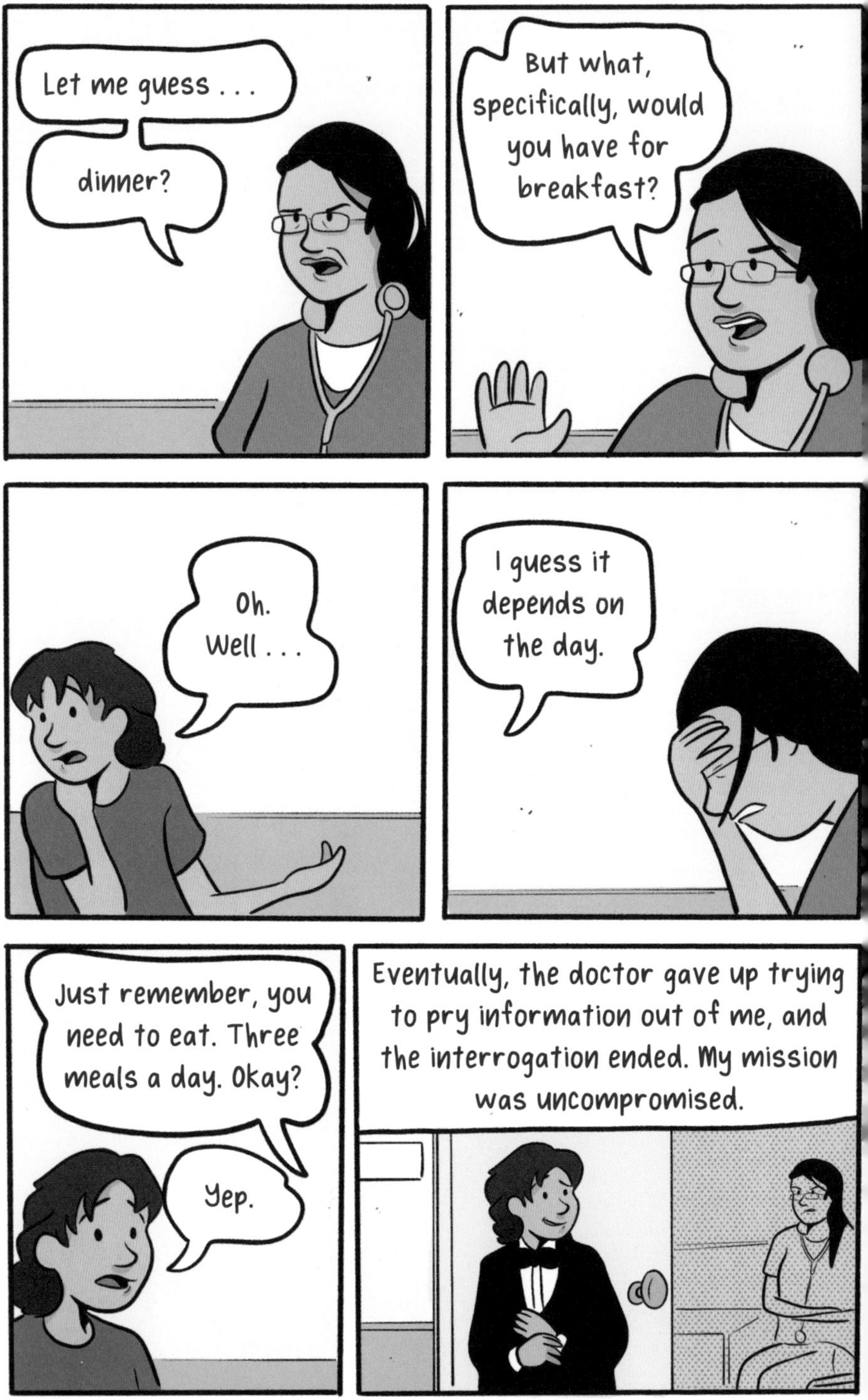
Let me guess . . .
dinner?
But what, specifically, would you have for breakfast?
Oh. Well . . .
I guess it depends on the day.
Just remember, you need to eat. Three meals a day. Okay?
Yep.
Eventually, the doctor gave up trying to pry information out of me, and the interrogation ended. My mission was uncompromised.

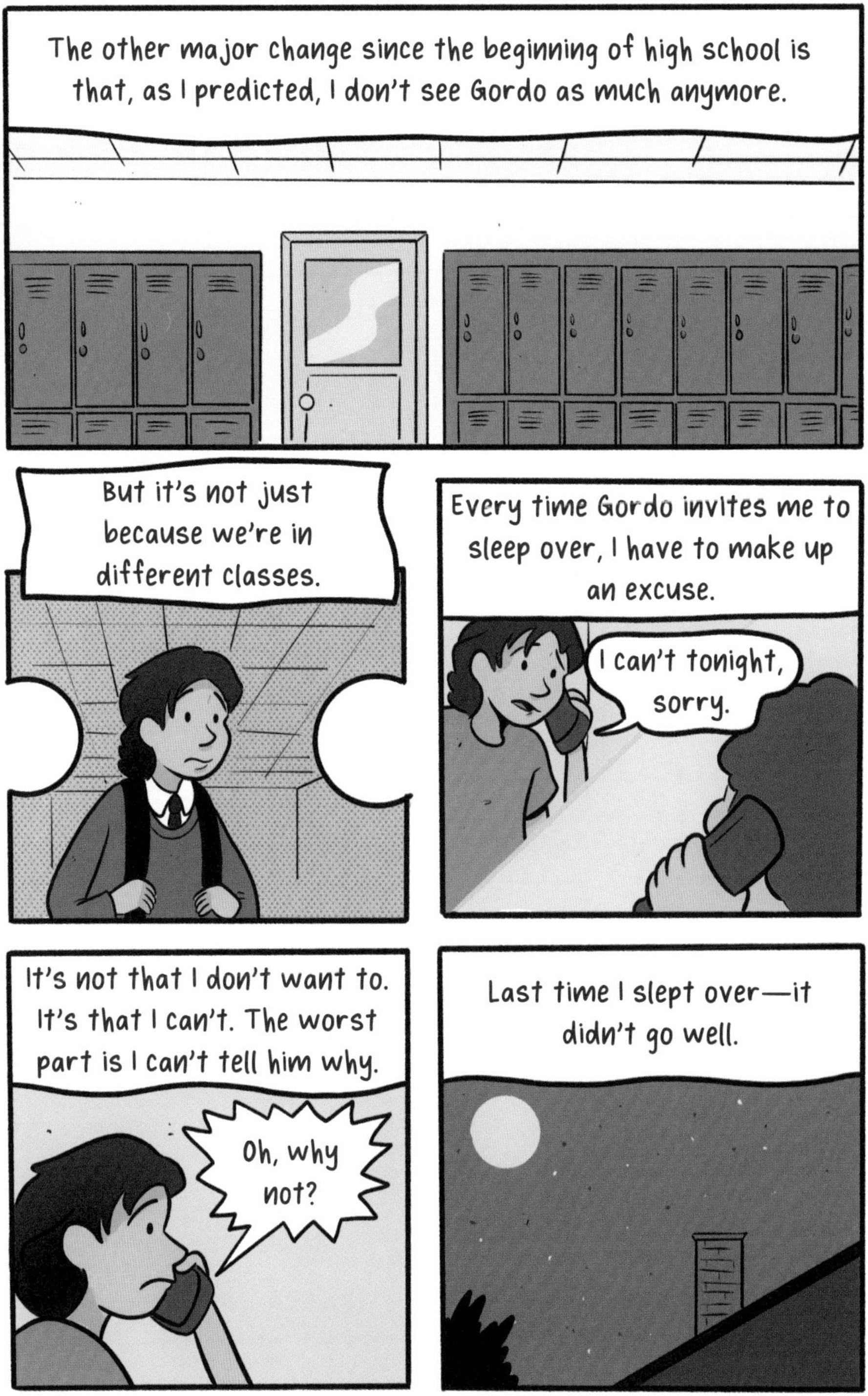
The other major change since the beginning of high school is that, as I predicted, I don't see Gordo as much anymore.
But it's not just because we're in different classes.
Every time Gordo invites me to sleep over, I have to make up an excuse.
I can't tonight, sorry.
It's not that I don't want to. It's that I can't. The worst part is I can't tell him why.
Oh, why not?
Last time I slept over—it didn't go well.

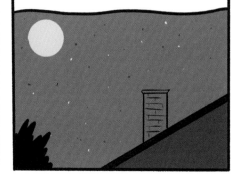

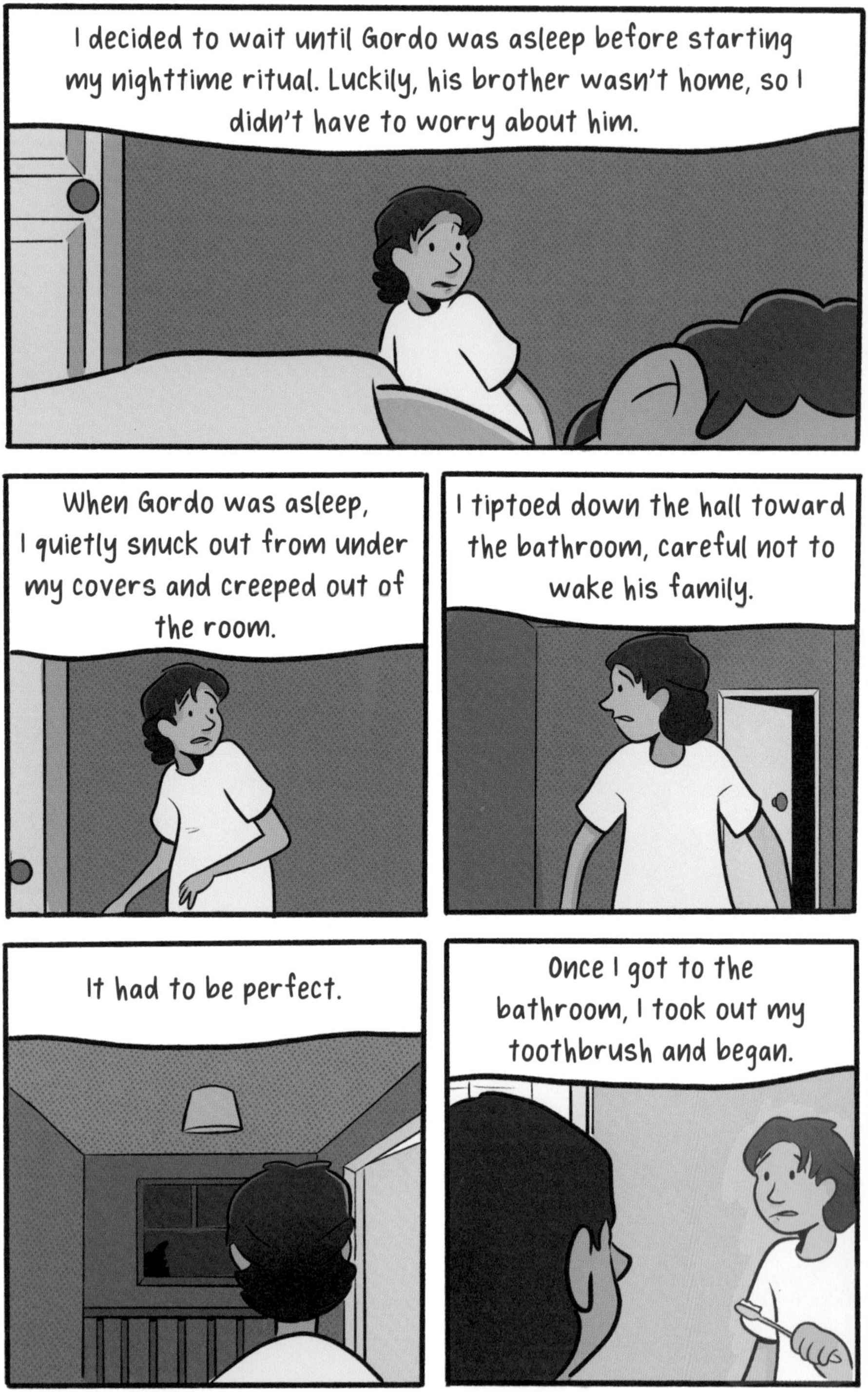
I decided to wait until Gordo was asleep before starting my nighttime ritual. Luckily, his brother wasn't home, so I didn't have to worry about him.
When Gordo was asleep, I quietly snuck out from under my covers and creeped out of the room.
I tiptoed down the hall toward the bathroom, careful not to wake his family.
It had to be perfect.
Once I got to the bathroom, I took out my toothbrush and began.

I counted brush strokes,

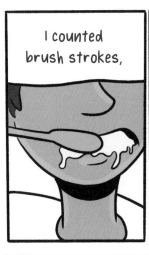

placed my toothbrush back down perfectly,

then I made it out of the bathroom and started my walk back to Gordo's room.

Then, just when I was home free, only a few steps away . . .

What are you doing?

Dennis.

Nothing! I was just brushing my teeth. What are you doing here?

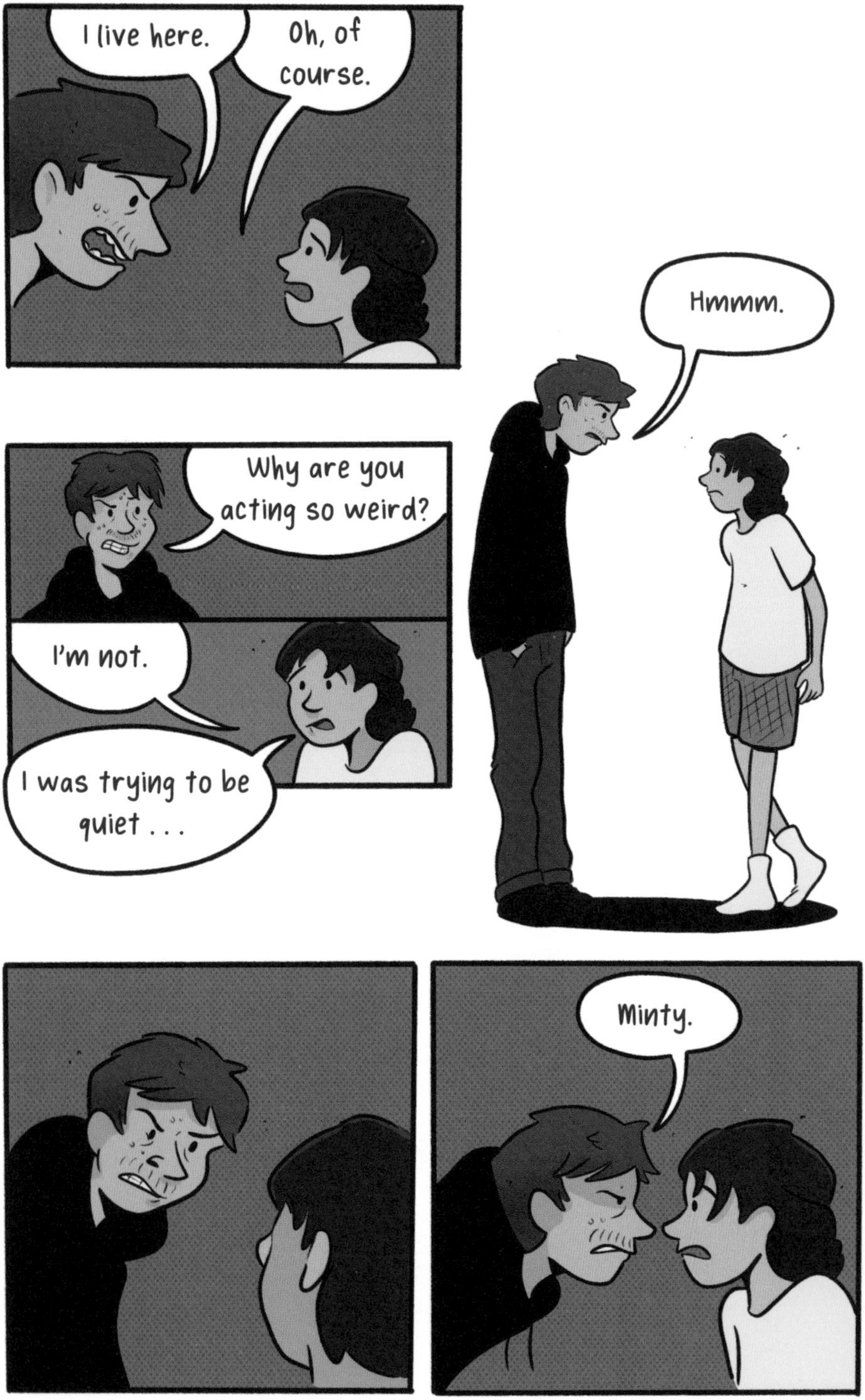
I live here.
Oh, of course.
Why are you acting so weird?
I'm not.
I was trying to be quiet . . .
Hmmm.
Minty.

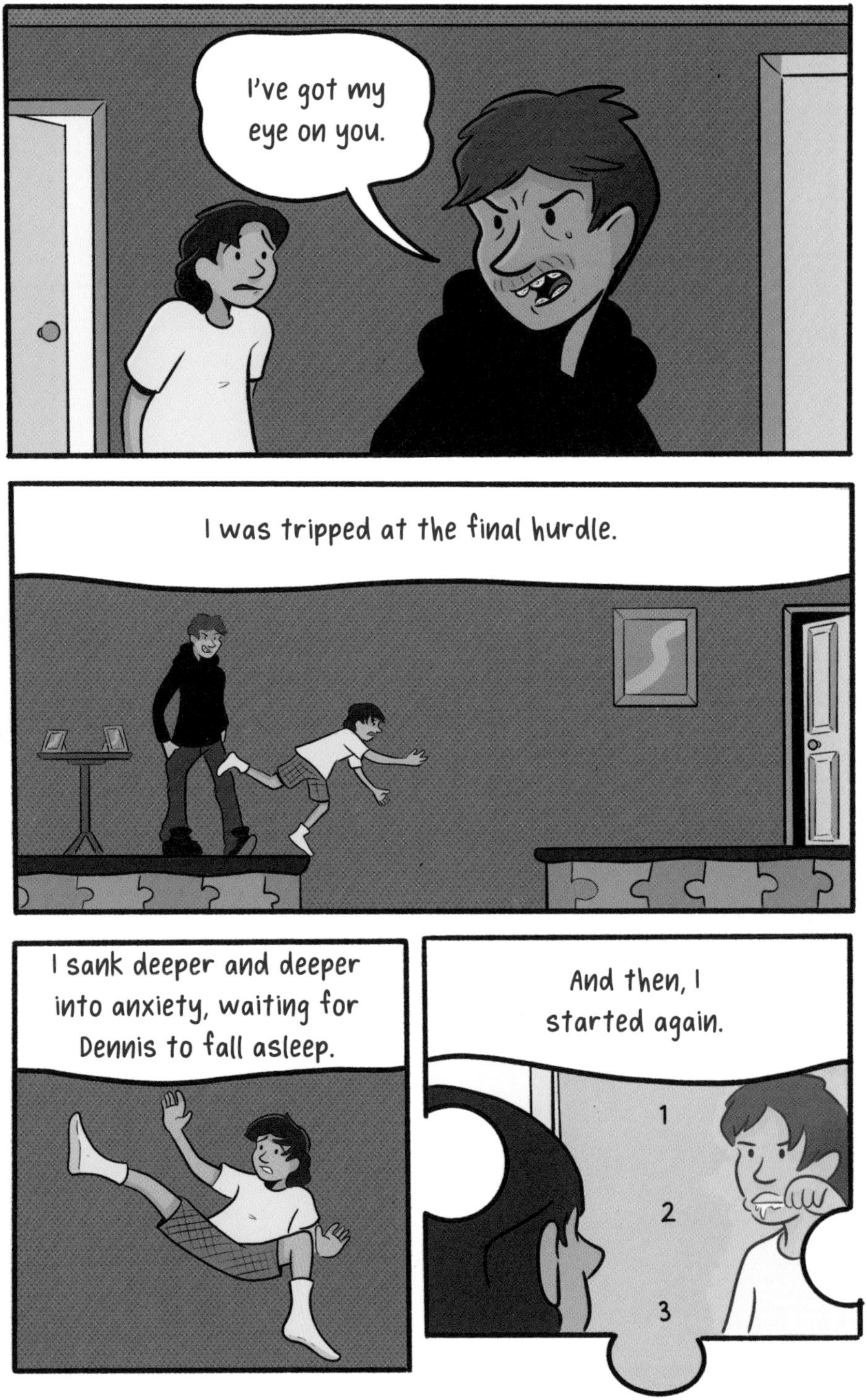
I've got my eye on you.
I was tripped at the final hurdle.
I sank deeper and deeper into anxiety, waiting for Dennis to fall asleep.
And then, I started again.
1
2
3

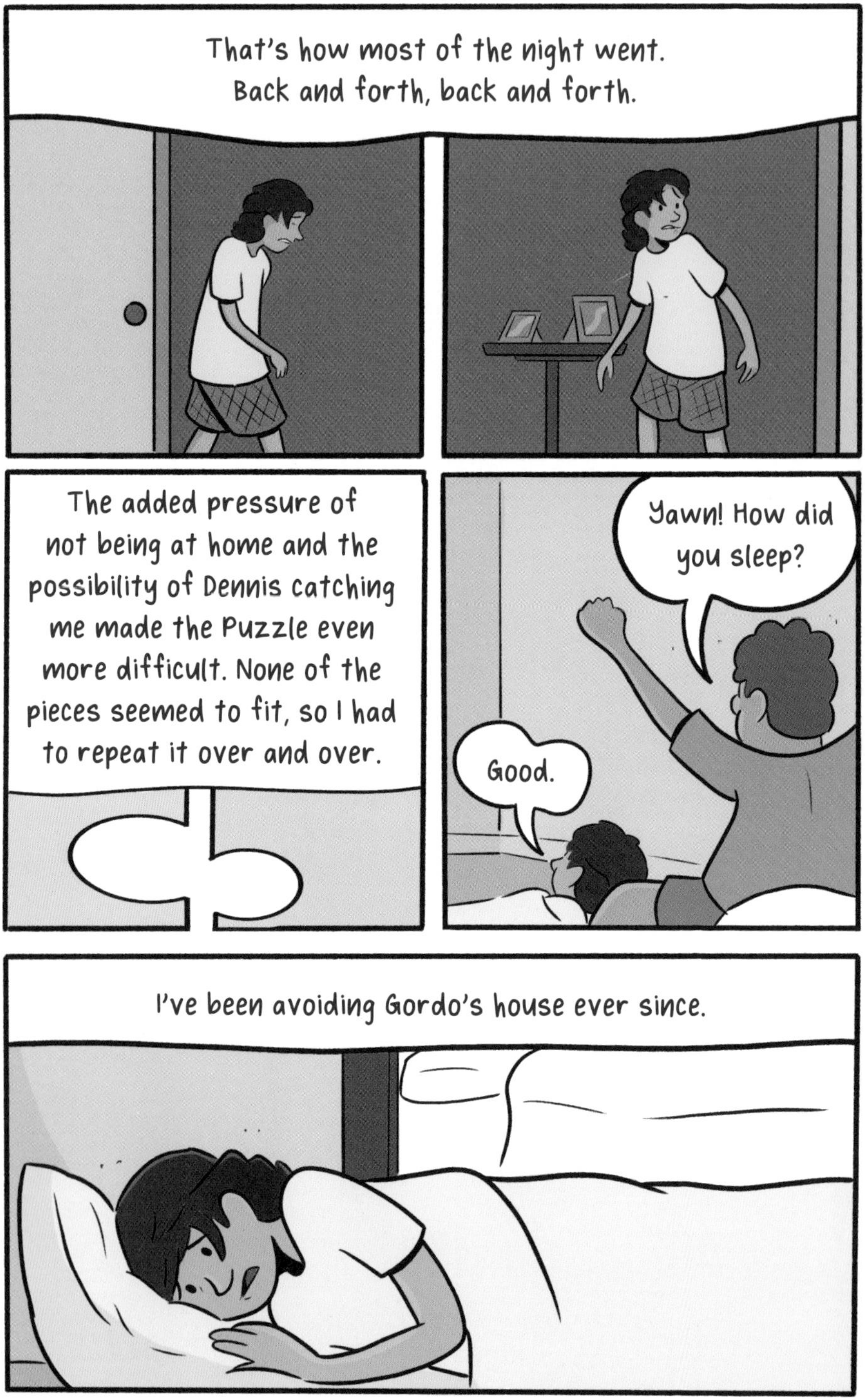

That's how most of the night went.
Back and forth, back and forth.
The added pressure of not being at home and the possibility of Dennis catching me made the Puzzle even more difficult. None of the pieces seemed to fit, so I had to repeat it over and over.
Yawn! How did you sleep?
Good.
I've been avoiding Gordo's house ever since.

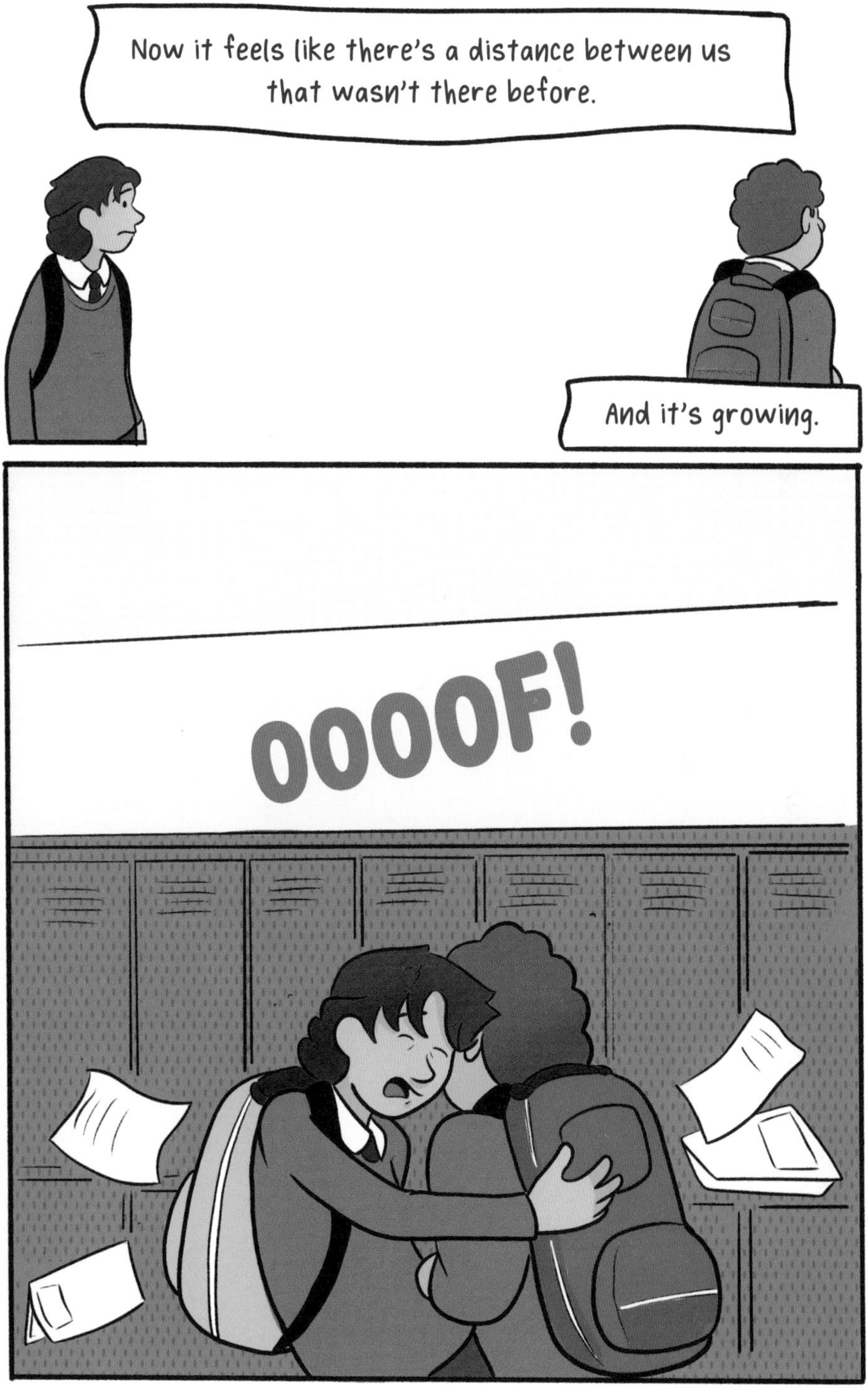
Now it feels like there's a distance between us that wasn't there before.
And it's growing.
OOOOF!

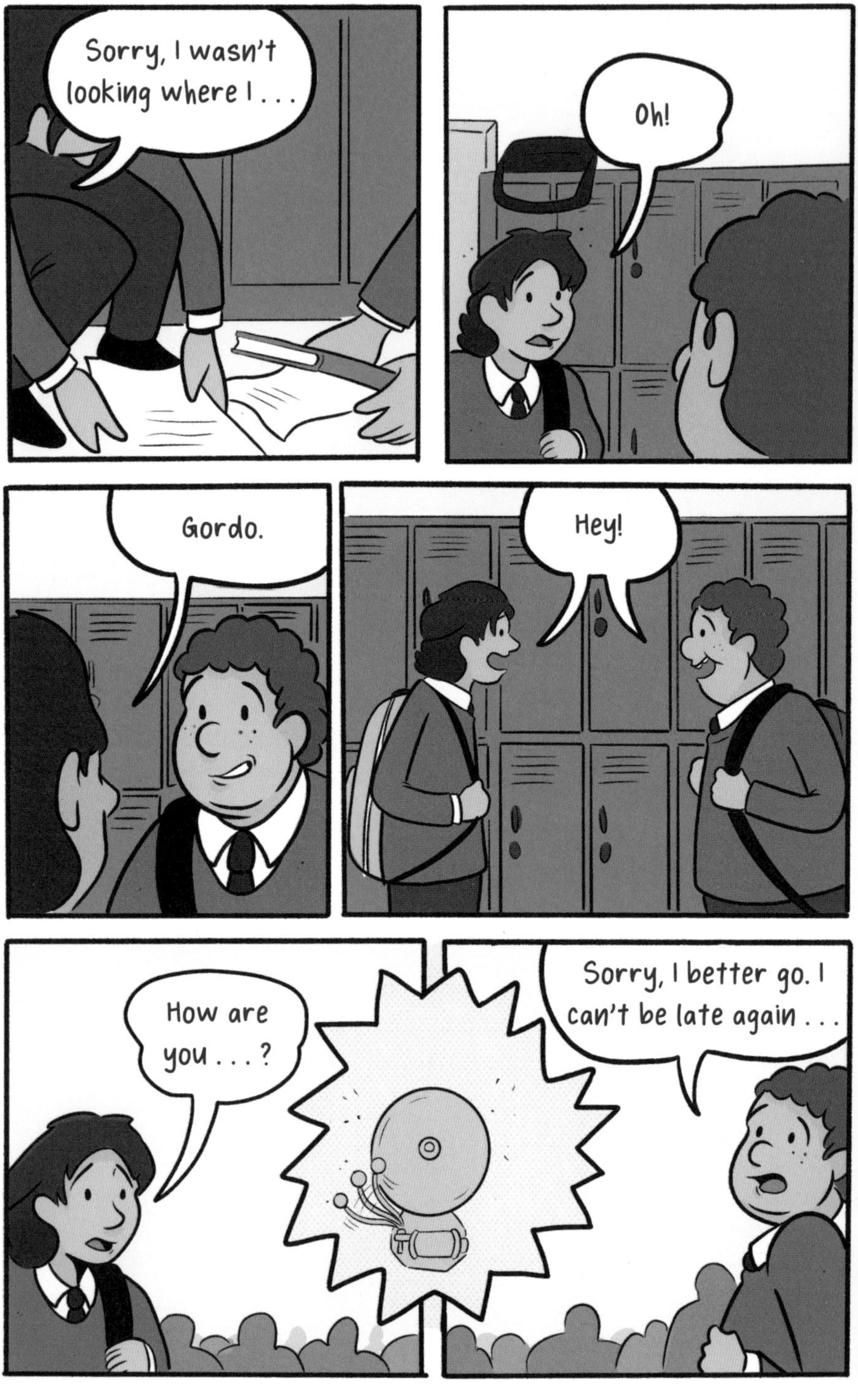
Sorry, I wasn't looking where I . . .
Oh!
Gordo.
Hey!
How are you . . . ?
Sorry, I better go. I can't be late again . . .

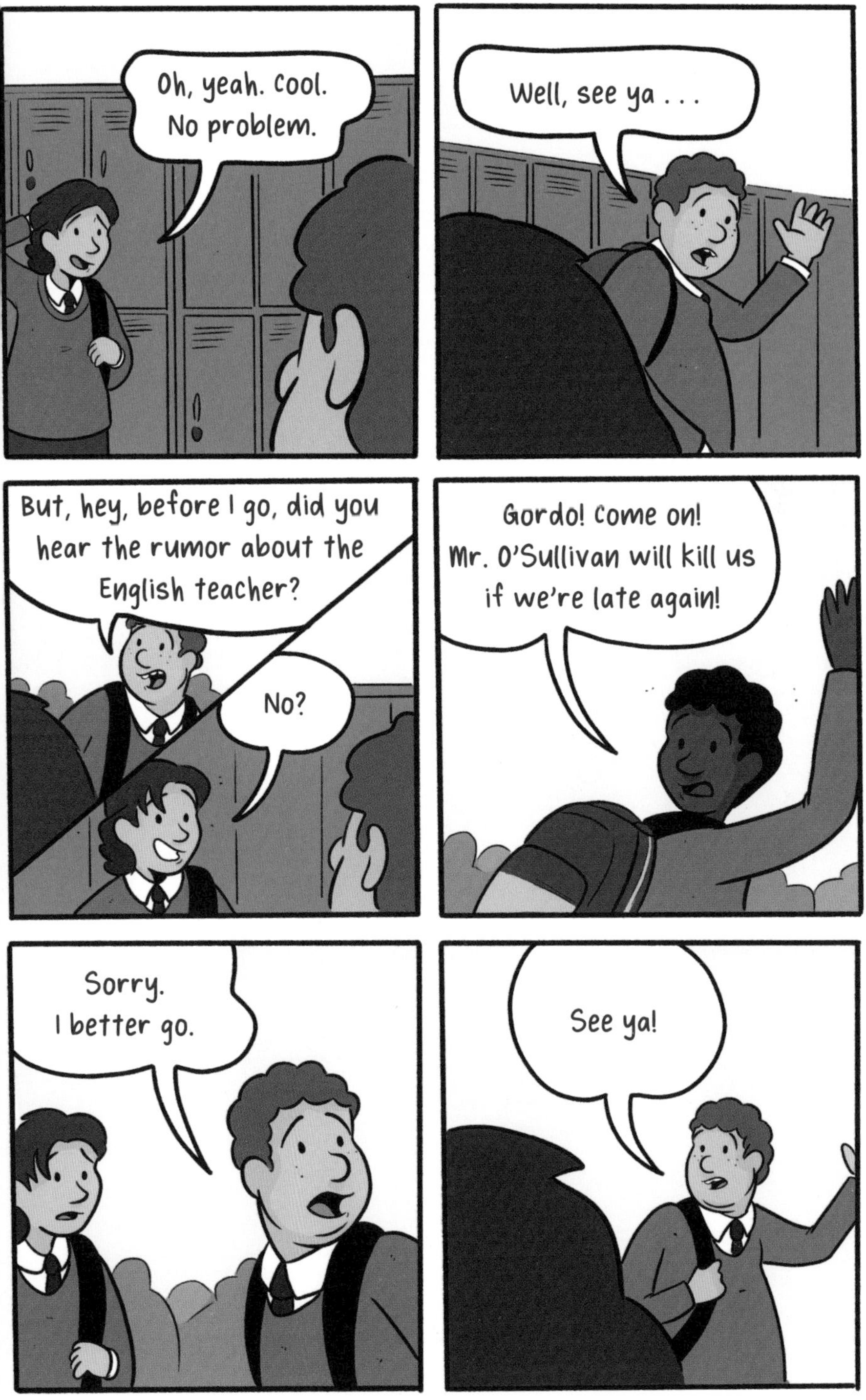
Oh, yeah. Cool. No problem.
Well, see ya . . .
But, hey, before I go, did you hear the rumor about the English teacher?
No?
Gordo! Come on! Mr. O'Sullivan will kill us if we're late again!
Sorry. I better go.
See ya!

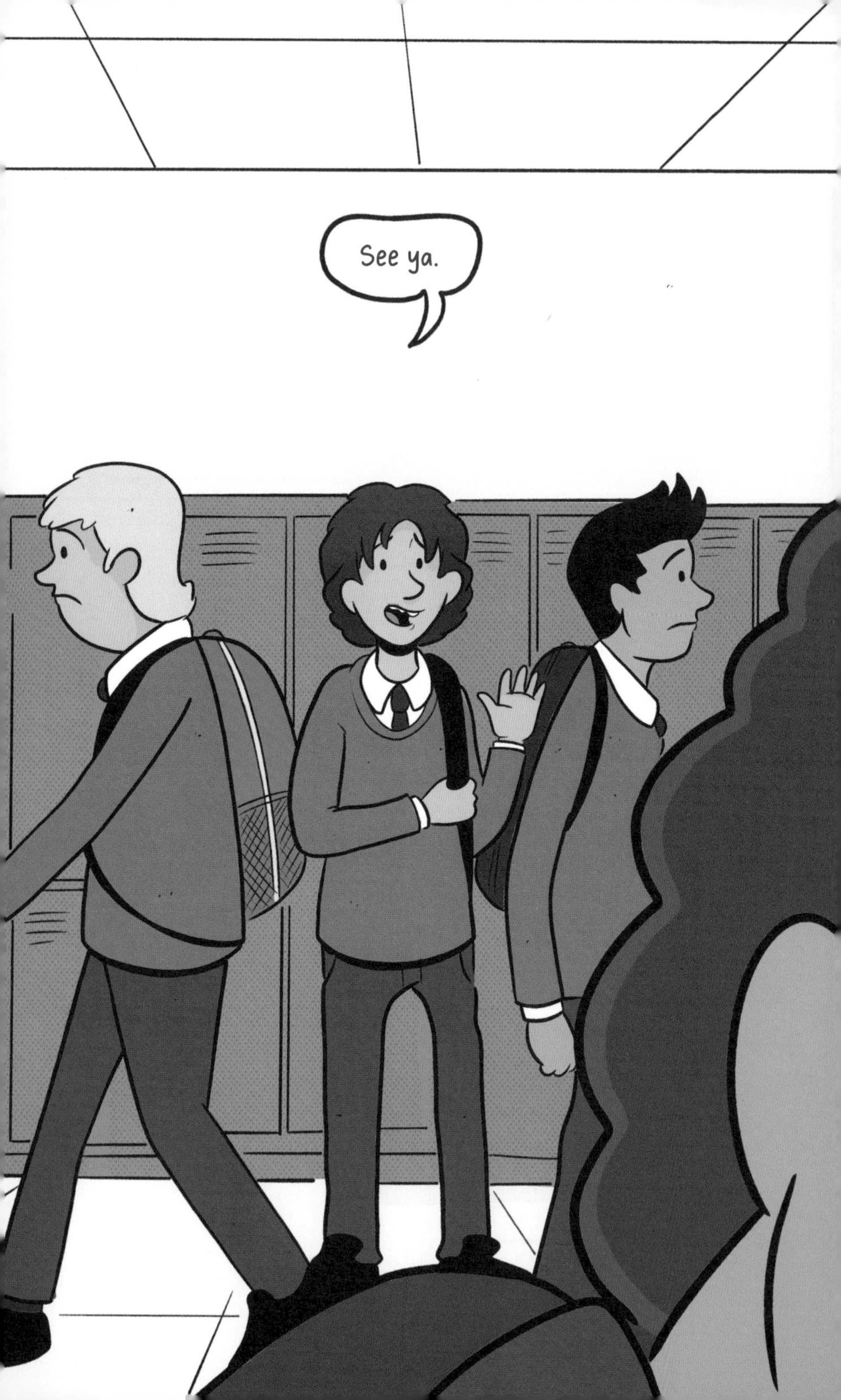
See ya.

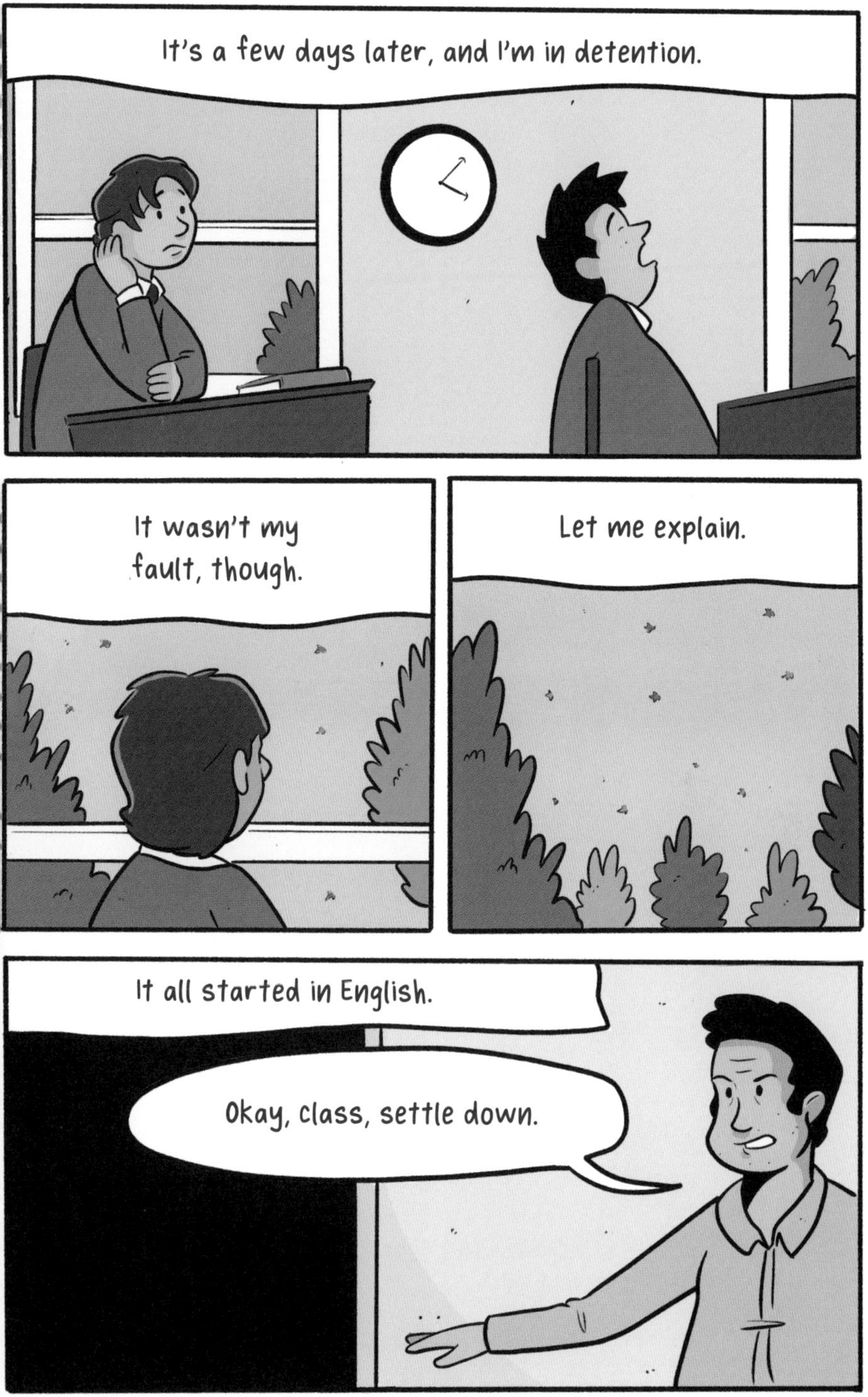
It's a few days later, and I'm in detention.
It wasn't my fault, though.
Let me explain.
It all started in English.
Okay, class, settle down.

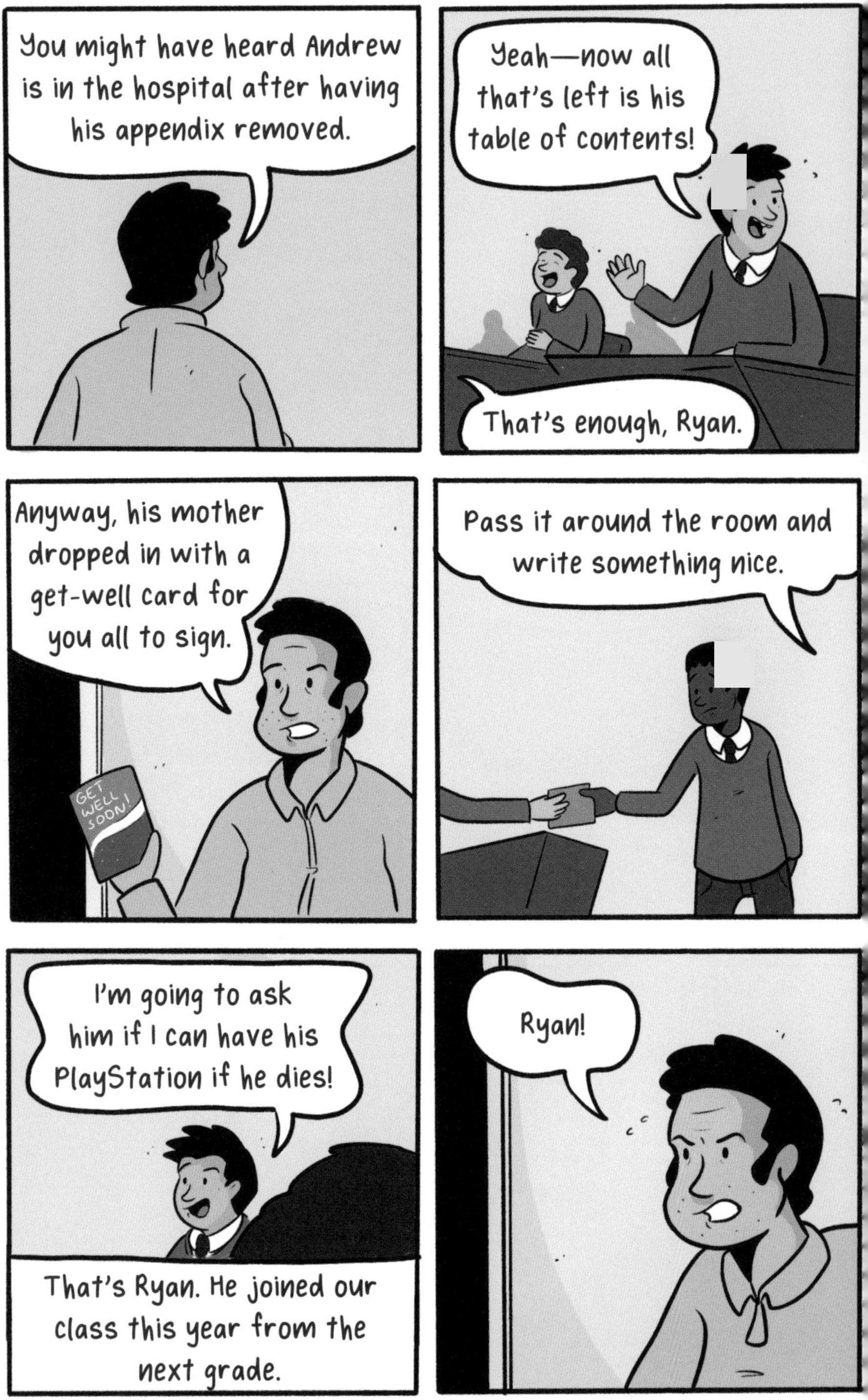
You might have heard Andrew is in the hospital after having his appendix removed.
Yeah—now all that's left is his table of contents!
That's enough, Ryan.
Anyway, his mother dropped in with a get-well card for you all to sign.
GET WELL SOON!
Pass it around the room and write something nice.
I'm going to ask him if I can have his PlayStation if he dies!
That's Ryan. He joined our class this year from the next grade.
Ryan!

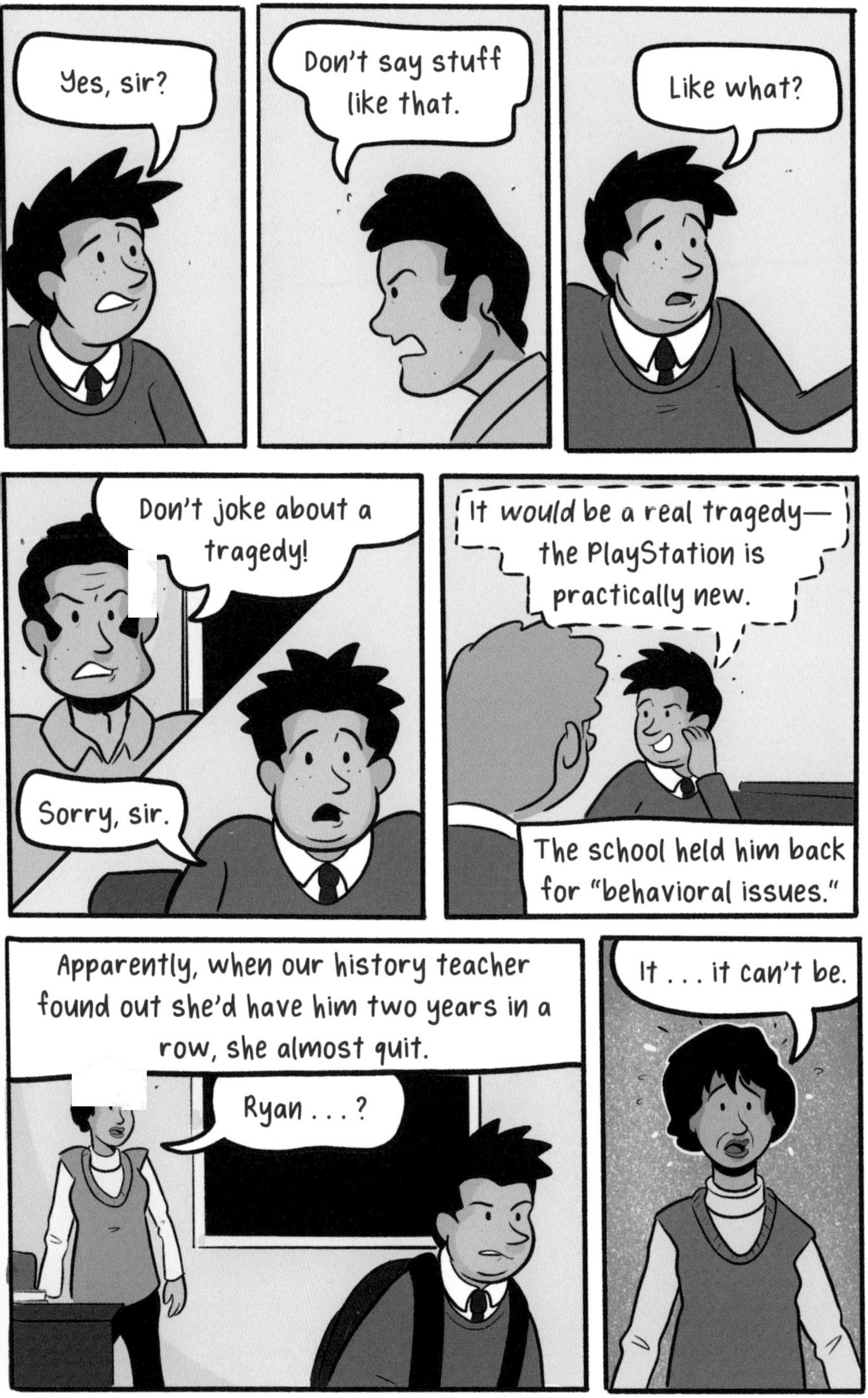
Yes, sir?
Don't say stuff like that.
Like what?
Don't joke about a tragedy!
Sorry, sir.
It *would* be a real tragedy—the PlayStation is practically new.
The school held him back for "behavioral issues."
Apparently, when our history teacher found out she'd have him two years in a row, she almost quit.
Ryan . . . ?
It . . . it can't be.

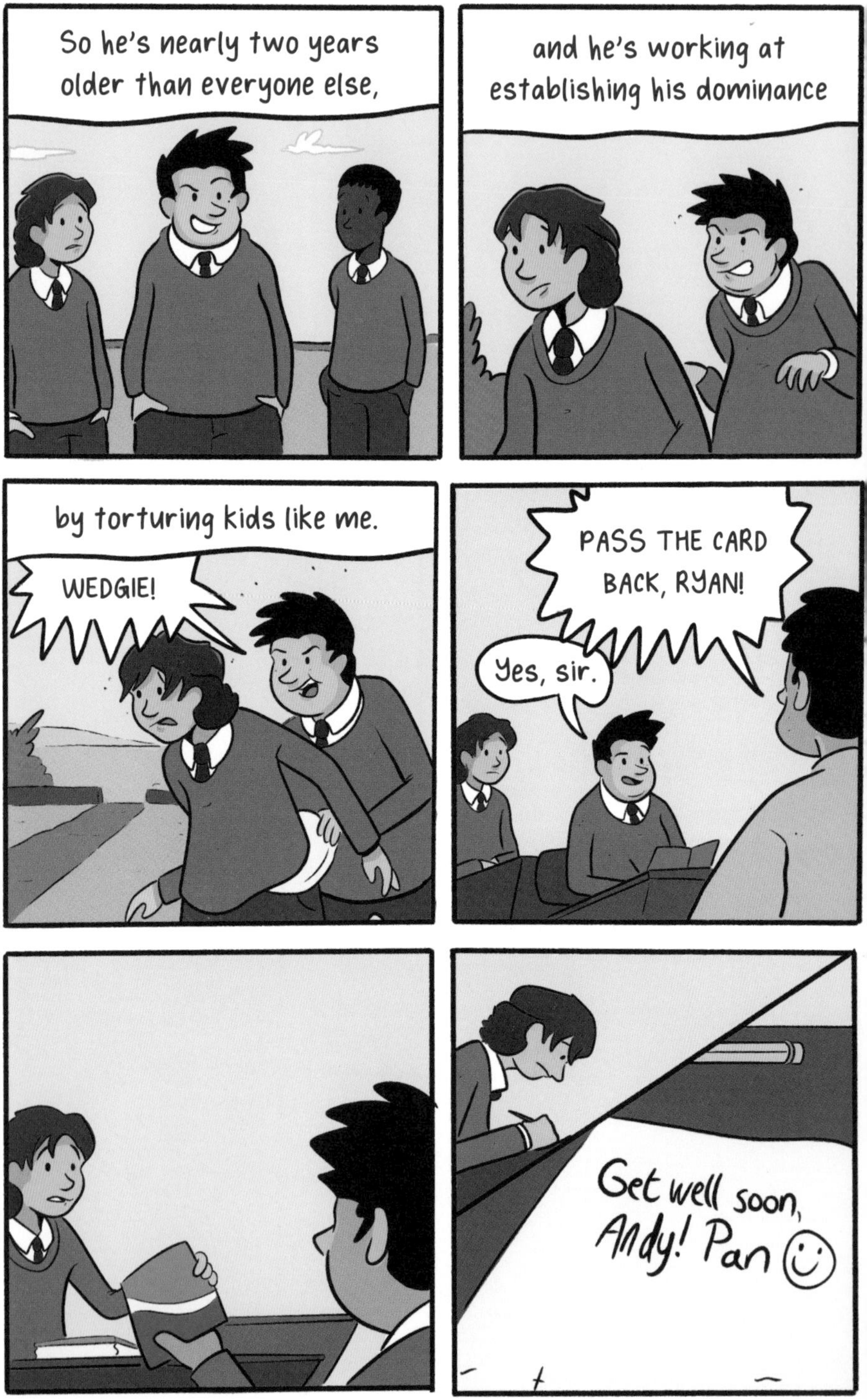
So he's nearly two years older than everyone else,
and he's working at establishing his dominance
by torturing kids like me.
WEDGIE!
PASS THE CARD BACK, RYAN!
Yes, sir.
Get well soon, Andy! Pan

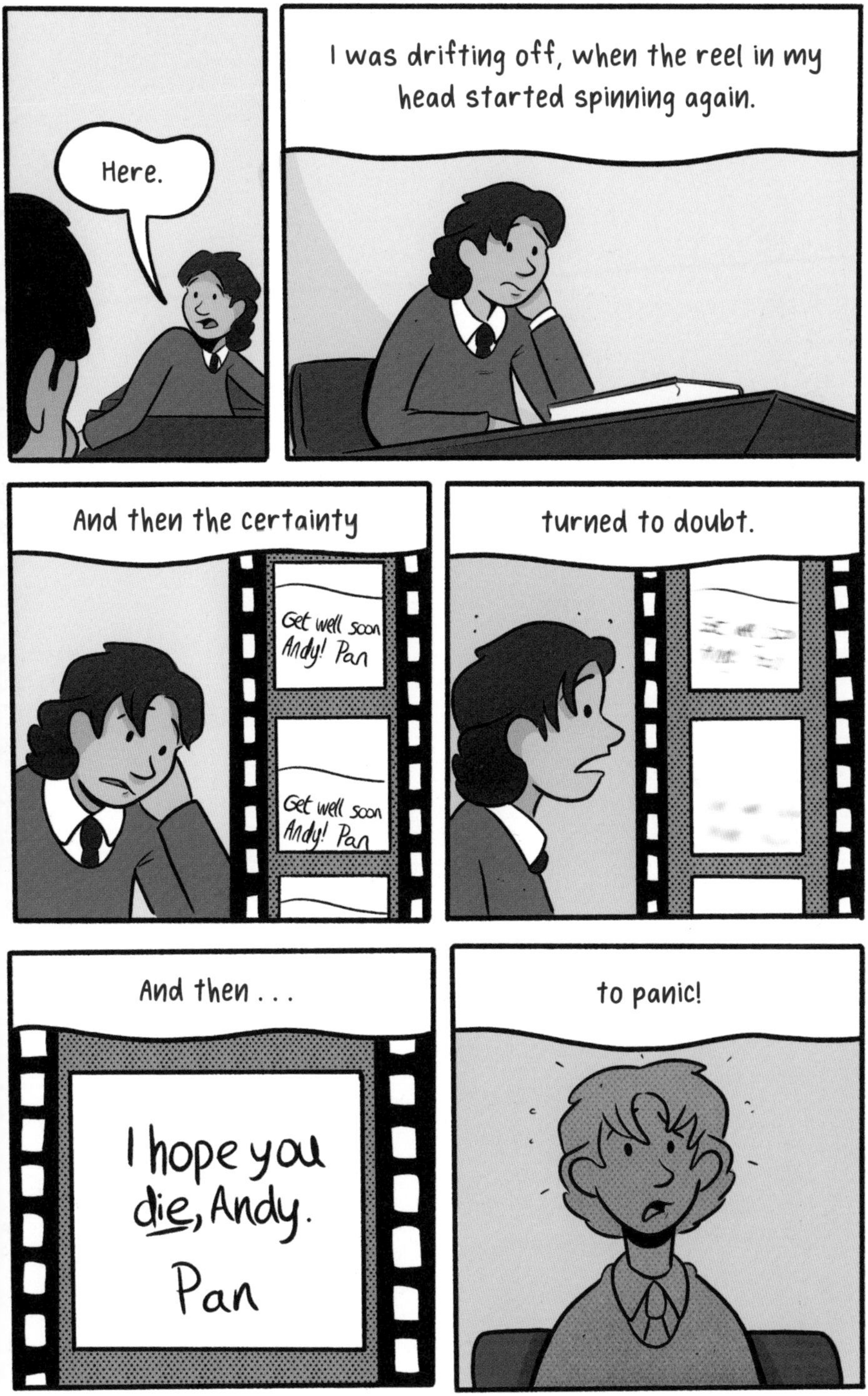
Here.
I was drifting off, when the reel in my head started spinning again.
And then the certainty
Get well soon Andy! Pan
Get well soon Andy! Pan
turned to doubt.
And then . . .
I hope you die, Andy. Pan
to panic!

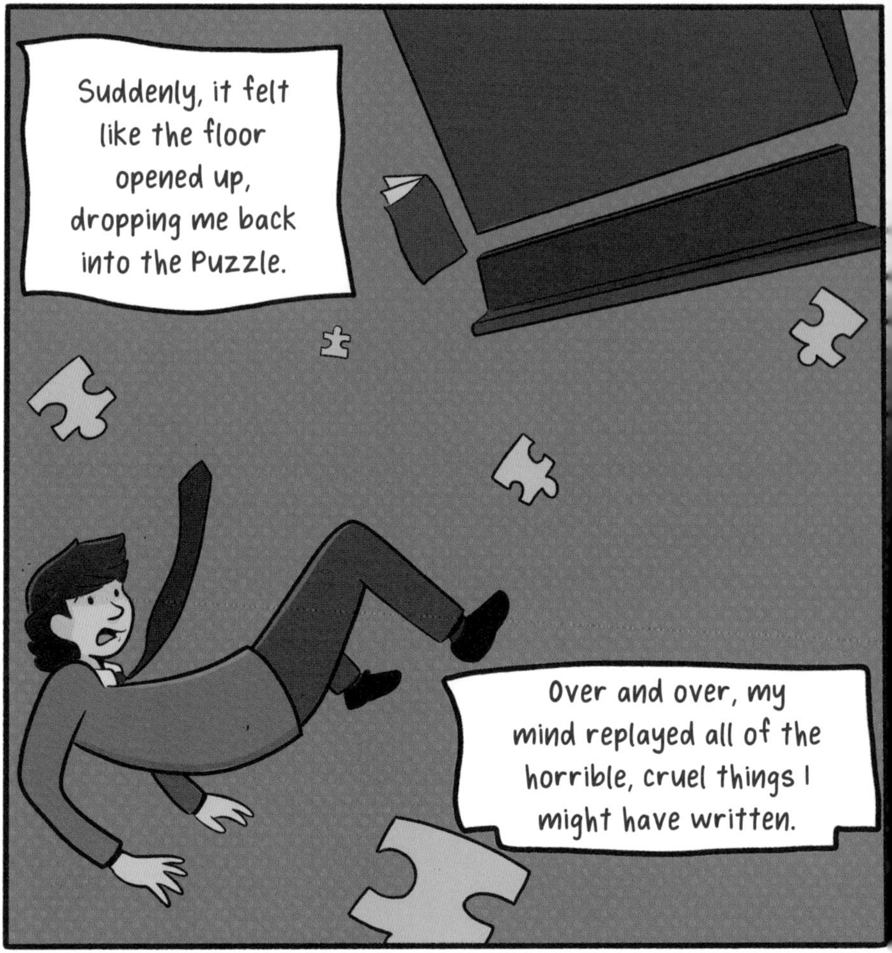
Suddenly, it felt like the floor opened up, dropping me back into the Puzzle.
Over and over, my mind replayed all of the horrible, cruel things I might have written.

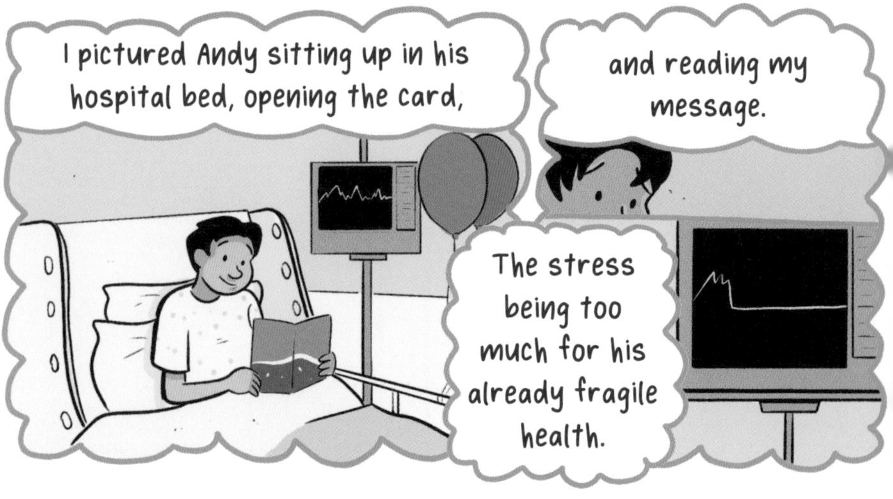
I pictured Andy sitting up in his hospital bed, opening the card,
and reading my message.
The stress being too much for his already fragile health.

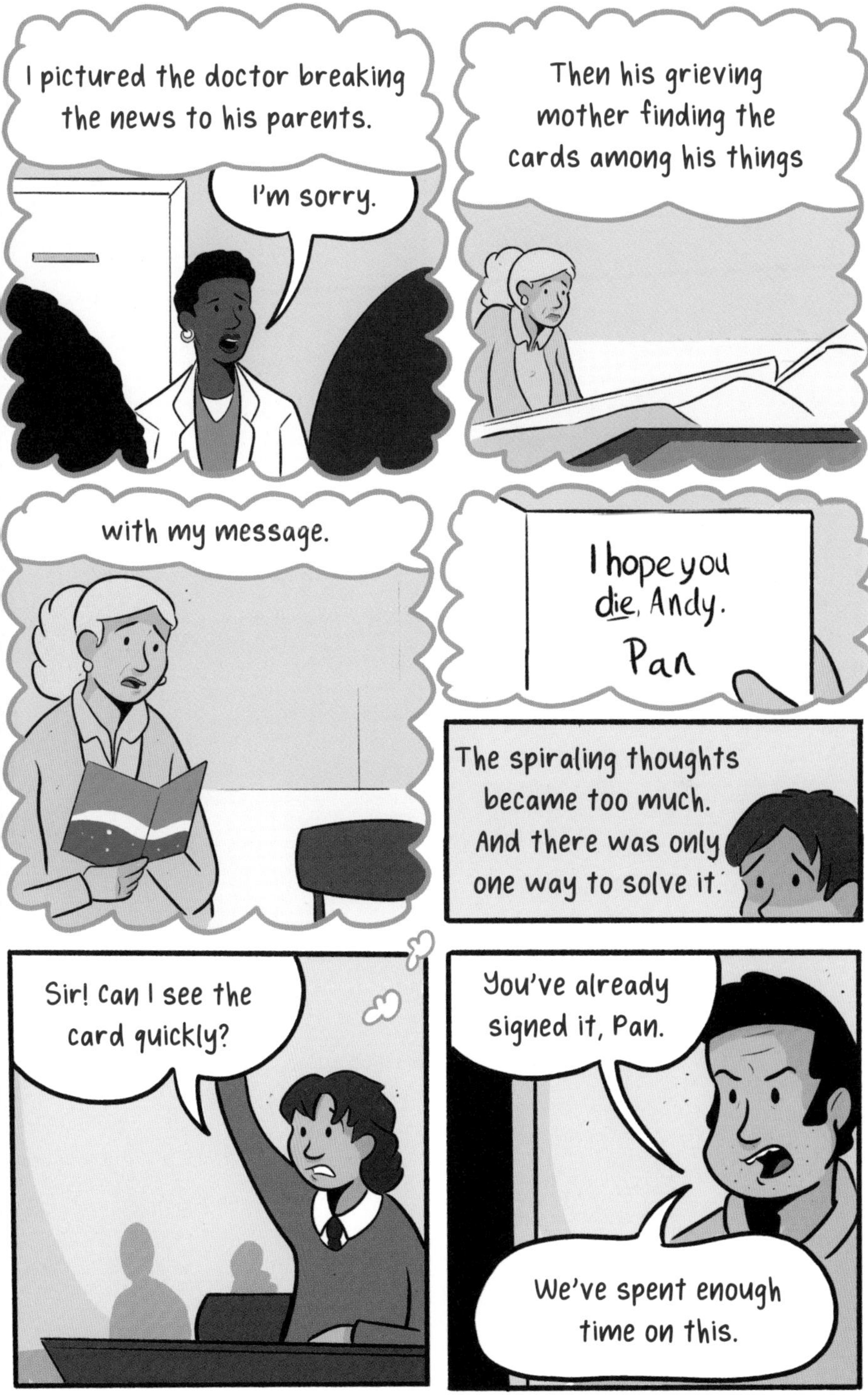
I pictured the doctor breaking the news to his parents.
I'm sorry.
Then his grieving mother finding the cards among his things
with my message.
I hope you die, Andy. Pan
The spiraling thoughts became too much. And there was only one way to solve it.
Sir! Can I see the card quickly?
You've already signed it, Pan.
We've spent enough time on this.

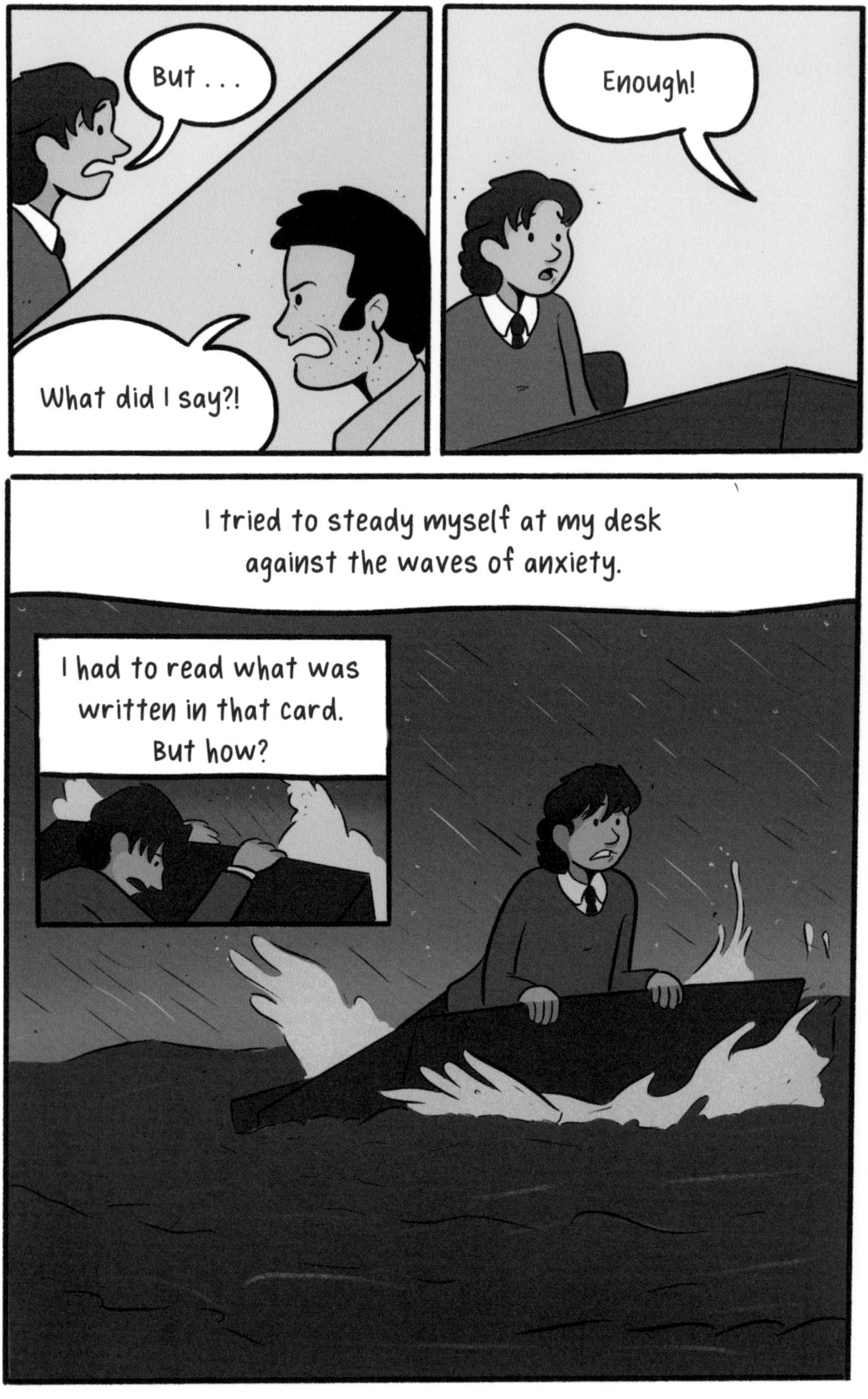
But . . .
What did I say?!
Enough!
I tried to steady myself at my desk against the waves of anxiety.
I had to read what was written in that card. But how?

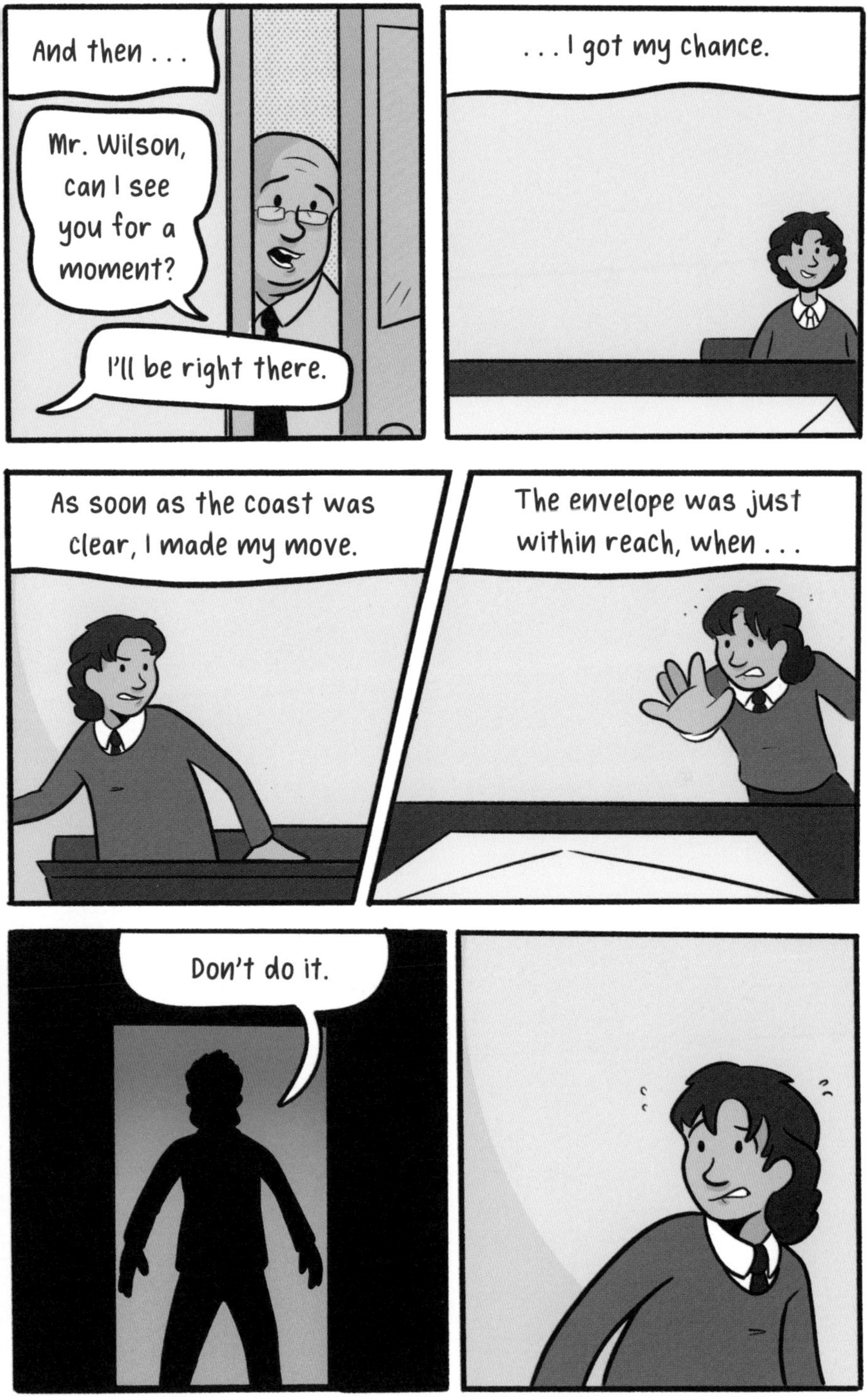
And then . . .
Mr. Wilson, can I see you for a moment?
I'll be right there.
. . . I got my chance.
As soon as the coast was clear, I made my move.
The envelope was just within reach, when . . .
Don't do it.

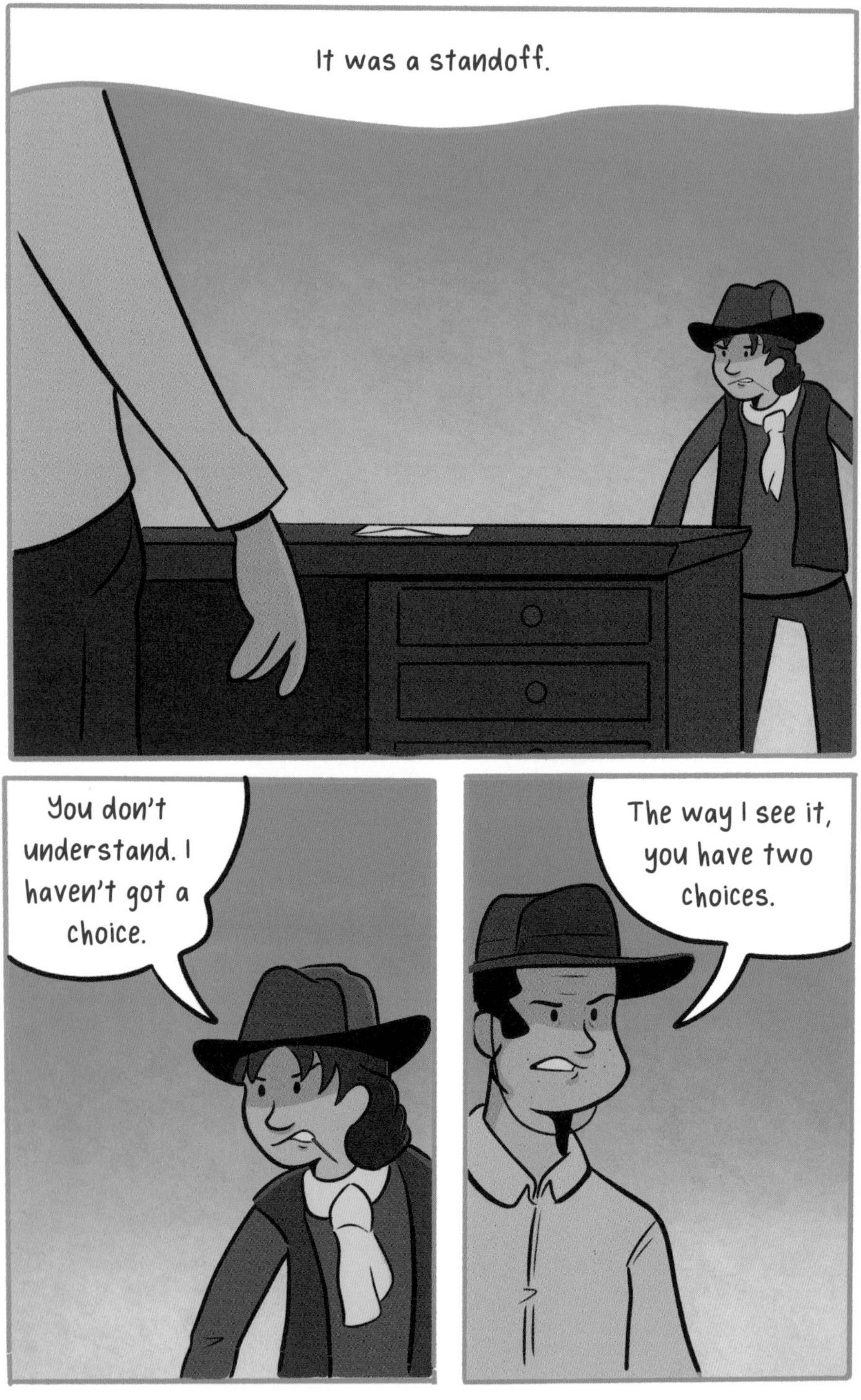
It was a standoff.
You don't understand. I haven't got a choice.
The way I see it, you have two choices.

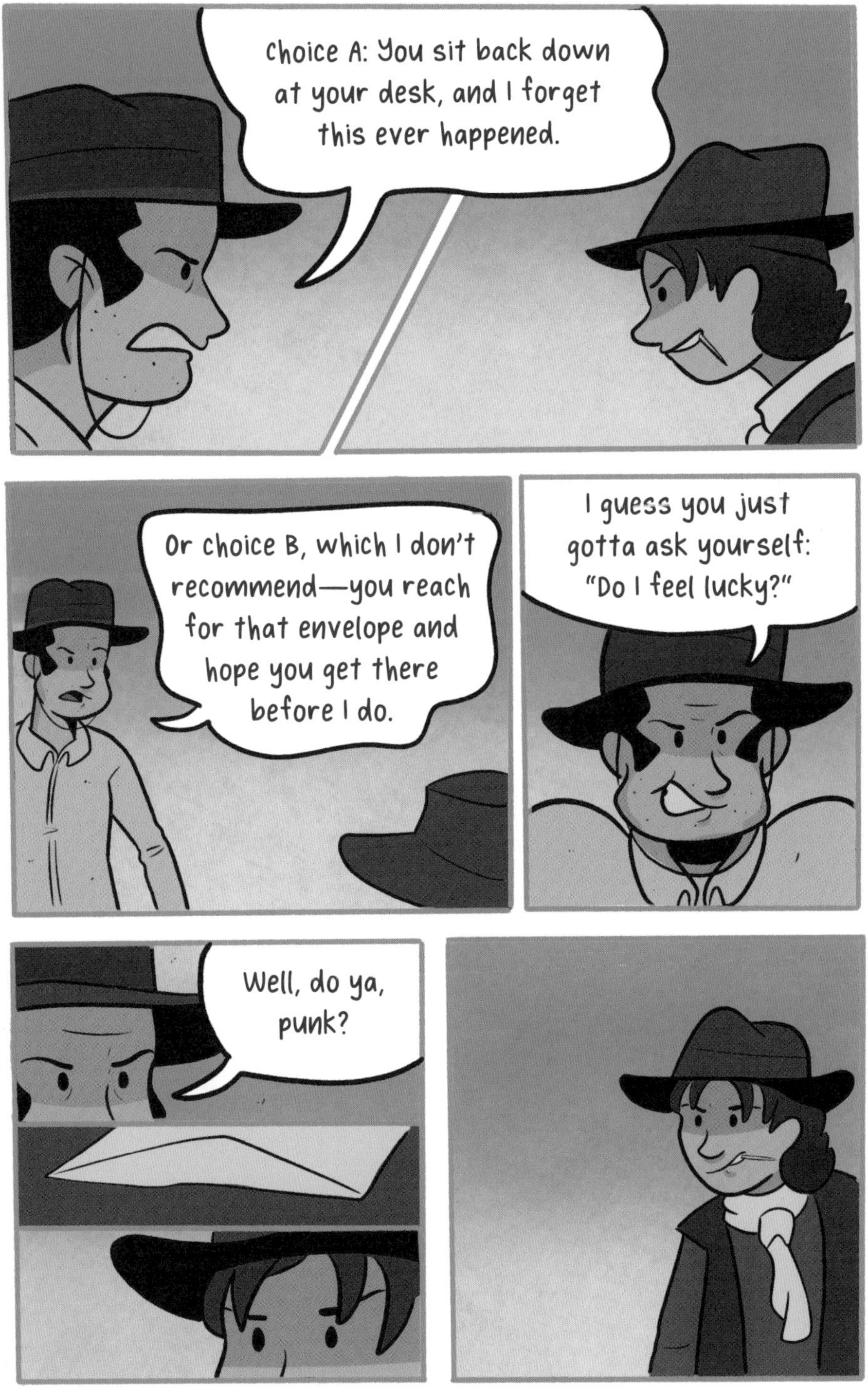
Choice A: You sit back down at your desk, and I forget this ever happened.
Or choice B, which I don't recommend—you reach for that envelope and hope you get there before I do.
I guess you just gotta ask yourself: "Do I feel lucky?"
Well, do ya, punk?

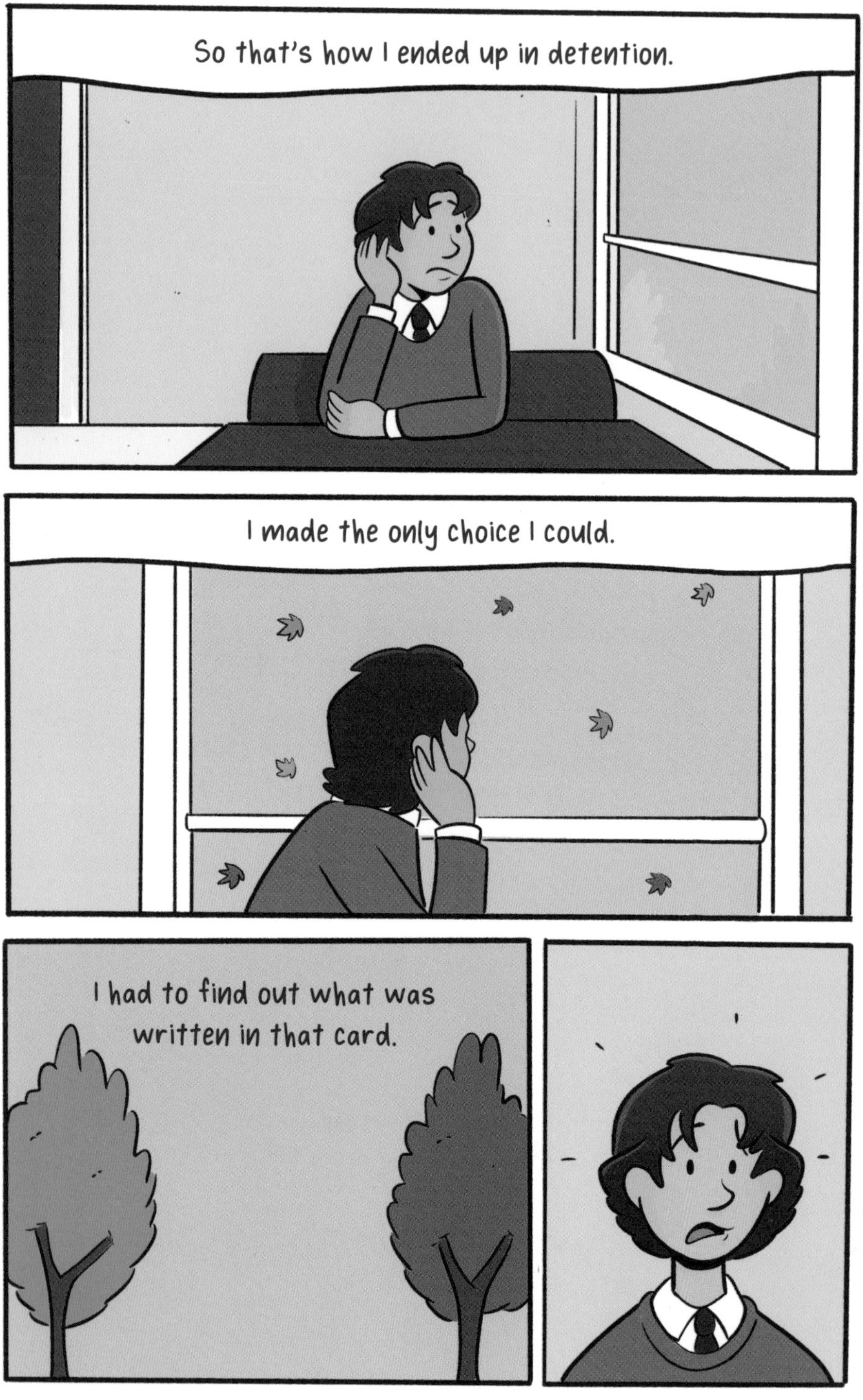
So that's how I ended up in detention.
I made the only choice I could.
I had to find out what was written in that card.

What was it, again?

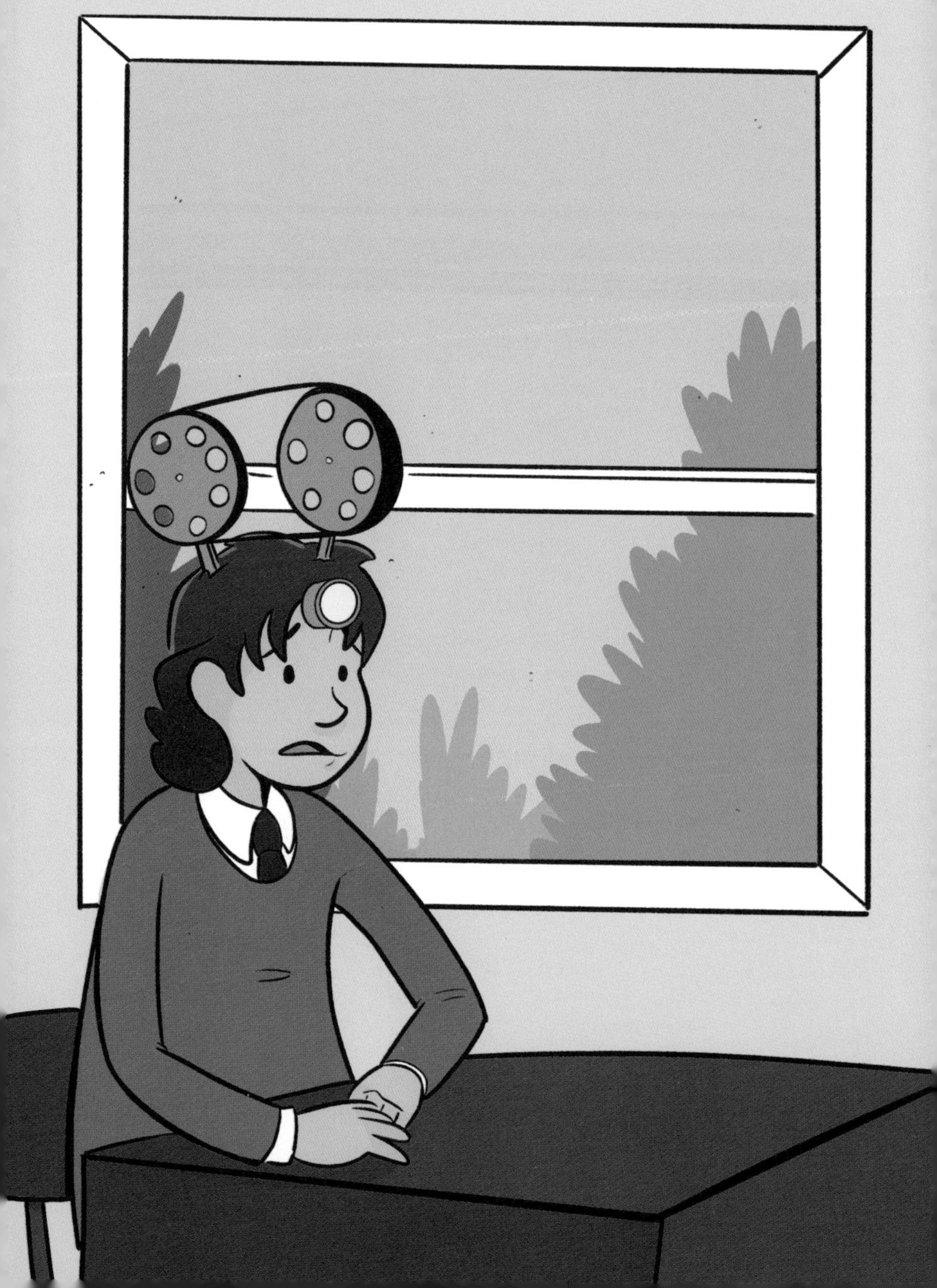

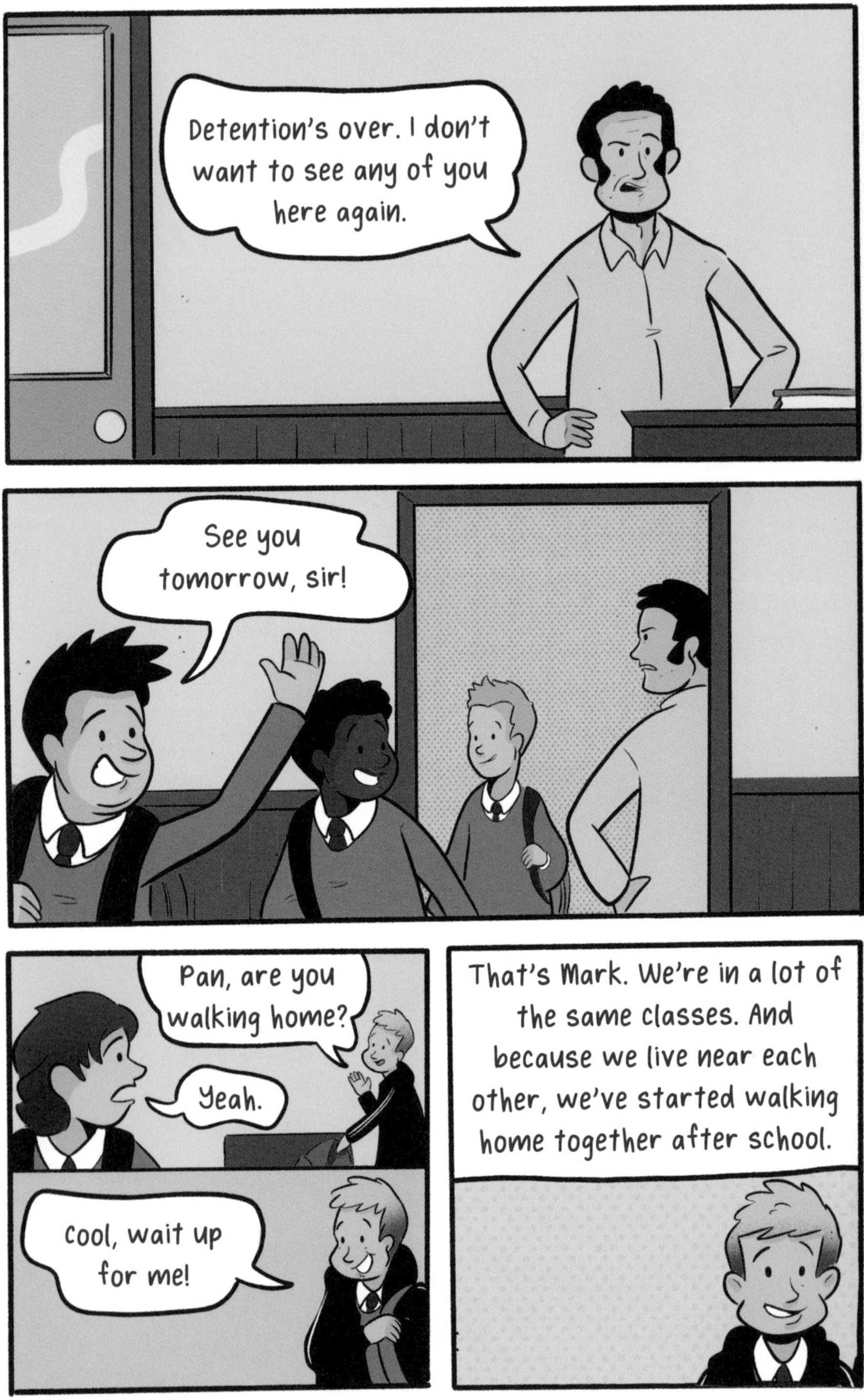

Detention's over. I don't want to see any of you here again.
See you tomorrow, sir!
Pan, are you walking home?
Yeah.
Cool, wait up for me!
That's Mark. We're in a lot of the same classes. And because we live near each other, we've started walking home together after school.

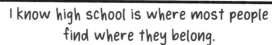

I know high school is where most people
find where they belong.

But I still feel a bit like I'm stumbling in the dark.

So I'm glad I have Mark to help show me the way.

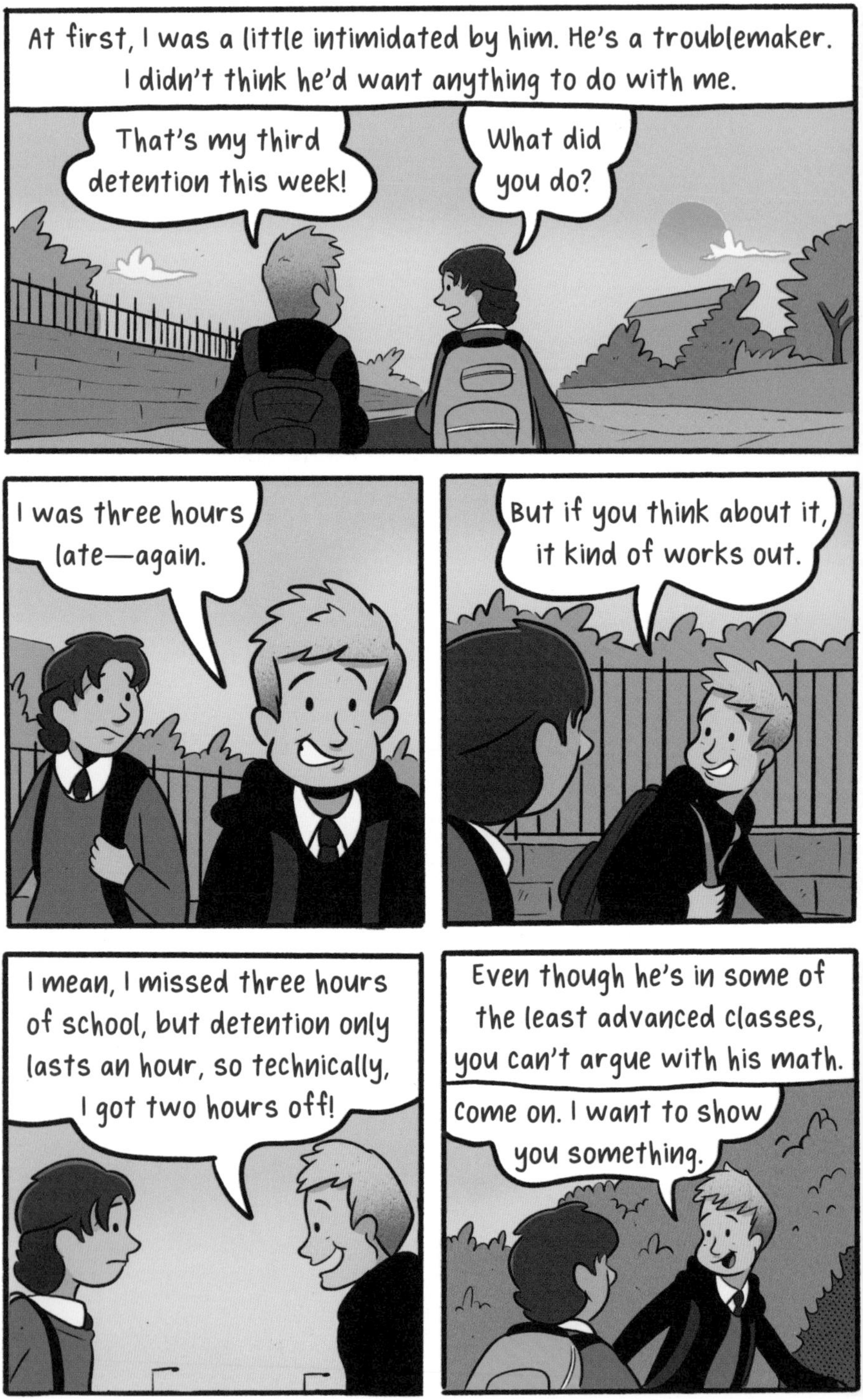
At first, I was a little intimidated by him. He's a troublemaker. I didn't think he'd want anything to do with me.
That's my third detention this week!
What did you do?
I was three hours late—again.
But if you think about it, it kind of works out.
I mean, I missed three hours of school, but detention only lasts an hour, so technically, I got two hours off!
Even though he's in some of the least advanced classes, you can't argue with his math.
Come on. I want to show you something.

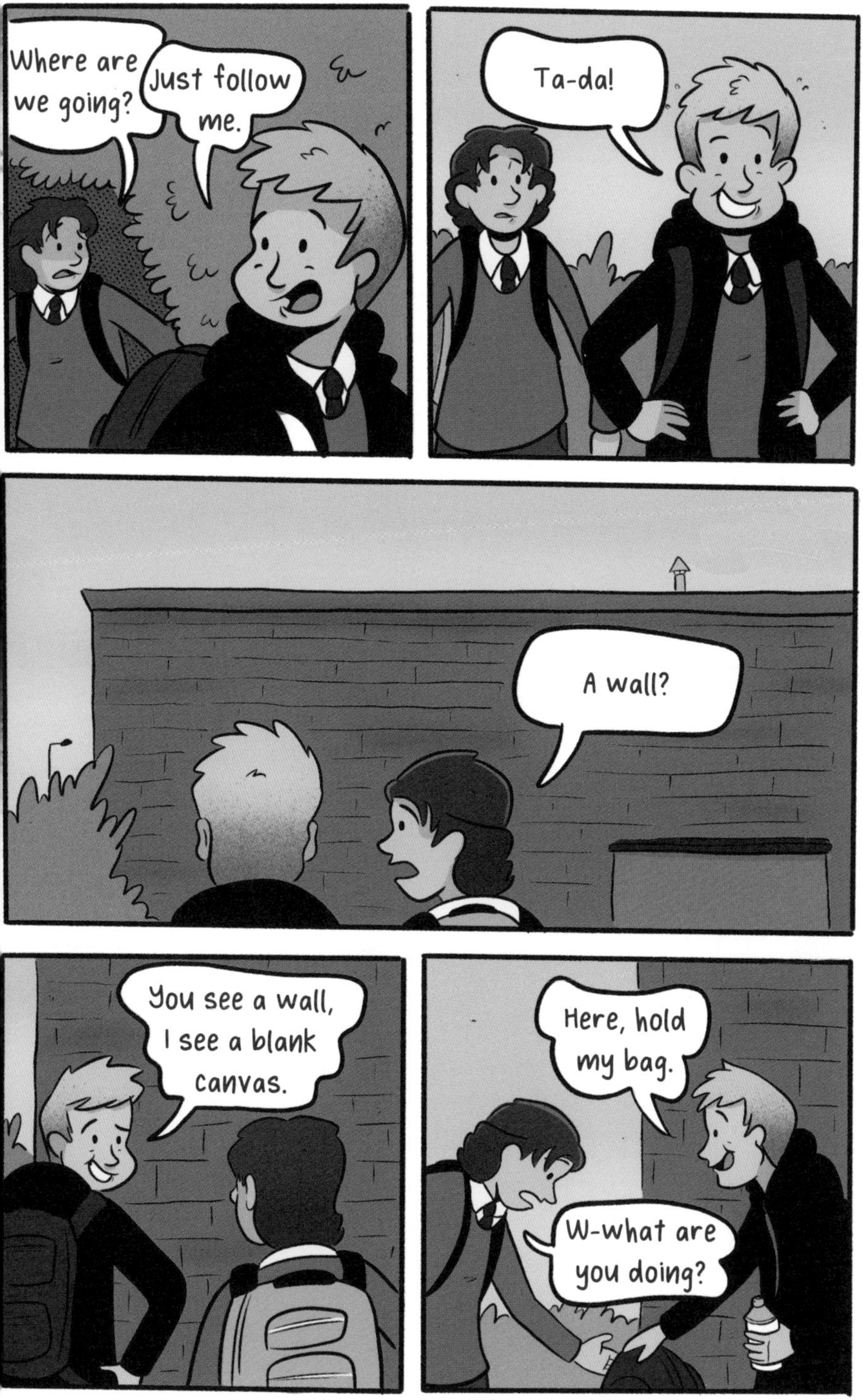

Where are we going?
Just follow me.
Ta-da!
A wall?
You see a wall, I see a blank canvas.
Here, hold my bag.
W-what are you doing?

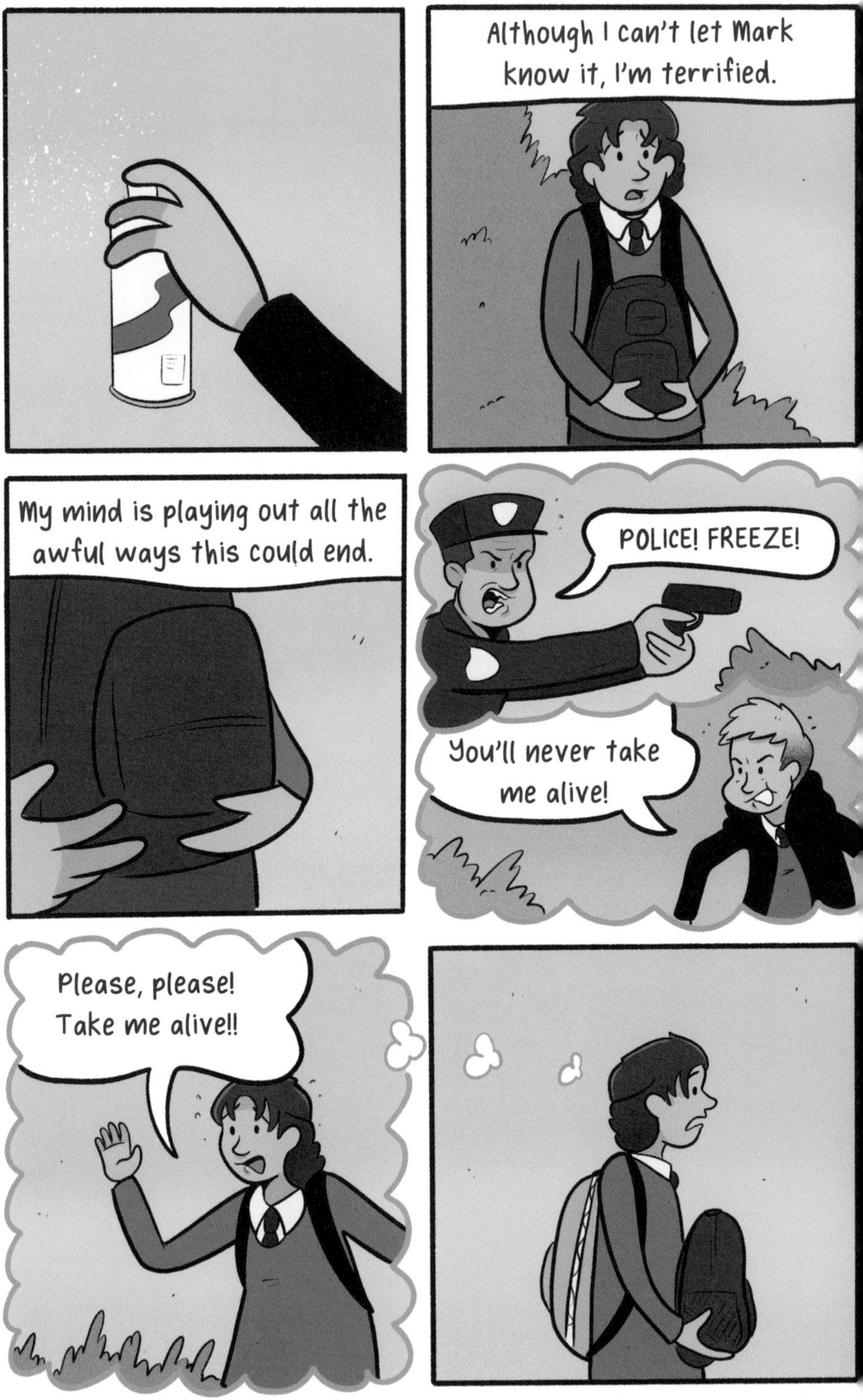
Although I can't let Mark know it, I'm terrified.
My mind is playing out all the awful ways this could end.
POLICE! FREEZE!
You'll never take me alive!
Please, please! Take me alive!!

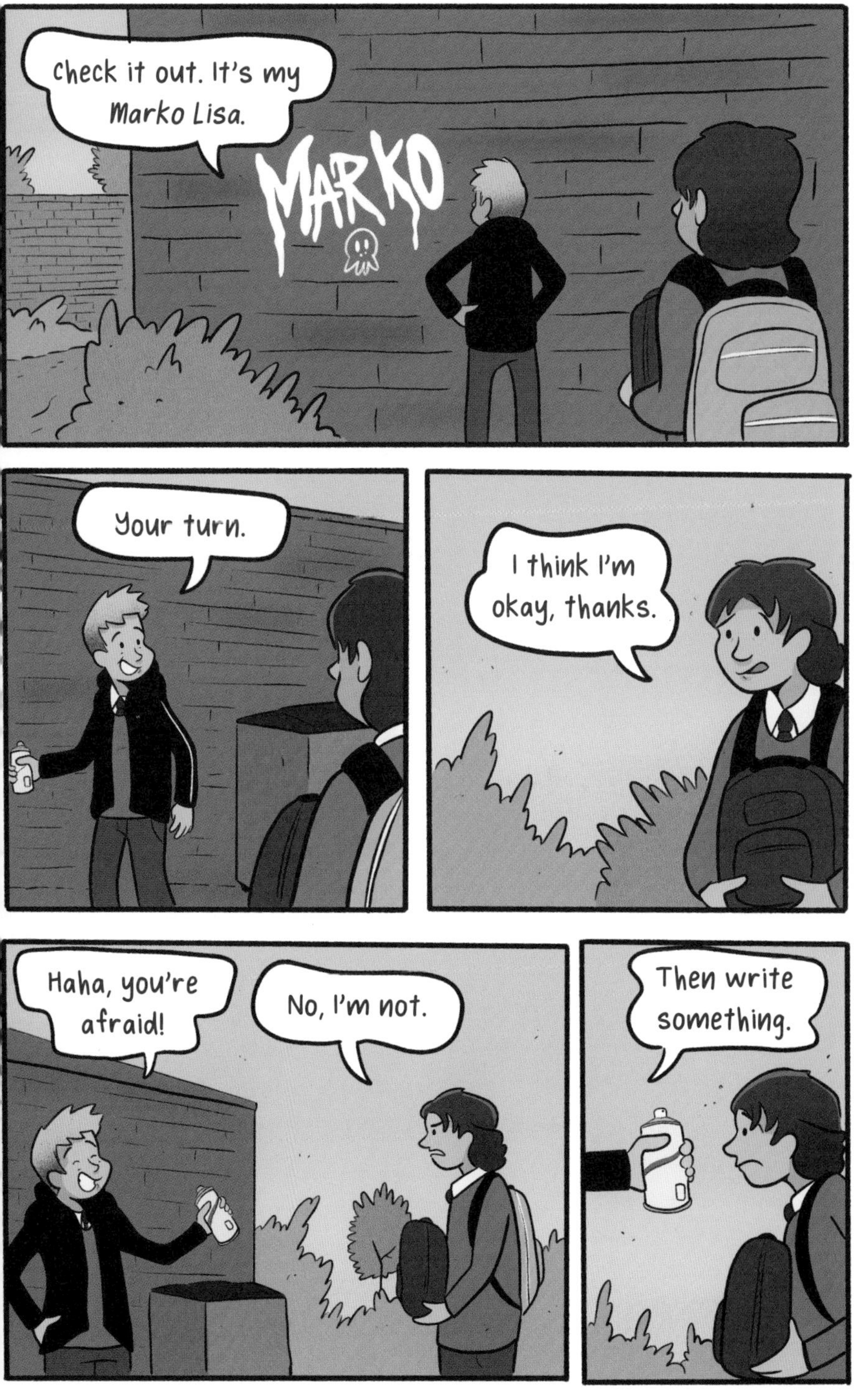
Check it out. It's my Marko Lisa.
MARKO
Your turn.
I think I'm okay, thanks.
Haha, you're afraid!
No, I'm not.
Then write something.

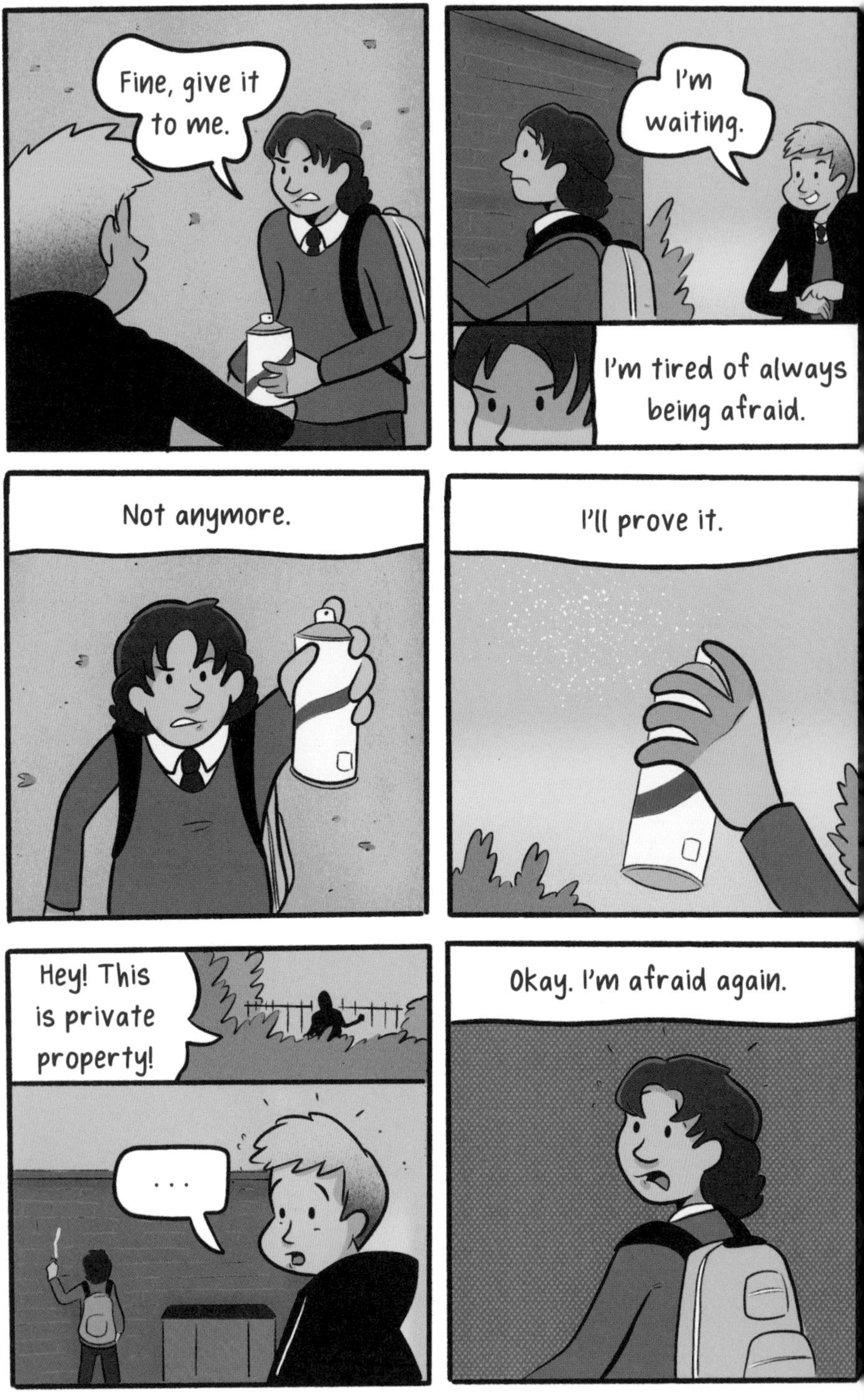

Fine, give it to me.
I'm waiting.
I'm tired of always being afraid.
Not anymore.
I'll prove it.
Hey! This is private property!
. . .
Okay. I'm afraid again.

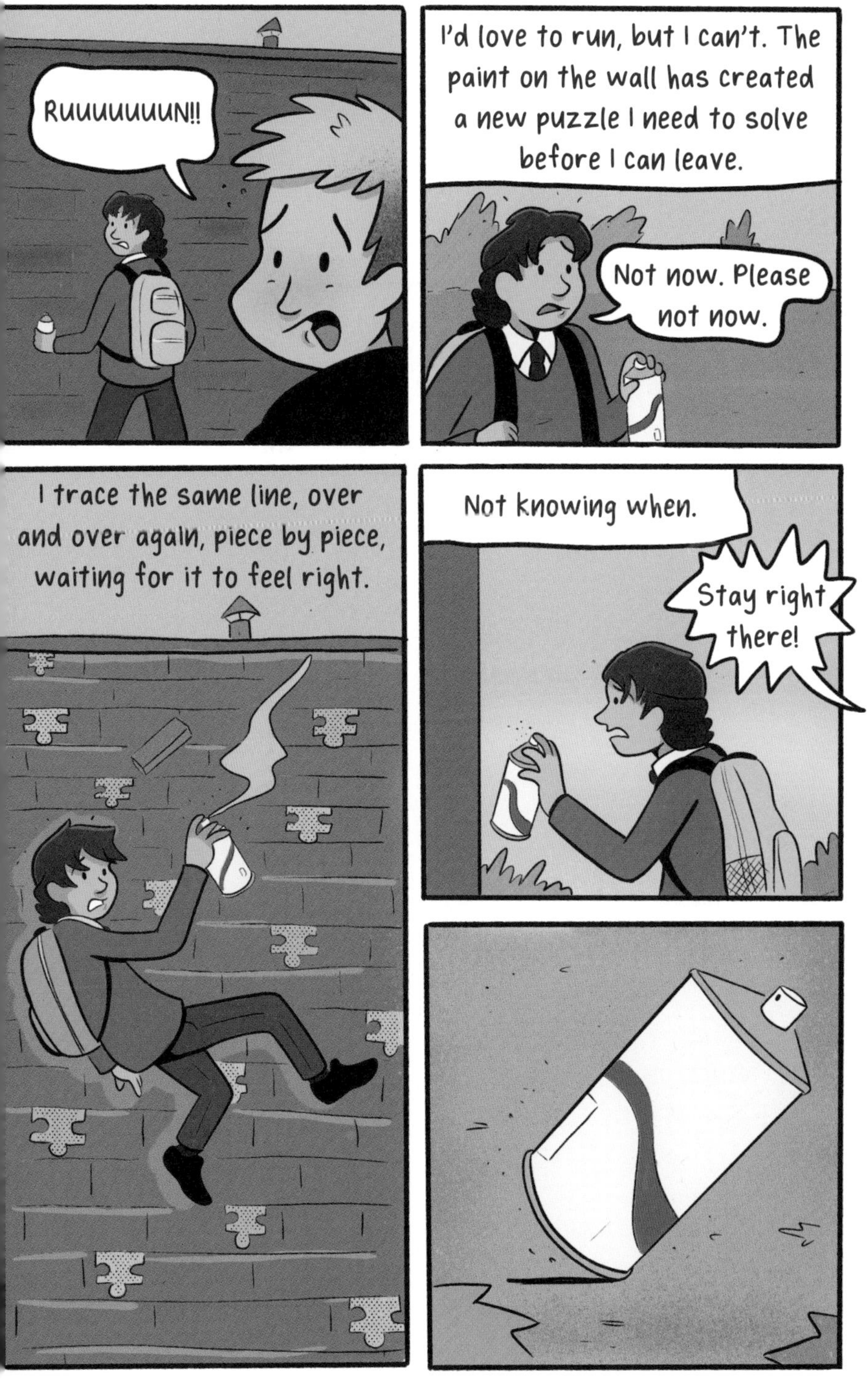
RUUUUUUUN!!
I'd love to run, but I can't. The paint on the wall has created a new puzzle I need to solve before I can leave.
Not now. Please not now.
I trace the same line, over and over again, piece by piece, waiting for it to feel right.
Not knowing when.
Stay right there!

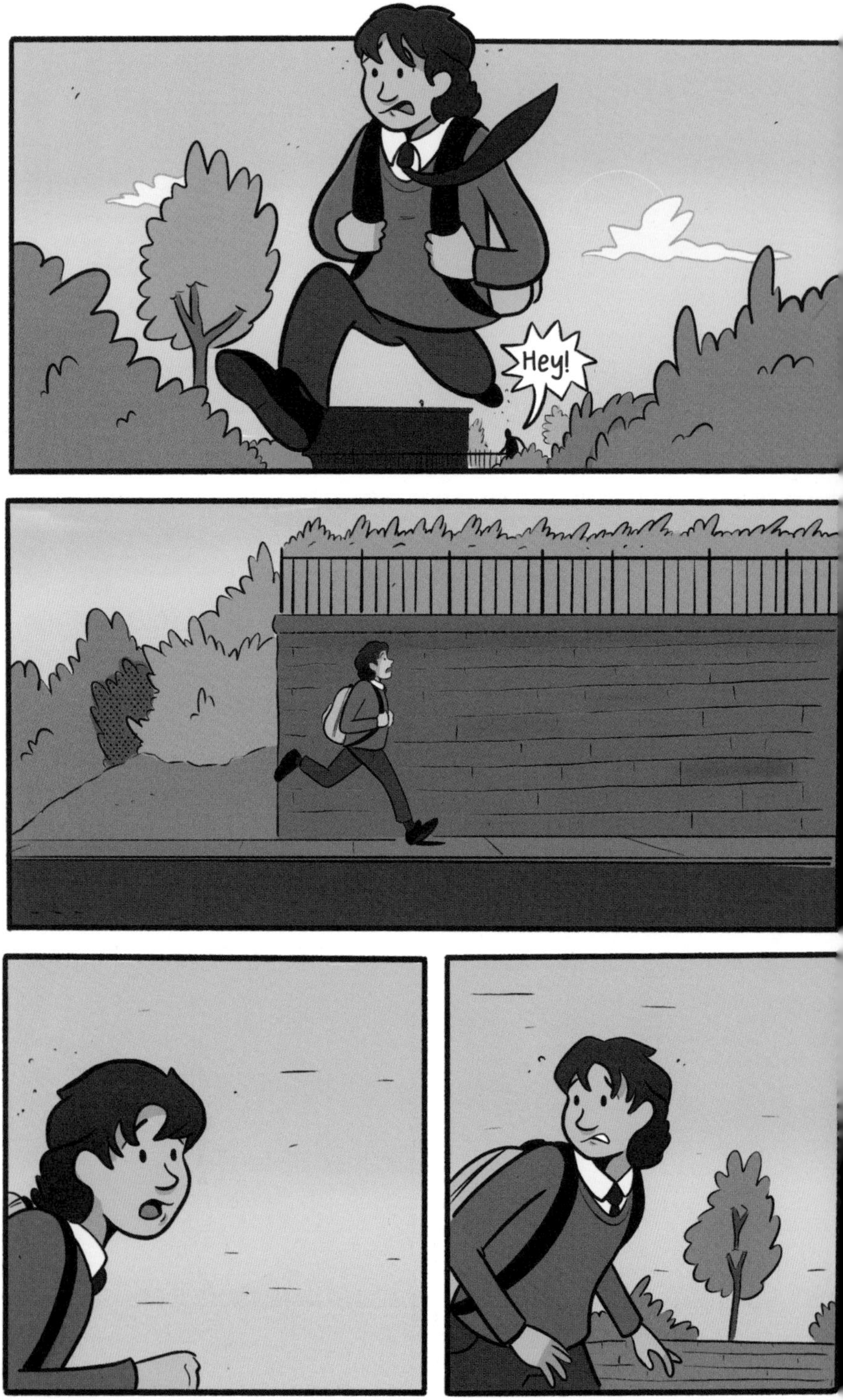
Hey!

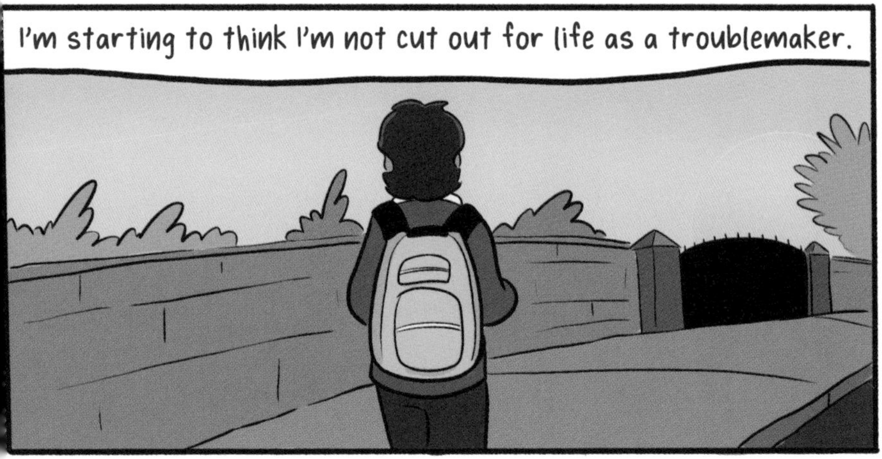
I'm starting to think I'm not cut out for life as a troublemaker.

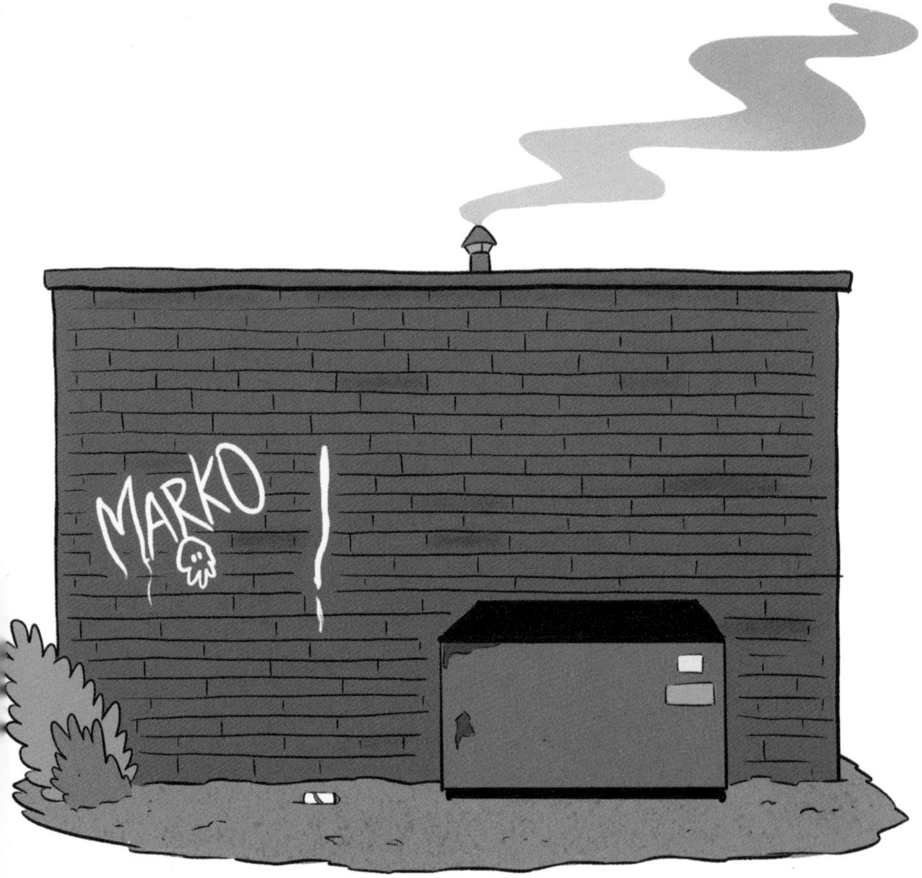
MARKO

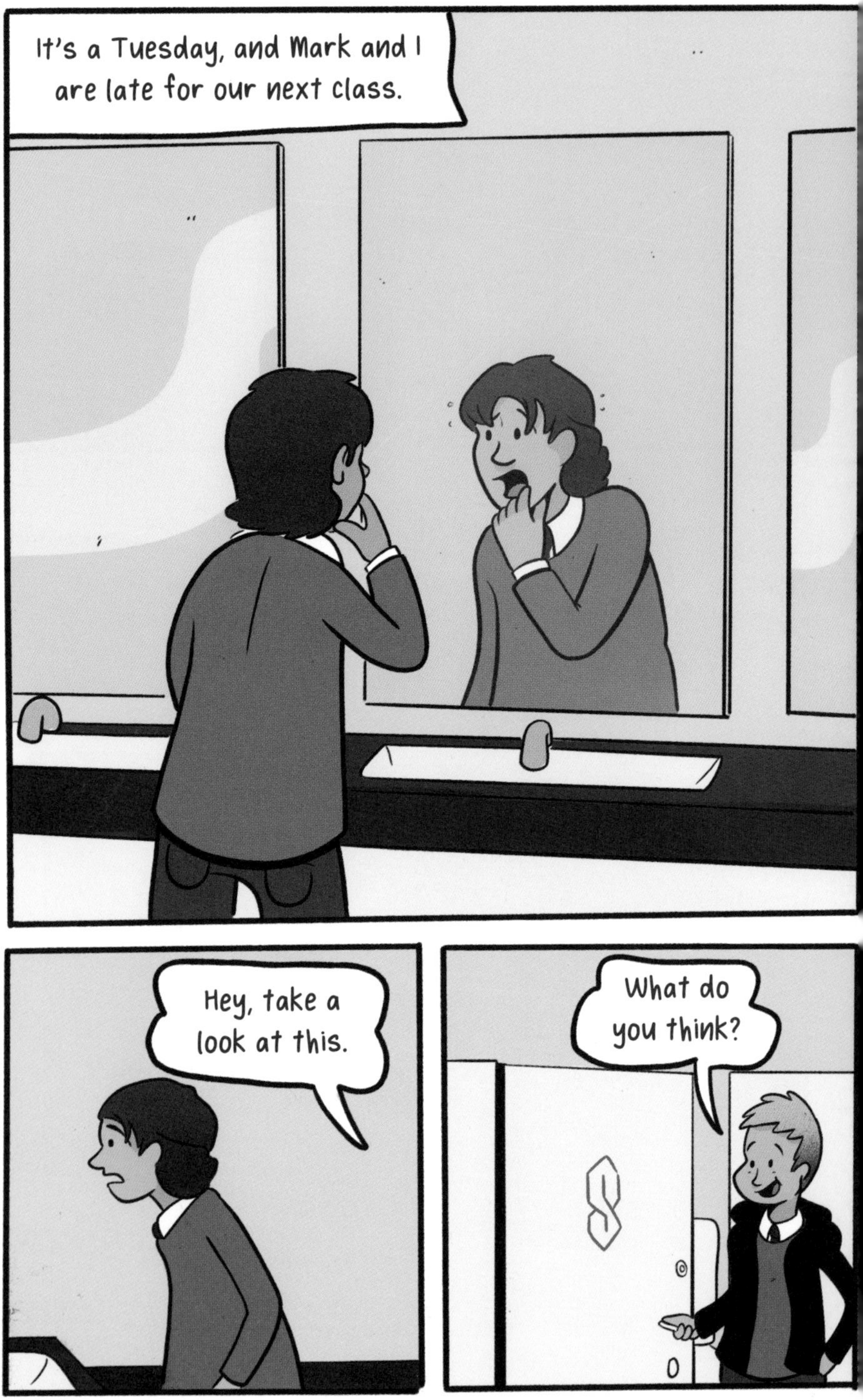

It's a Tuesday, and Mark and I are late for our next class.
Hey, take a look at this.
What do you think?

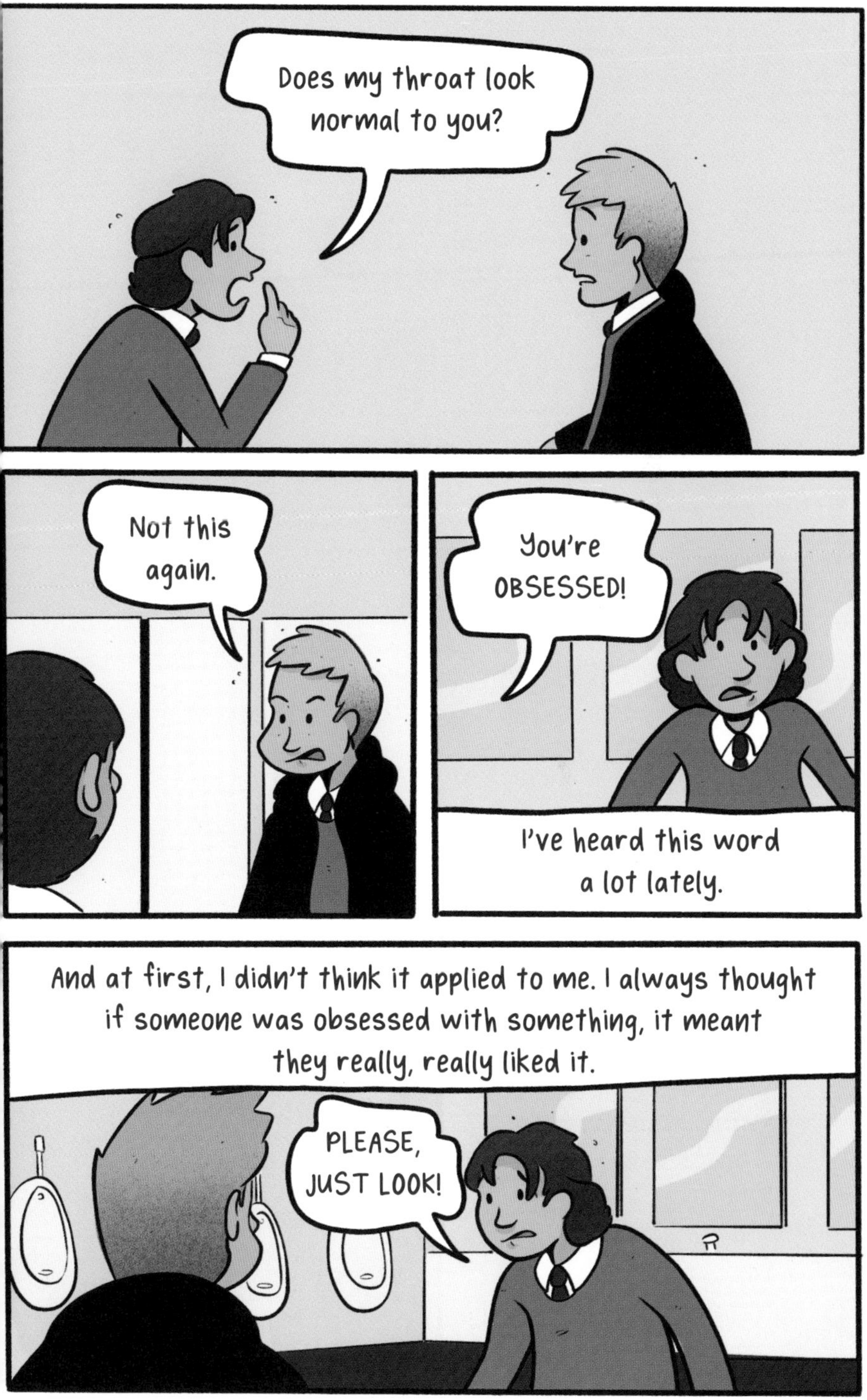
Does my throat look normal to you?
Not this again.
You're OBSESSED!
I've heard this word a lot lately.
And at first, I didn't think it applied to me. I always thought if someone was obsessed with something, it meant they really, really liked it.
PLEASE, JUST LOOK!

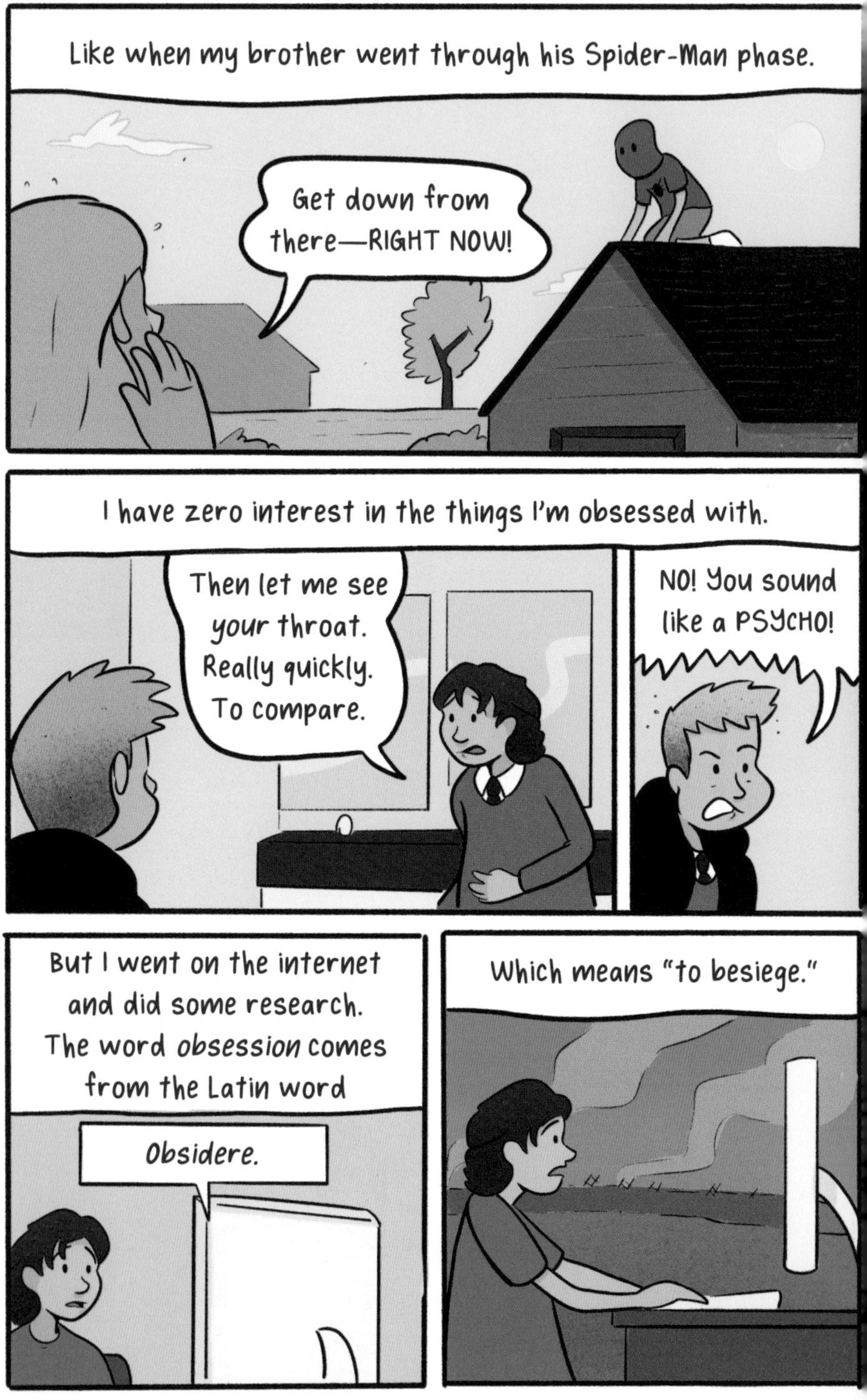

Like when my brother went through his Spider-Man phase.
Get down from there—RIGHT NOW!
I have zero interest in the things I'm obsessed with.
Then let me see your throat. Really quickly. To compare.
NO! You sound like a PSYCHO!
But I went on the internet and did some research. The word *obsession* comes from the Latin word
Obsidere.
Which means "to besiege."

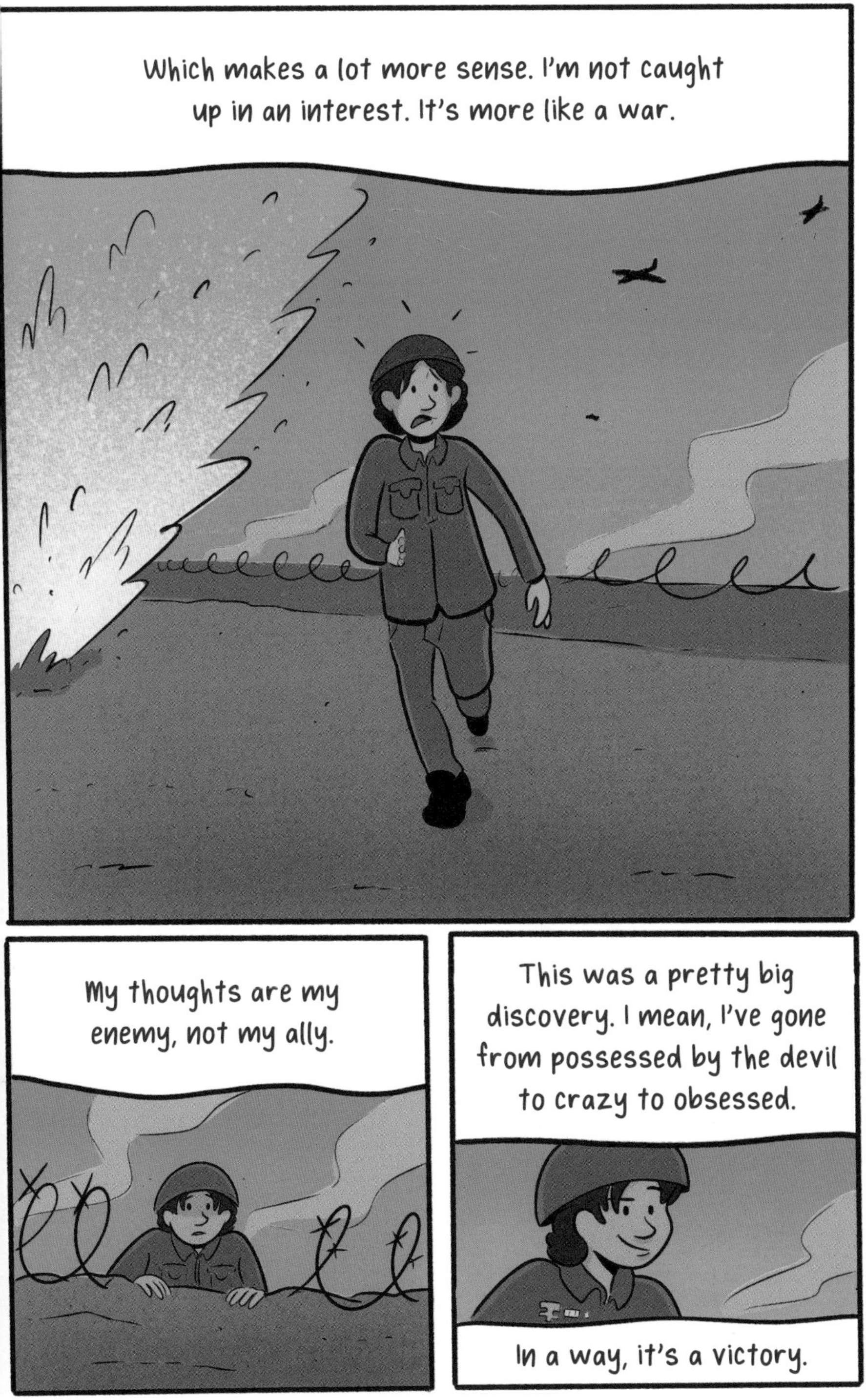
Which makes a lot more sense. I'm not caught up in an interest. It's more like a war.
My thoughts are my enemy, not my ally.
This was a pretty big discovery. I mean, I've gone from possessed by the devil to crazy to obsessed.
In a way, it's a victory.

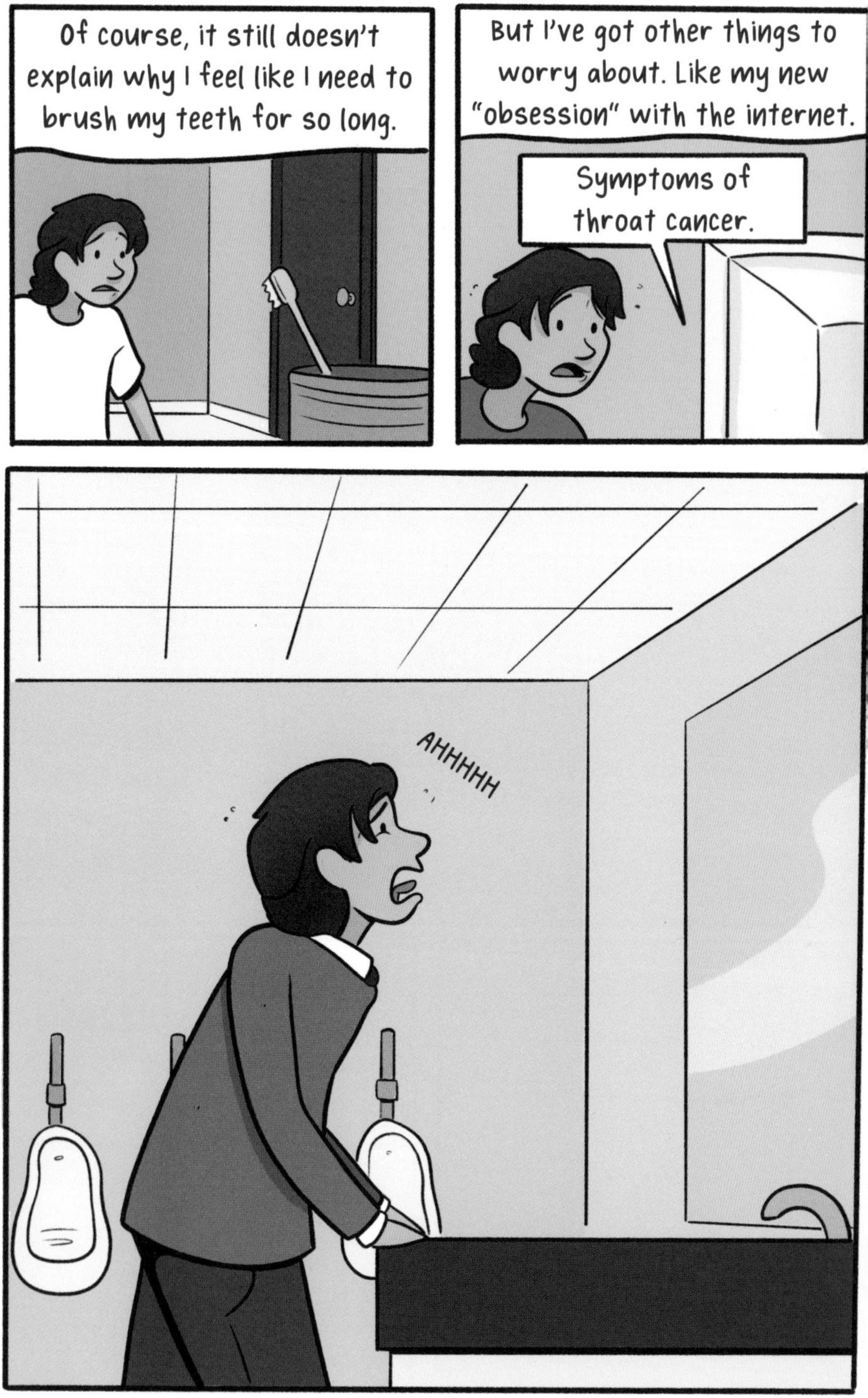

Of course, it still doesn't explain why I feel like I need to brush my teeth for so long.
But I've got other things to worry about. Like my new "obsession" with the internet.
Symptoms of throat cancer.
AHHHHH

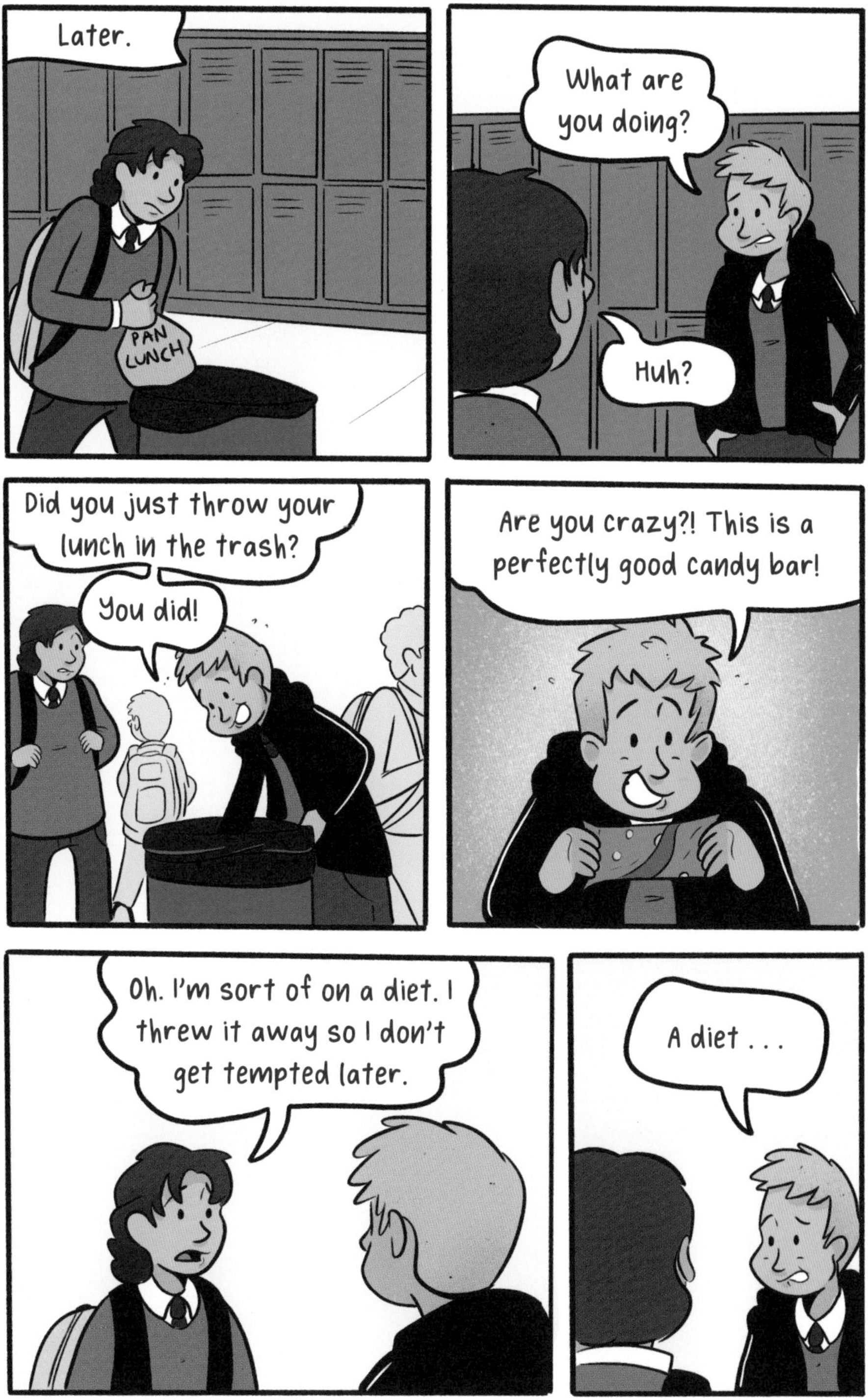
Later.
PAN LUNCH
What are you doing?
Huh?
Did you just throw your lunch in the trash?
You did!
Are you crazy?! This is a perfectly good candy bar!
Oh. I'm sort of on a diet. I threw it away so I don't get tempted later.
A diet . . .

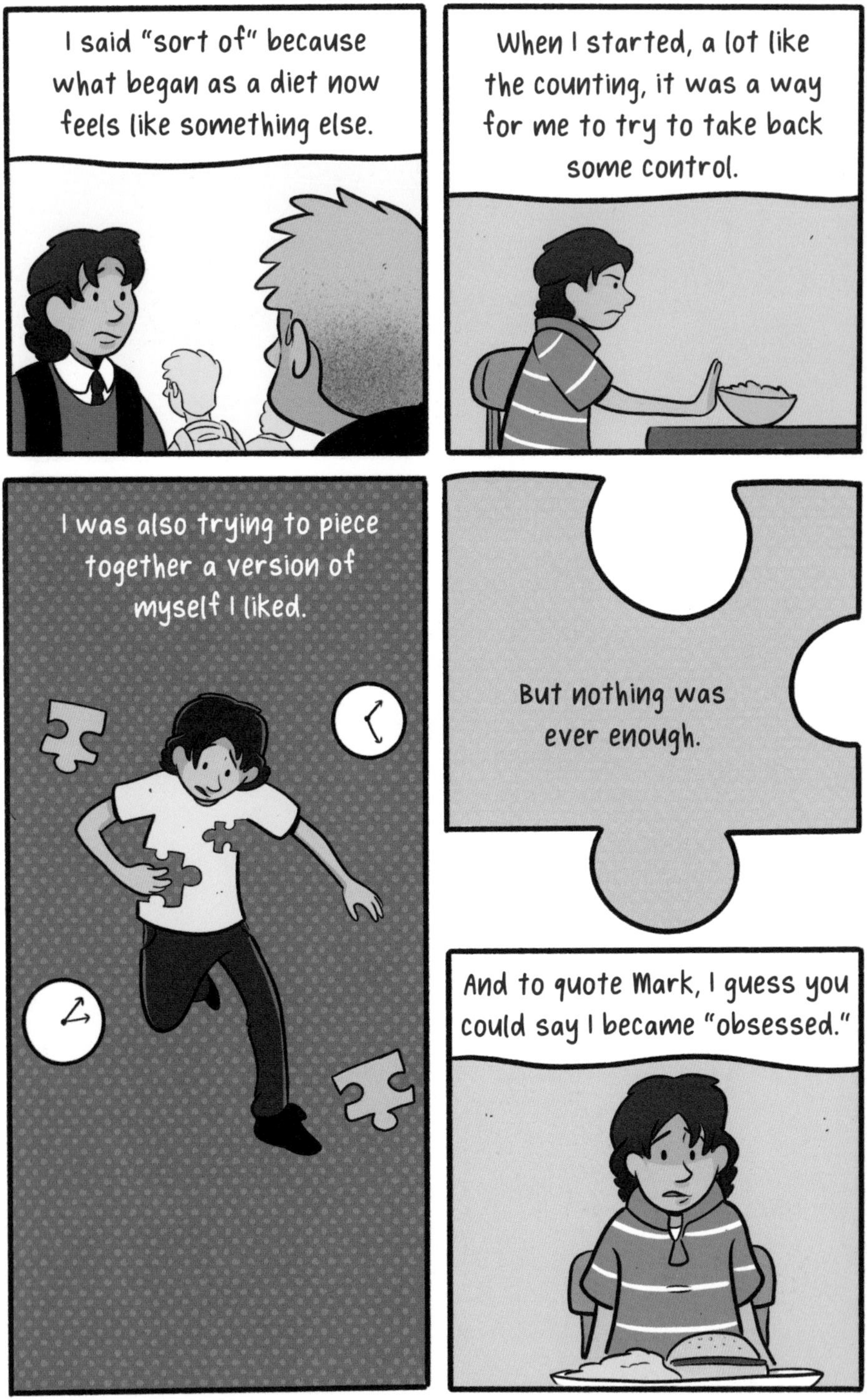
I said "sort of" because what began as a diet now feels like something else.
When I started, a lot like the counting, it was a way for me to try to take back some control.
I was also trying to piece together a version of myself I liked.
But nothing was ever enough.
And to quote Mark, I guess you could say I became "obsessed."

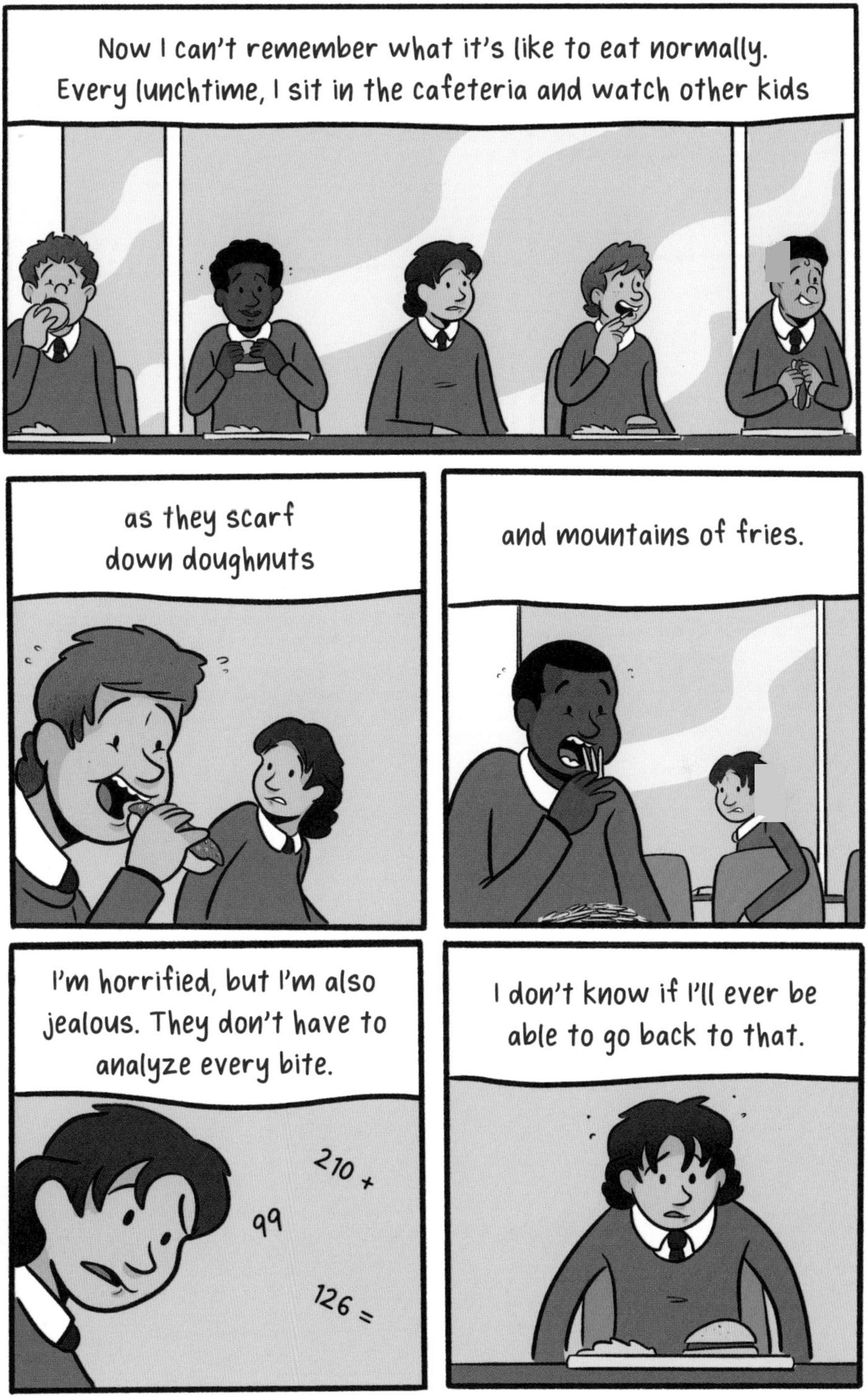
Now I can't remember what it's like to eat normally. Every lunchtime, I sit in the cafeteria and watch other kids
as they scarf down doughnuts
and mountains of fries.
I'm horrified, but I'm also jealous. They don't have to analyze every bite.
210 +
99
126 =
I don't know if I'll ever be able to go back to that.

Even as my weight drops,

the moment I've been waiting for—when I'll look into the mirror and everything will make sense—still hasn't come.

But just like when the Puzzle whispers "one more time" while I brush my teeth,

it tells me I'm getting closer and to keep going.

I just need to try again.

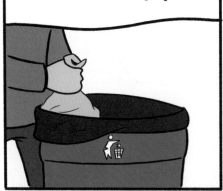

And again.

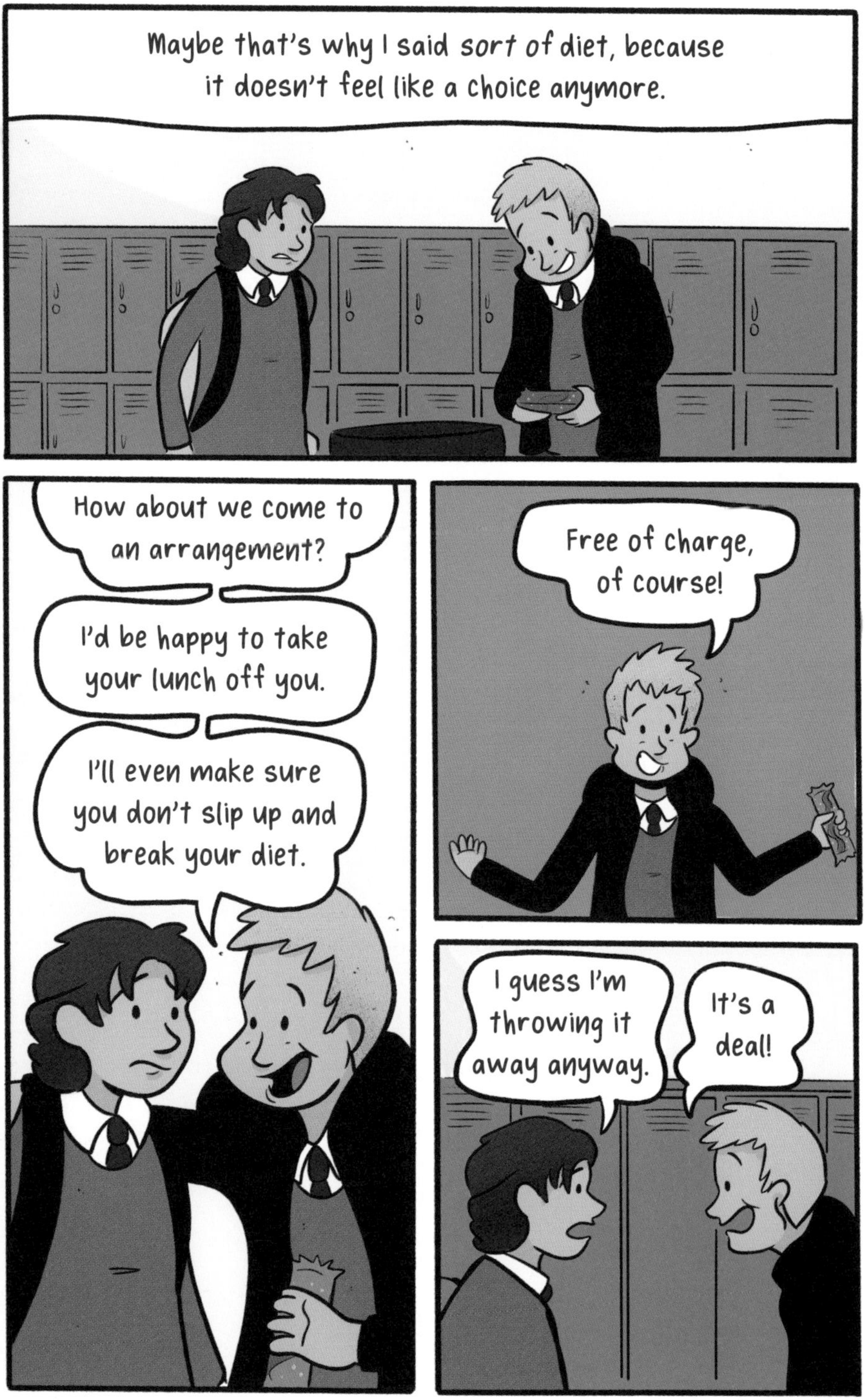

Maybe that's why I said *sort of* diet, because it doesn't feel like a choice anymore.
How about we come to an arrangement?
I'd be happy to take your lunch off you.
I'll even make sure you don't slip up and break your diet.
Free of charge, of course!
I guess I'm throwing it away anyway.
It's a deal!

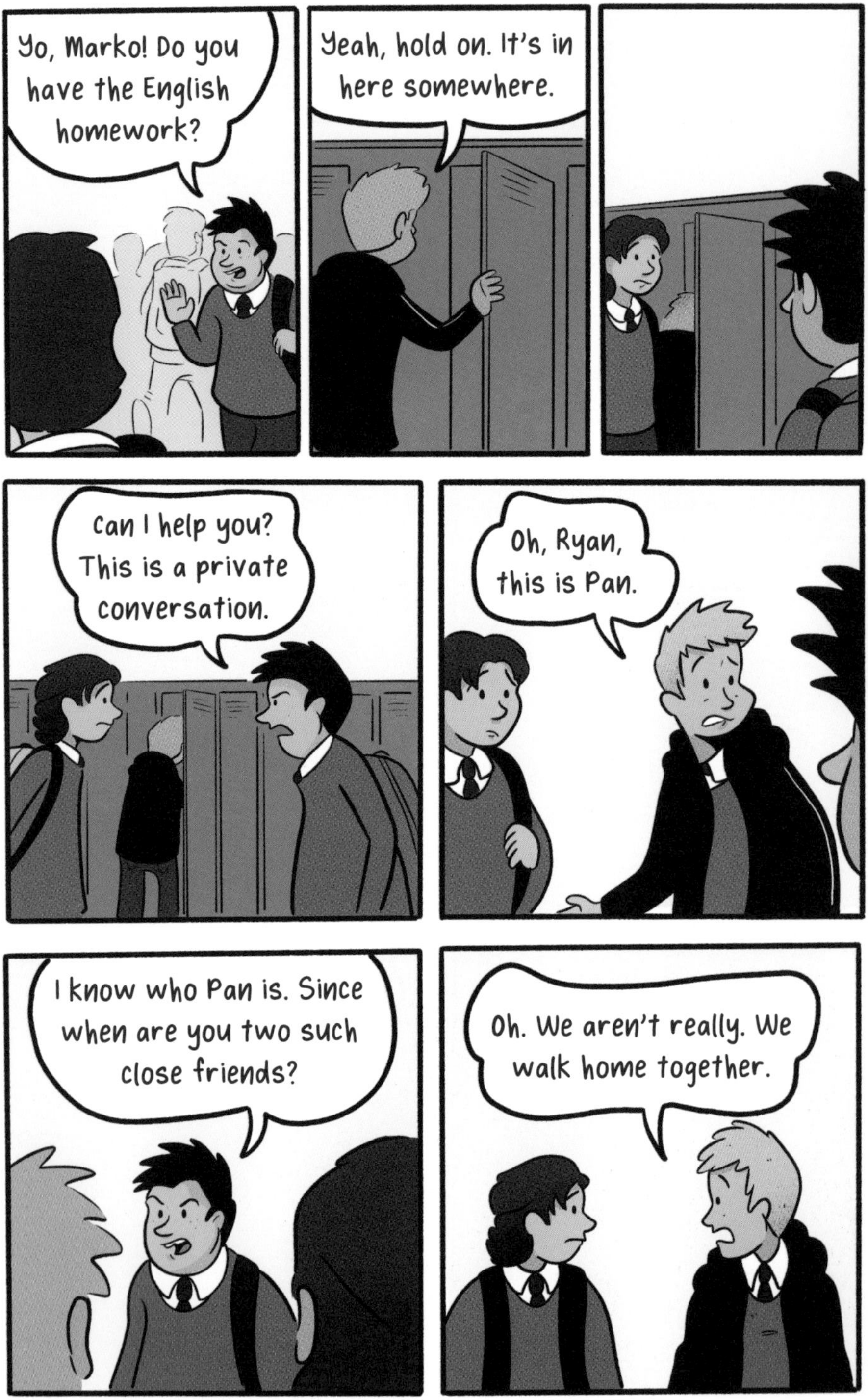
Yo, Marko! Do you have the English homework?
Yeah, hold on. It's in here somewhere.
Can I help you? This is a private conversation.
Oh, Ryan, this is Pan.
I know who Pan is. Since when are you two such close friends?
Oh. We aren't really. We walk home together.

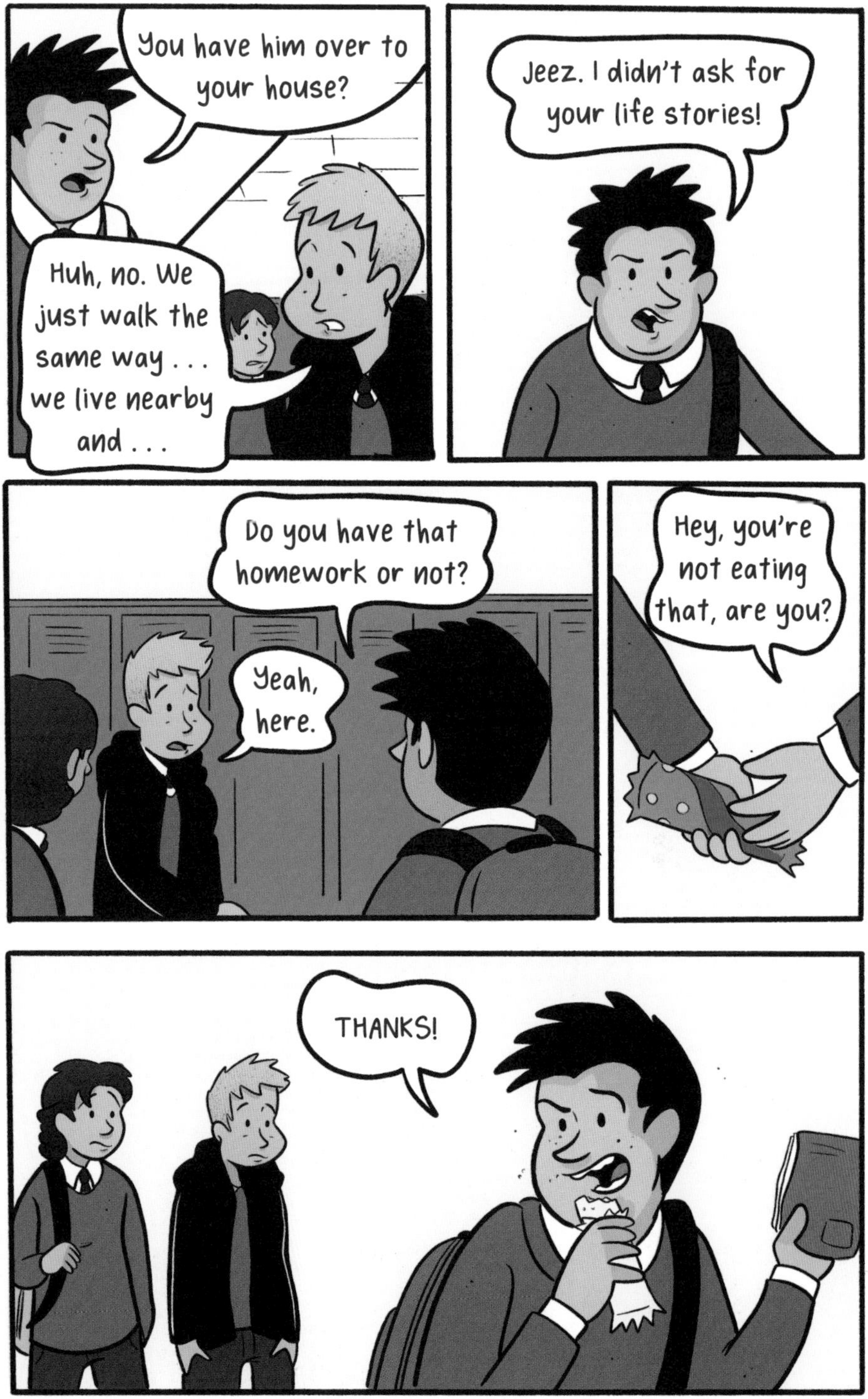
You have him over to your house?
Huh, no. We just walk the same way . . . we live nearby and . . .
Jeez. I didn't ask for your life stories!
Do you have that homework or not?
Yeah, here.
Hey, you're not eating that, are you?
THANKS!

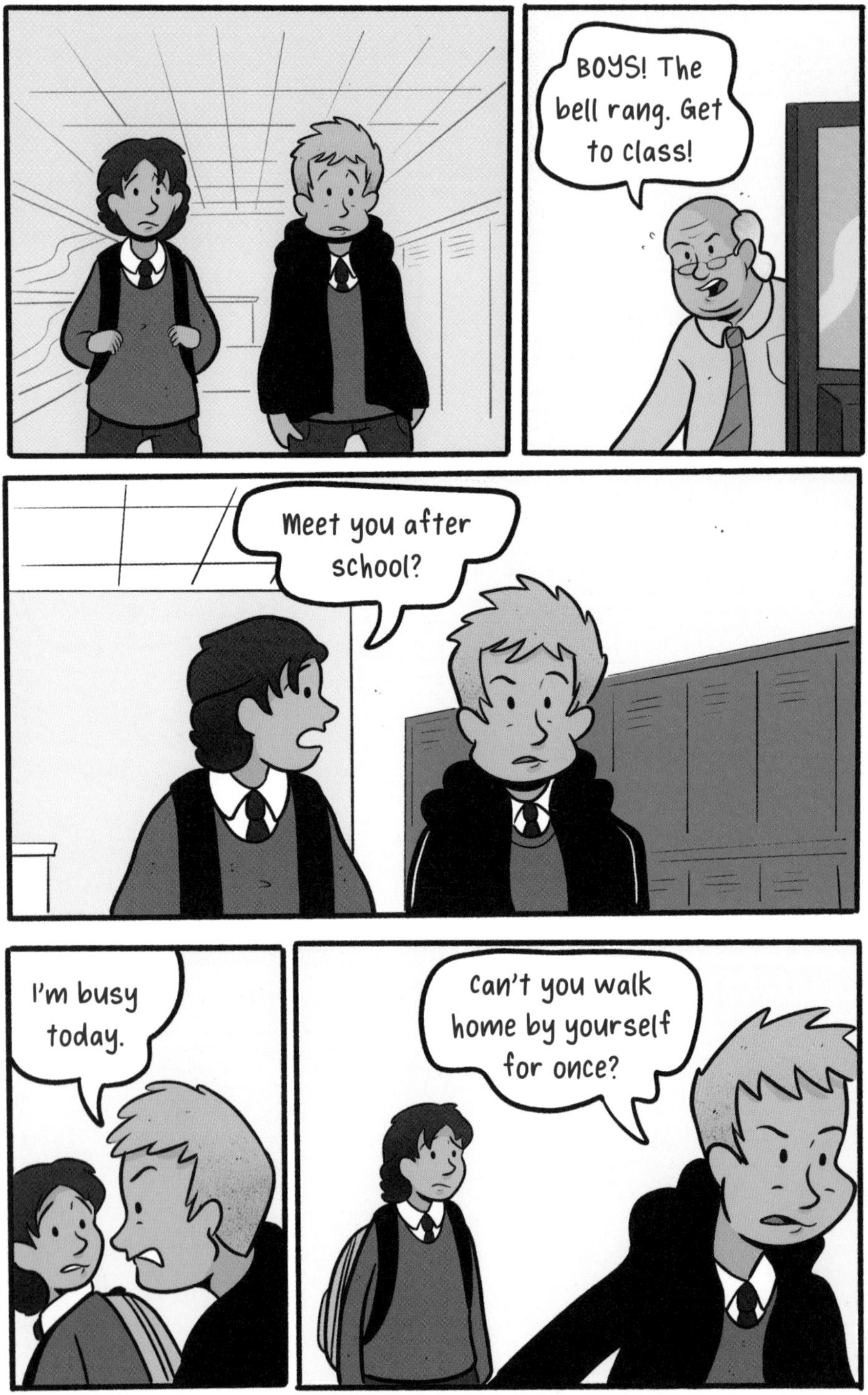
BOYS! The bell rang. Get to class!
Meet you after school?
I'm busy today.
Can't you walk home by yourself for once?

5

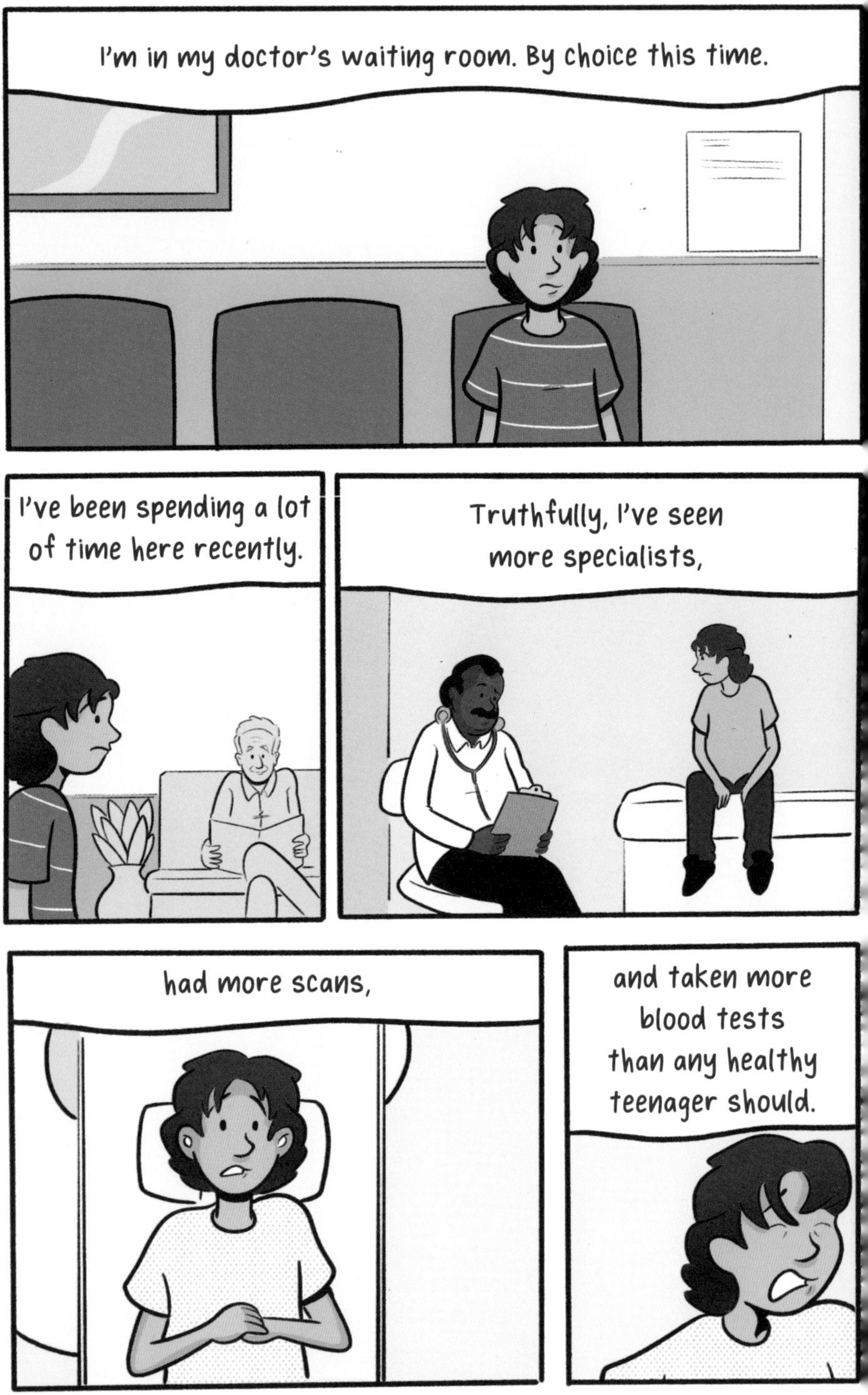
I'm in my doctor's waiting room. By choice this time.
I've been spending a lot of time here recently.
Truthfully, I've seen more specialists,
had more scans,
and taken more blood tests than any healthy teenager should.

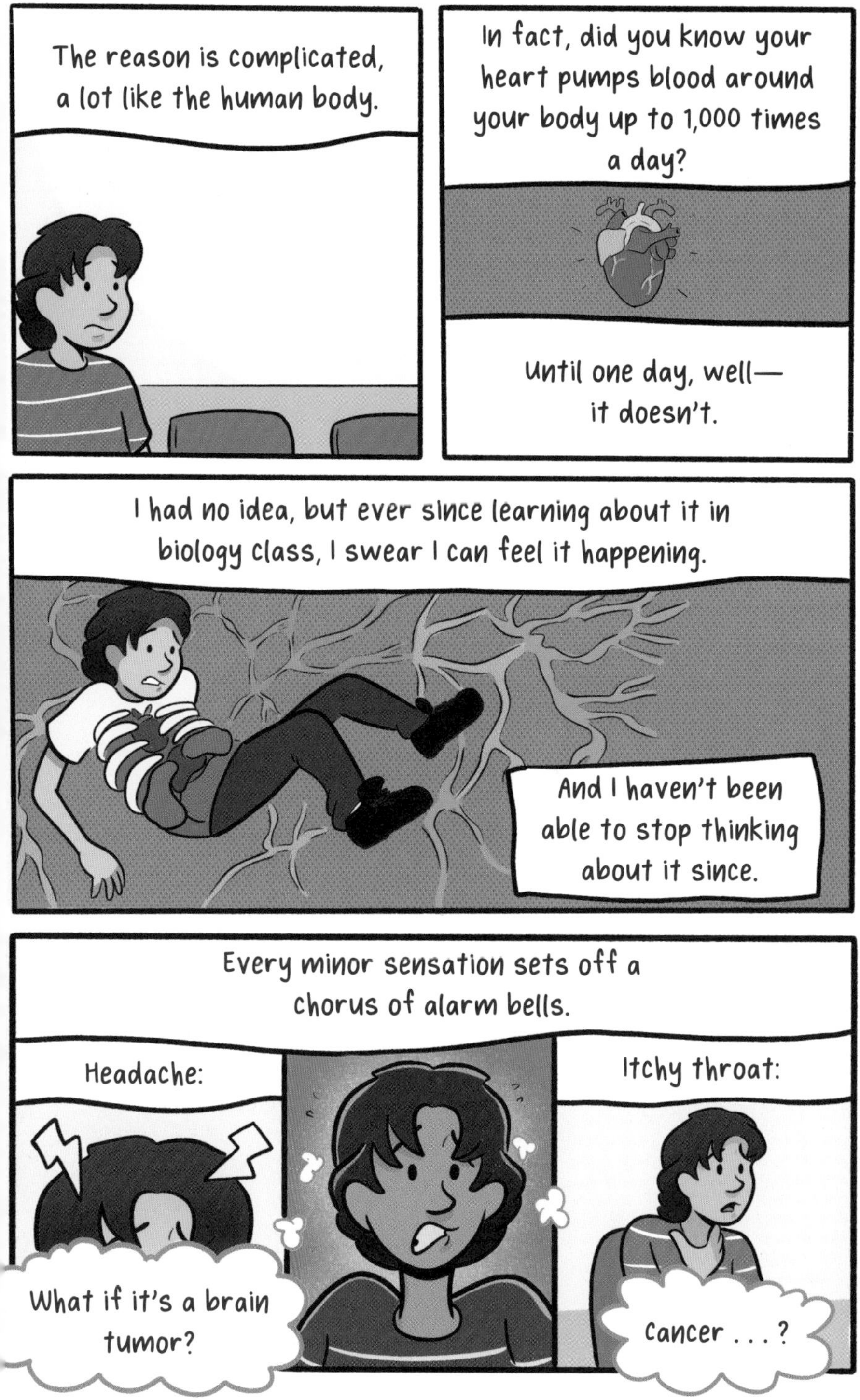

The reason is complicated, a lot like the human body.
In fact, did you know your heart pumps blood around your body up to 1,000 times a day?
Until one day, well— it doesn't.
I had no idea, but ever since learning about it in biology class, I swear I can feel it happening.
And I haven't been able to stop thinking about it since.
Every minor sensation sets off a chorus of alarm bells.
Headache:
What if it's a brain tumor?
Itchy throat:
Cancer . . . ?

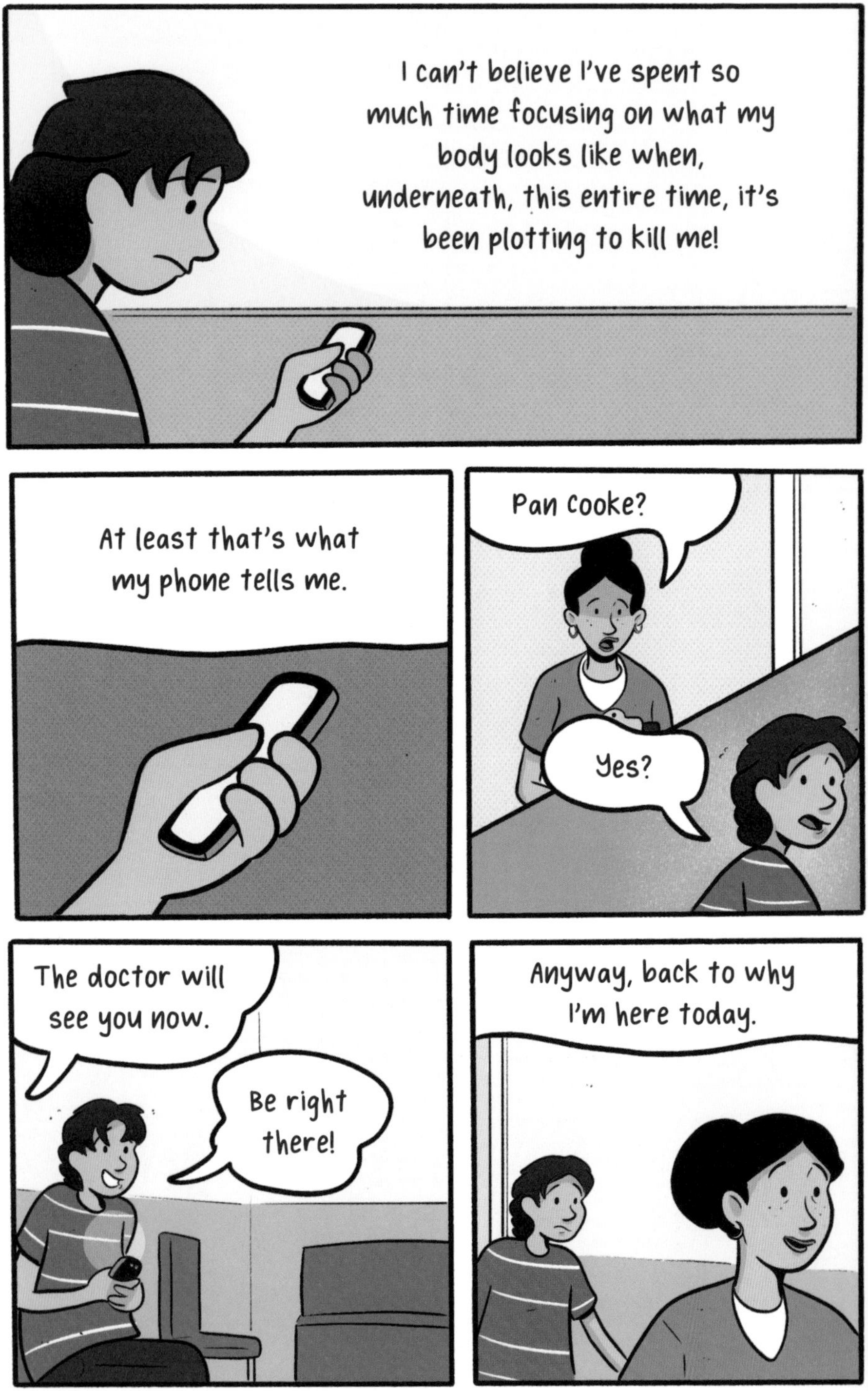
I can't believe I've spent so much time focusing on what my body looks like when, underneath, this entire time, it's been plotting to kill me!
At least that's what my phone tells me.
Pan Cooke?
Yes?
The doctor will see you now.
Be right there!
Anyway, back to why I'm here today.

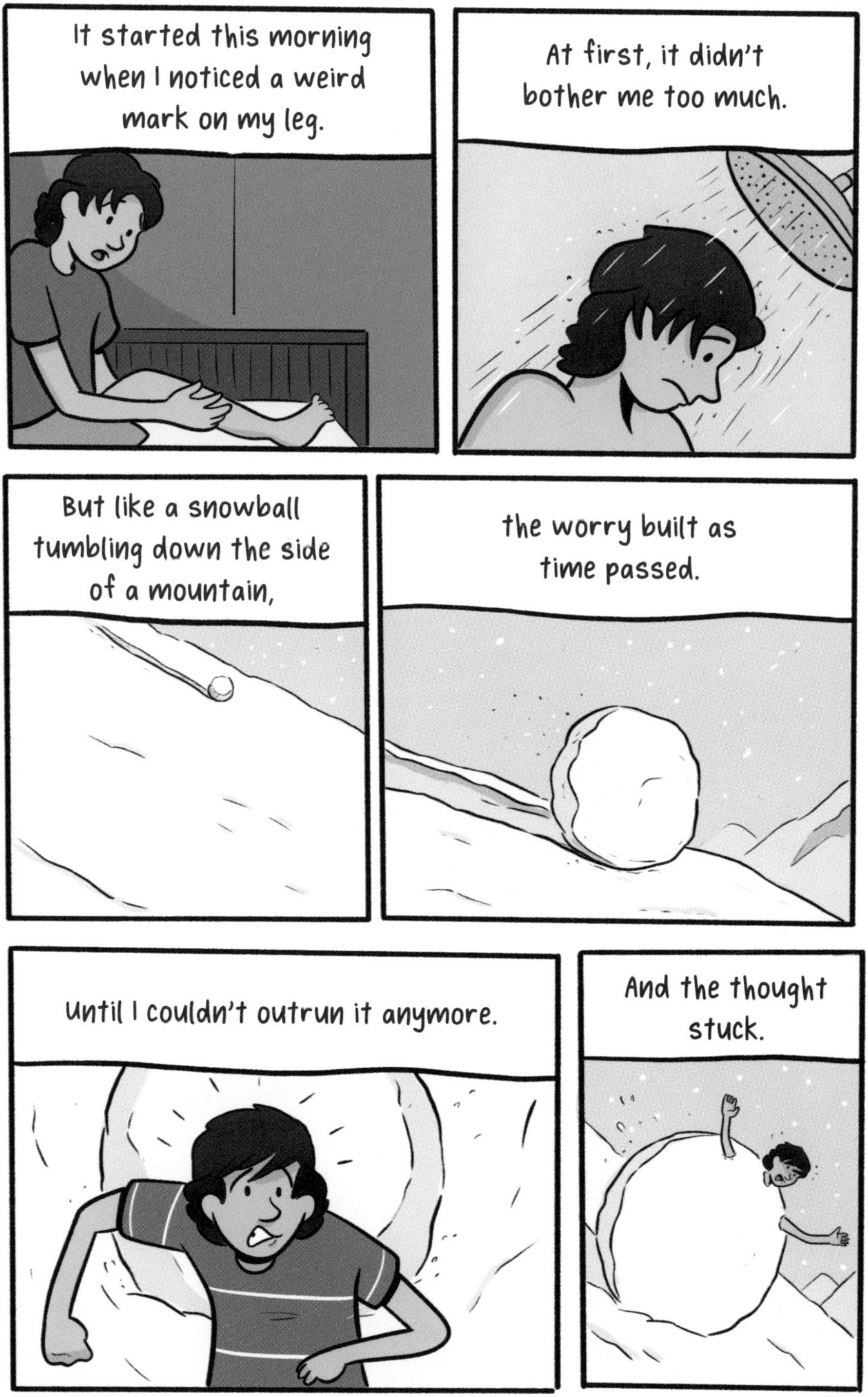
It started this morning when I noticed a weird mark on my leg.
At first, it didn't bother me too much.
But like a snowball tumbling down the side of a mountain,
the worry built as time passed.
Until I couldn't outrun it anymore.
And the thought stuck.

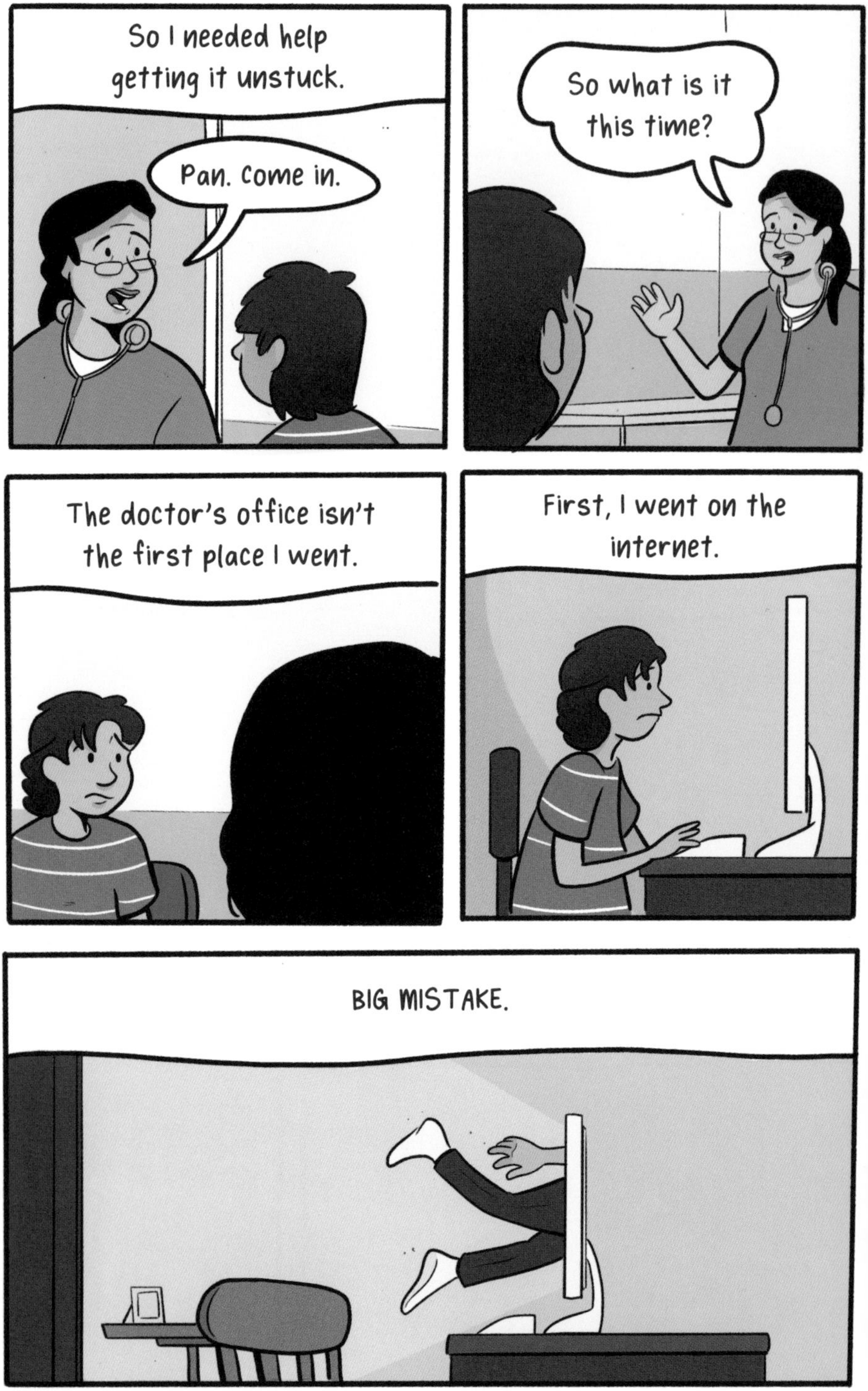
So I needed help getting it unstuck.
Pan. Come in.
So what is it this time?
The doctor's office isn't the first place I went.
First, I went on the internet.
BIG MISTAKE.

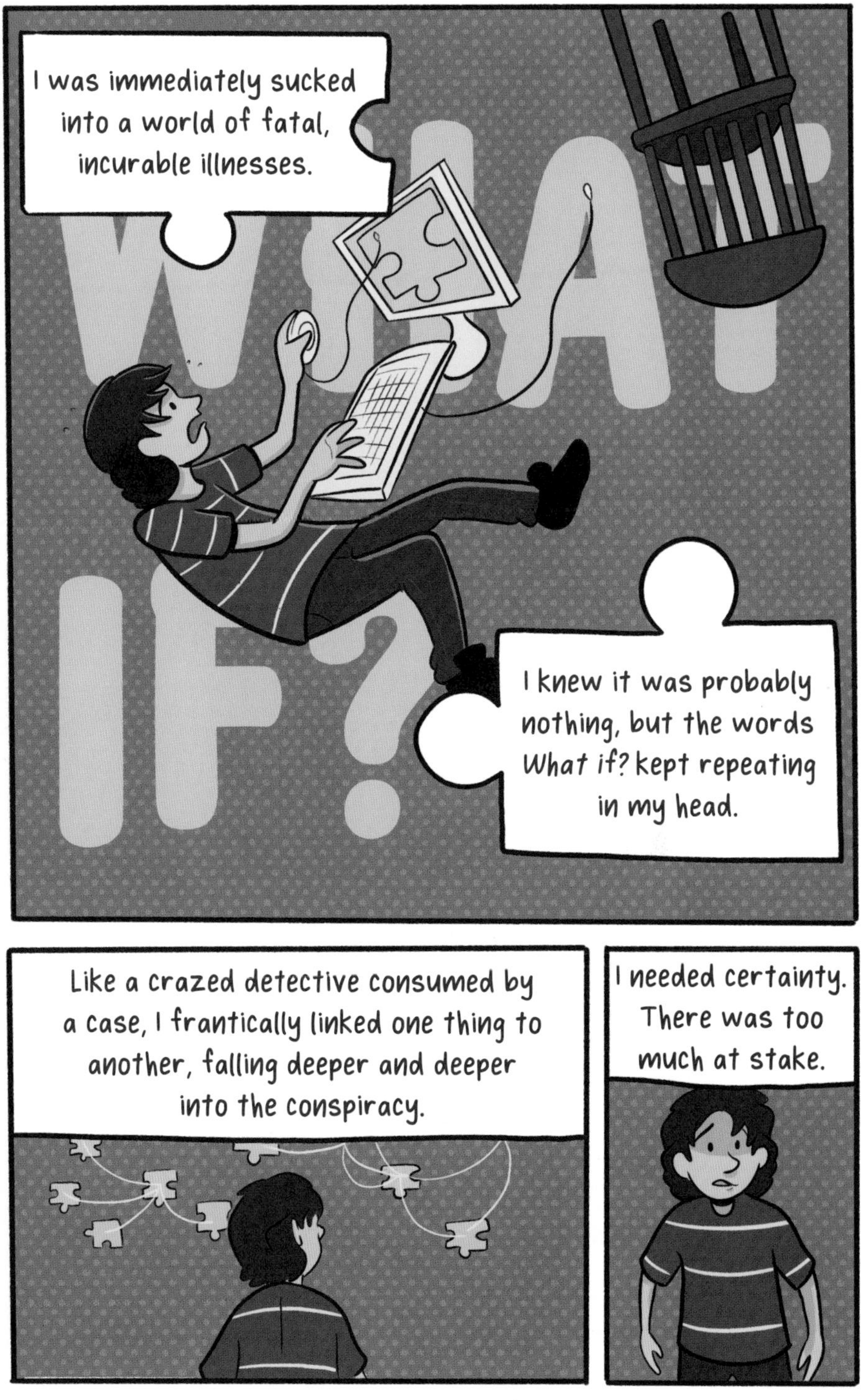
I was immediately sucked into a world of fatal, incurable illnesses.
WHAT IF?
I knew it was probably nothing, but the words *What if?* kept repeating in my head.
Like a crazed detective consumed by a case, I frantically linked one thing to another, falling deeper and deeper into the conspiracy.
I needed certainty. There was too much at stake.

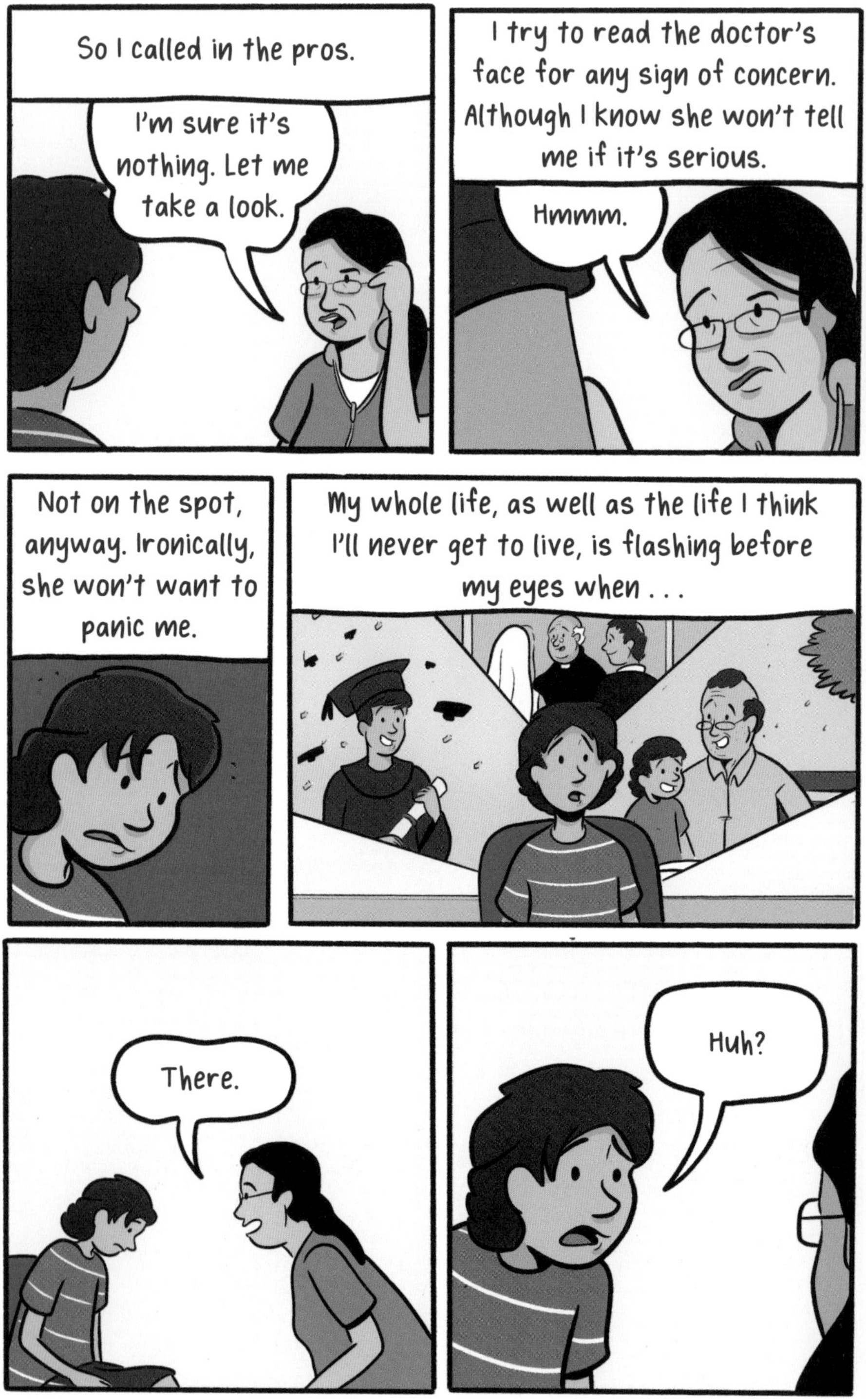
So I called in the pros.
I'm sure it's nothing. Let me take a look.
I try to read the doctor's face for any sign of concern. Although I know she won't tell me if it's serious.
Hmmm.
Not on the spot, anyway. Ironically, she won't want to panic me.
My whole life, as well as the life I think I'll never get to live, is flashing before my eyes when . . .
There.
Huh?

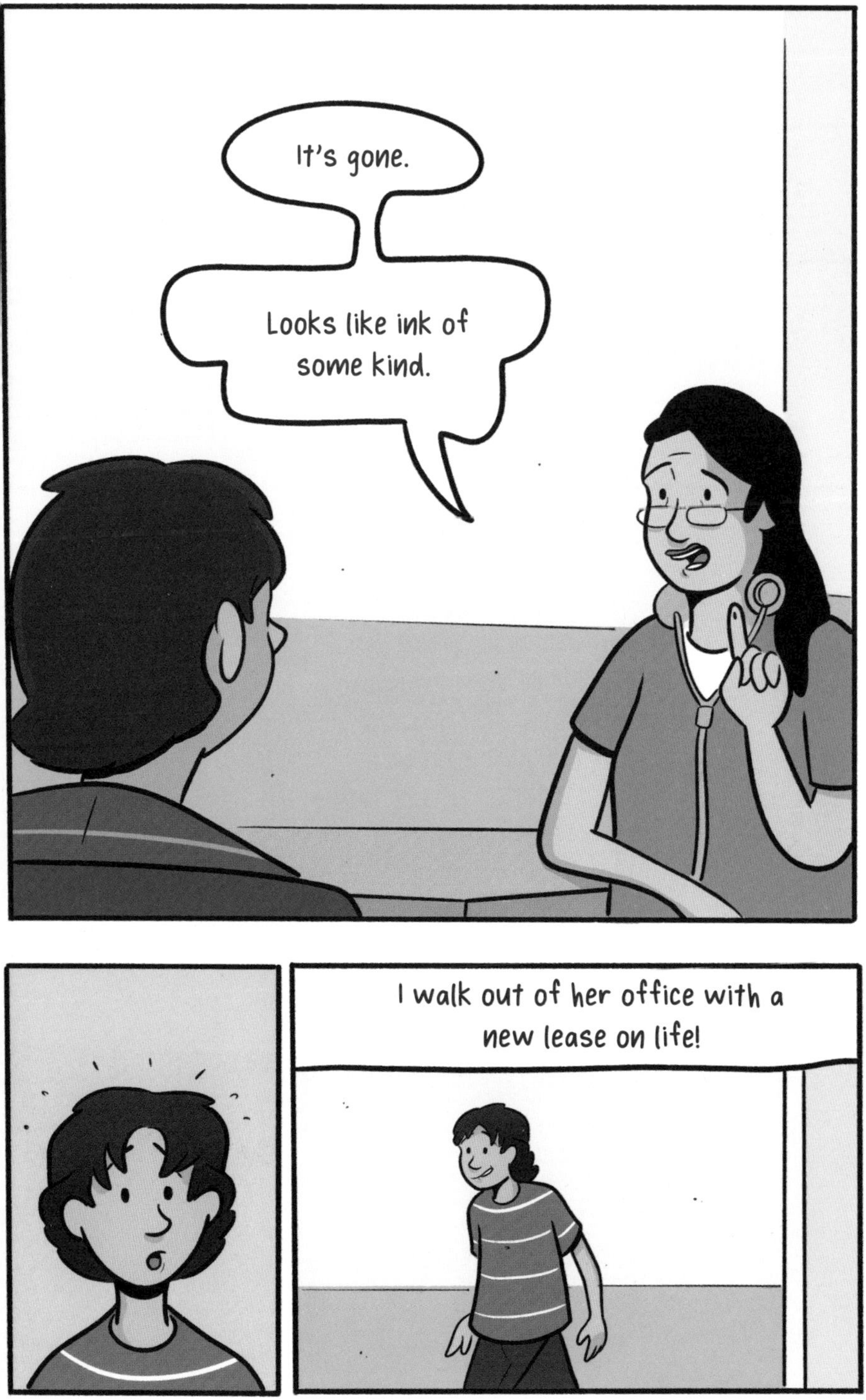
It's gone.
Looks like ink of some kind.
I walk out of her office with a new lease on life!

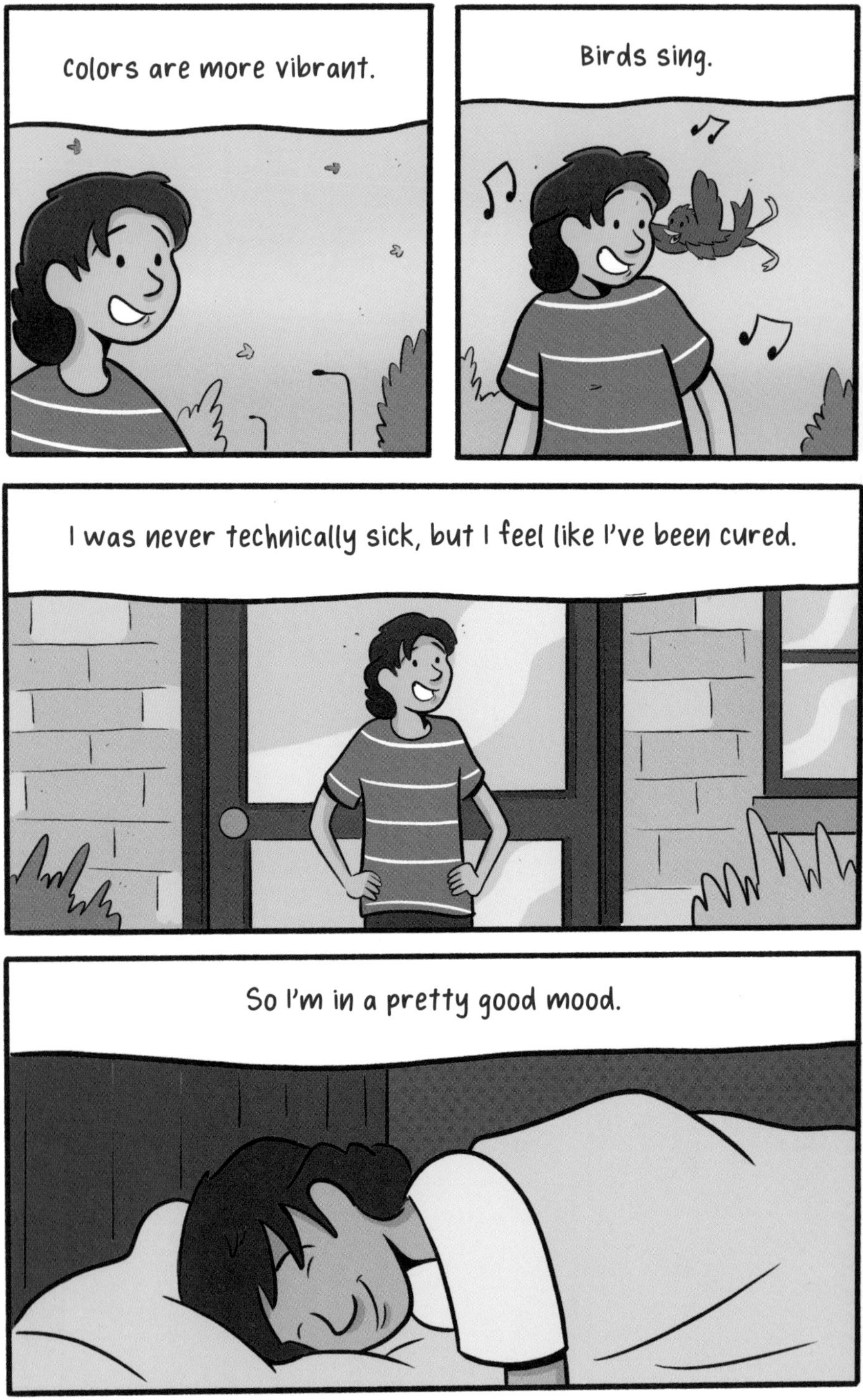

Colors are more vibrant.
Birds sing.
I was never technically sick, but I feel like I've been cured.
So I'm in a pretty good mood.

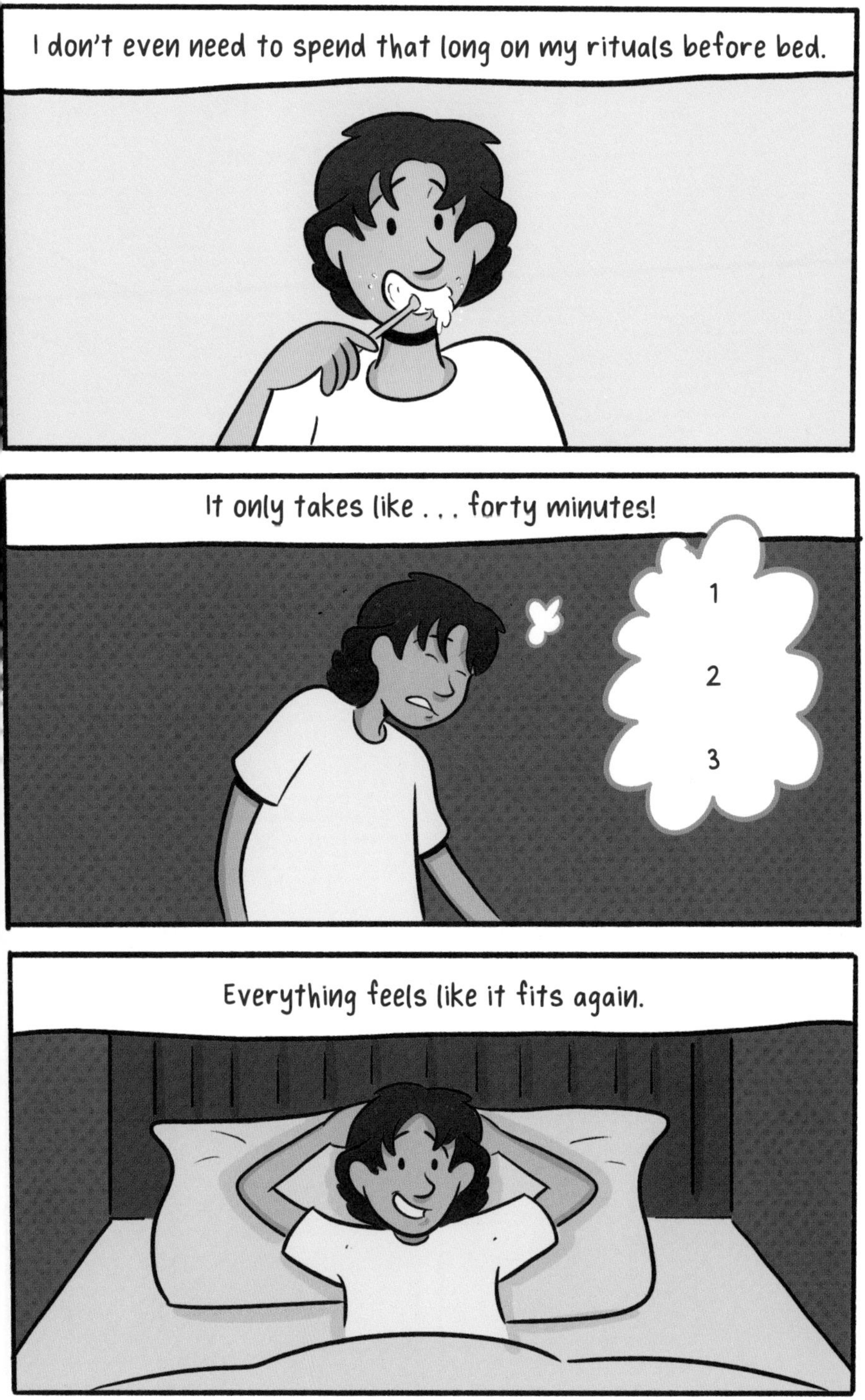
I don't even need to spend that long on my rituals before bed.
It only takes like . . . forty minutes!
1
2
3
Everything feels like it fits again.

Recently, I've realized, it's easier if I get others to solve the puzzle for me.

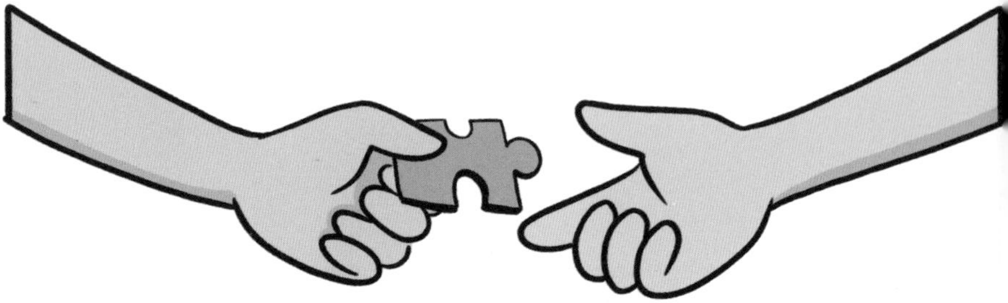

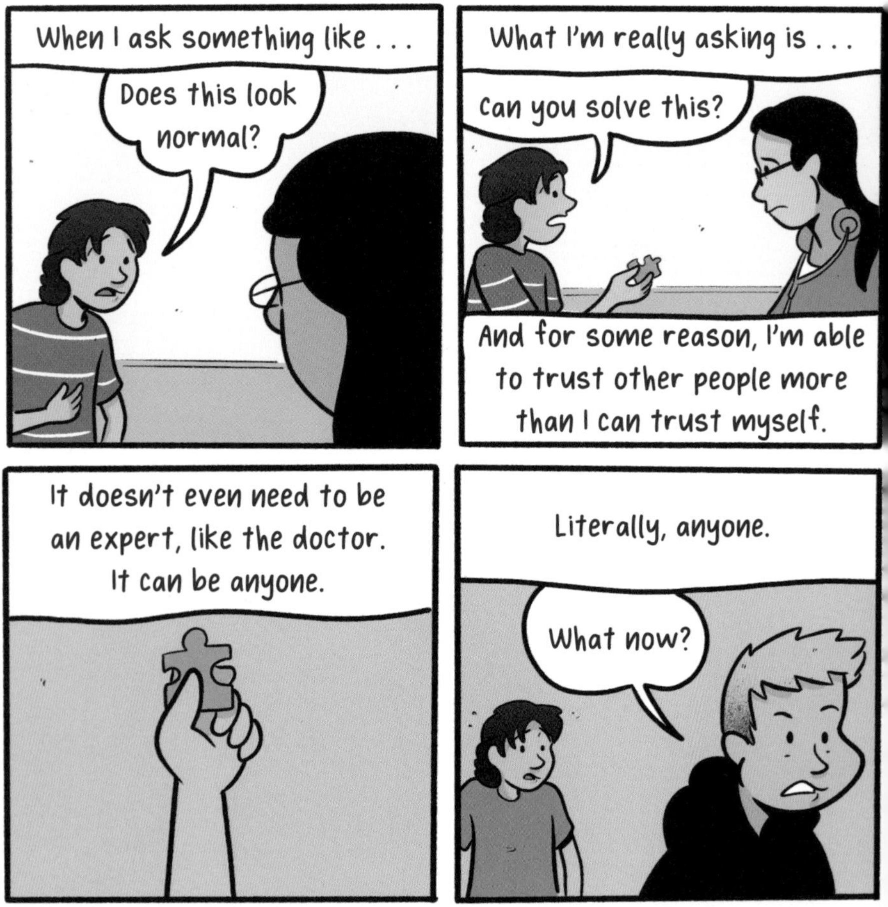
When I ask something like . . .
Does this look normal?
What I'm really asking is . . .
Can you solve this?
And for some reason, I'm able to trust other people more than I can trust myself.
It doesn't even need to be an expert, like the doctor. It can be anyone.
Literally, anyone.
What now?

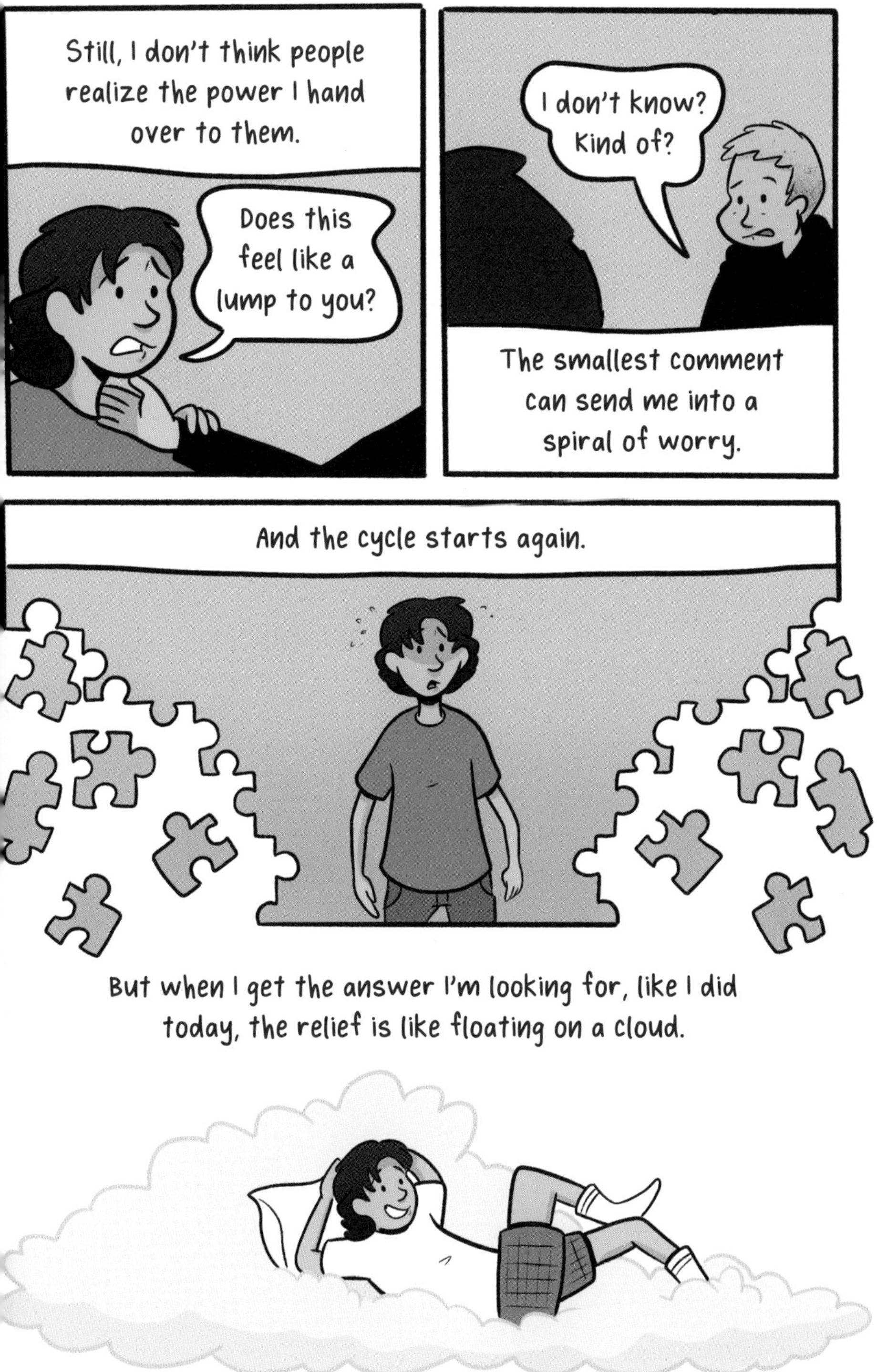
Still, I don't think people realize the power I hand over to them.
Does this feel like a lump to you?
I don't know? Kind of?
The smallest comment can send me into a spiral of worry.
And the cycle starts again.
But when I get the answer I'm looking for, like I did today, the relief is like floating on a cloud.

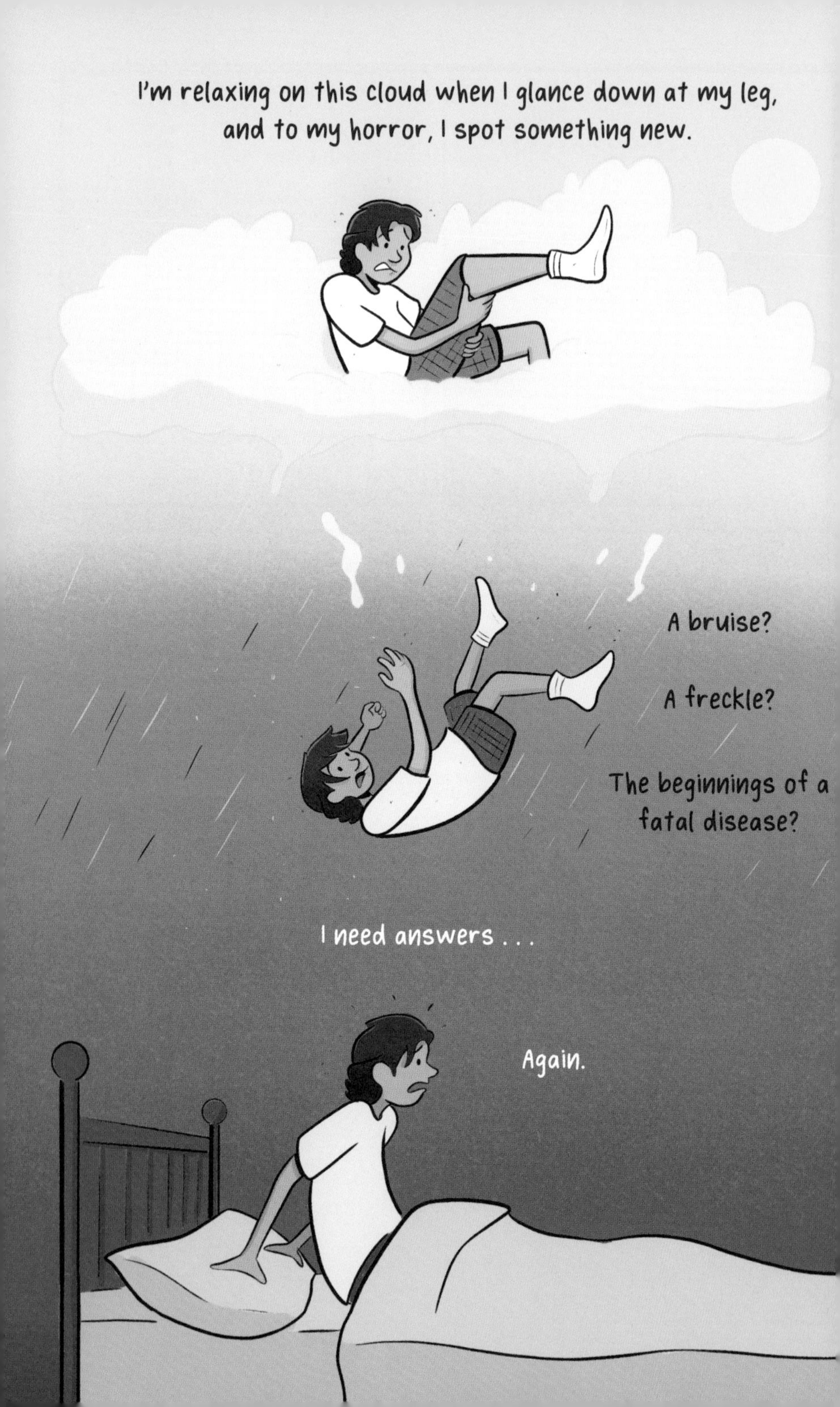
I'm relaxing on this cloud when I glance down at my leg, and to my horror, I spot something new.
A bruise?
A freckle?
The beginnings of a fatal disease?
I need answers . . .
Again.

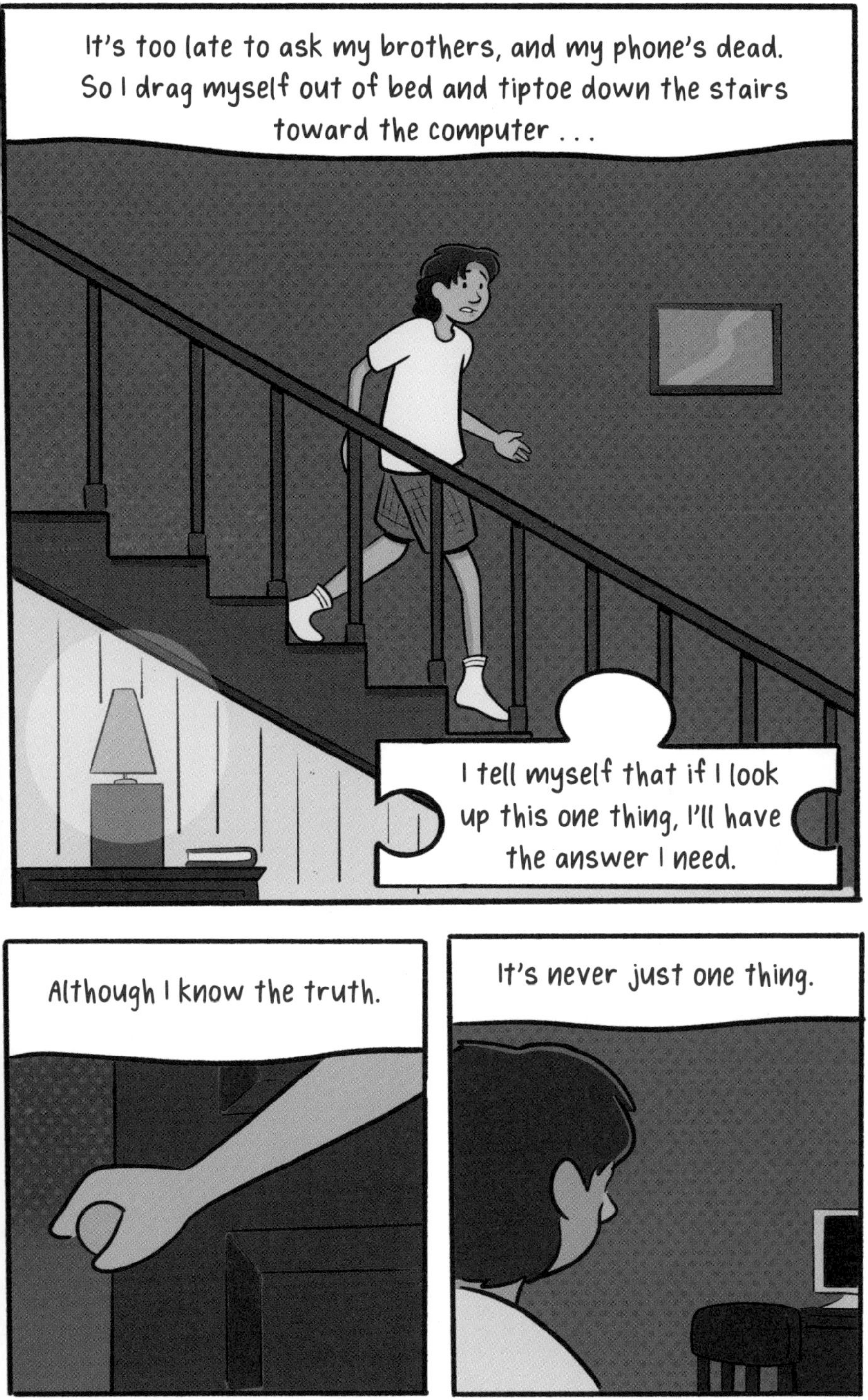

It's too late to ask my brothers, and my phone's dead. So I drag myself out of bed and tiptoe down the stairs toward the computer . . .
I tell myself that if I look up this one thing, I'll have the answer I need.
Although I know the truth.
It's never just one thing.

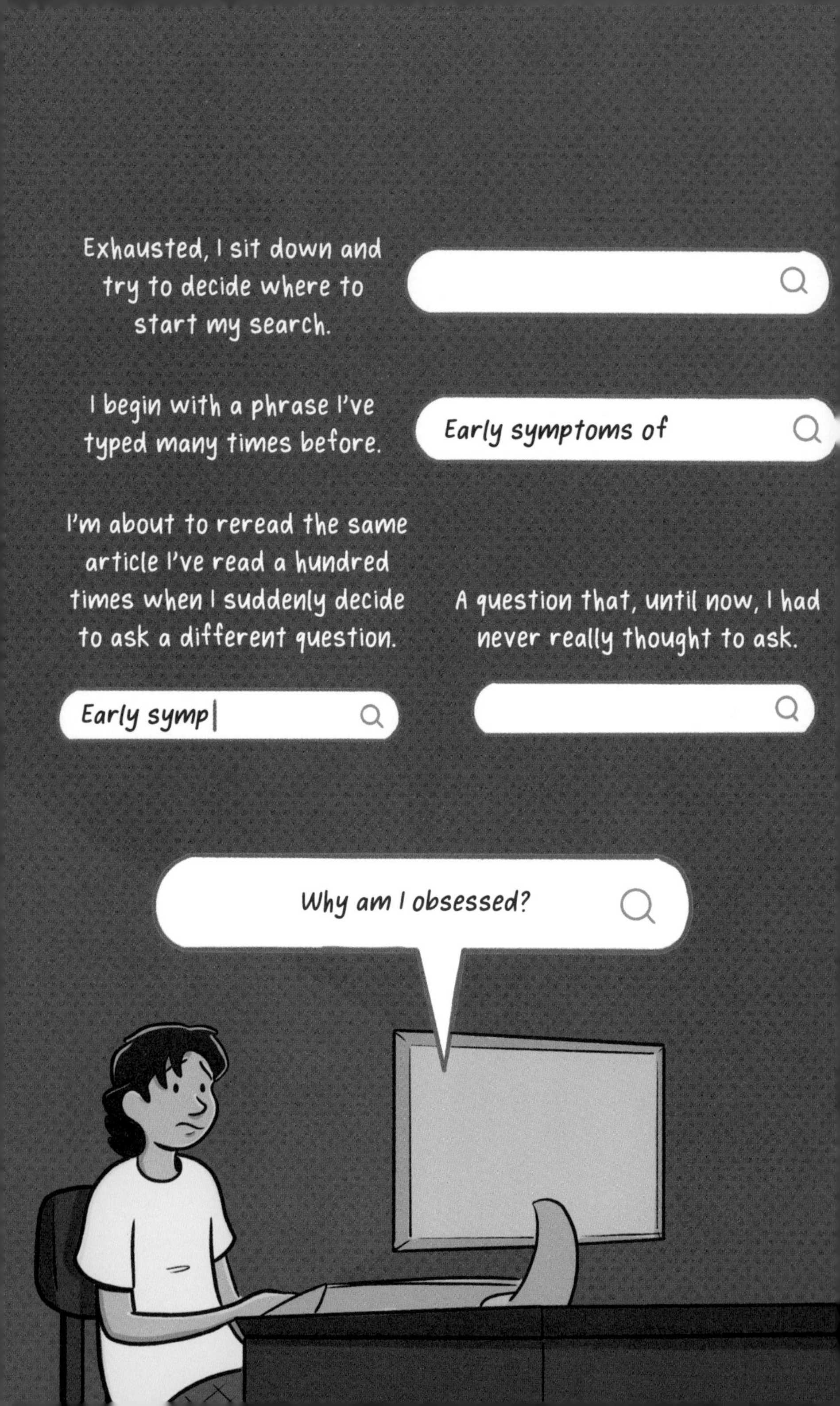
Exhausted, I sit down and try to decide where to start my search.
I begin with a phrase I've typed many times before.
Early symptoms of
I'm about to reread the same article I've read a hundred times when I suddenly decide to ask a different question.
Early symp
A question that, until now, I had never really thought to ask.
Why am I obsessed?

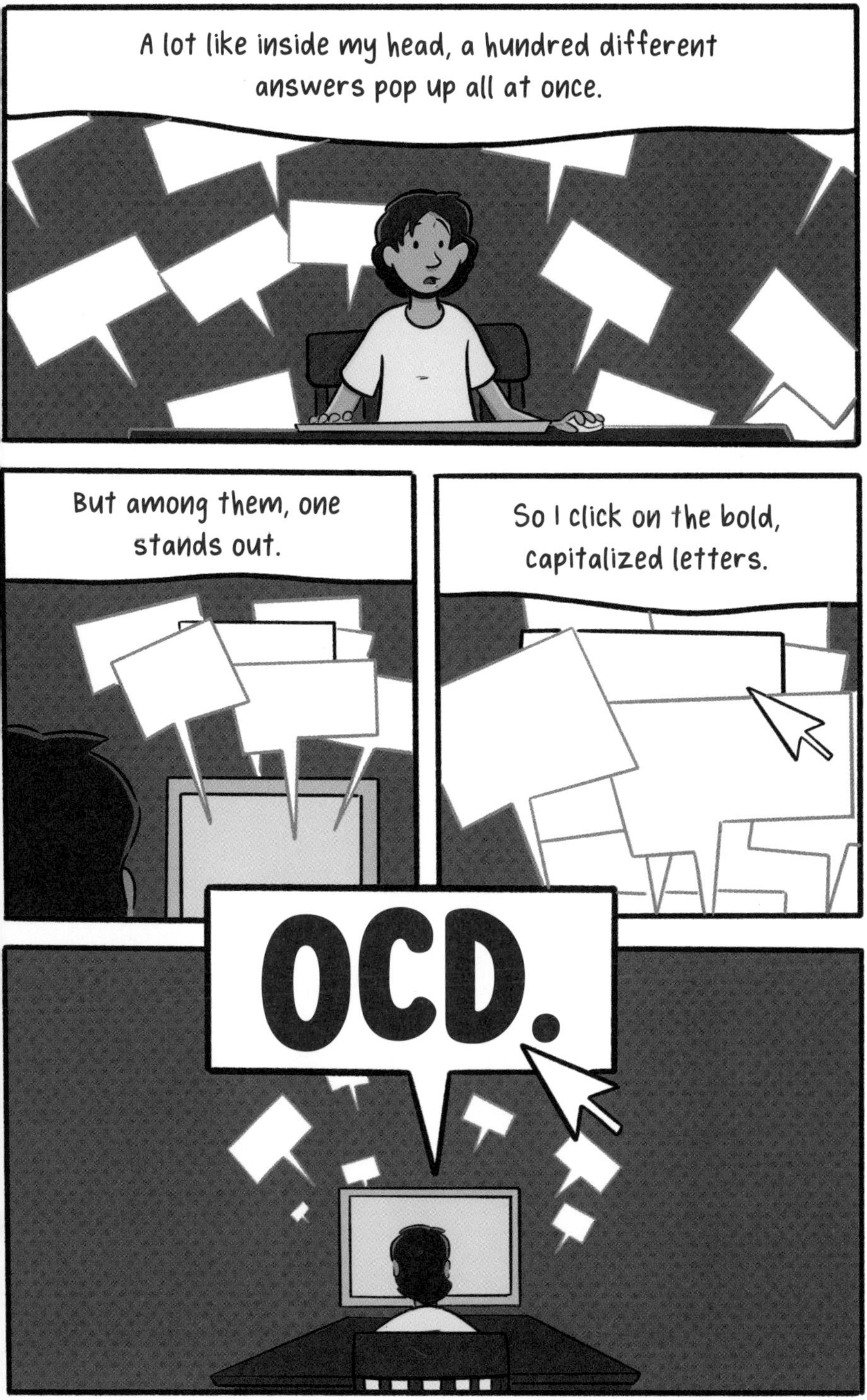
A lot like inside my head, a hundred different answers pop up all at once.
But among them, one stands out.
So I click on the bold, capitalized letters.
OCD.

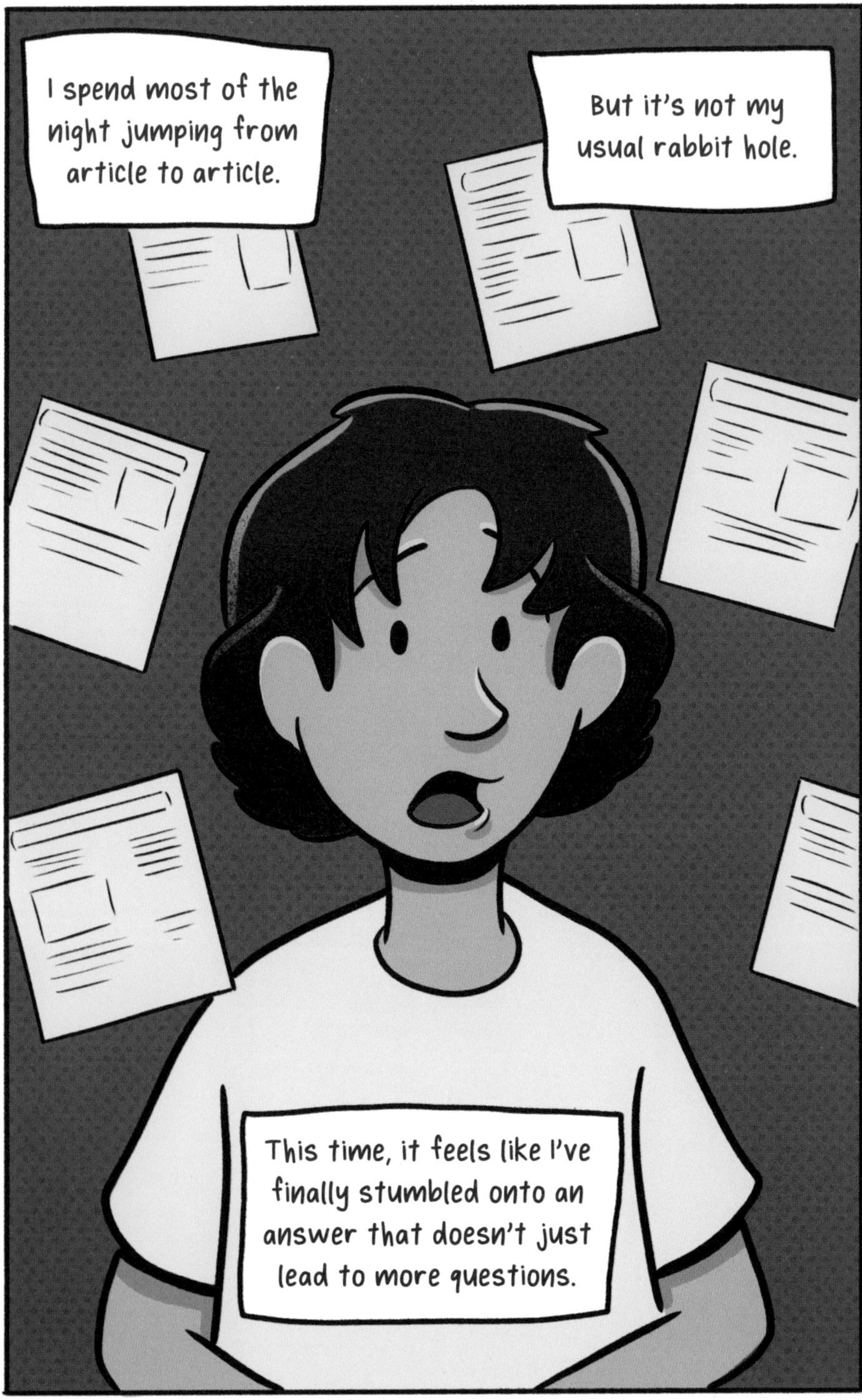
I spend most of the night jumping from article to article.
But it's not my usual rabbit hole.
This time, it feels like I've finally stumbled onto an answer that doesn't just lead to more questions.

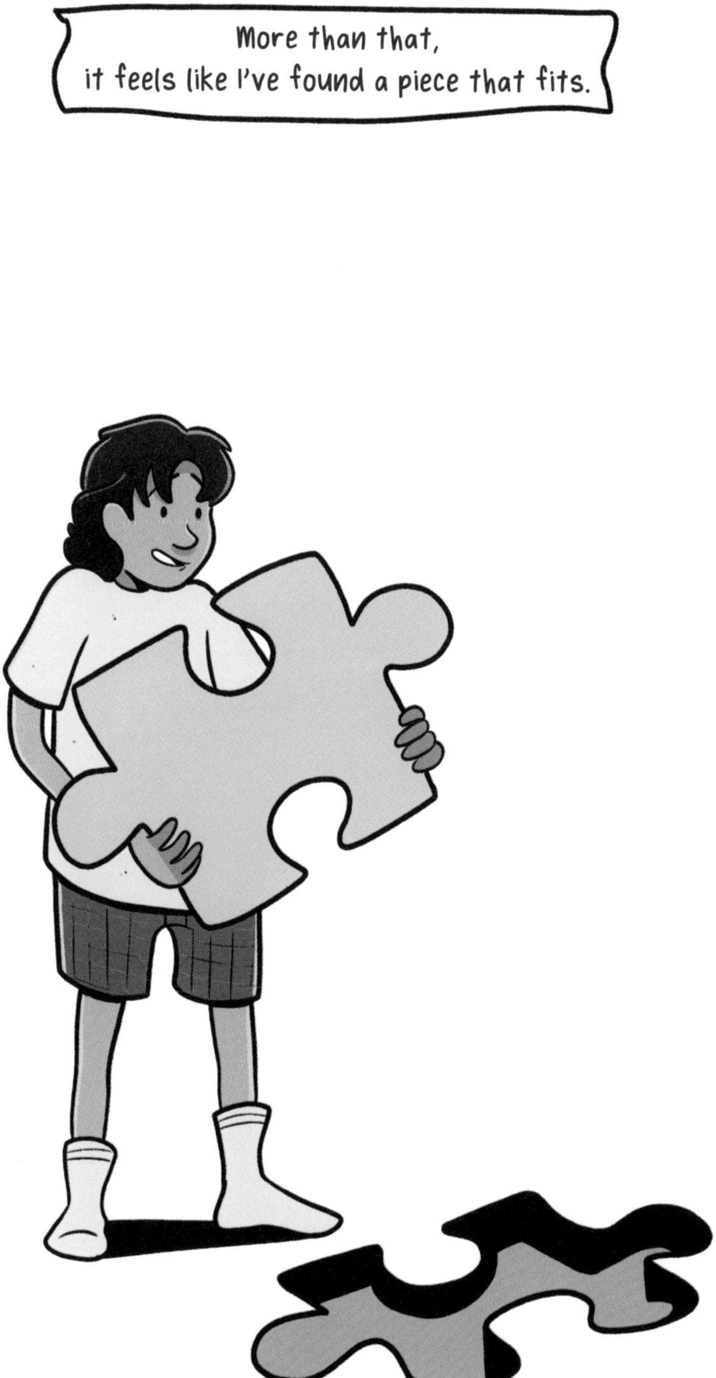
More than that,
it feels like I've found a piece that fits.

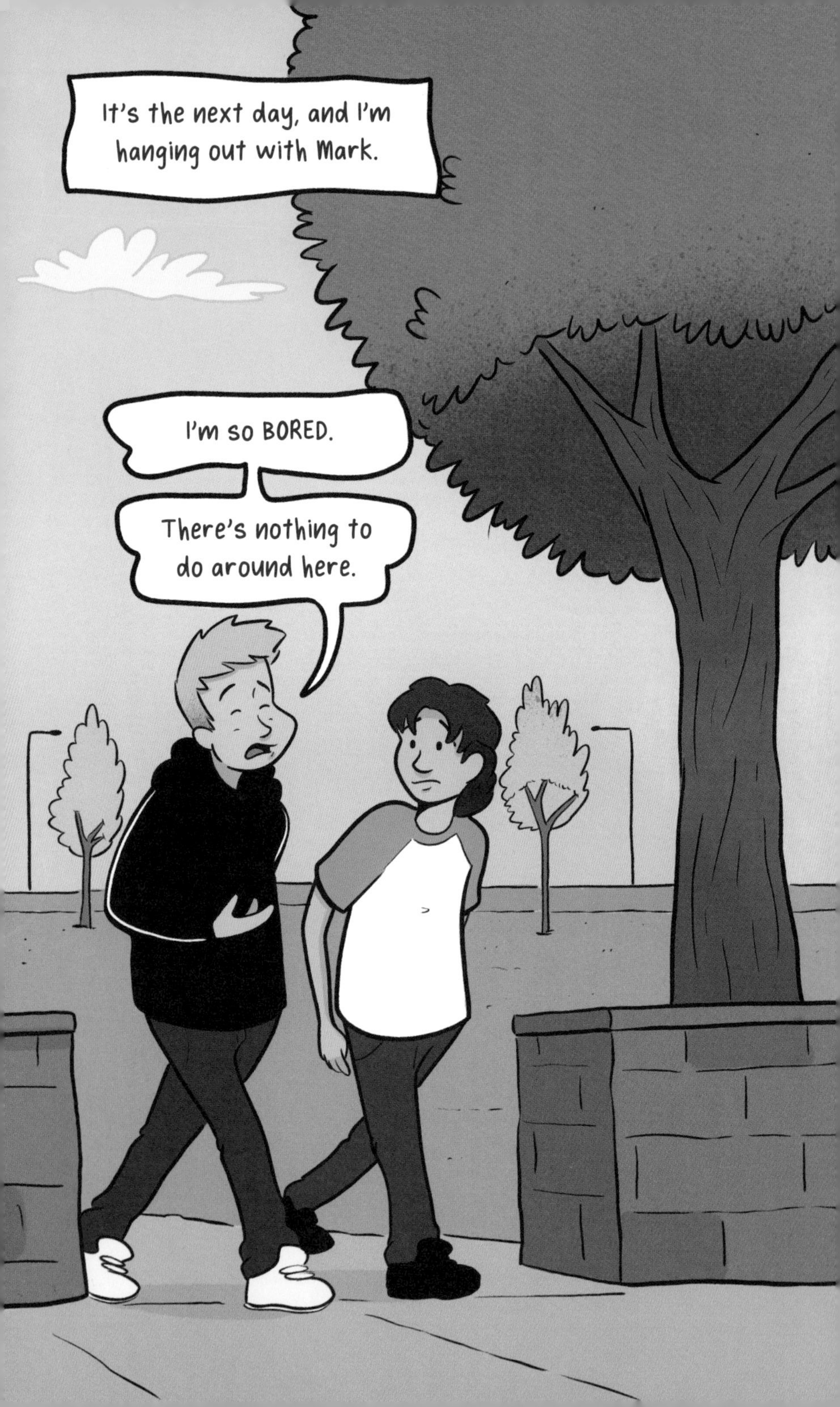
It's the next day, and I'm hanging out with Mark.
I'm so BORED.
There's nothing to do around here.

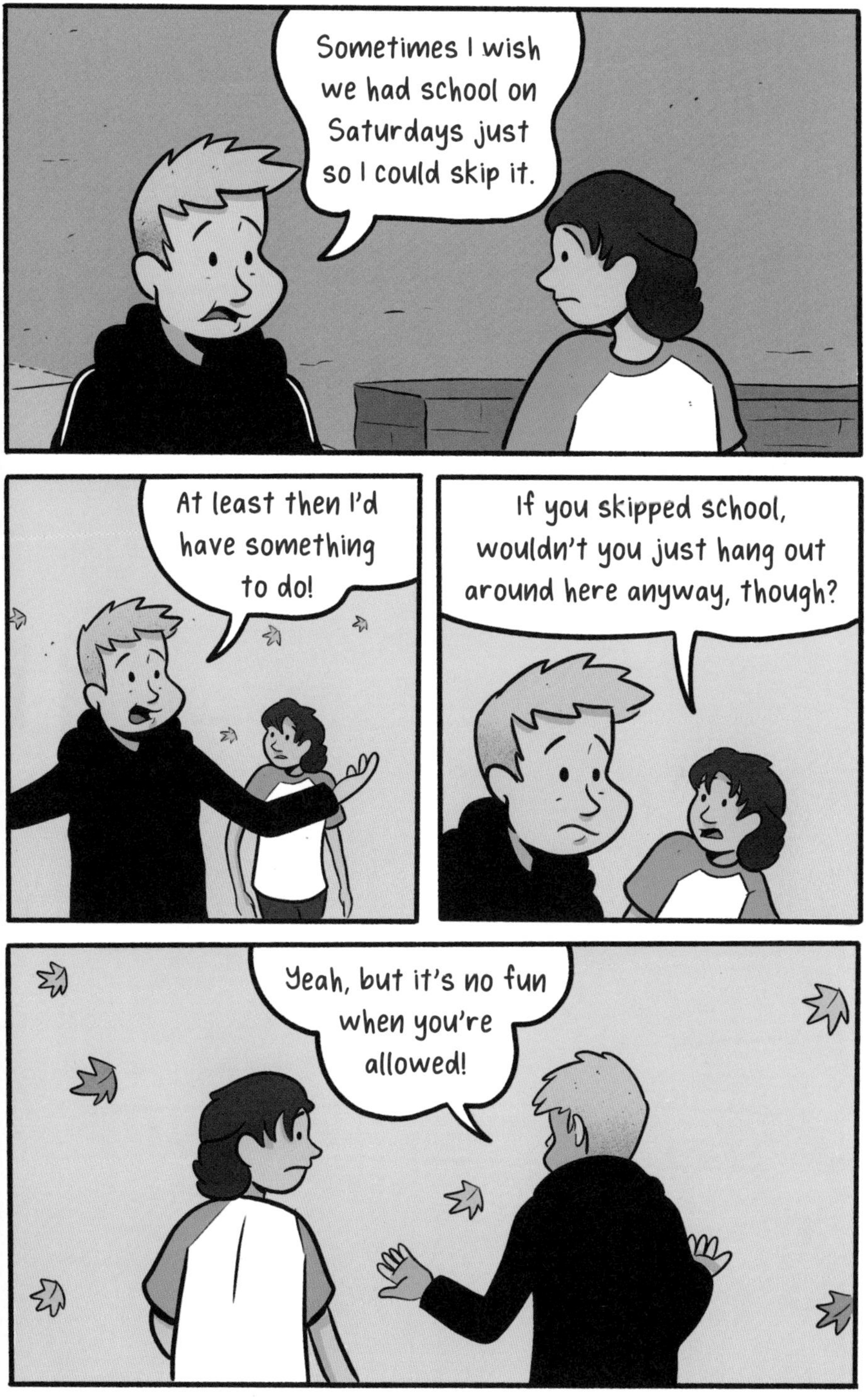

Sometimes I wish we had school on Saturdays just so I could skip it.
At least then I'd have something to do!
If you skipped school, wouldn't you just hang out around here anyway, though?
Yeah, but it's no fun when you're allowed!

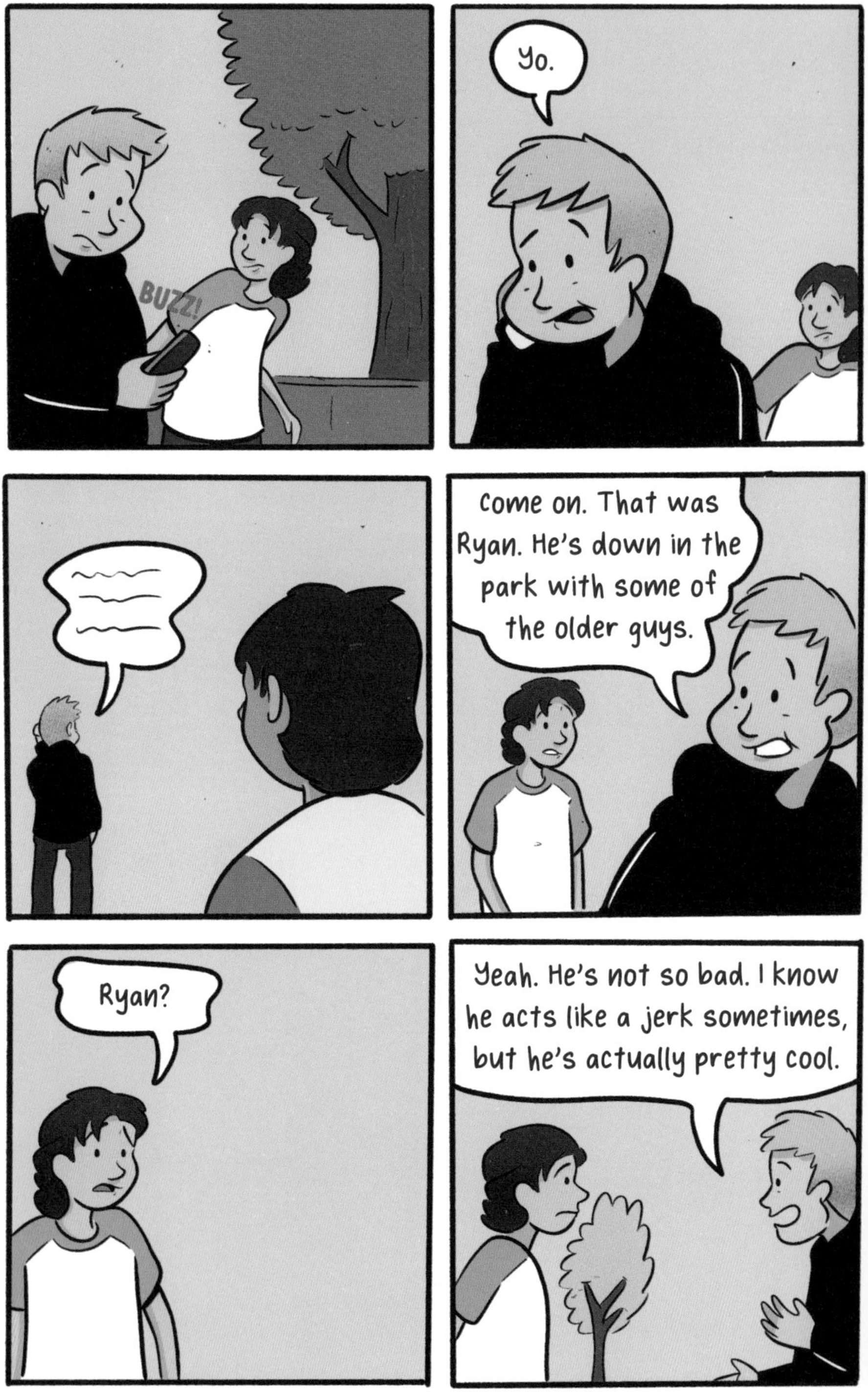
BUZZ!
Yo.
Come on. That was Ryan. He's down in the park with some of the older guys.
Ryan?
Yeah. He's not so bad. I know he acts like a jerk sometimes, but he's actually pretty cool.

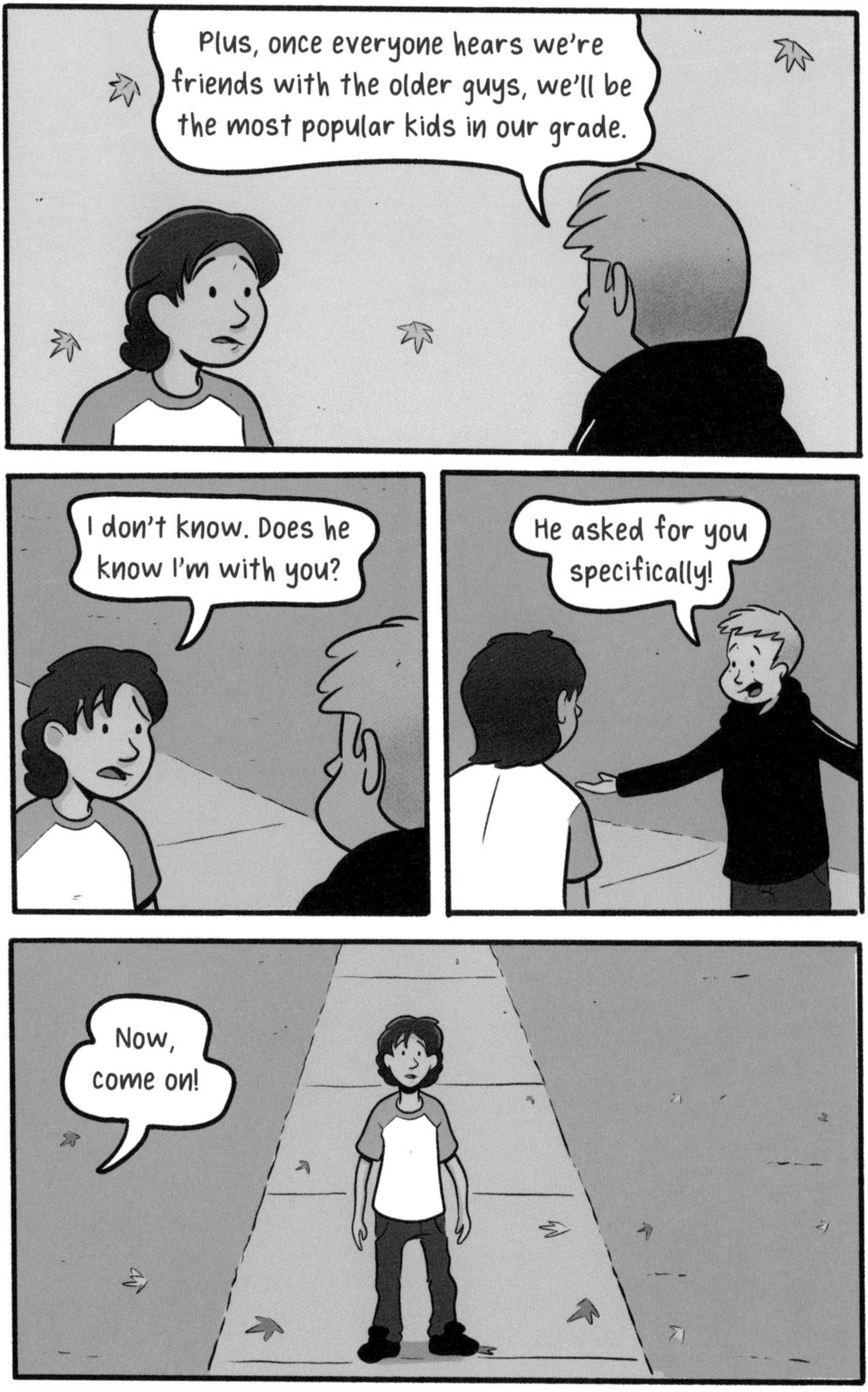
Plus, once everyone hears we're friends with the older guys, we'll be the most popular kids in our grade.
I don't know. Does he know I'm with you?
He asked for you specifically!
Now, come on!

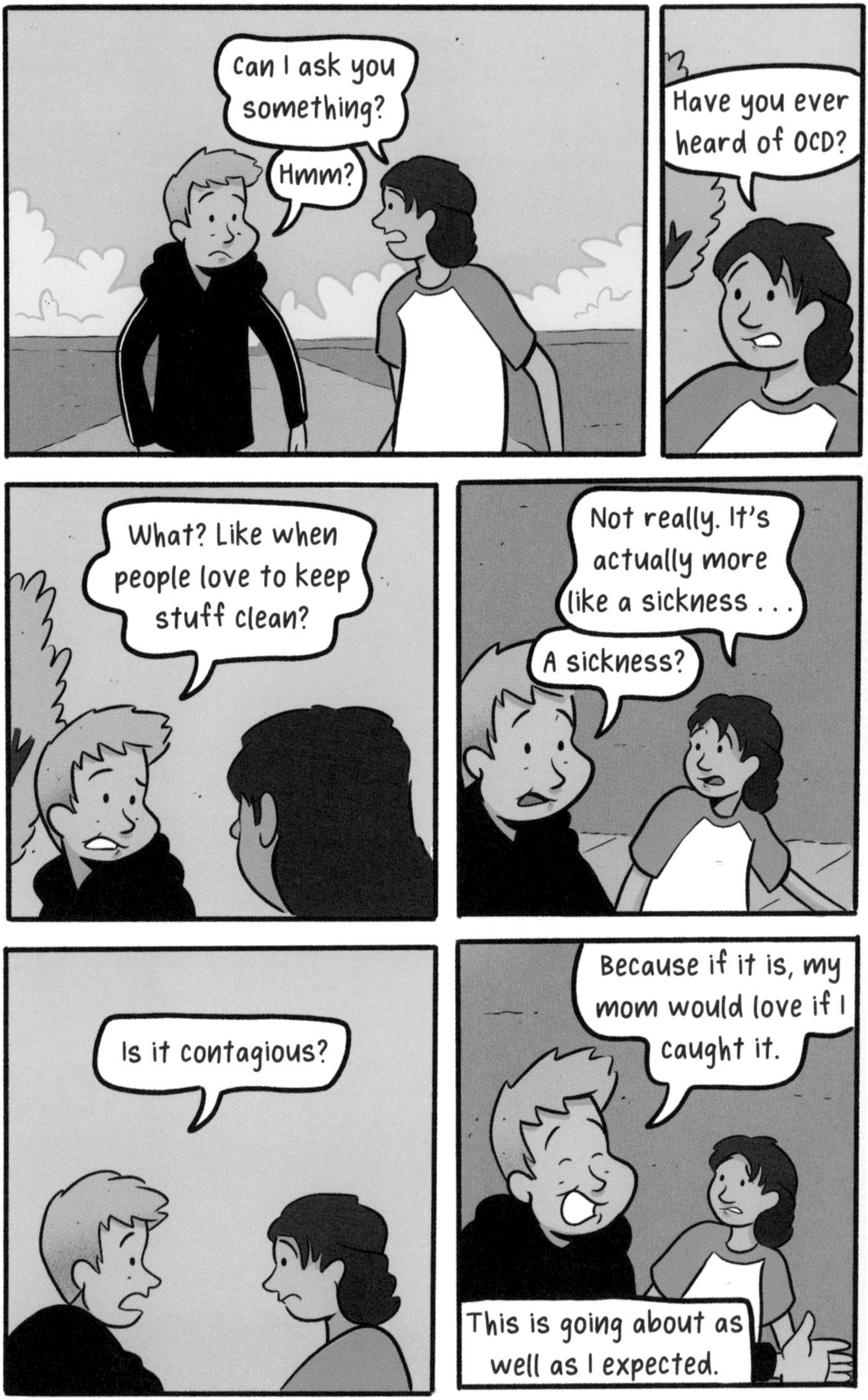
Can I ask you something?
Hmm?
Have you ever heard of OCD?
What? Like when people love to keep stuff clean?
Not really. It's actually more like a sickness . . .
A sickness?
Is it contagious?
Because if it is, my mom would love if I caught it.
This is going about as well as I expected.

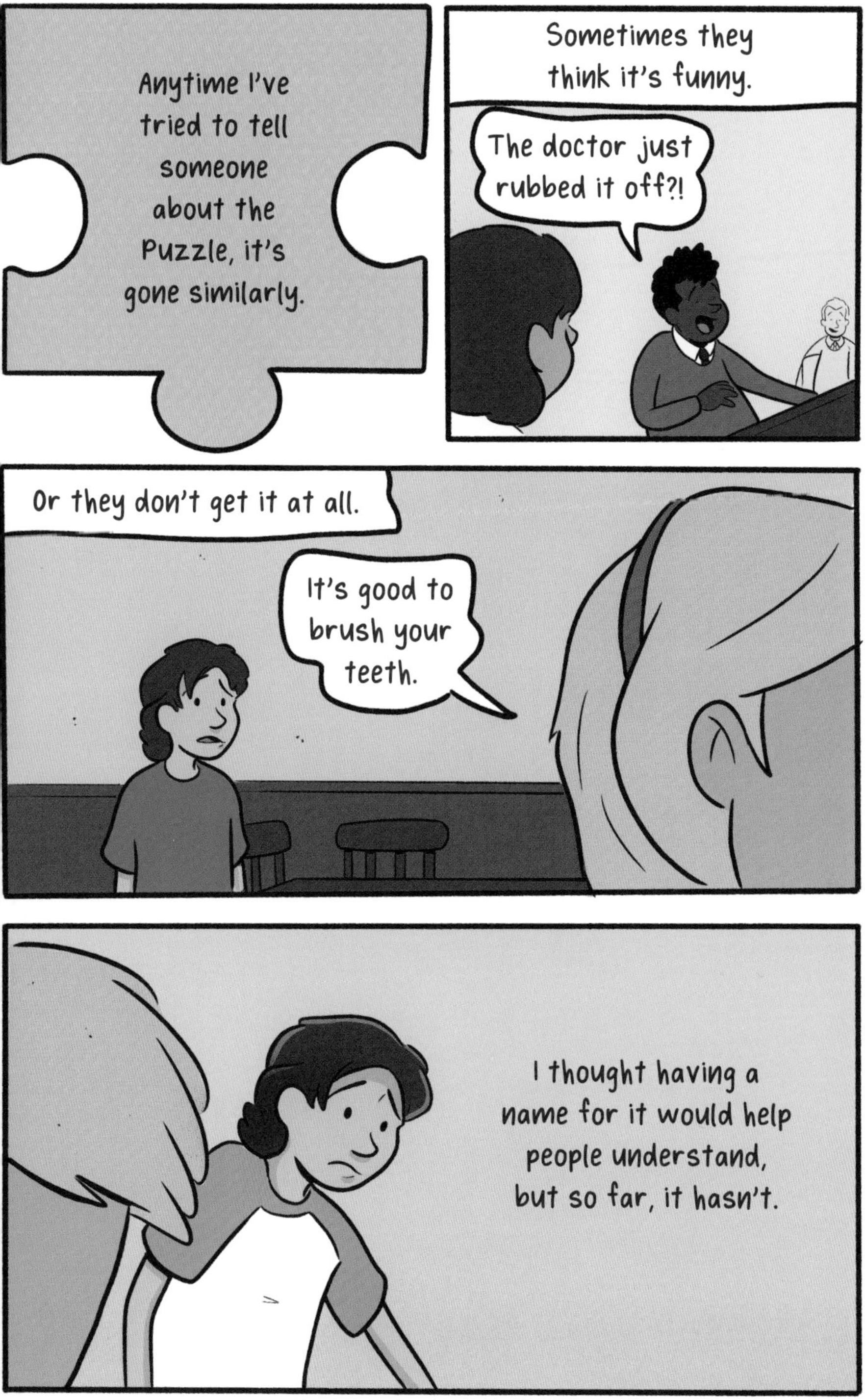
Anytime I've tried to tell someone about the Puzzle, it's gone similarly.
Sometimes they think it's funny.
The doctor just rubbed it off?!
Or they don't get it at all.
It's good to brush your teeth.
I thought having a name for it would help people understand, but so far, it hasn't.

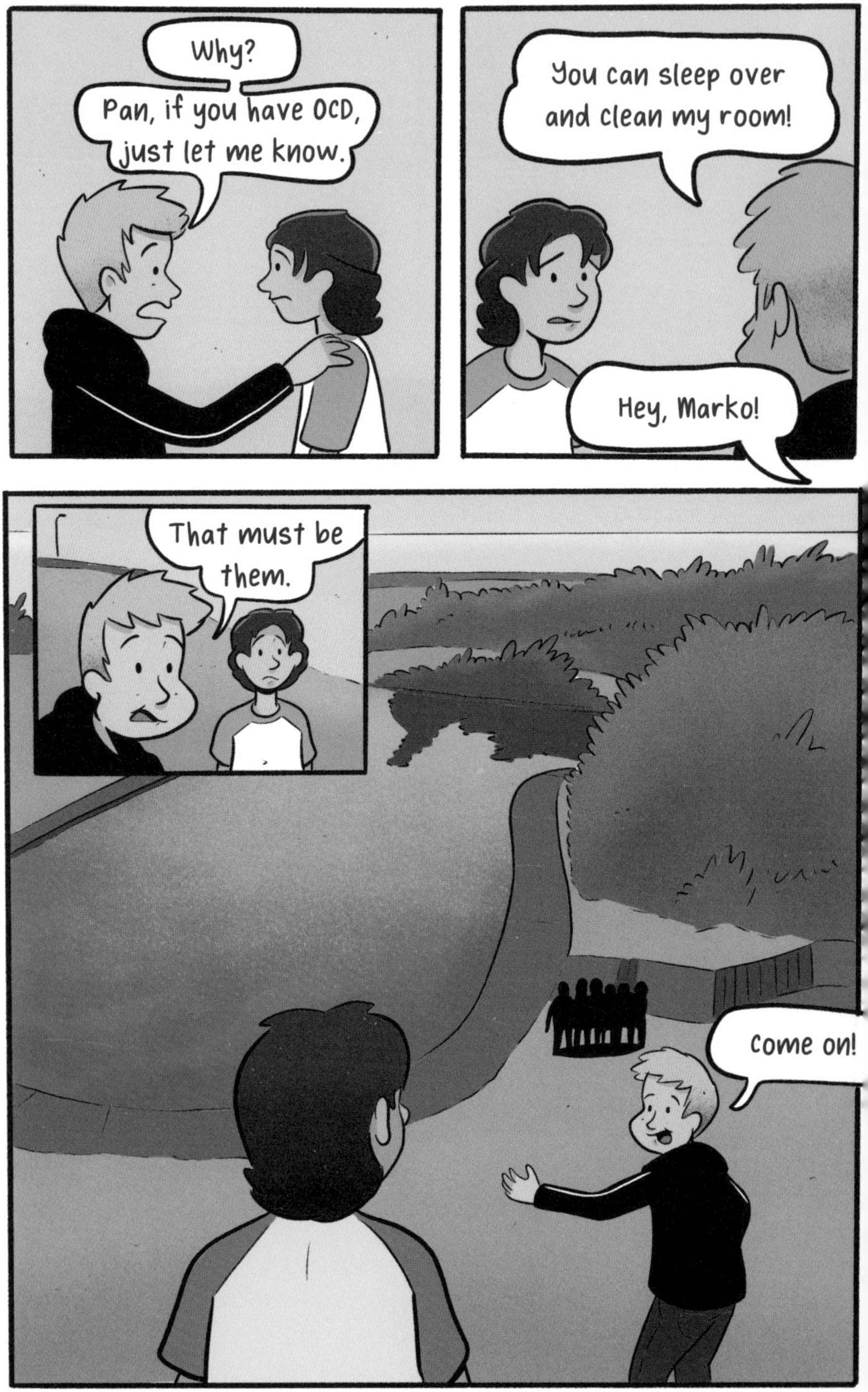

Why?
Pan, if you have OCD, just let me know.
You can sleep over and clean my room!
Hey, Marko!
That must be them.
Come on!

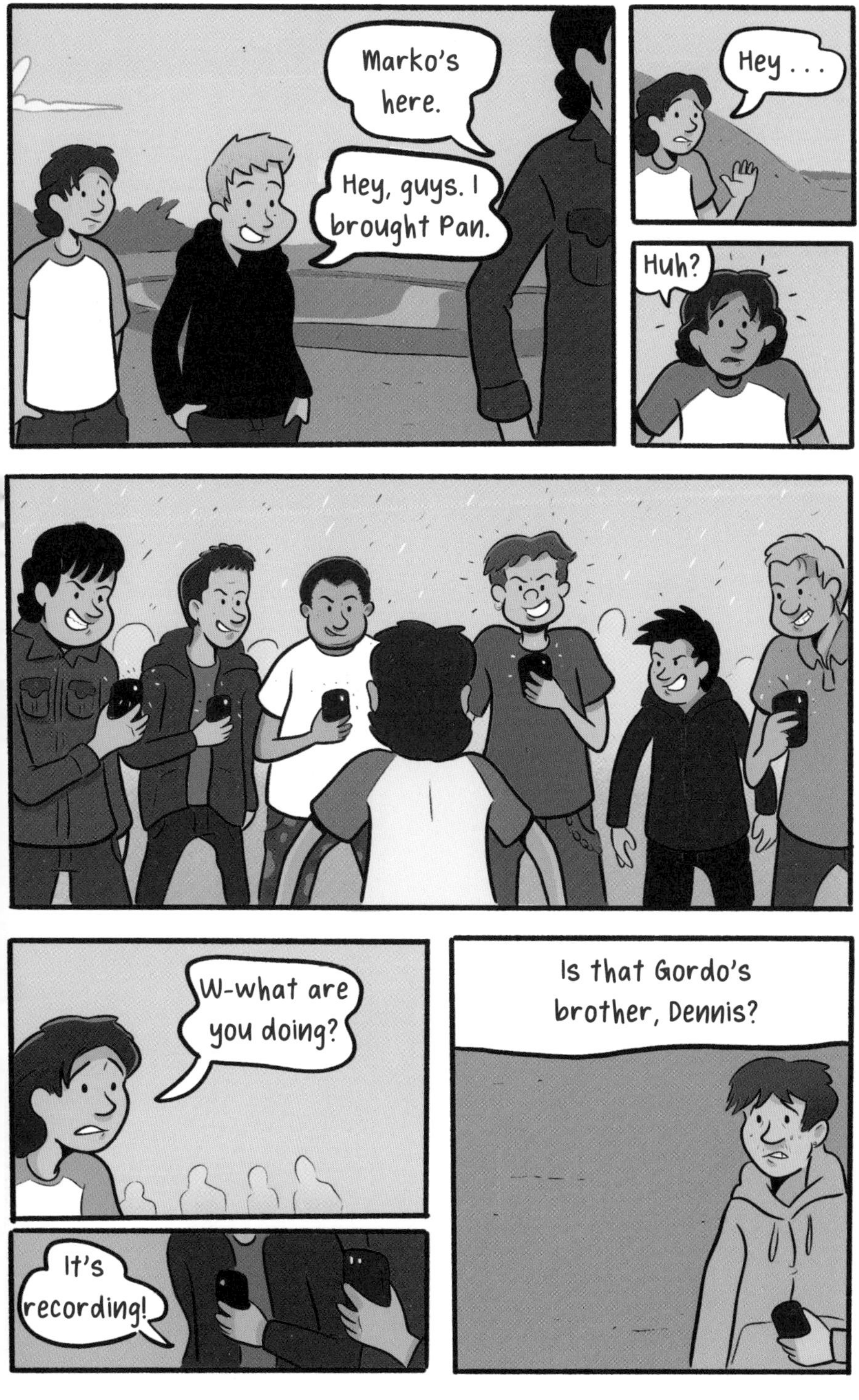
Marko's here.
Hey, guys. I brought Pan.
Hey . . .
Huh?
W-what are you doing?
It's recording!
Is that Gordo's brother, Dennis?

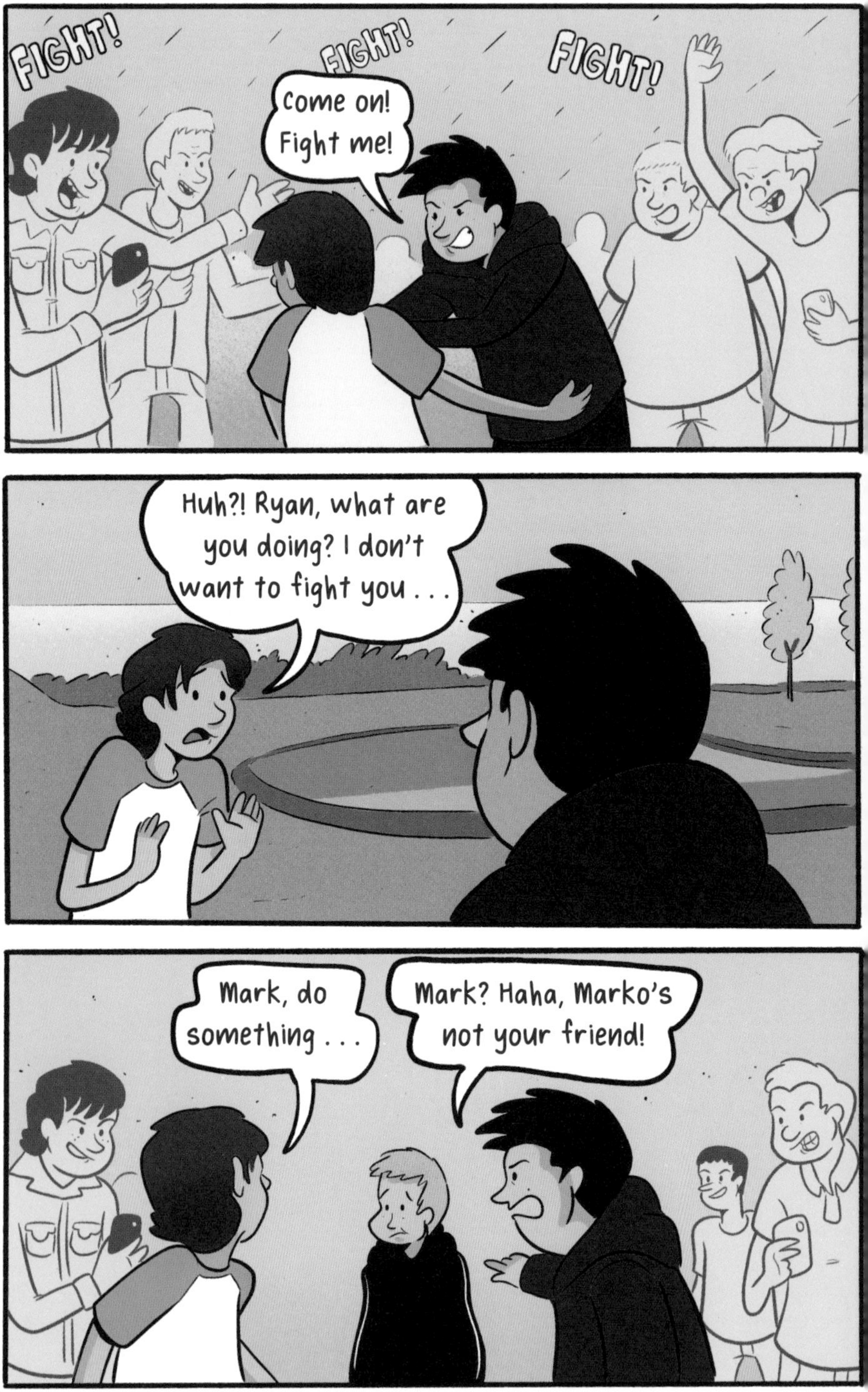
FIGHT!
FIGHT!
FIGHT!
Come on! Fight me!
Huh?! Ryan, what are you doing? I don't want to fight you . . .
Mark, do something . . .
Mark? Haha, Marko's not your friend!

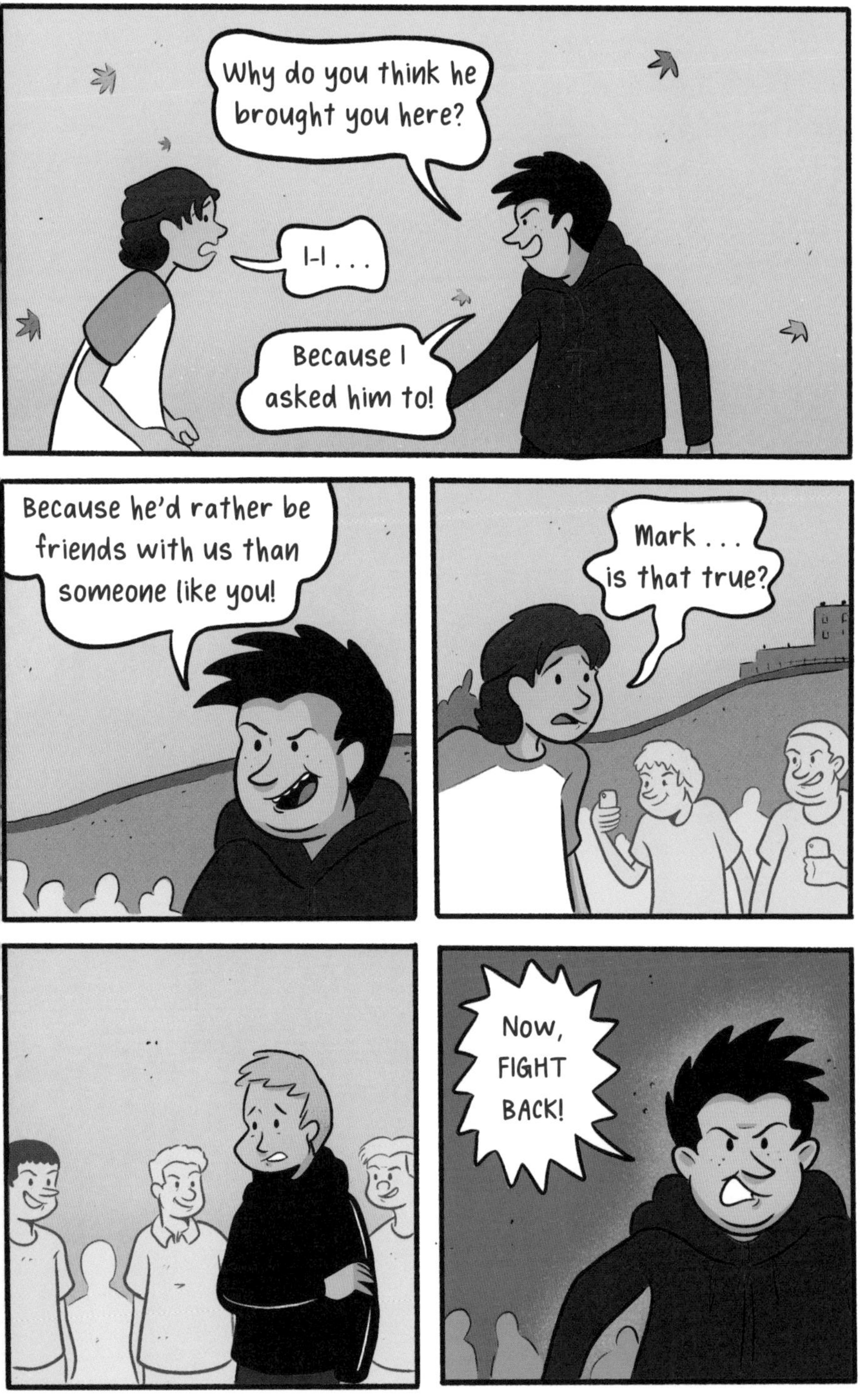
Why do you think he brought you here?
I-I . . .
Because I asked him to!
Because he'd rather be friends with us than someone like you!
Mark . . . is that true?
Now, FIGHT BACK!

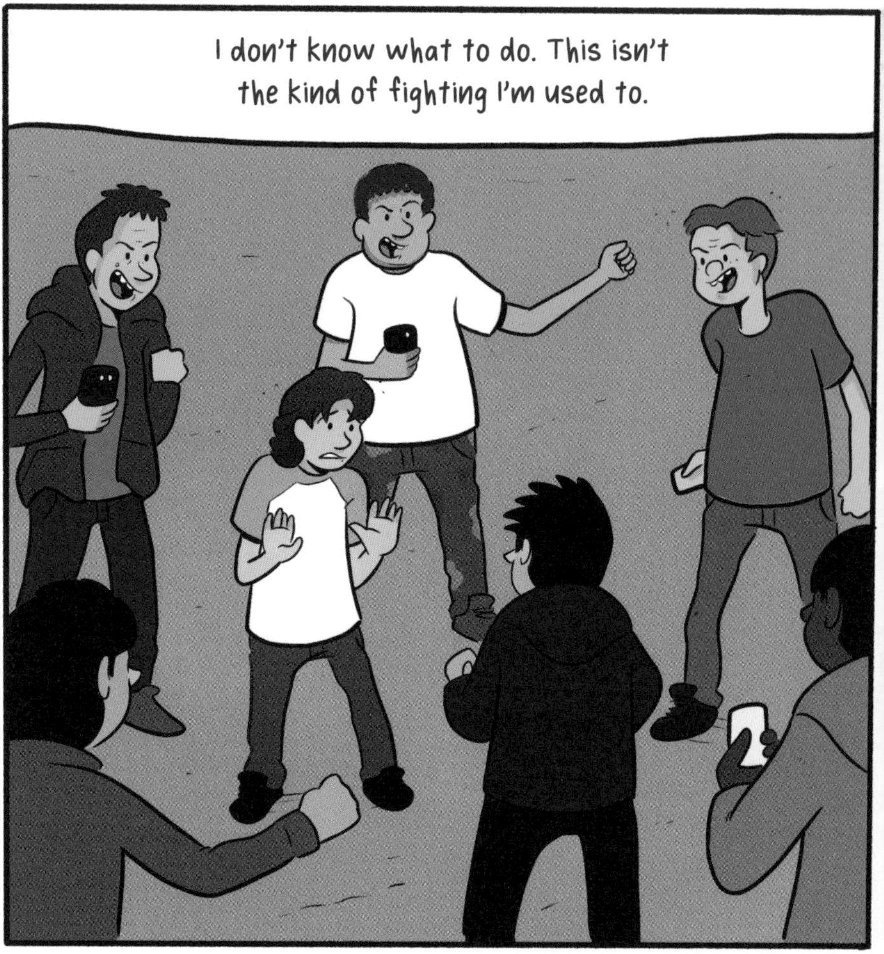
I don't know what to do. This isn't the kind of fighting I'm used to.

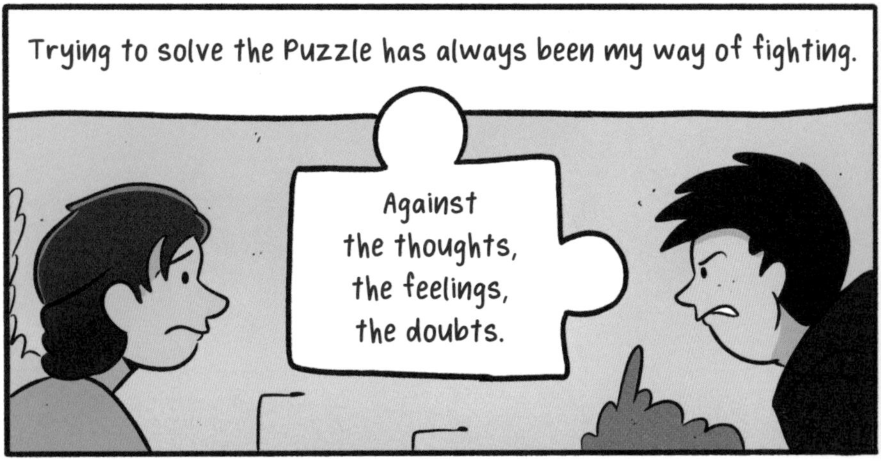
Trying to solve the Puzzle has always been my way of fighting.
Against the thoughts, the feelings, the doubts.

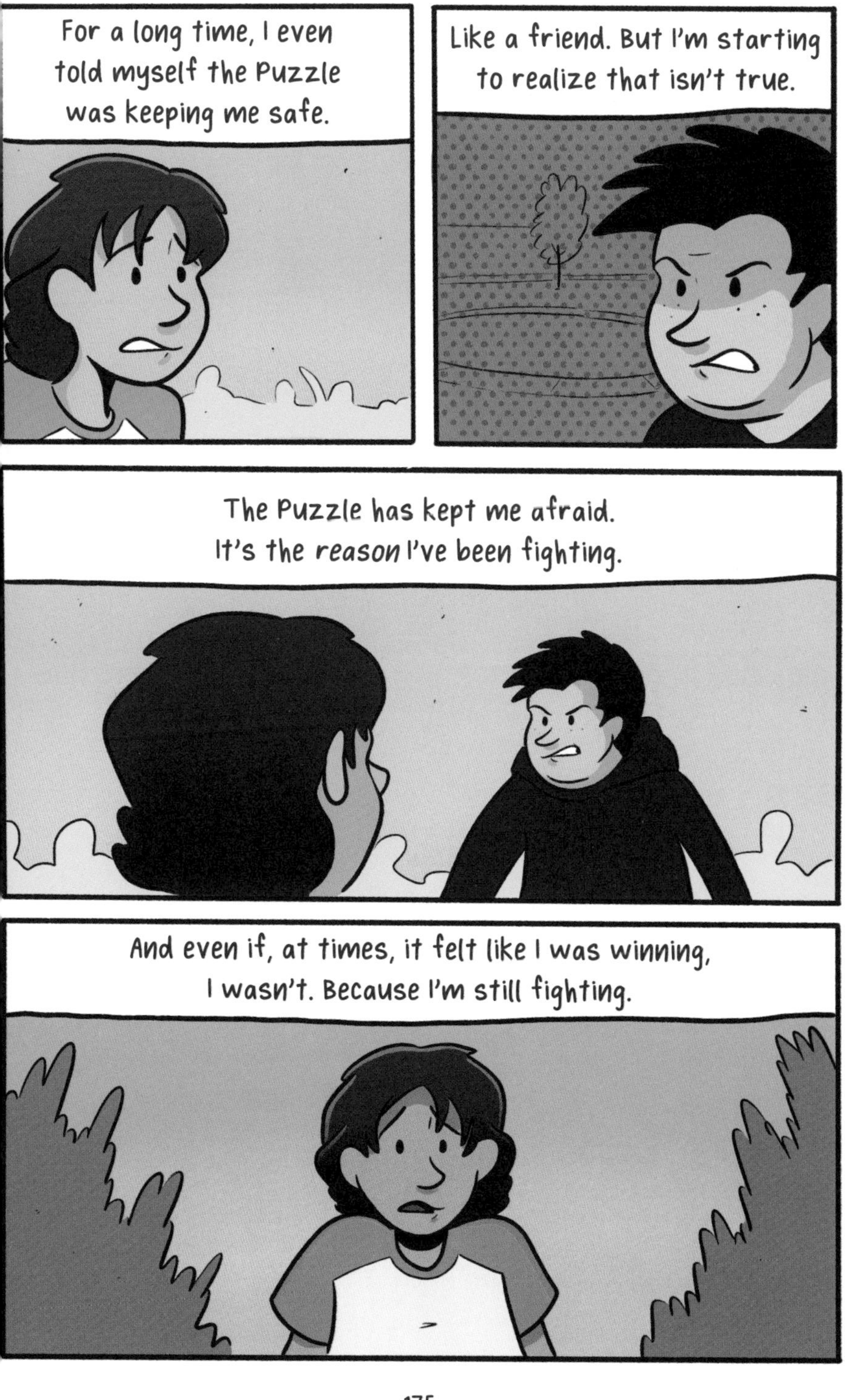
For a long time, I even told myself the Puzzle was keeping me safe.
Like a friend. But I'm starting to realize that isn't true.
The Puzzle has kept me afraid. It's the *reason* I've been fighting.
And even if, at times, it felt like I was winning, I wasn't. Because I'm still fighting.

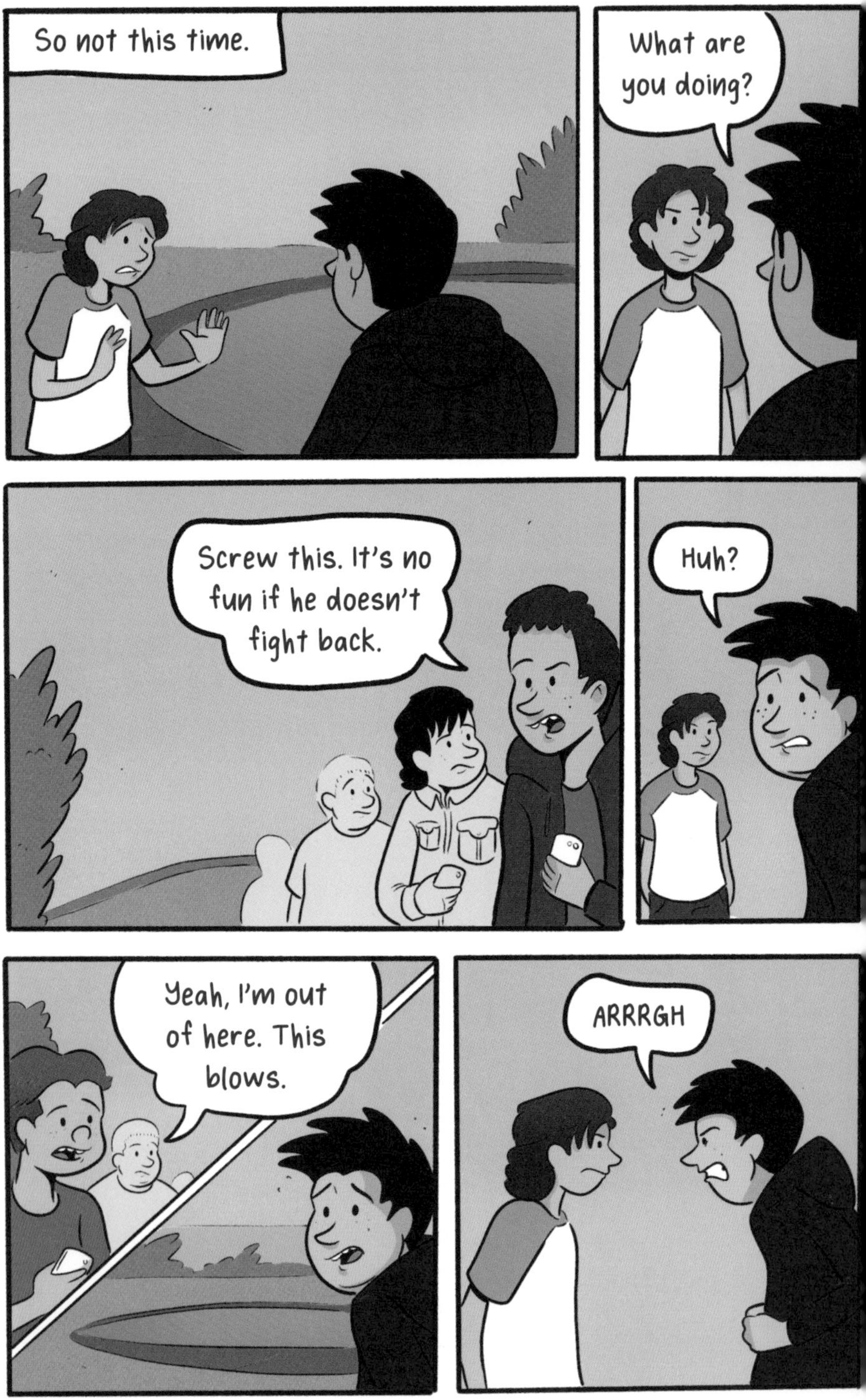
So not this time.
What are you doing?
Screw this. It's no fun if he doesn't fight back.
Huh?
Yeah, I'm out of here. This blows.
ARRRGH

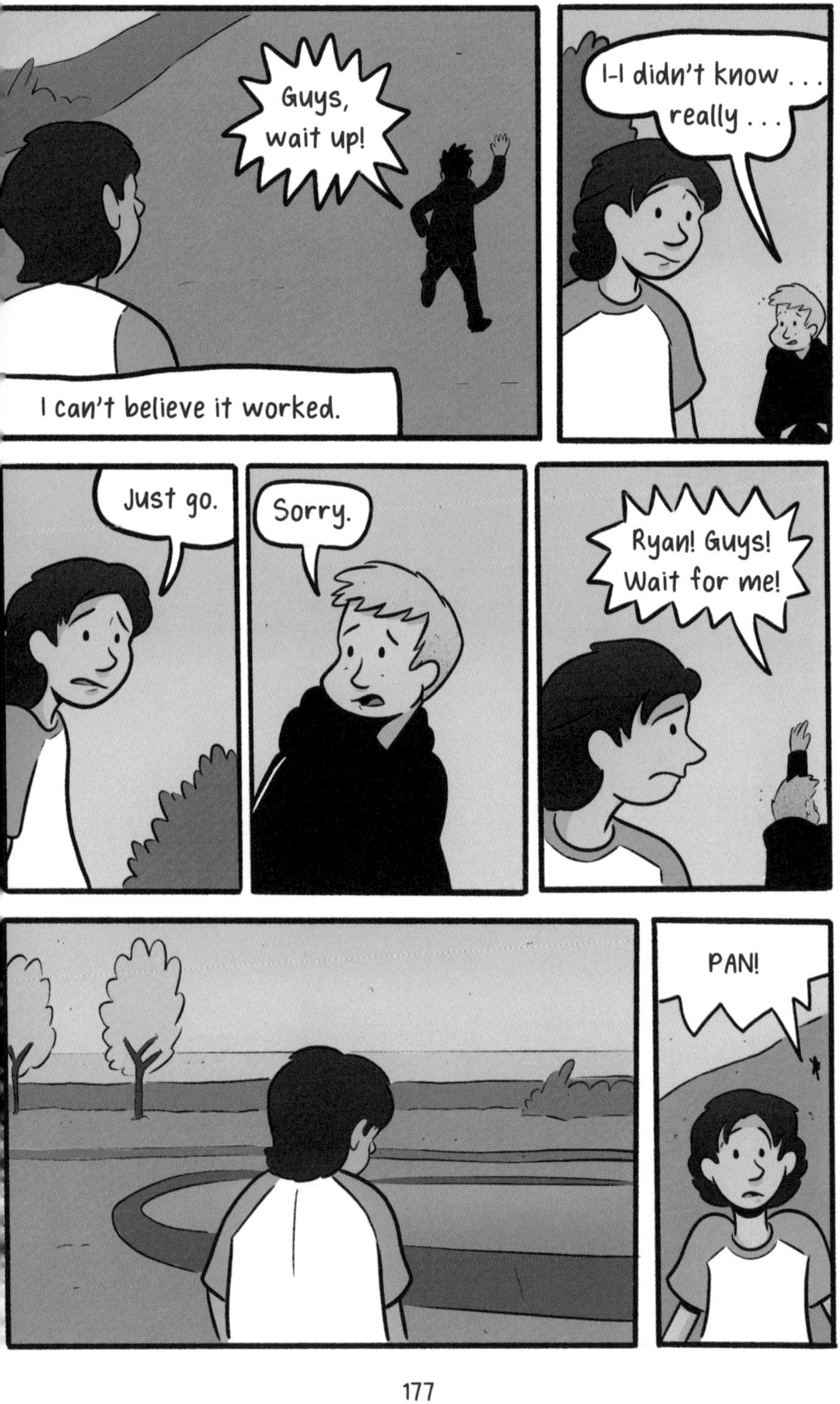

Guys, wait up!
I can't believe it worked.
I-I didn't know . . . really . . .
Just go.
Sorry.
Ryan! Guys! Wait for me!
PAN!

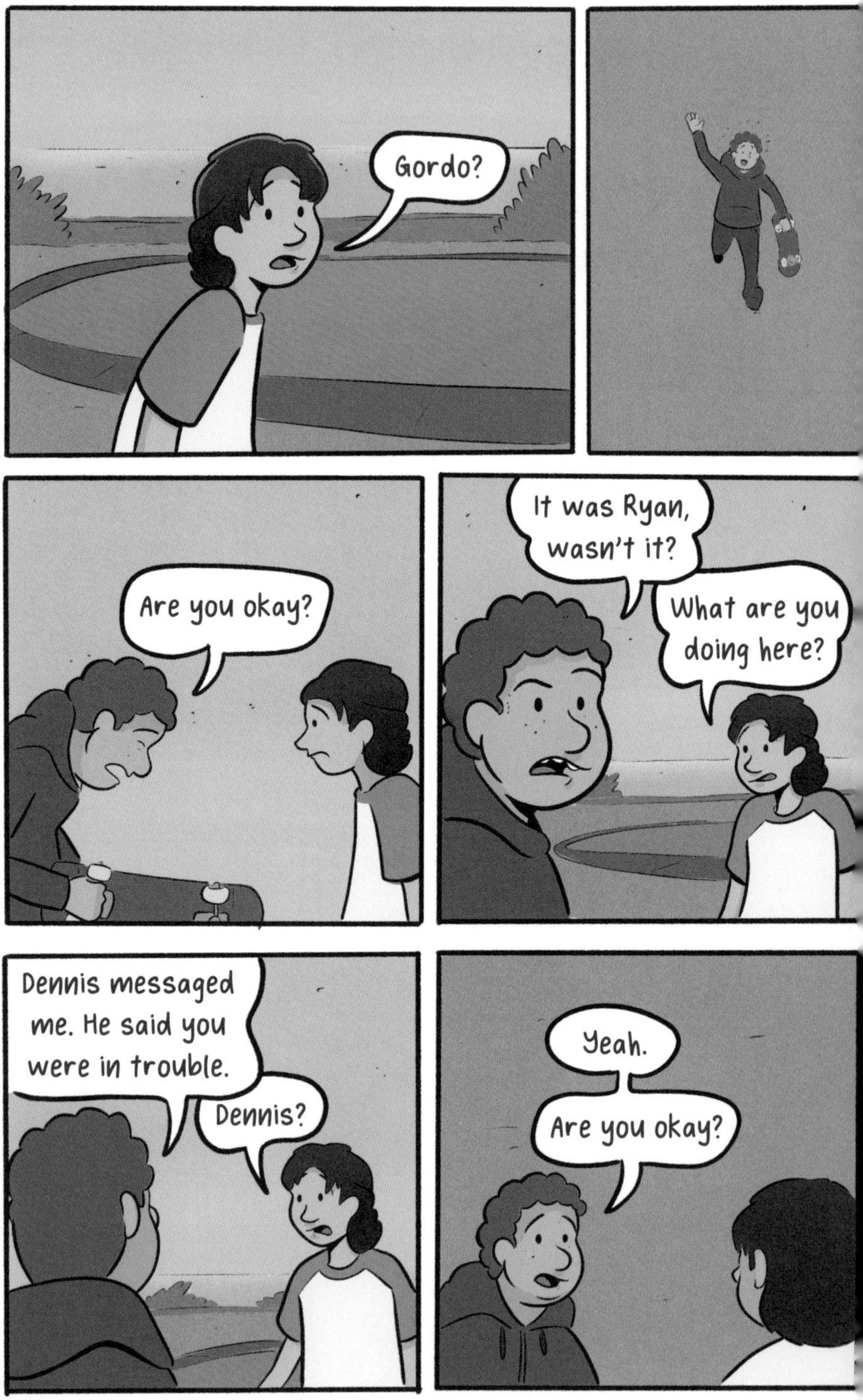
Gordo?
Are you okay?
It was Ryan, wasn't it?
What are you doing here?
Dennis messaged me. He said you were in trouble.
Dennis?
Yeah.
Are you okay?

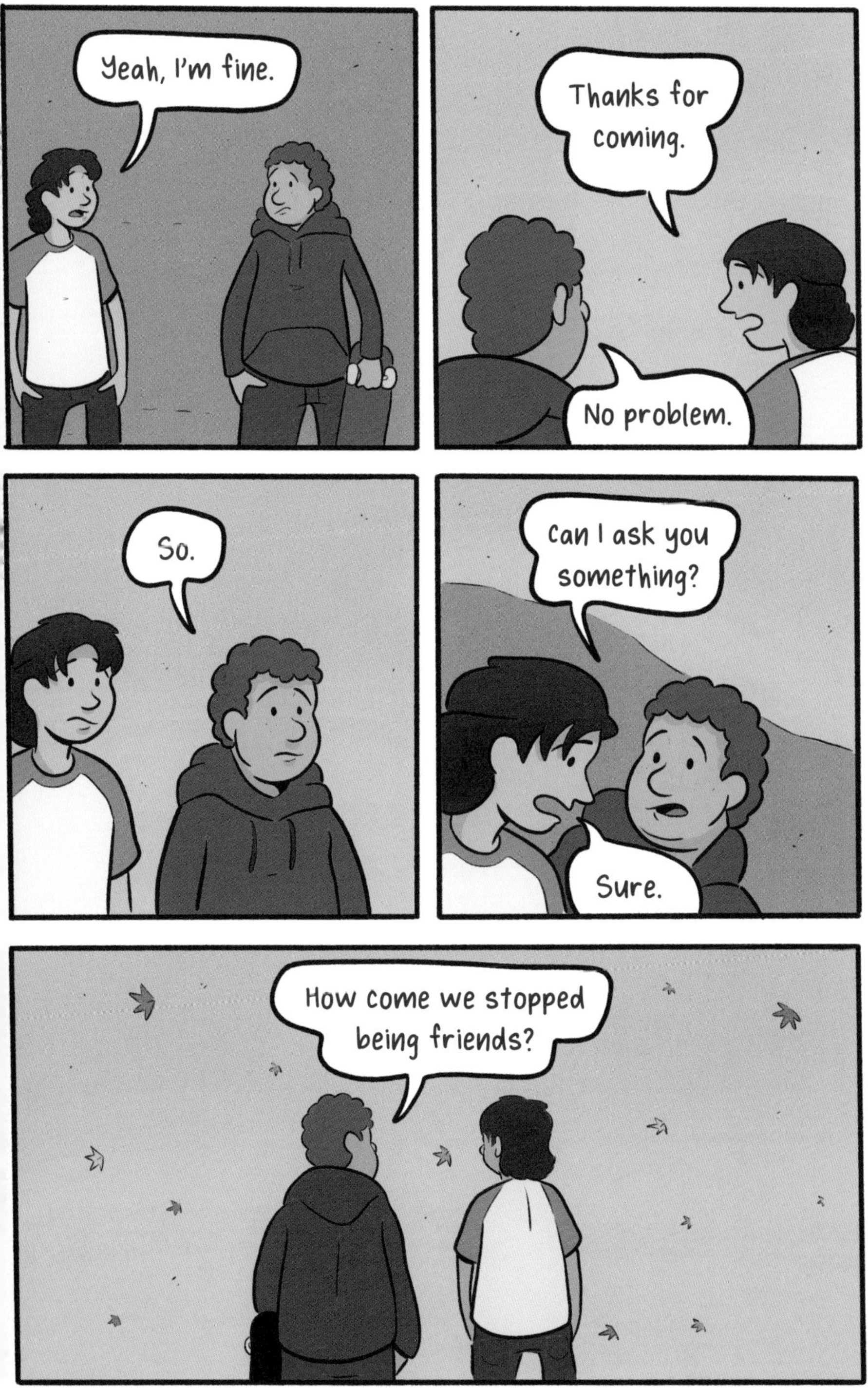
Yeah, I'm fine.
Thanks for coming.
No problem.
So.
Can I ask you something?
Sure.
How come we stopped being friends?

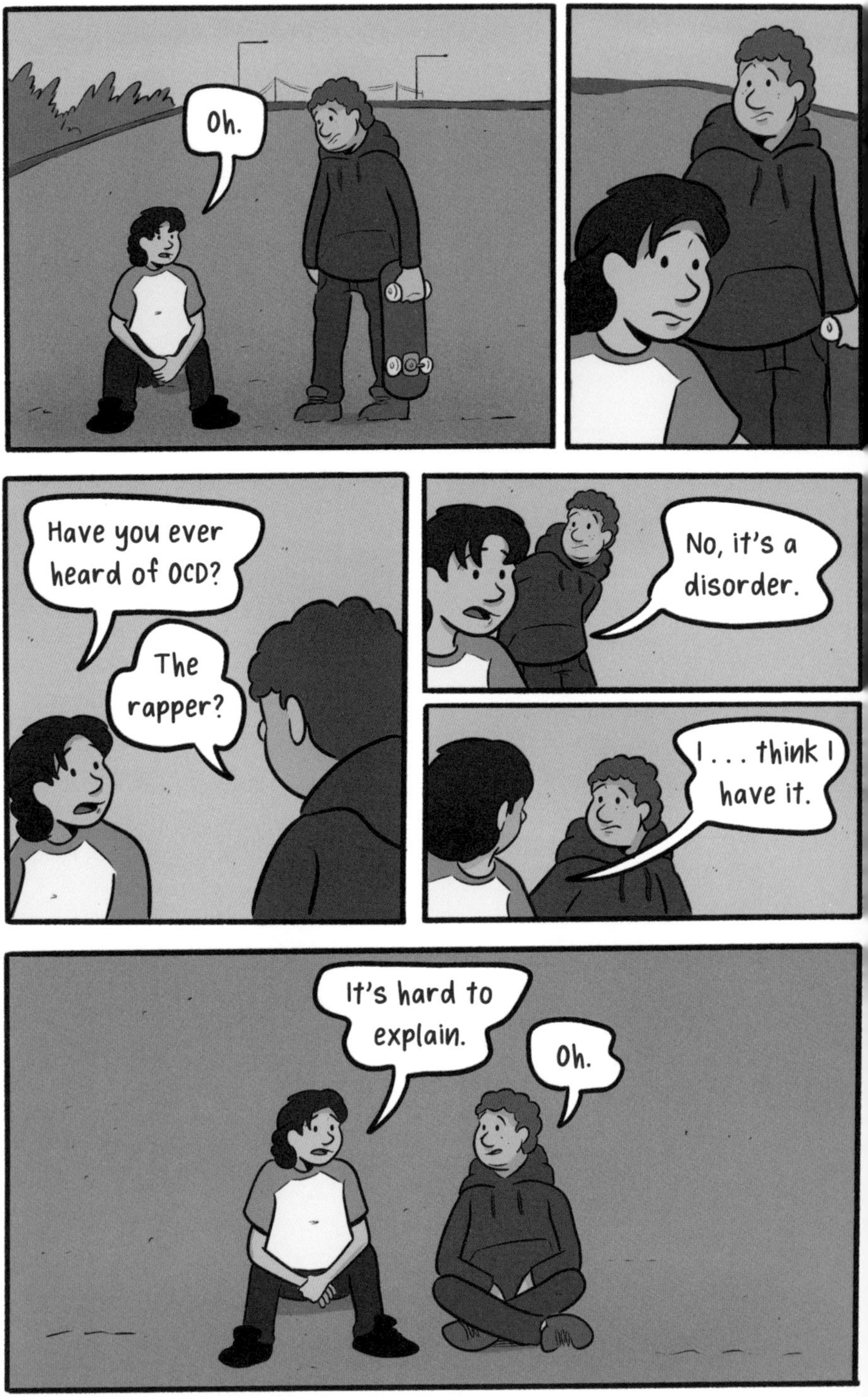
Oh.
Have you ever heard of OCD?
The rapper?
No, it's a disorder.
I . . . think I have it.
It's hard to explain.
Oh.

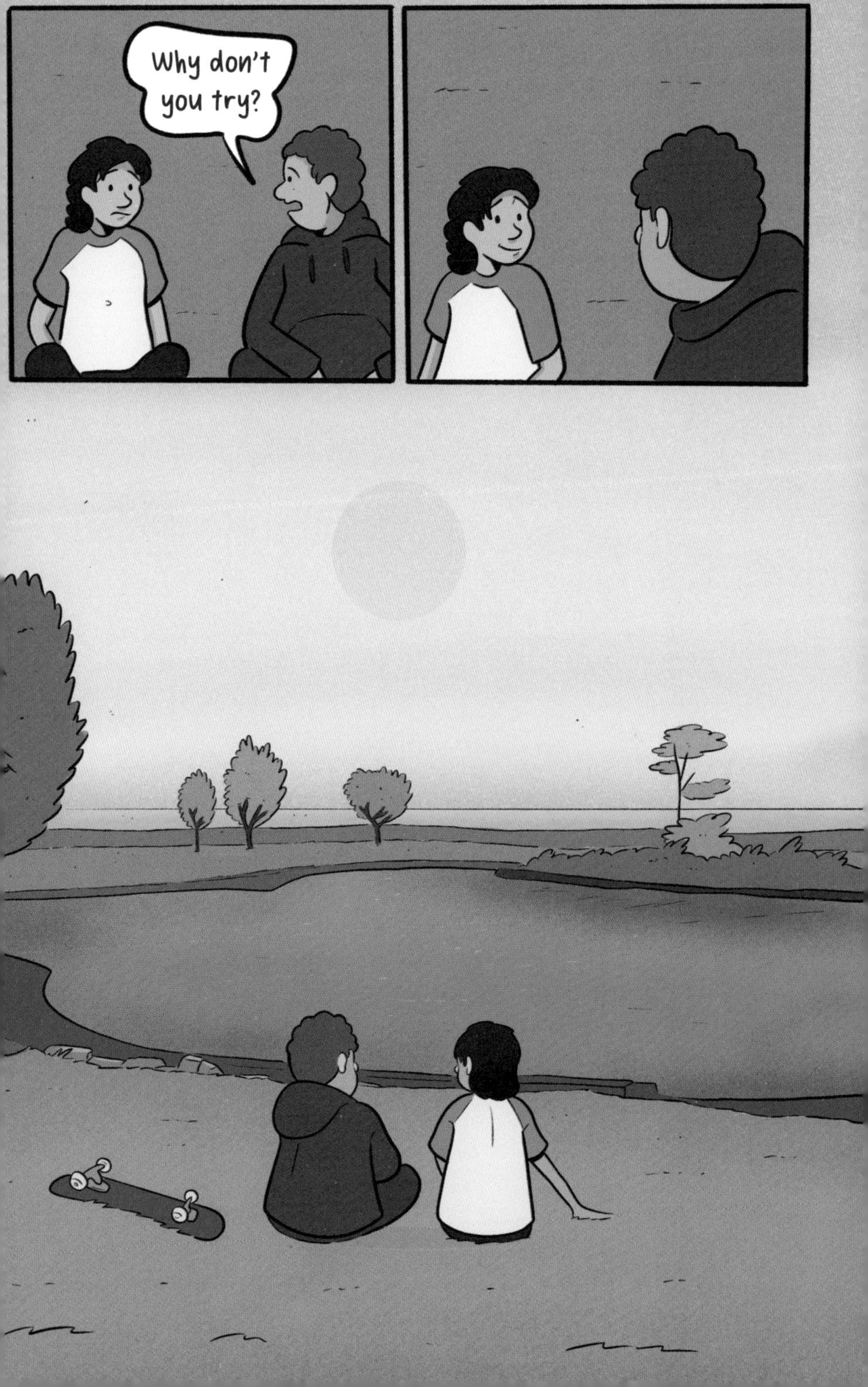
Why don't you try?

6

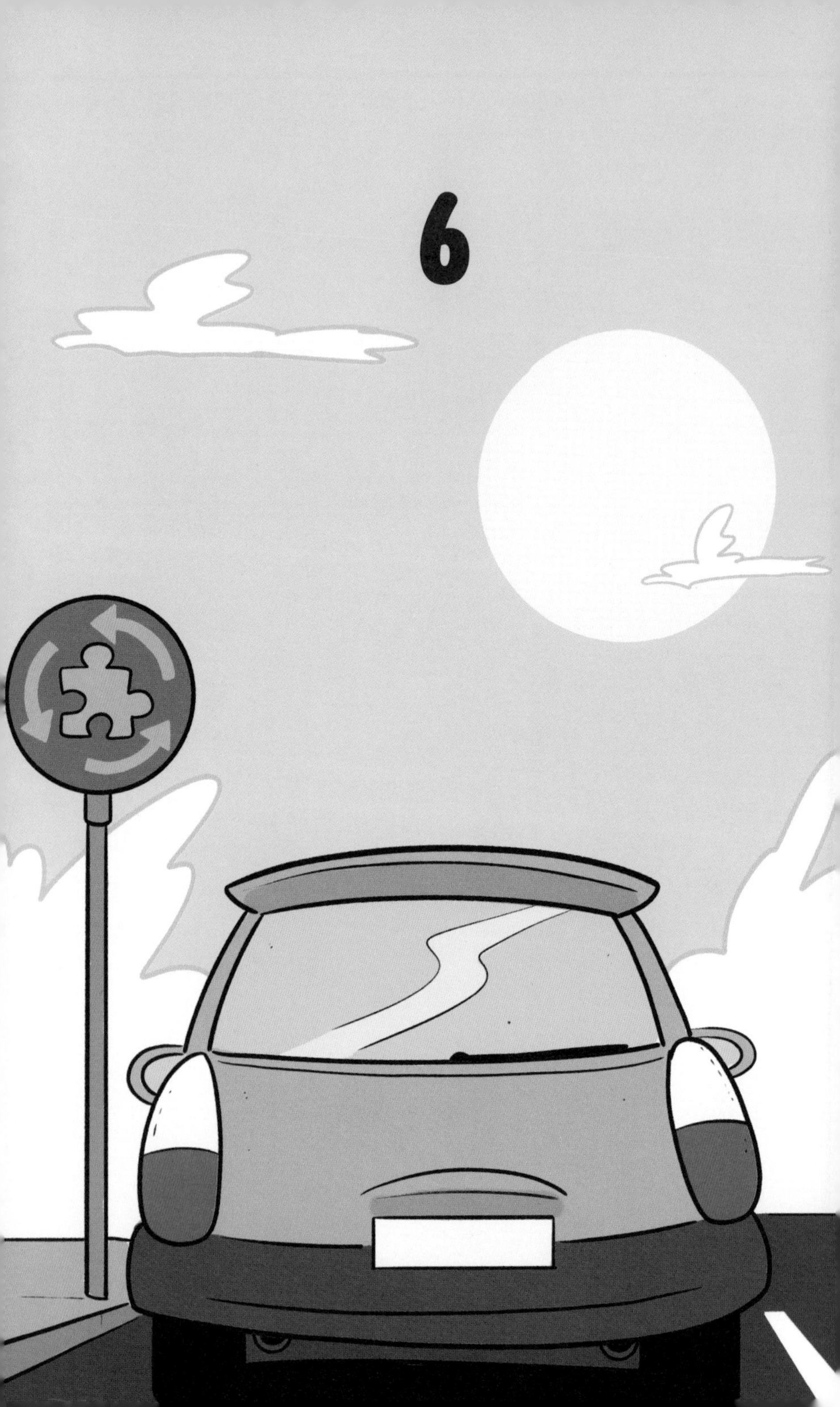

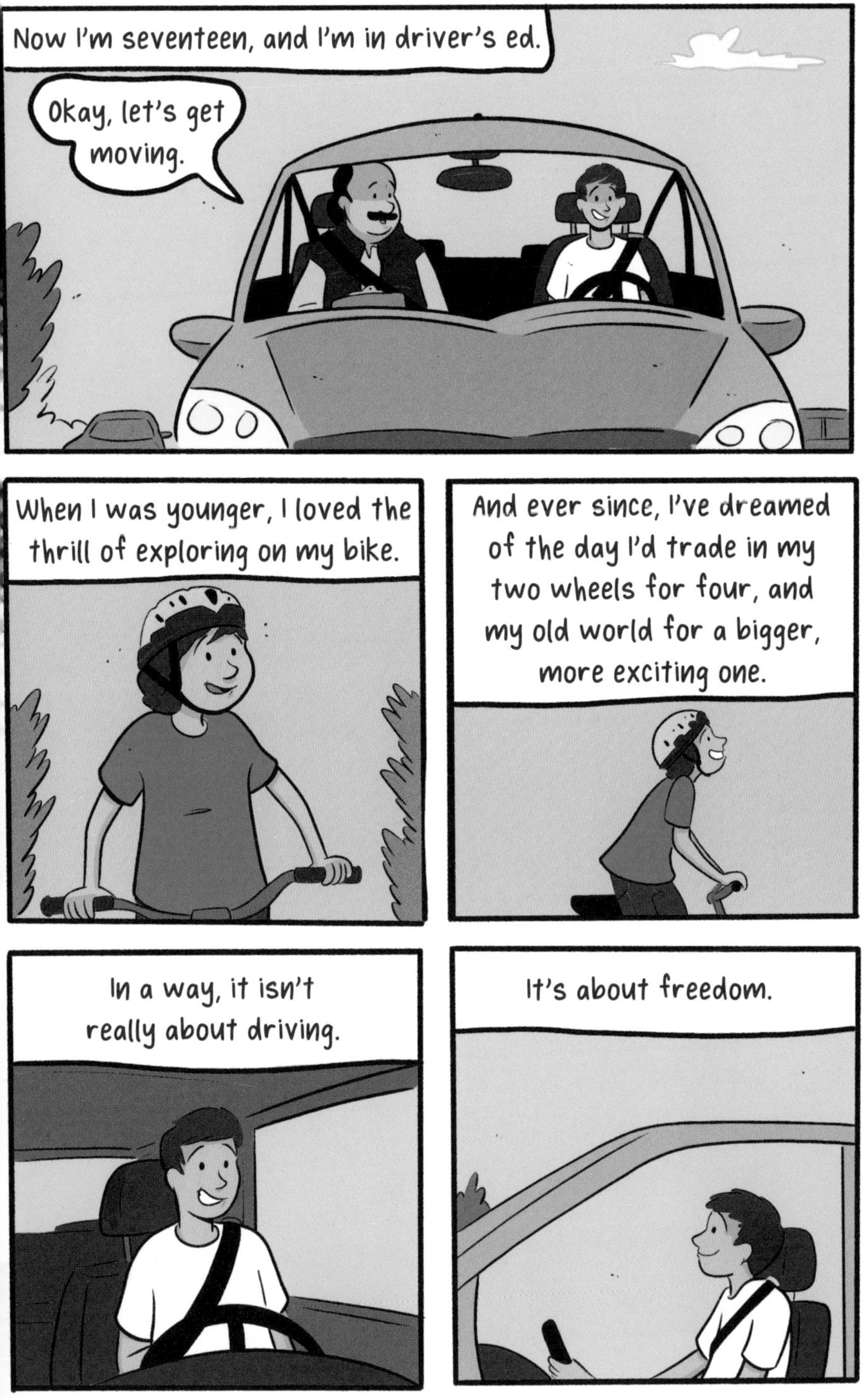
Now I'm seventeen, and I'm in driver's ed.
Okay, let's get moving.
When I was younger, I loved the thrill of exploring on my bike.
And ever since, I've dreamed of the day I'd trade in my two wheels for four, and my old world for a bigger, more exciting one.
In a way, it isn't really about driving.
It's about freedom.

Although, it's hard to feel free when I still spend so much time in my head.

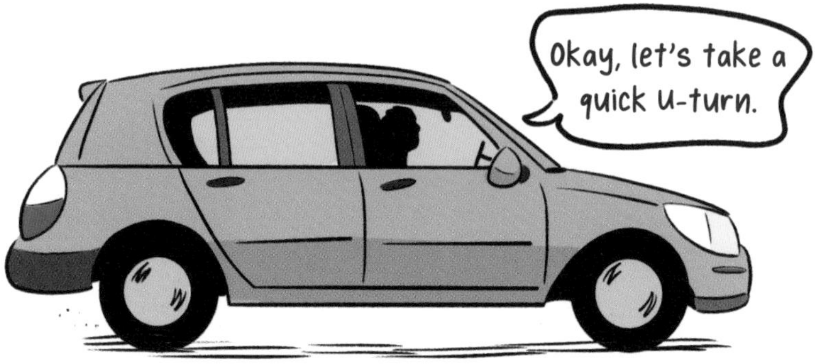
Okay, let's take a quick U-turn.

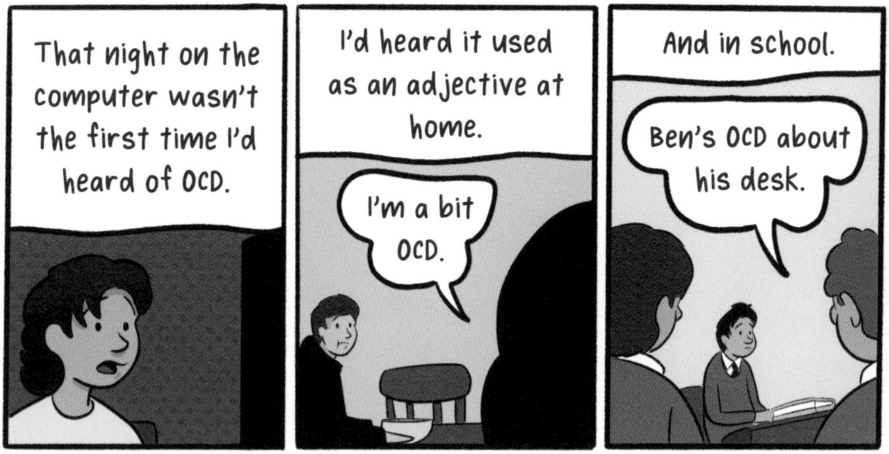
That night on the computer wasn't the first time I'd heard of OCD.
I'd heard it used as an adjective at home.
I'm a bit OCD.
And in school.
Ben's OCD about his desk.

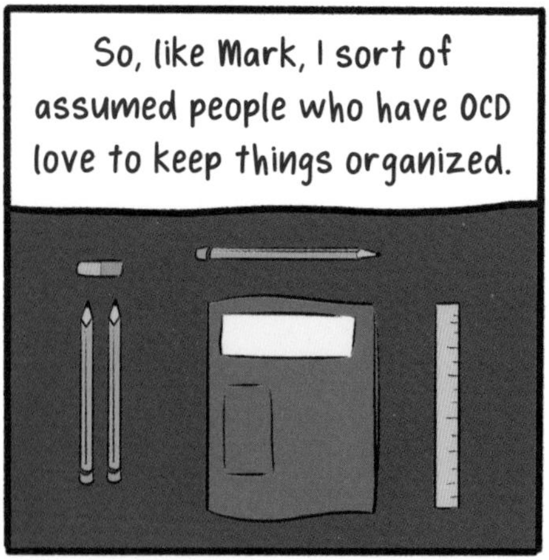
So, like Mark, I sort of assumed people who have OCD love to keep things organized.

For example, Monica Geller, the quirky neat freak in *Friends*.

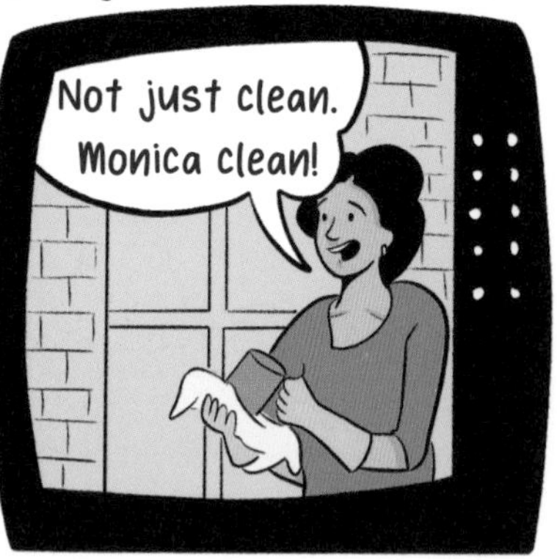
Not just clean. Monica clean!

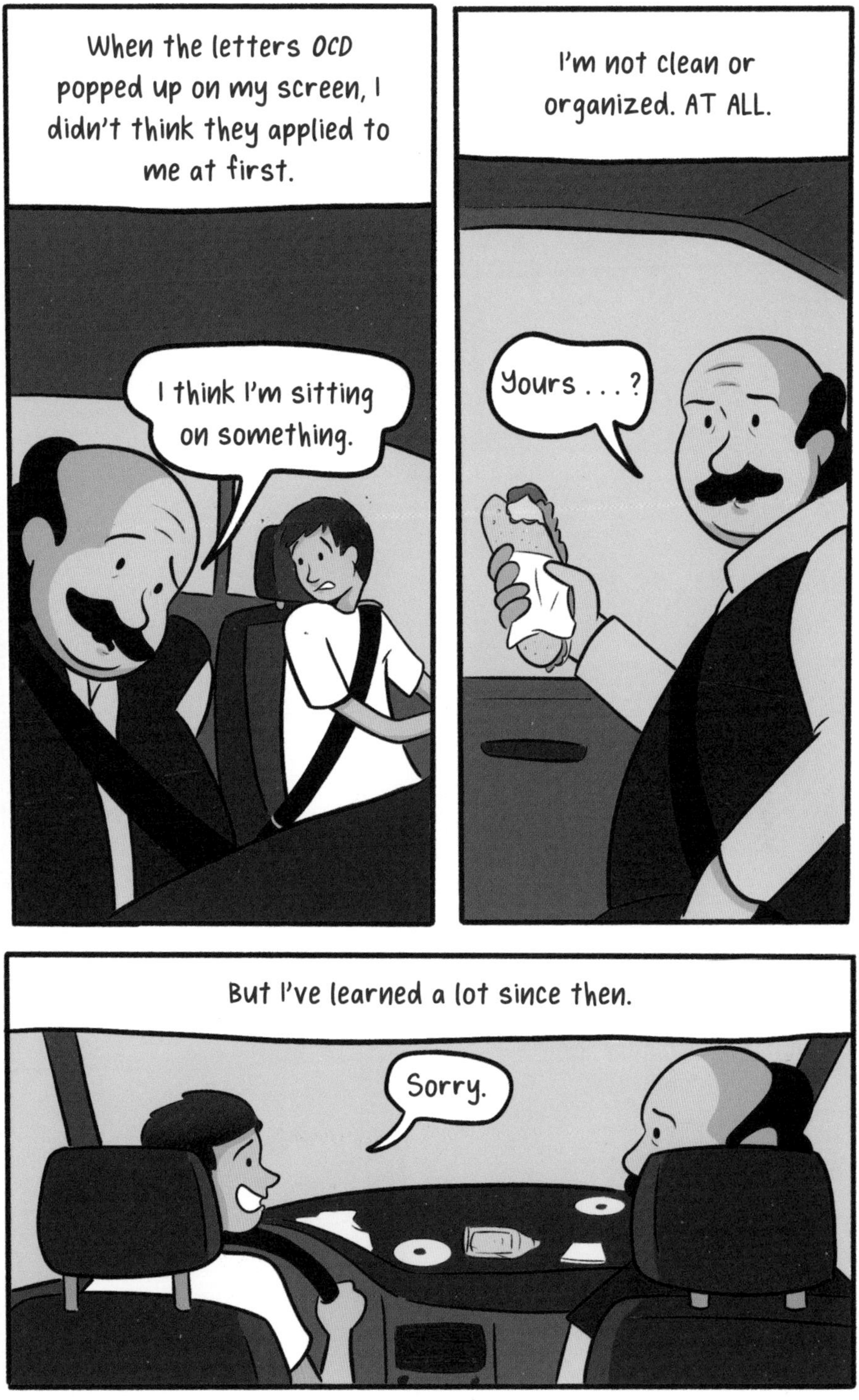
When the letters *OCD* popped up on my screen, I didn't think they applied to me at first.
I think I'm sitting on something.
I'm not clean or organized. AT ALL.
Yours . . . ?
But I've learned a lot since then.
Sorry.

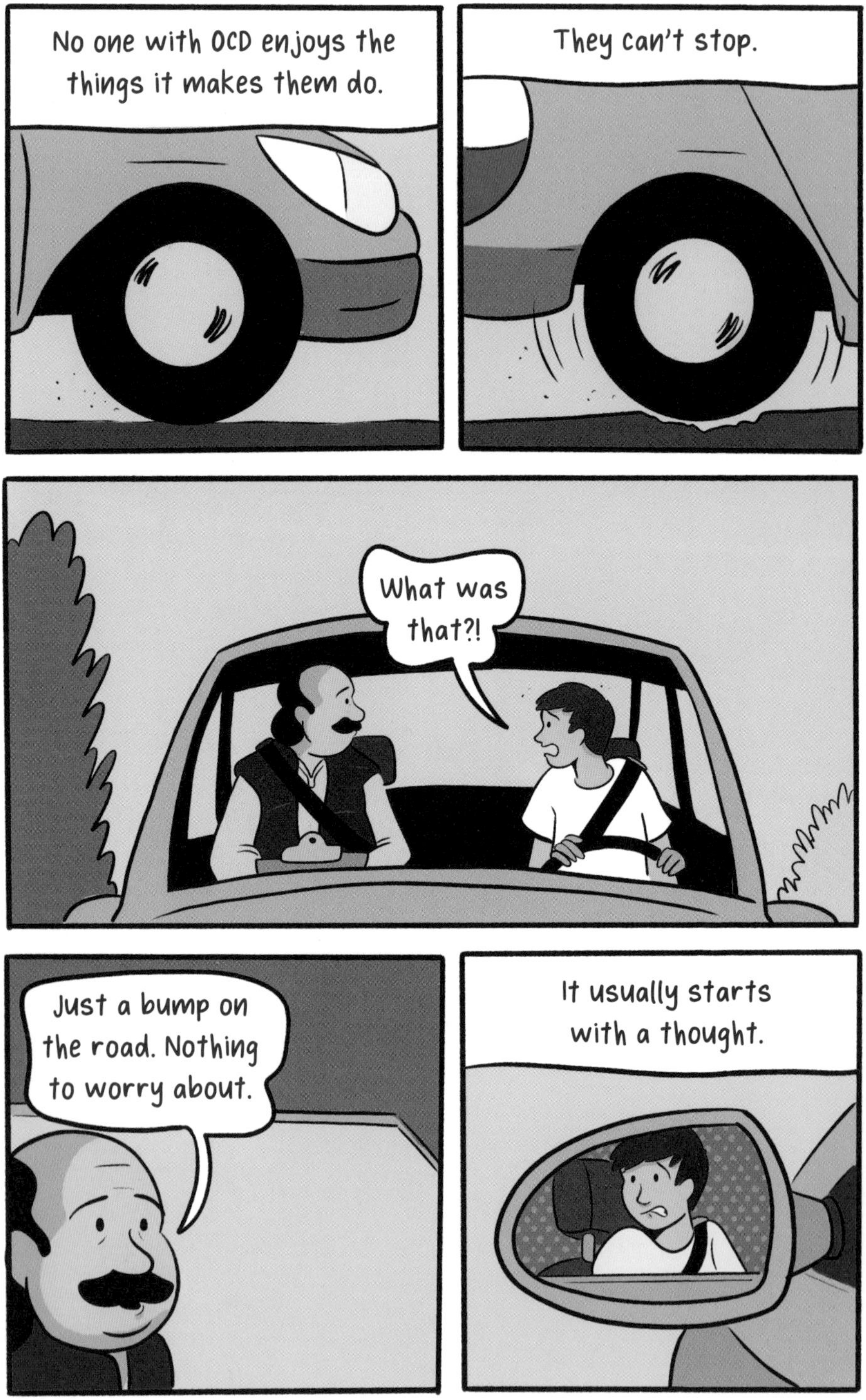
No one with OCD enjoys the things it makes them do.
They can't stop.
What was that?!
Just a bump on the road. Nothing to worry about.
It usually starts with a thought.

Like the one I'm having right now.

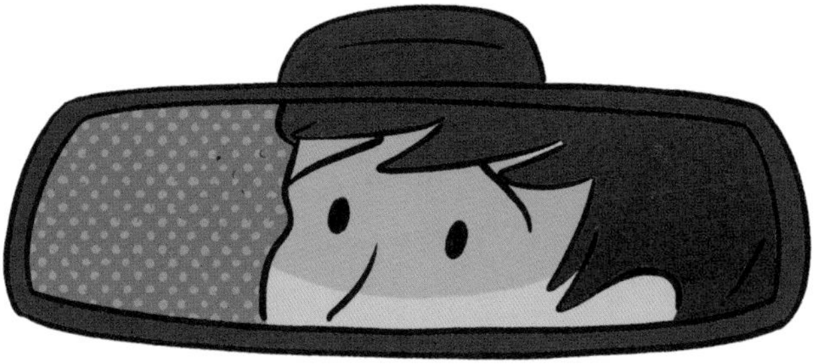

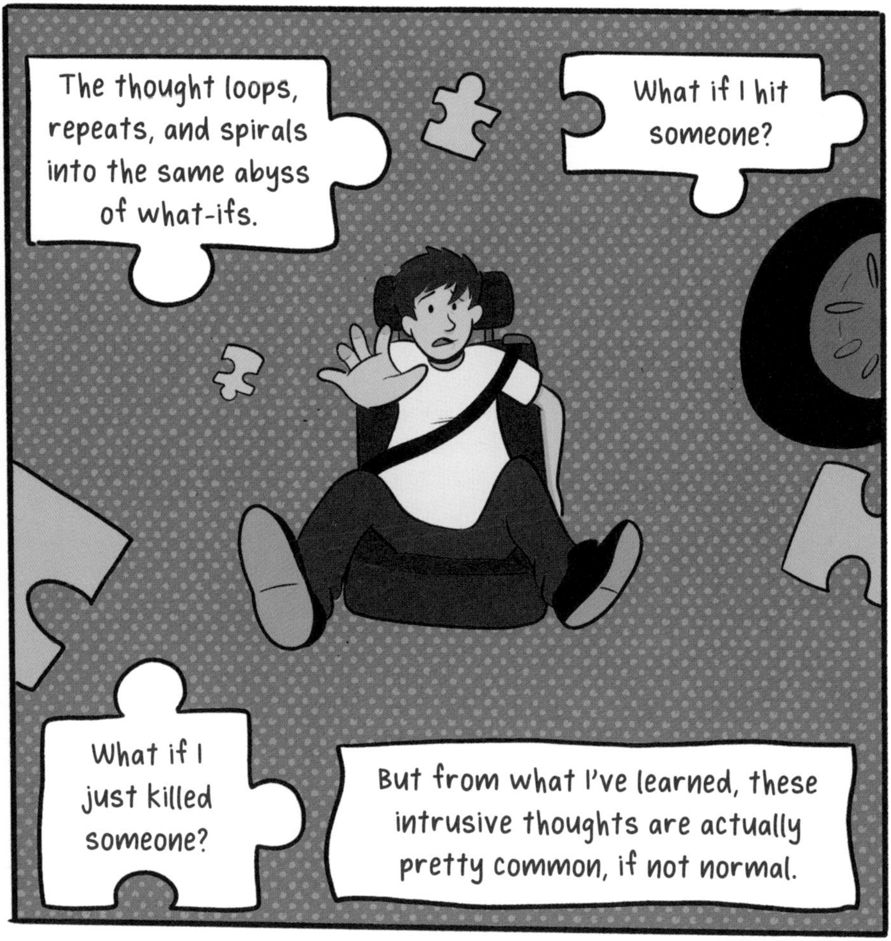

The thought loops, repeats, and spirals into the same abyss of what-ifs.
What if I hit someone?
What if I just killed someone?
But from what I've learned, these intrusive thoughts are actually pretty common, if not normal.

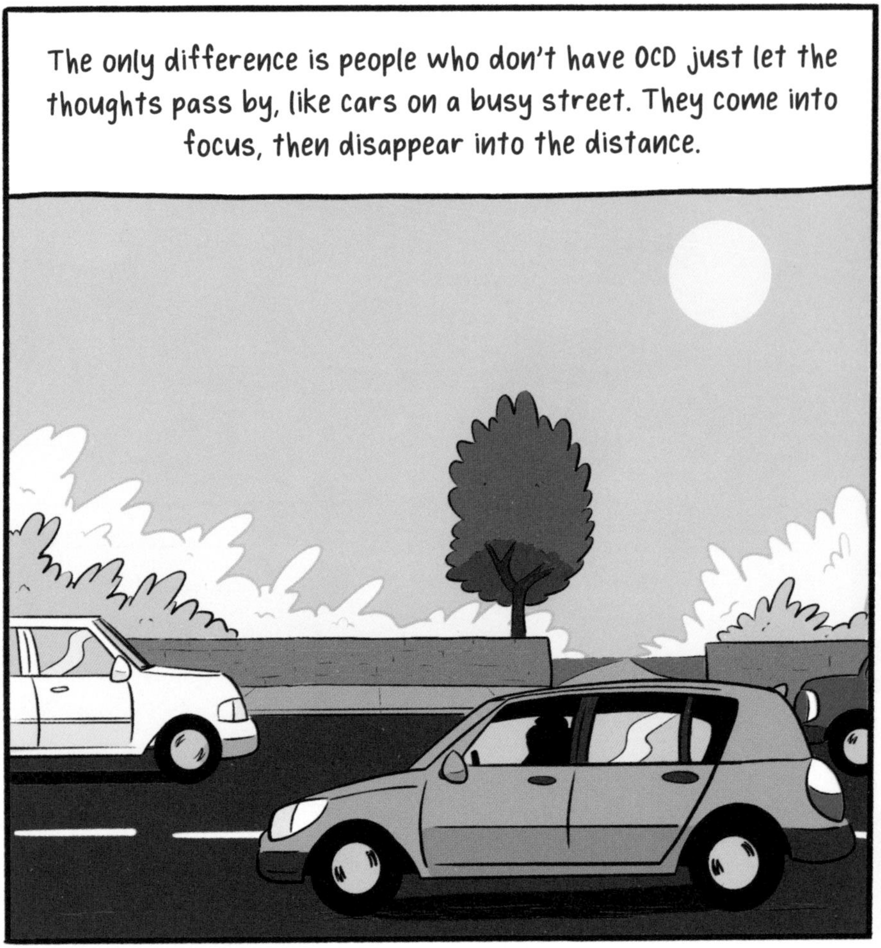
The only difference is people who don't have OCD just let the thoughts pass by, like cars on a busy street. They come into focus, then disappear into the distance.

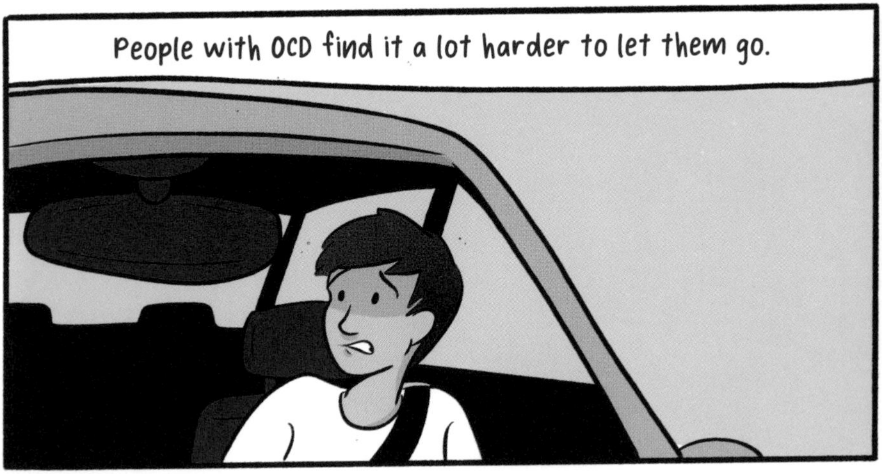
People with OCD find it a lot harder to let them go.

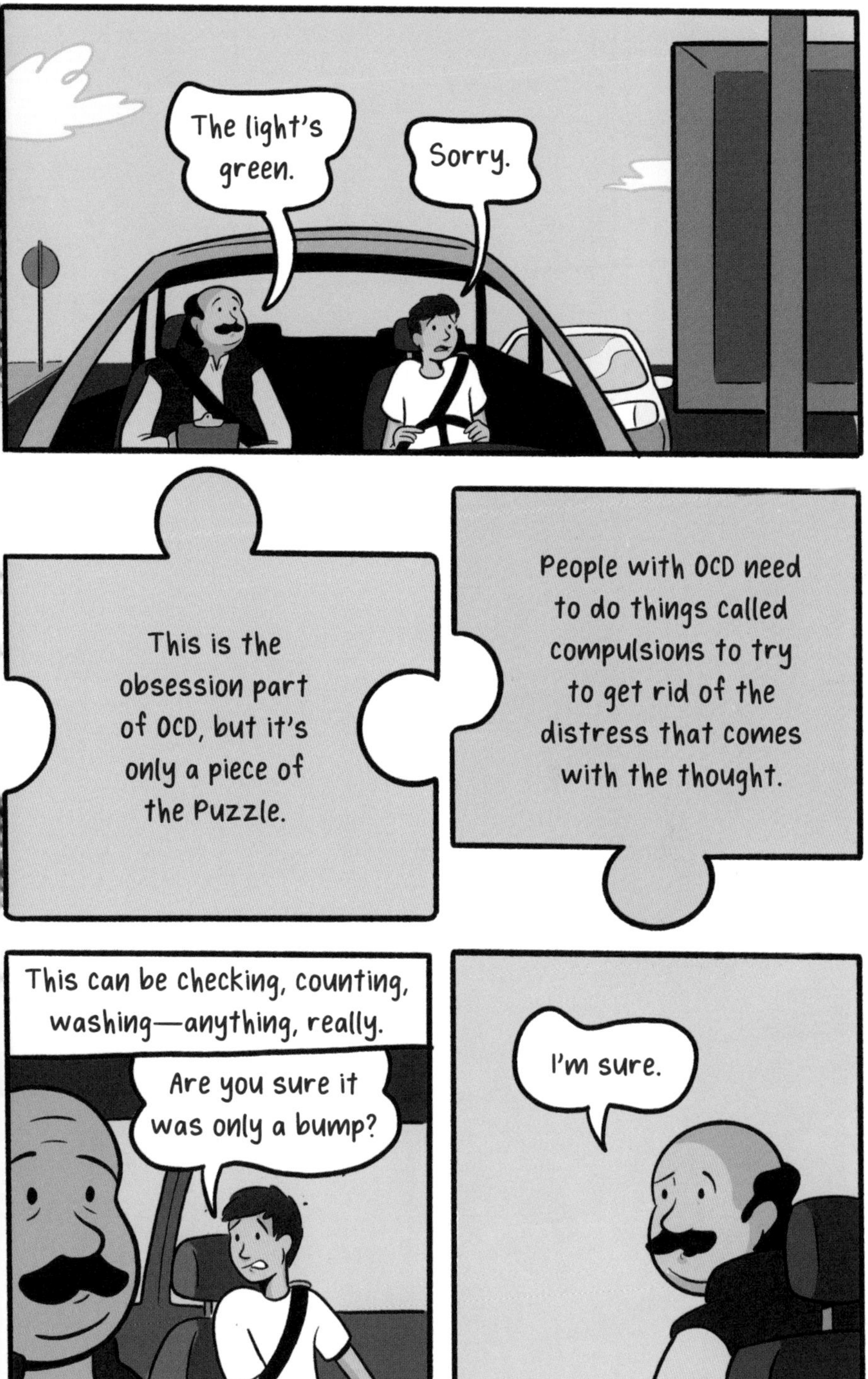

The light's green.
Sorry.
This is the obsession part of OCD, but it's only a piece of the puzzle.
People with OCD need to do things called compulsions to try to get rid of the distress that comes with the thought.
This can be checking, counting, washing—anything, really.
Are you sure it was only a bump?
I'm sure.

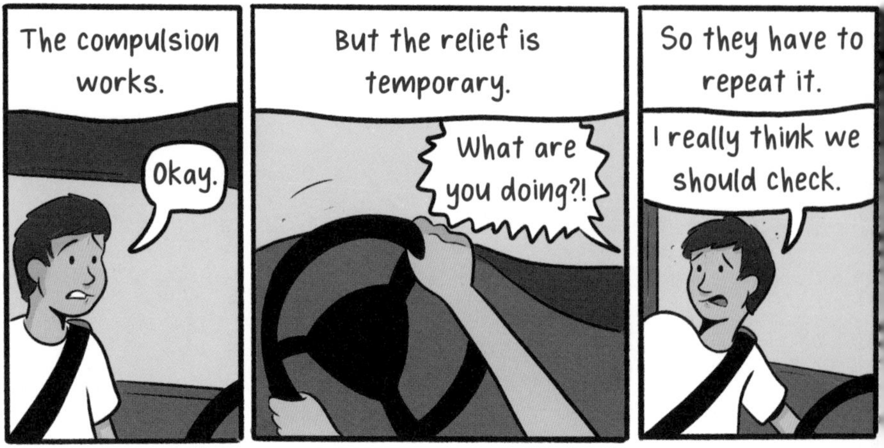
The compulsion works.
Okay.
But the relief is temporary.
What are you doing?!
So they have to repeat it.
I really think we should check.

The person gets trapped in a loop of having an intrusive thought, performing a compulsion, getting relief, the relief fading, then having to begin again.

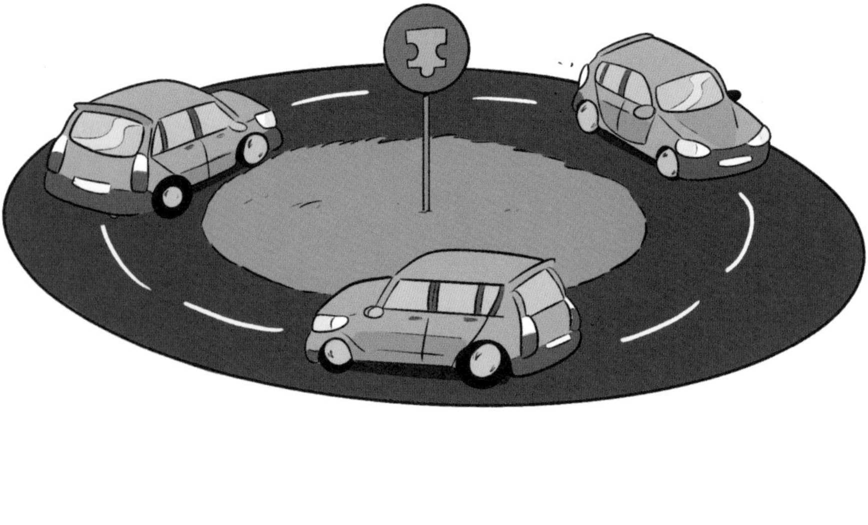

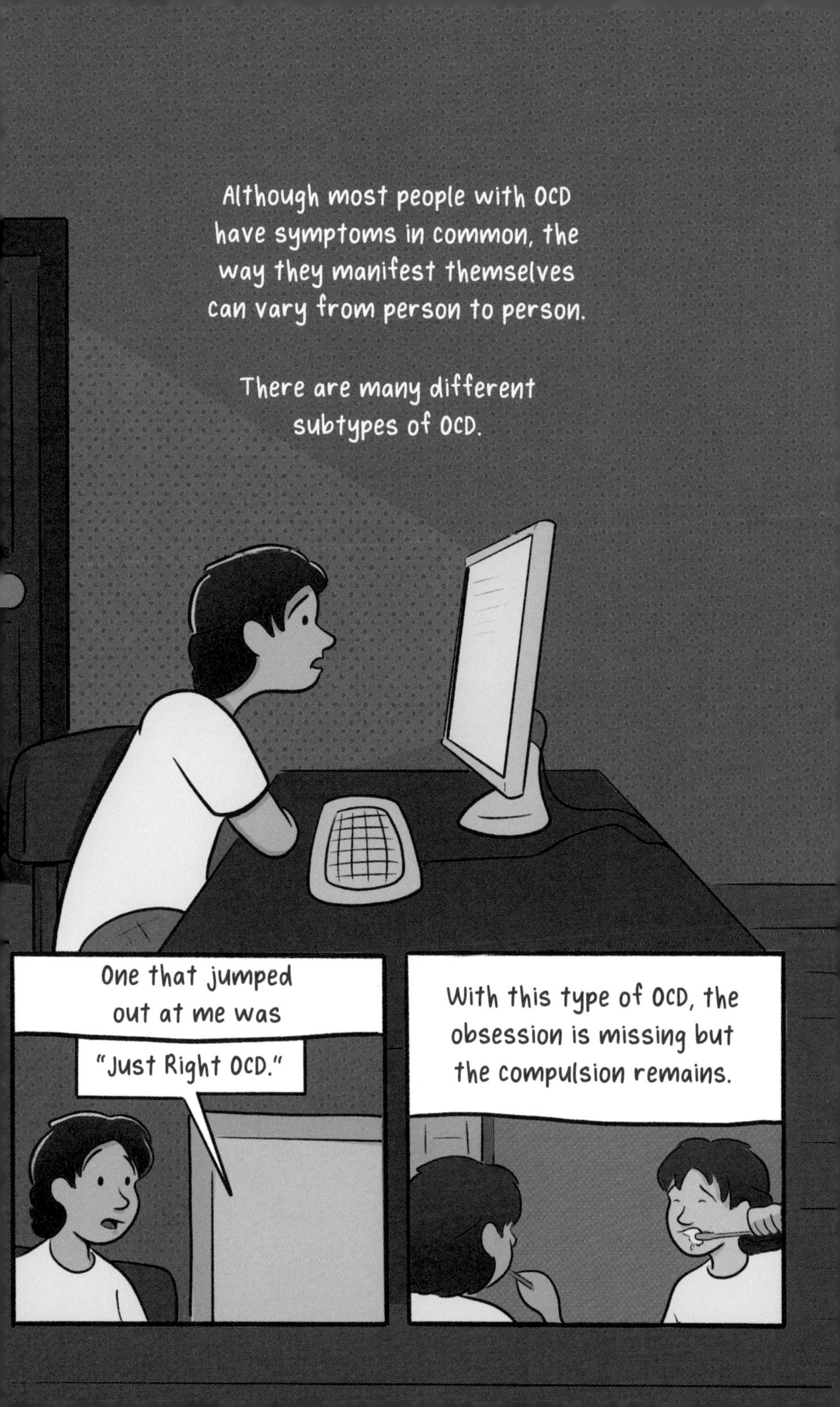
Although most people with OCD have symptoms in common, the way they manifest themselves can vary from person to person.
There are many different subtypes of OCD.
One that jumped out at me was
"Just Right OCD."
With this type of OCD, the obsession is missing but the compulsion remains.

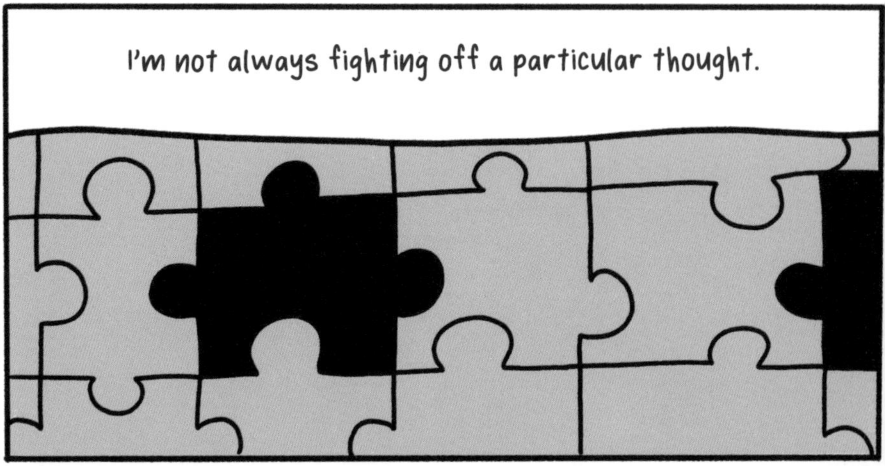
I'm not always fighting off a particular thought.

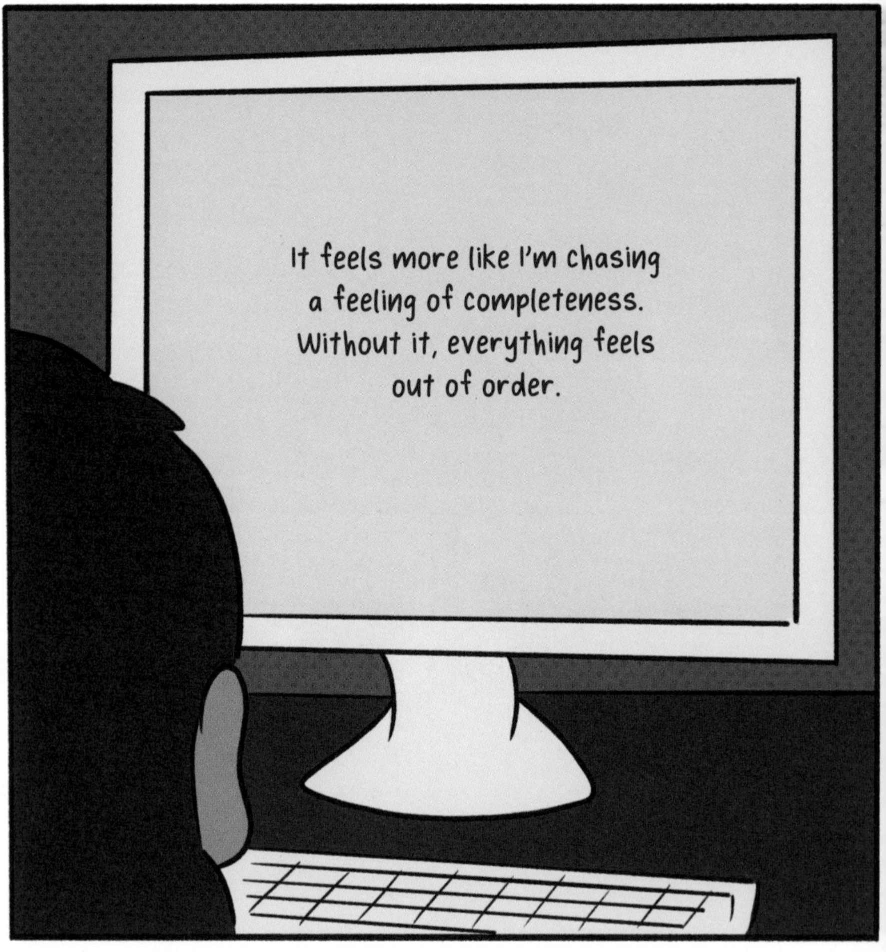
It feels more like I'm chasing a feeling of completeness. Without it, everything feels out of order.

I couldn't believe how varied OCD is. It's nothing like what I had thought.

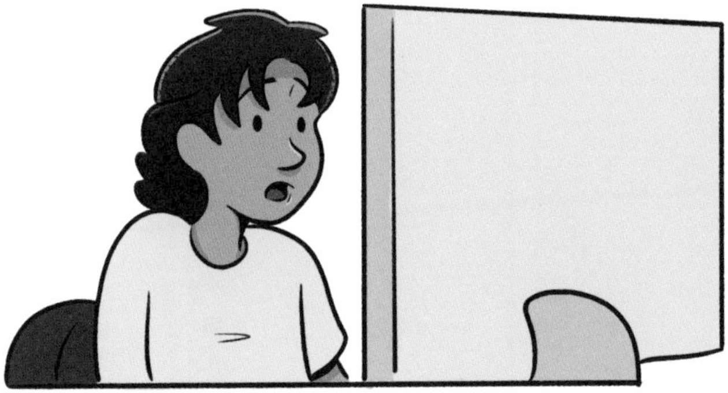

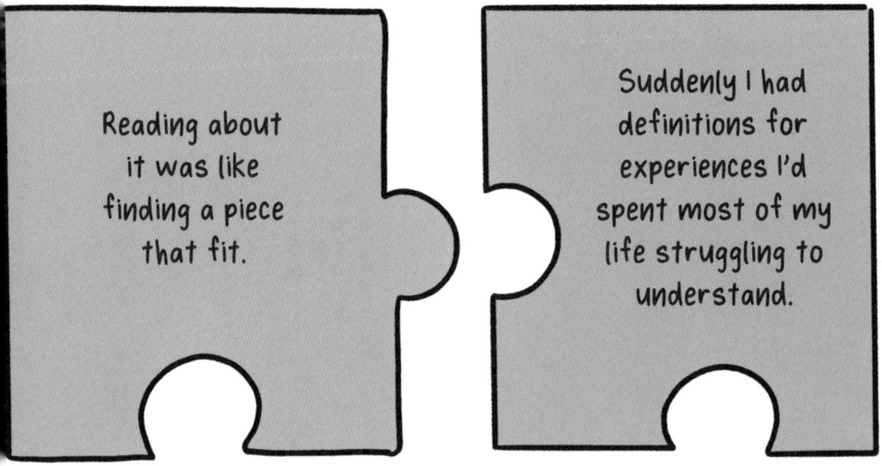
Reading about it was like finding a piece that fit.
Suddenly I had definitions for experiences I'd spent most of my life struggling to understand.

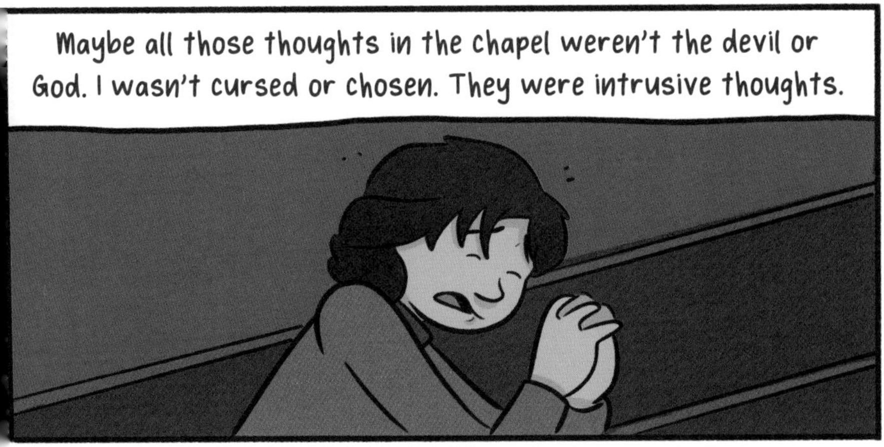
Maybe all those thoughts in the chapel weren't the devil or God. I wasn't cursed or chosen. They were intrusive thoughts.

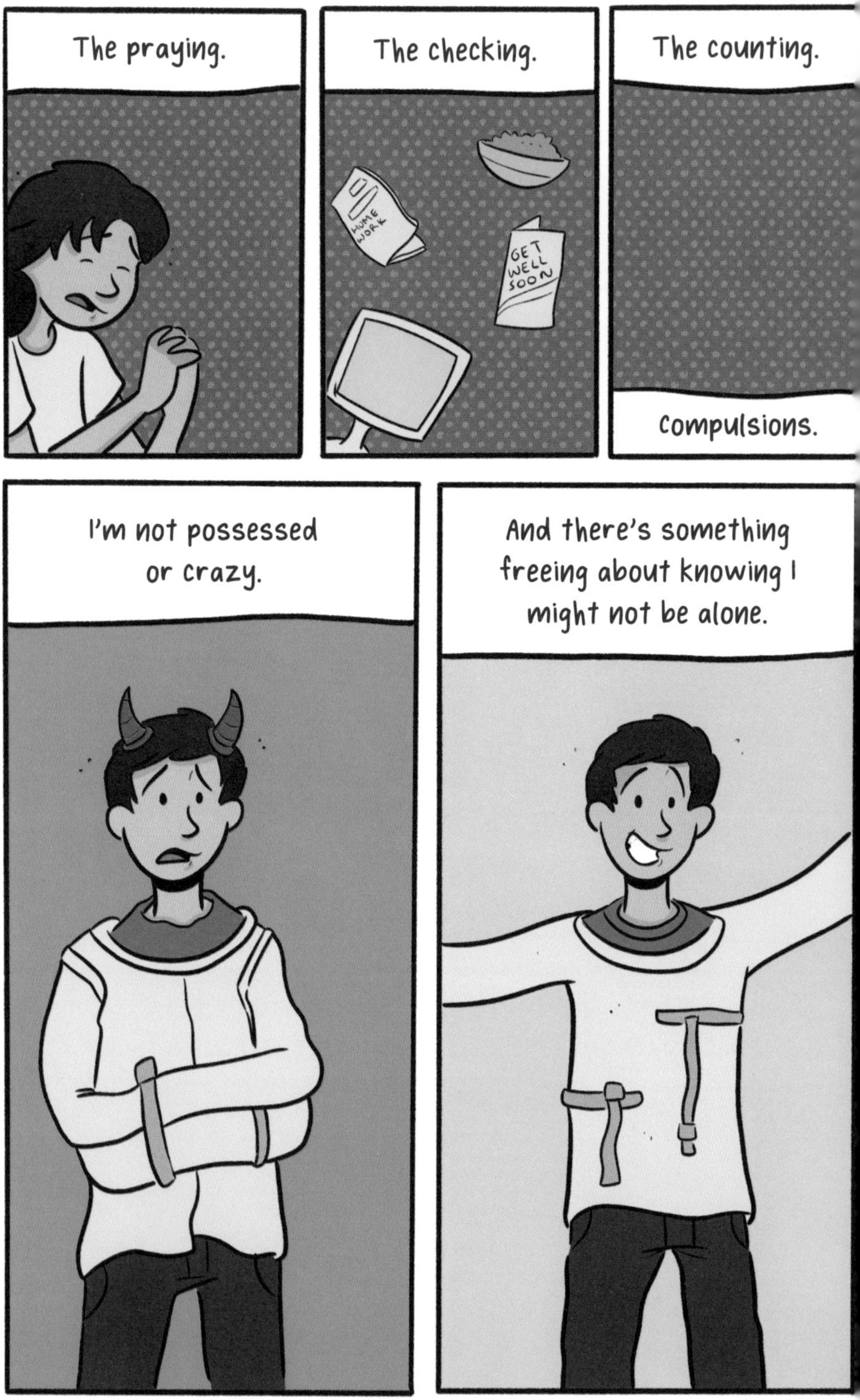
The praying.
The checking.
HOME WORK
GET WELL SOON
The counting.
Compulsions.
I'm not possessed or crazy.
And there's something freeing about knowing I might not be alone.

In fact, I'm in pretty good company.

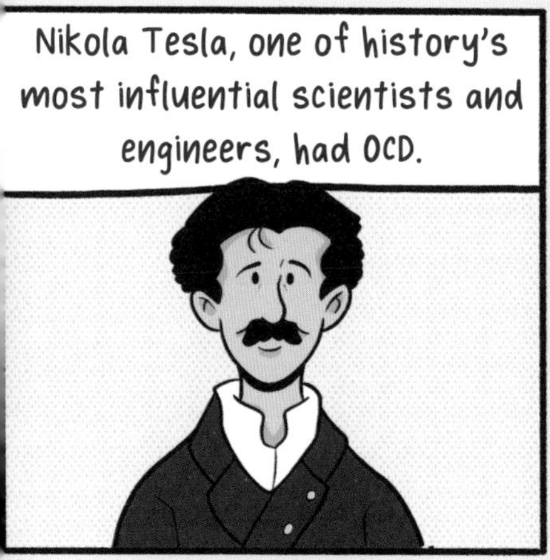
Nikola Tesla, one of history's most influential scientists and engineers, had OCD.

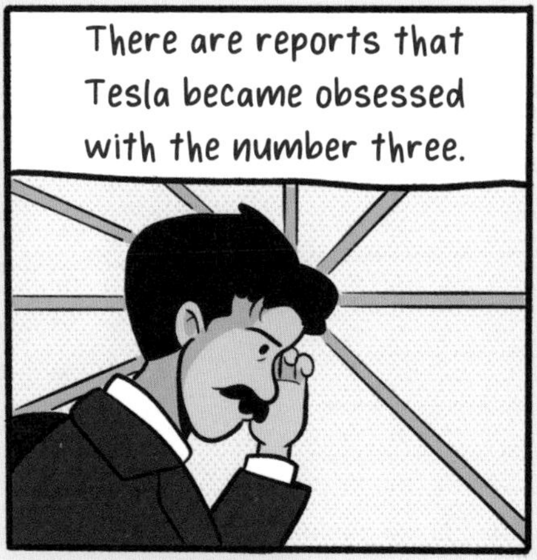
There are reports that Tesla became obsessed with the number three.

Apparently, he would swim thirty-three laps at his local pool as part of his daily routine.

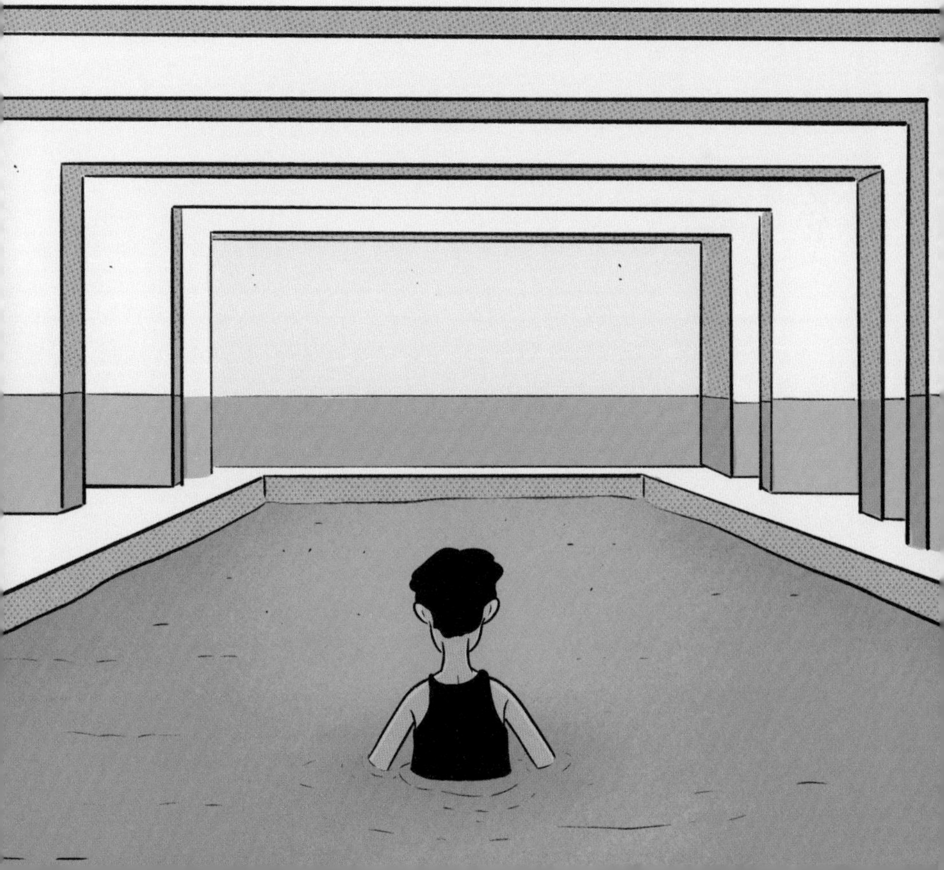

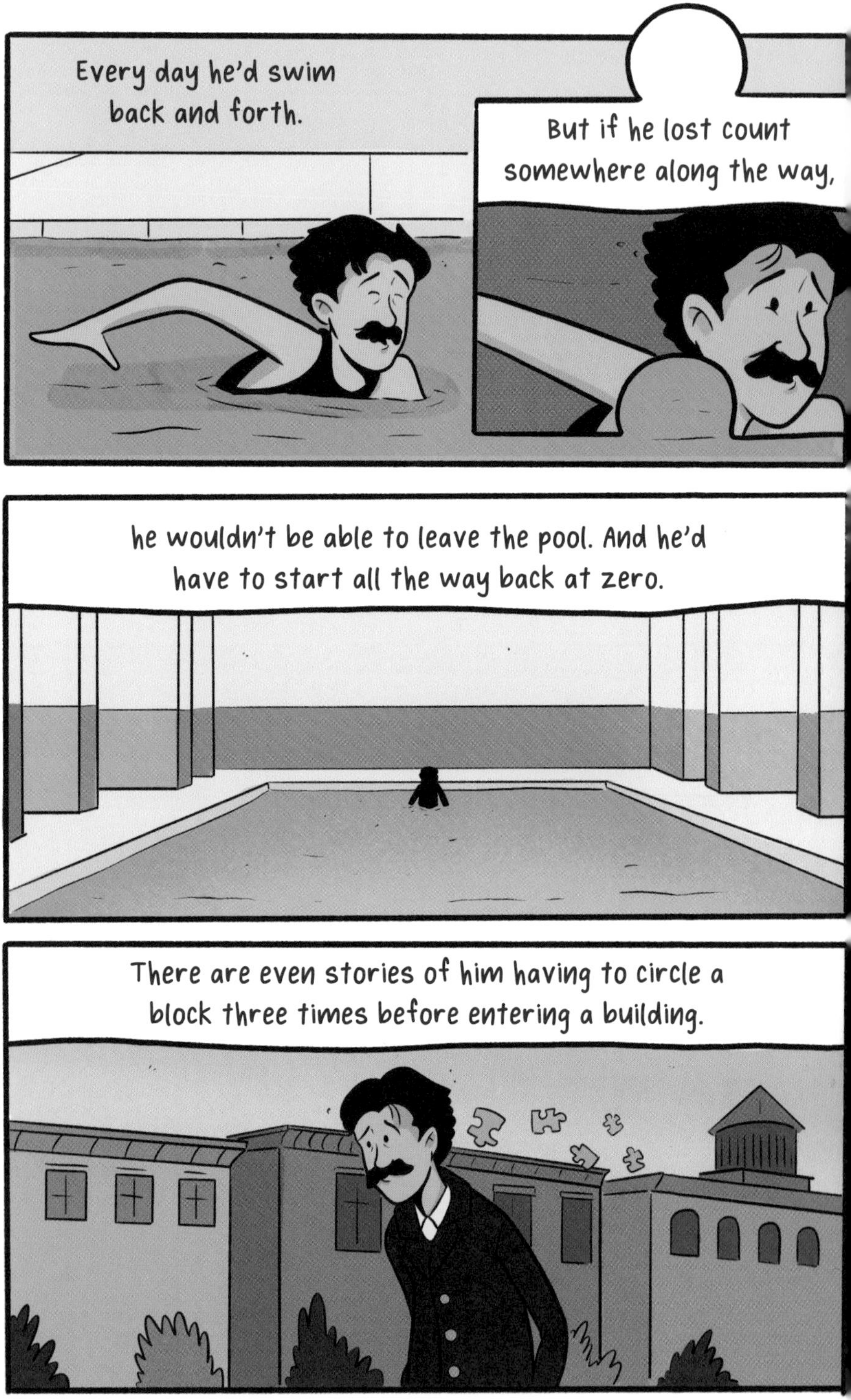
Every day he'd swim back and forth.
But if he lost count somewhere along the way,
he wouldn't be able to leave the pool. And he'd have to start all the way back at zero.
There are even stories of him having to circle a block three times before entering a building.

Another influential person with OCD was American manufacturer, aviator, motion-picture producer, and director Howard Hughes.

In 1937, Hughes broke the transcontinental US speed record in one of his planes.

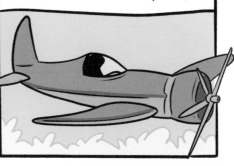

But despite this fearlessness in the cockpit, later in his life, Hughes became consumed by obsessive thoughts.

He would burn his entire wardrobe if he felt it had been exposed to germs.

Toward the end of his life, his health fears became so intense, he fired all his staff and isolated himself inside a hotel suite.

Where he would spend all day lying naked in bed with tissue boxes on his feet in what he considered a germ-free zone.

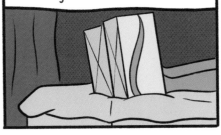

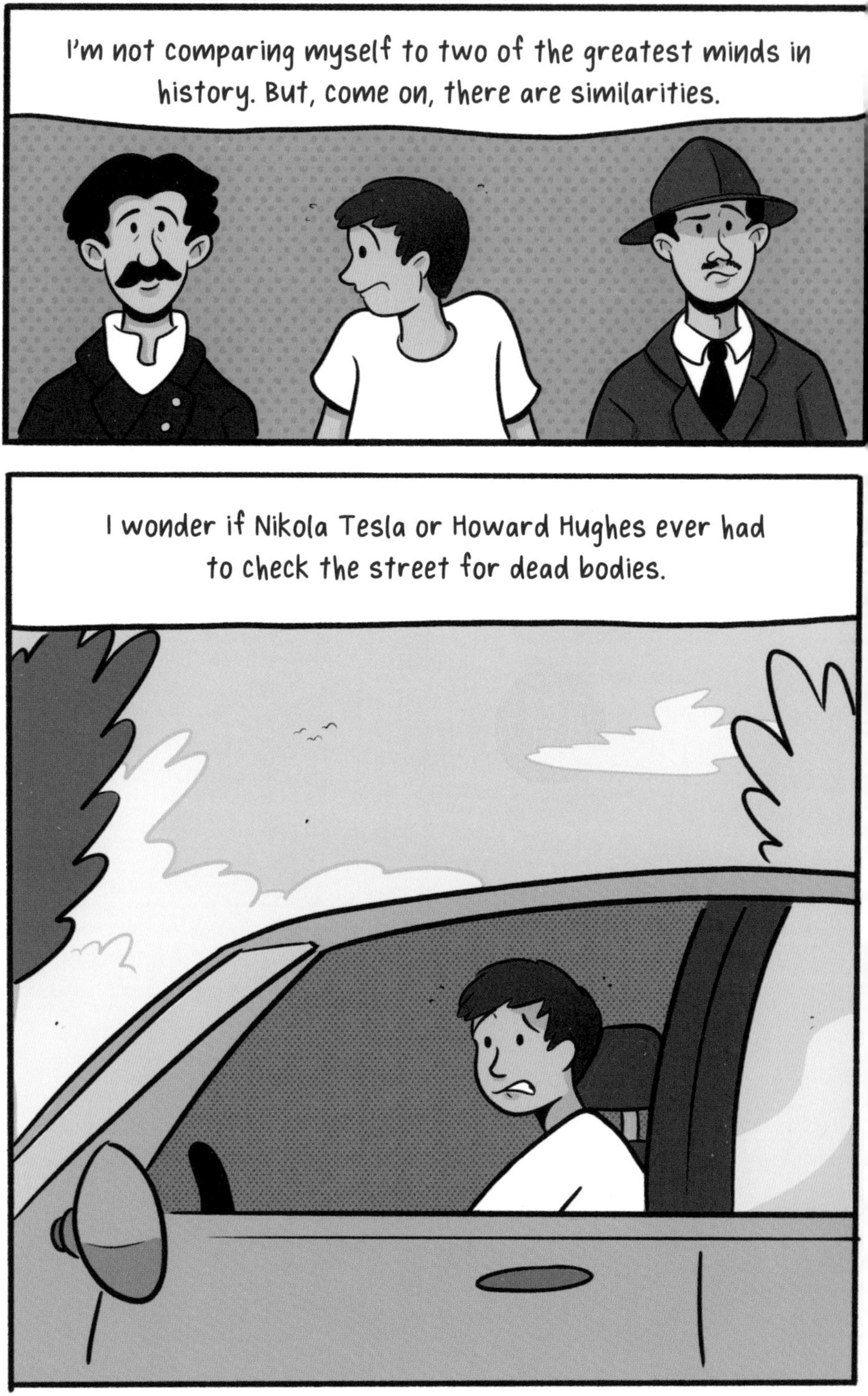
I'm not comparing myself to two of the greatest minds in history. But, come on, there are similarities.
I wonder if Nikola Tesla or Howard Hughes ever had to check the street for dead bodies.

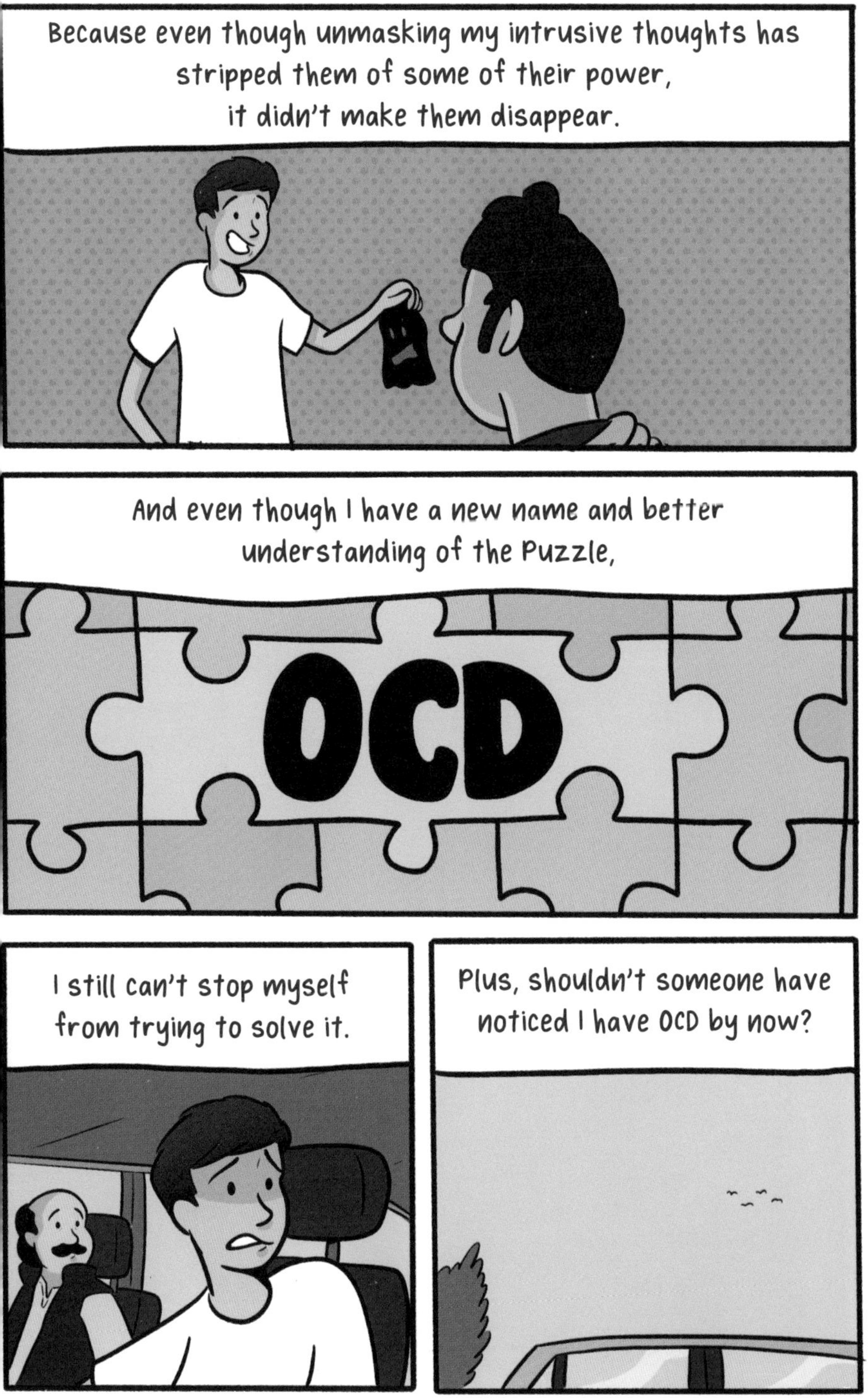
Because even though unmasking my intrusive thoughts has stripped them of some of their power, it didn't make them disappear.
And even though I have a new name and better understanding of the Puzzle,
OCD
I still can't stop myself from trying to solve it.
Plus, shouldn't someone have noticed I have OCD by now?

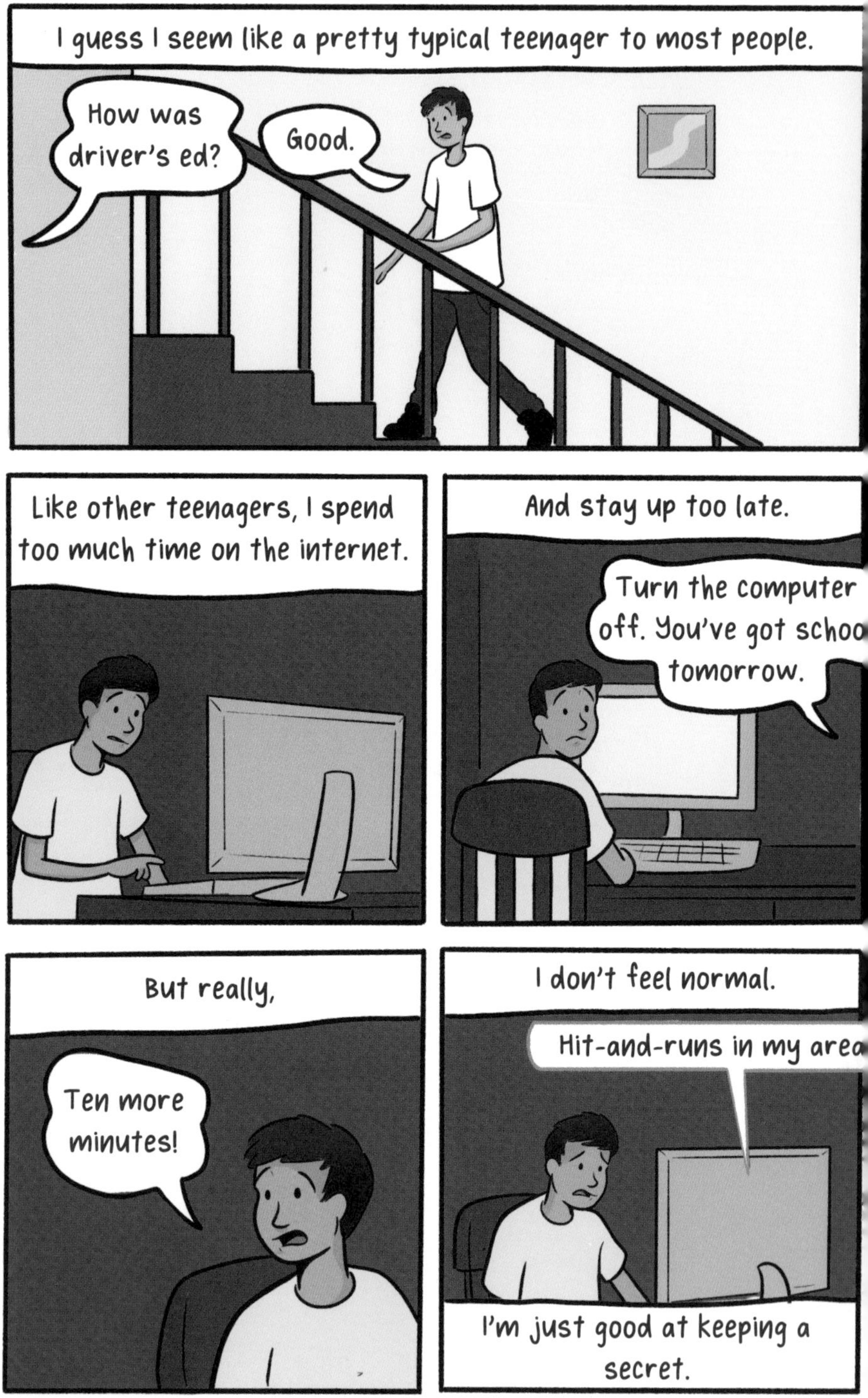
I guess I seem like a pretty typical teenager to most people.
How was driver's ed?
Good.
Like other teenagers, I spend too much time on the internet.
And stay up too late.
Turn the computer off. You've got schoo
tomorrow.
But really,
Ten more minutes!
I don't feel normal.
Hit-and-runs in my area
I'm just good at keeping a secret.

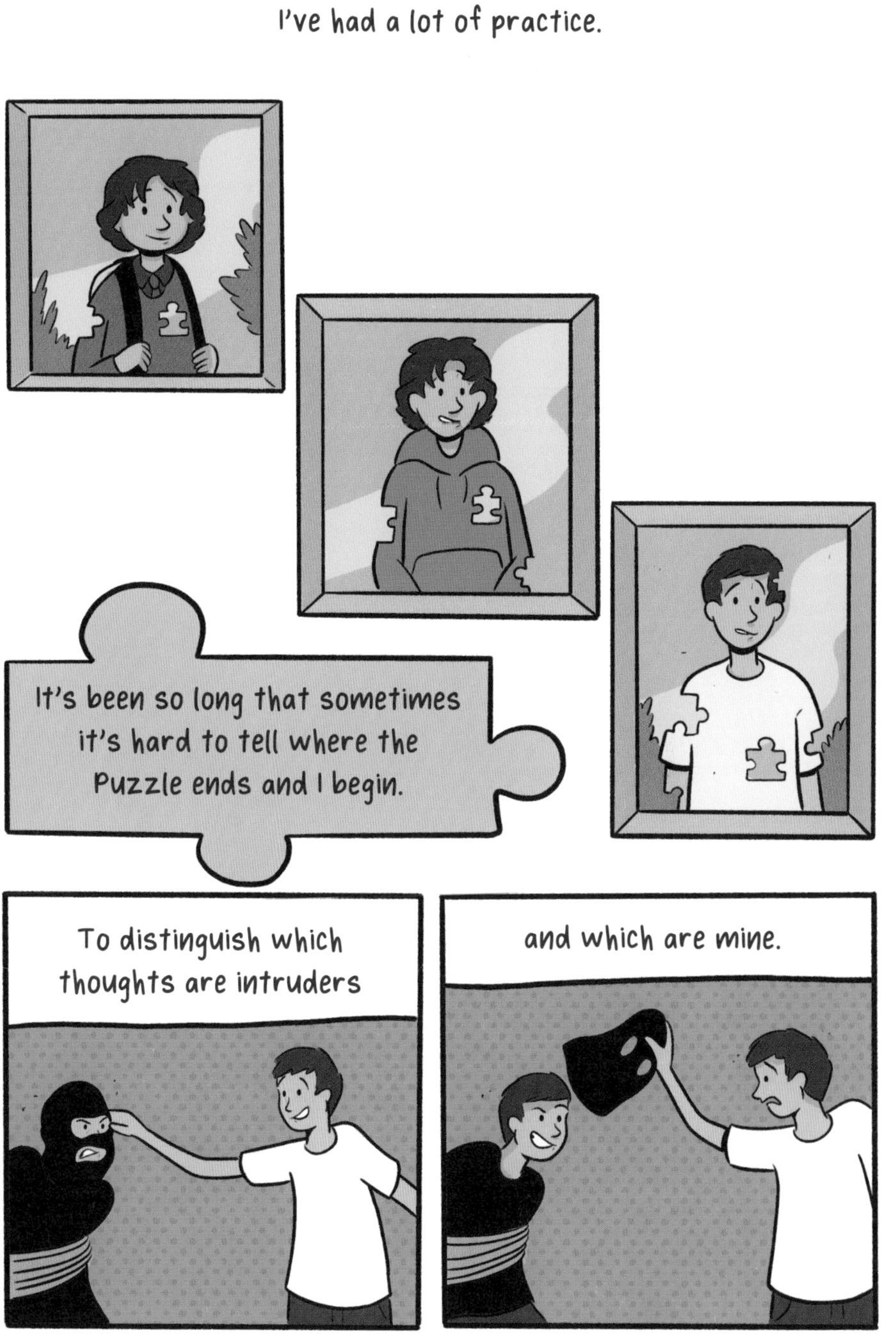

I've had a lot of practice.
It's been so long that sometimes it's hard to tell where the Puzzle ends and I begin.
To distinguish which thoughts are intruders
and which are mine.

But learning about OCD has made me realize the Puzzle isn't who I am, and more importantly—it's not my fault.

Which got me thinking—if it is a mental health issue, maybe I can get better?

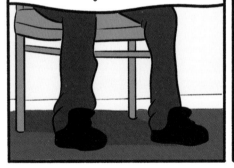

Maybe I just need to ask for help.

So here I am, nearly ten years after the Puzzle first showed up, about to do just that.

Pan? Come in.

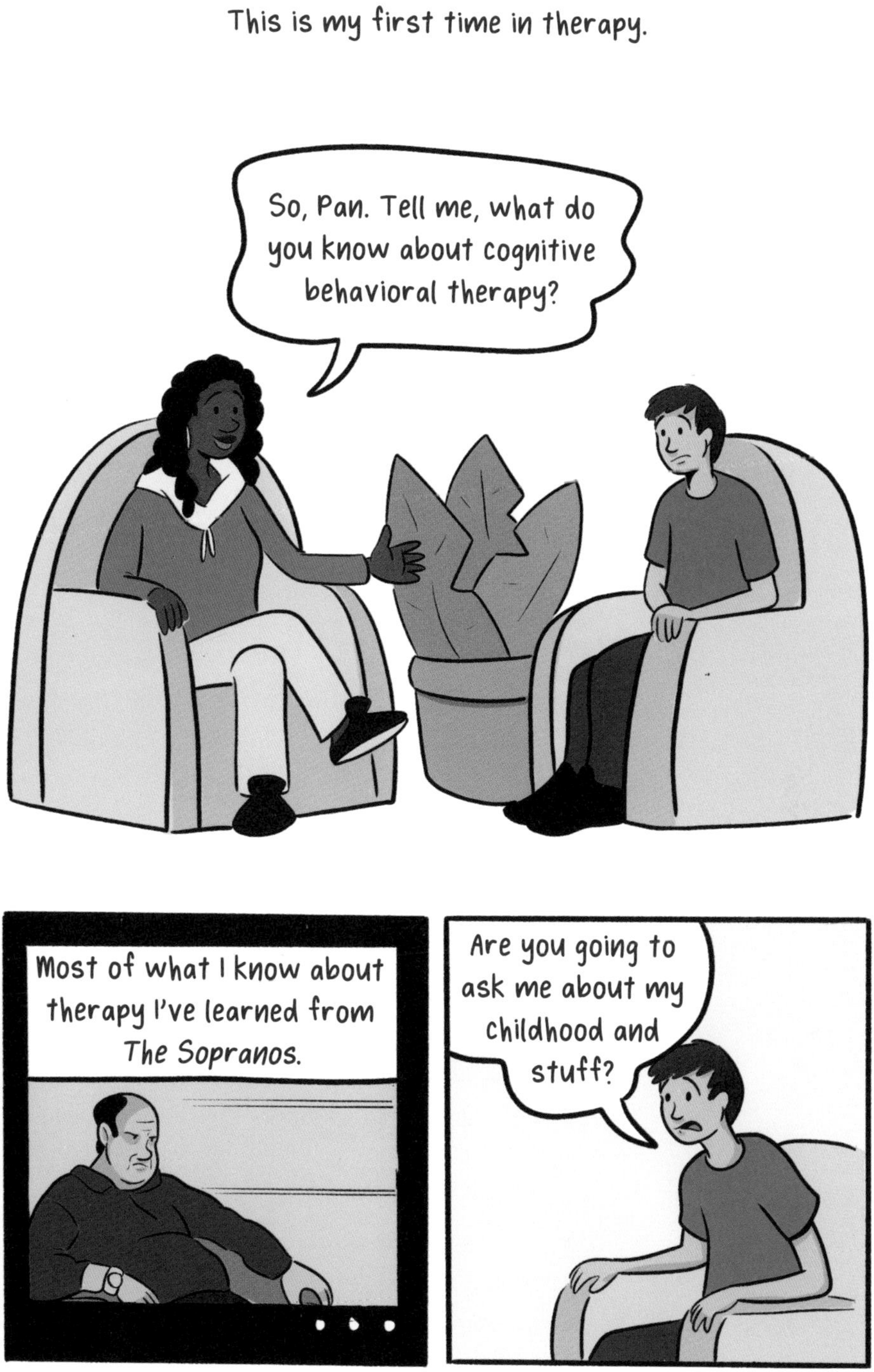
This is my first time in therapy.
So, Pan. Tell me, what do you know about cognitive behavioral therapy?
Most of what I know about therapy I've learned from *The Sopranos.*
Are you going to ask me about my childhood and stuff?

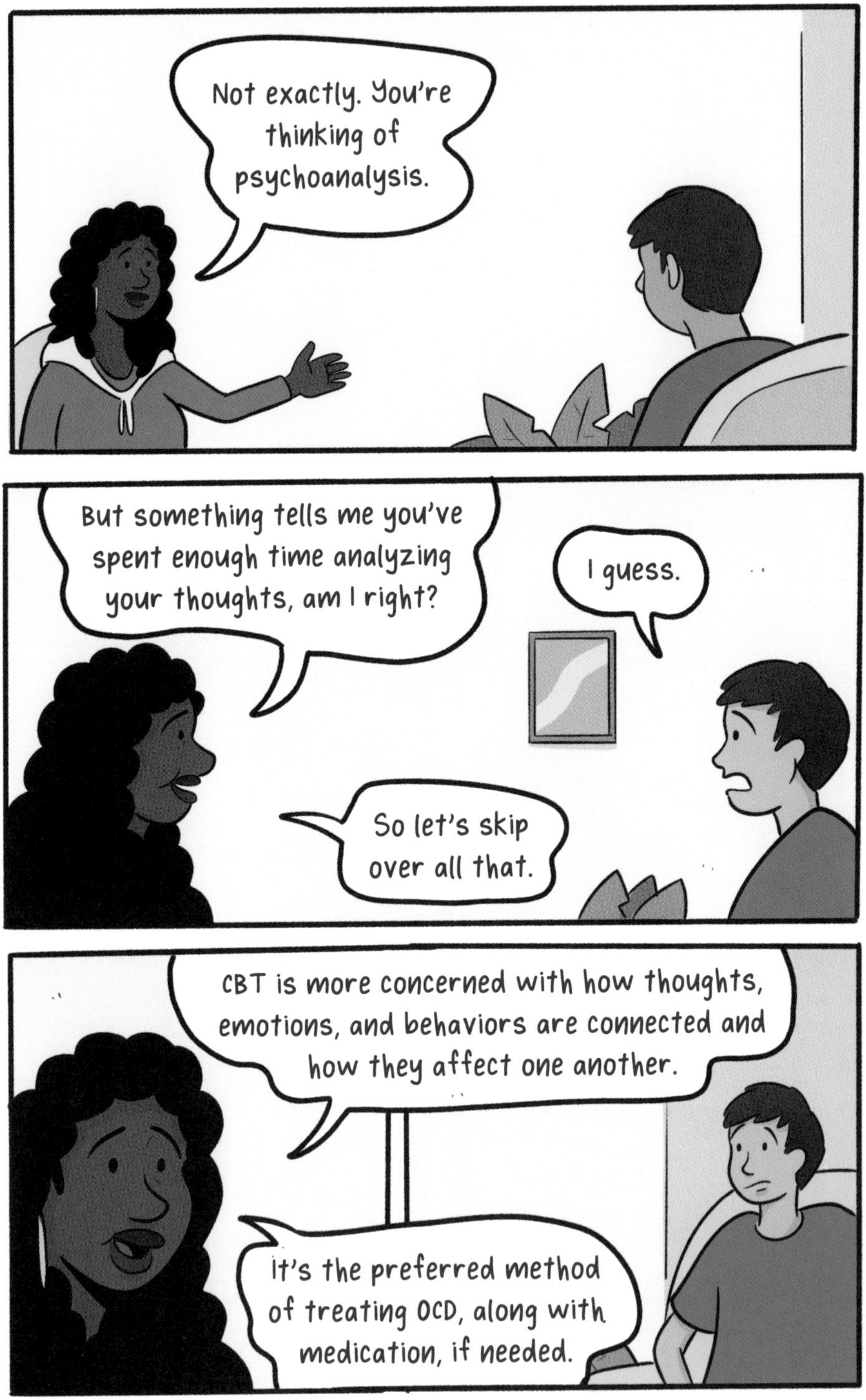
Not exactly. You're thinking of psychoanalysis.
But something tells me you've spent enough time analyzing your thoughts, am I right?
I guess.
So let's skip over all that.
CBT is more concerned with how thoughts, emotions, and behaviors are connected and how they affect one another.
It's the preferred method of treating OCD, along with medication, if needed.

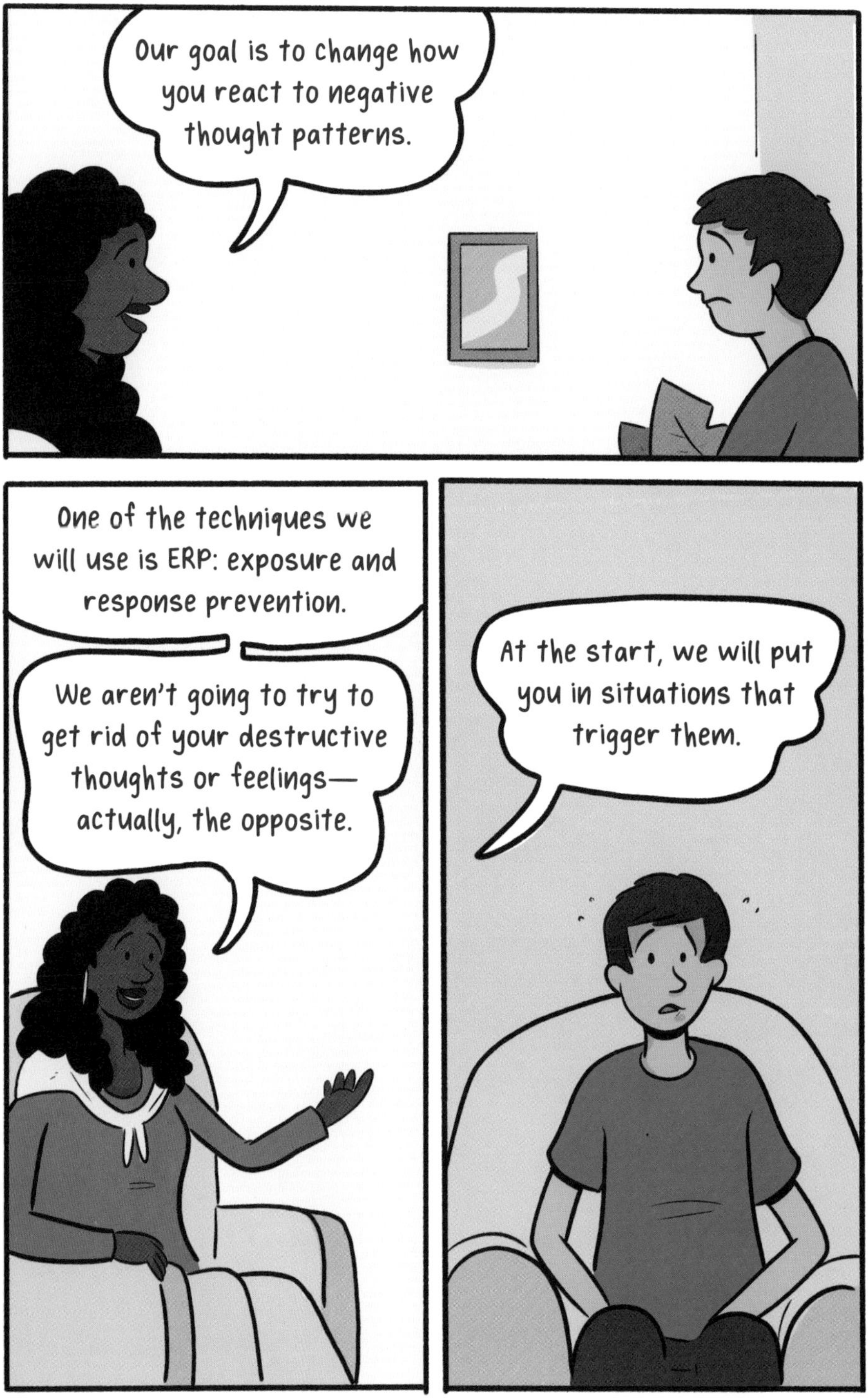
Our goal is to change how you react to negative thought patterns.
One of the techniques we will use is ERP: exposure and response prevention.
We aren't going to try to get rid of your destructive thoughts or feelings— actually, the opposite.
At the start, we will put you in situations that trigger them.

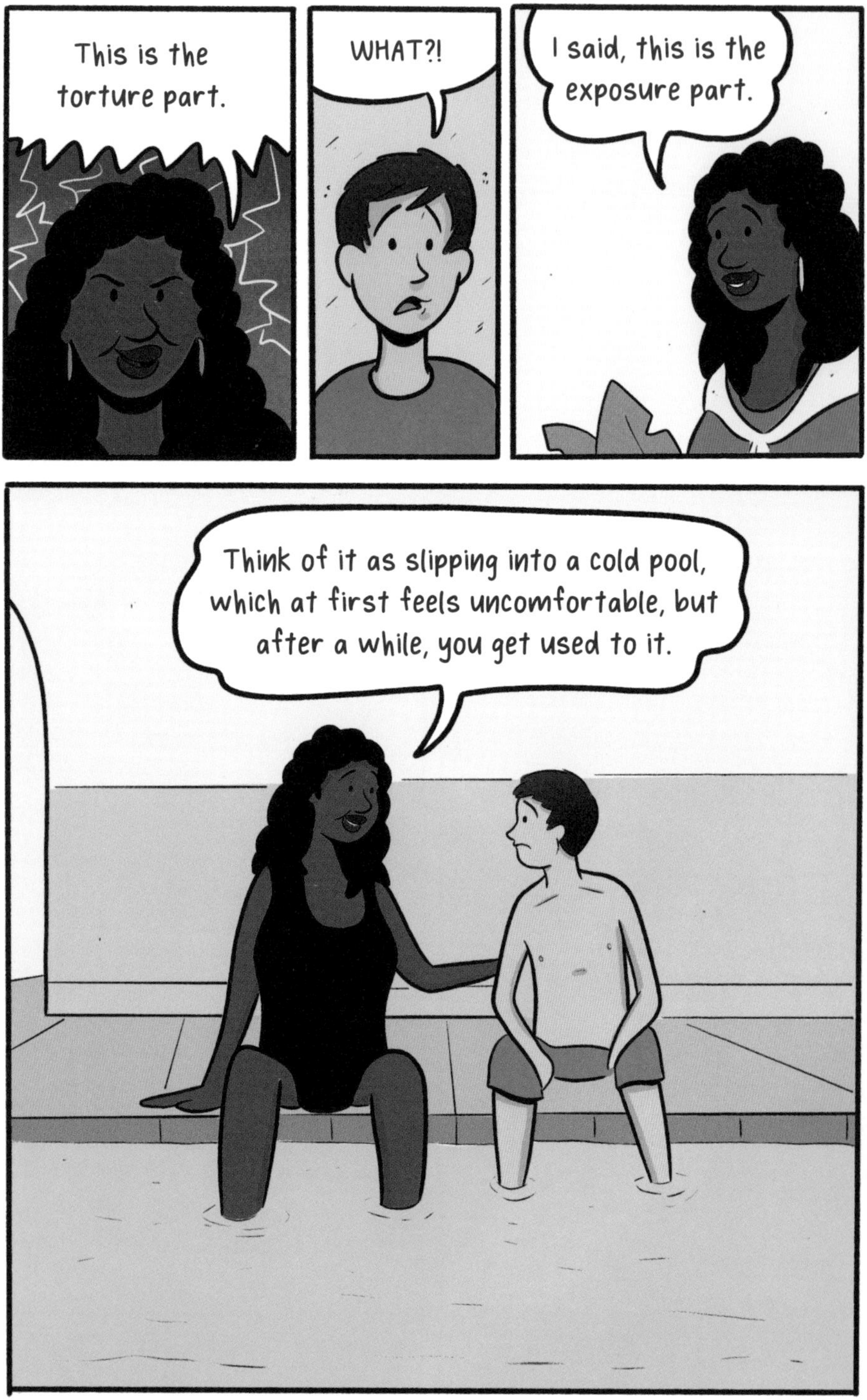
This is the torture part.
WHAT?!
I said, this is the exposure part.
Think of it as slipping into a cold pool, which at first feels uncomfortable, but after a while, you get used to it.

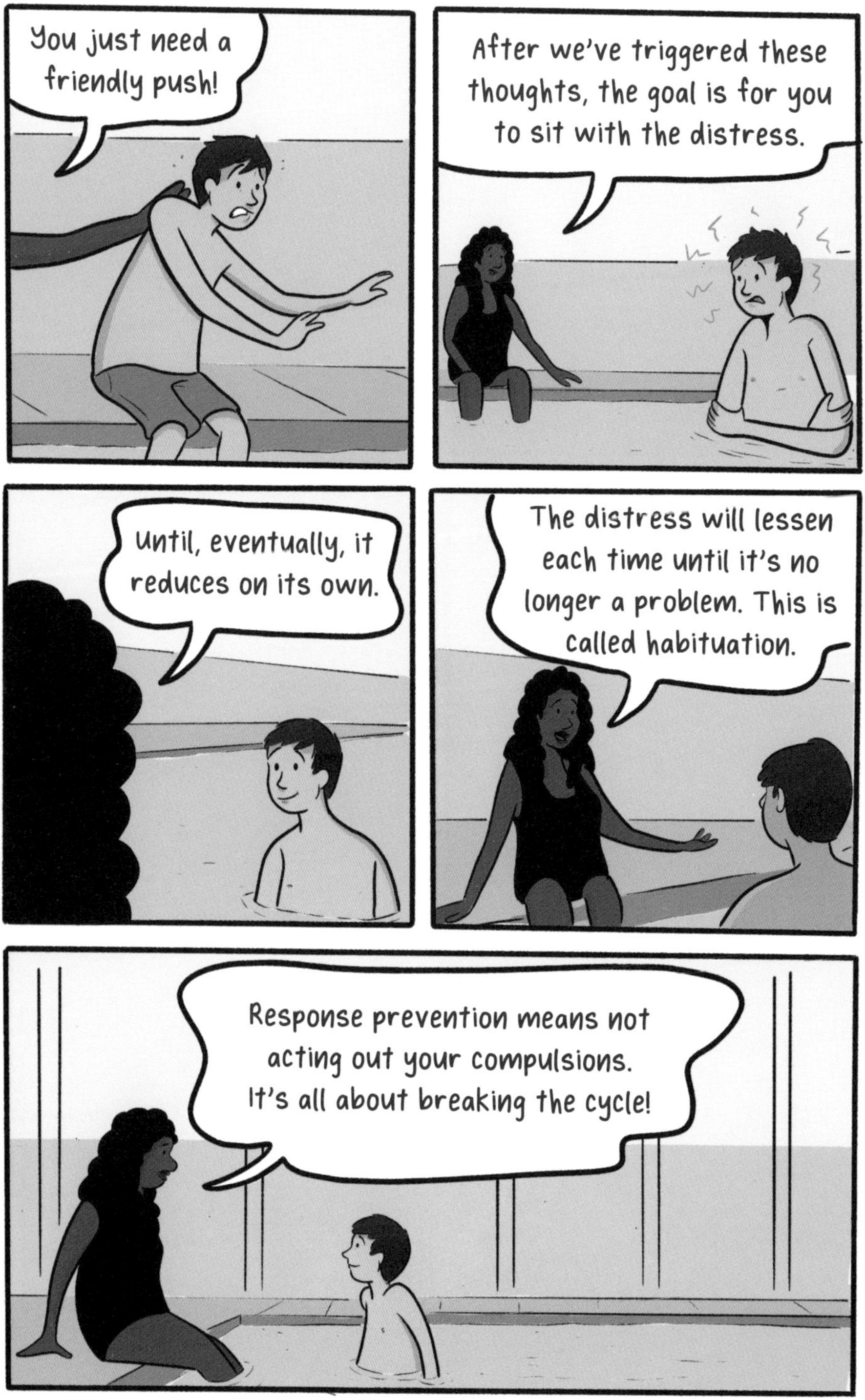

You just need a friendly push!
After we've triggered these thoughts, the goal is for you to sit with the distress.
Until, eventually, it reduces on its own.
The distress will lessen each time until it's no longer a problem. This is called habituation.
Response prevention means not acting out your compulsions. It's all about breaking the cycle!

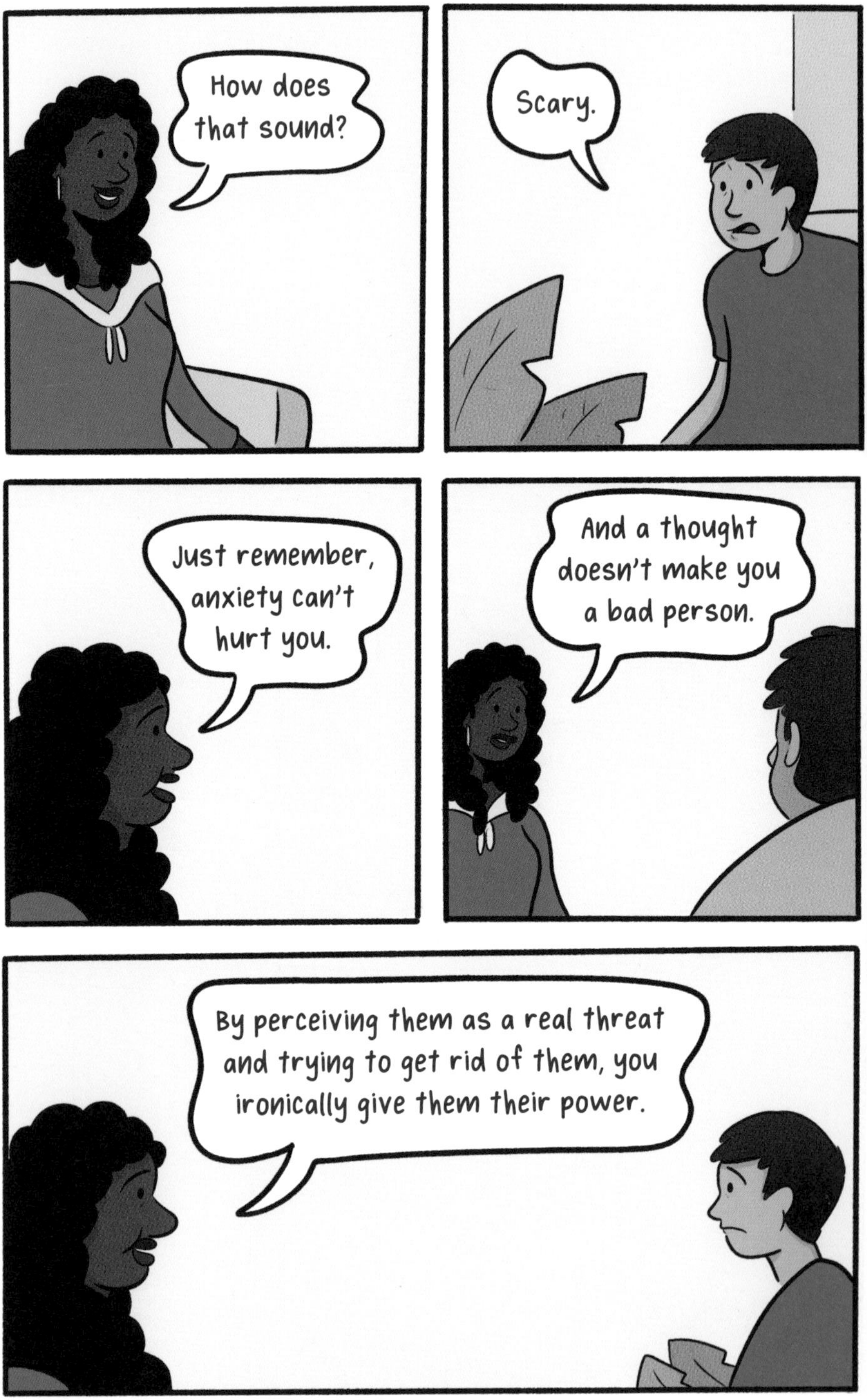
How does that sound?
Scary.
Just remember, anxiety can't hurt you.
And a thought doesn't make you a bad person.
By perceiving them as a real threat and trying to get rid of them, you ironically give them their power.

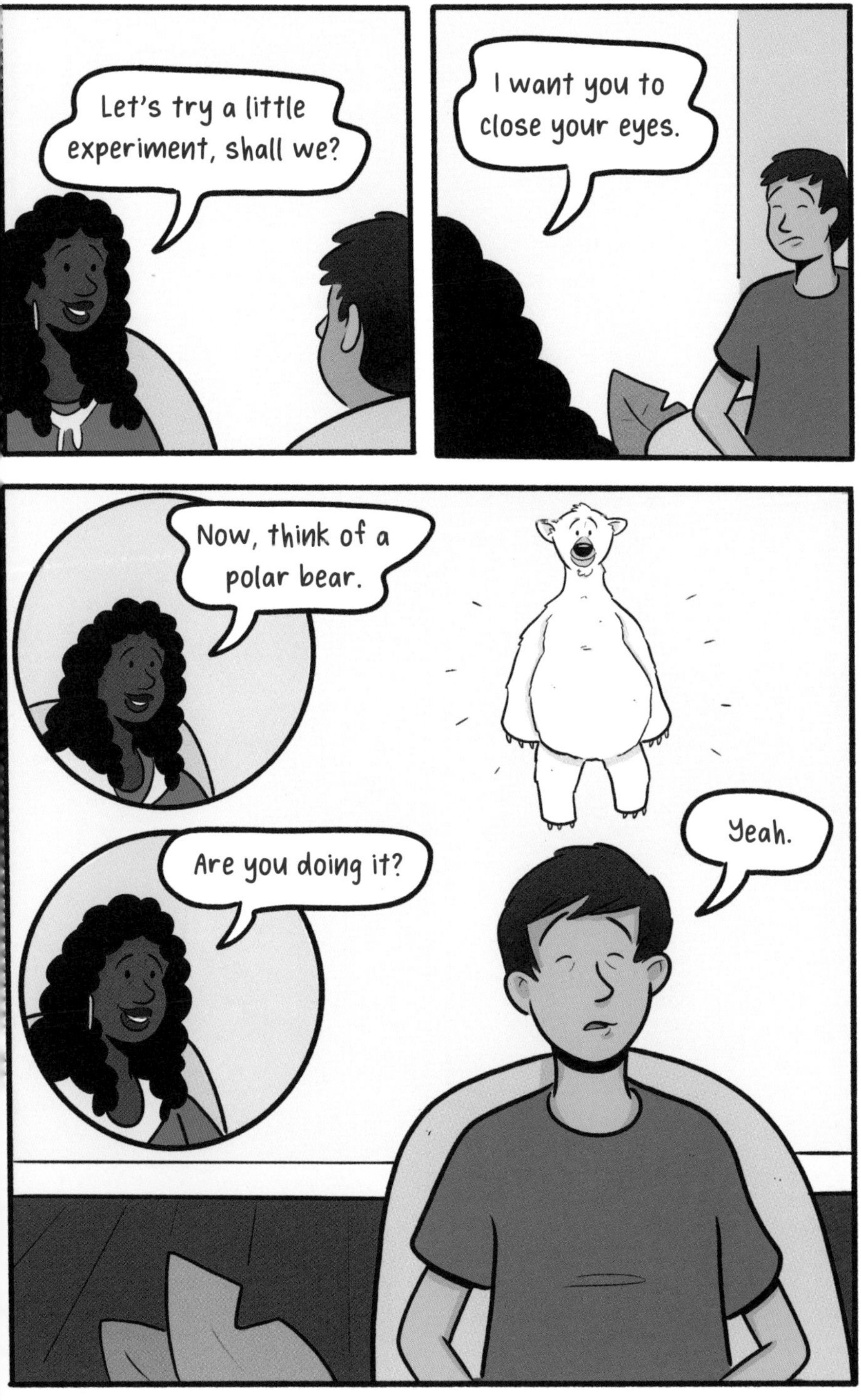
Let's try a little experiment, shall we?
I want you to close your eyes.
Now, think of a polar bear.
Are you doing it?
Yeah.

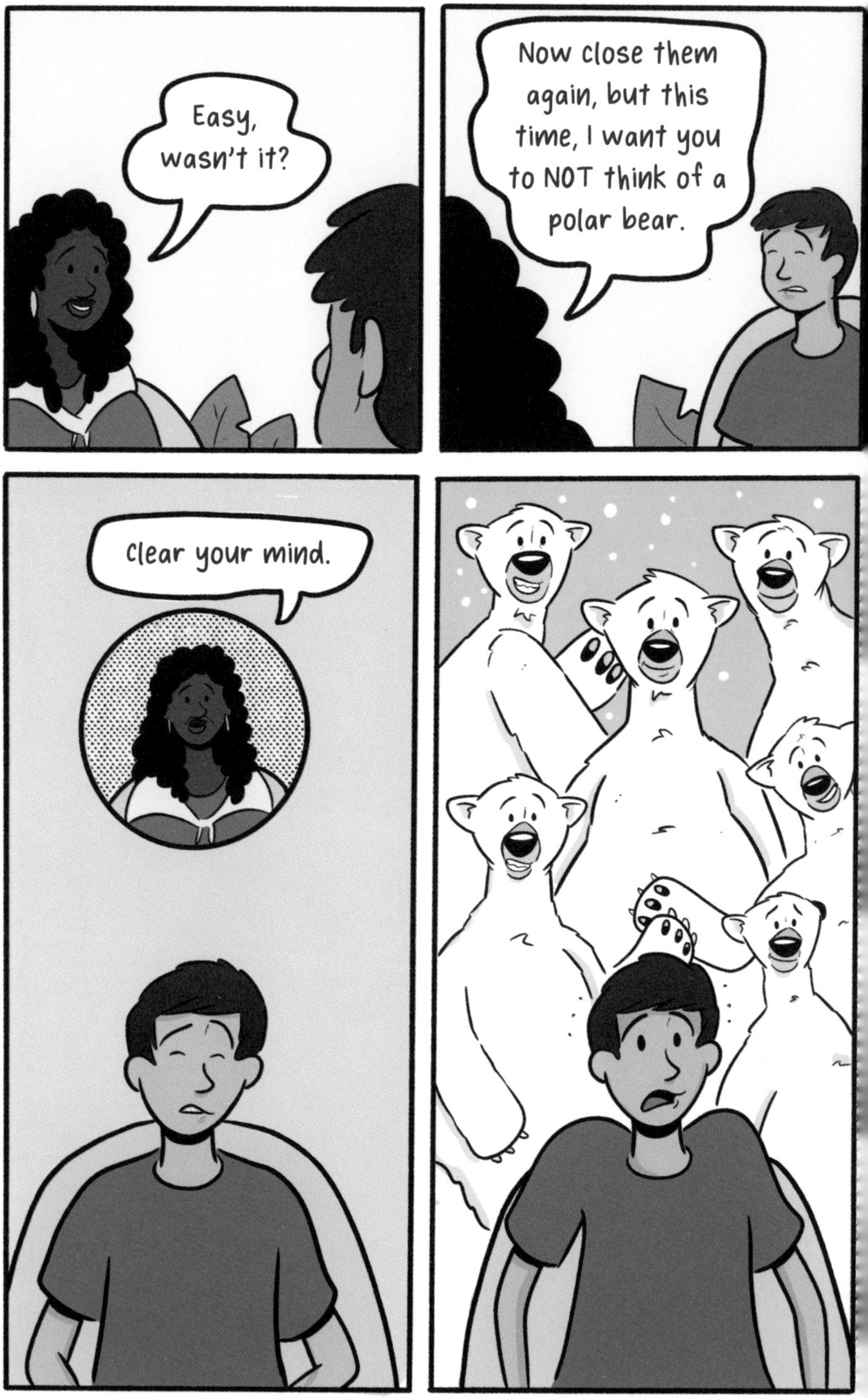
Easy, wasn't it?
Now close them again, but this time, I want you to NOT think of a polar bear.
Clear your mind.

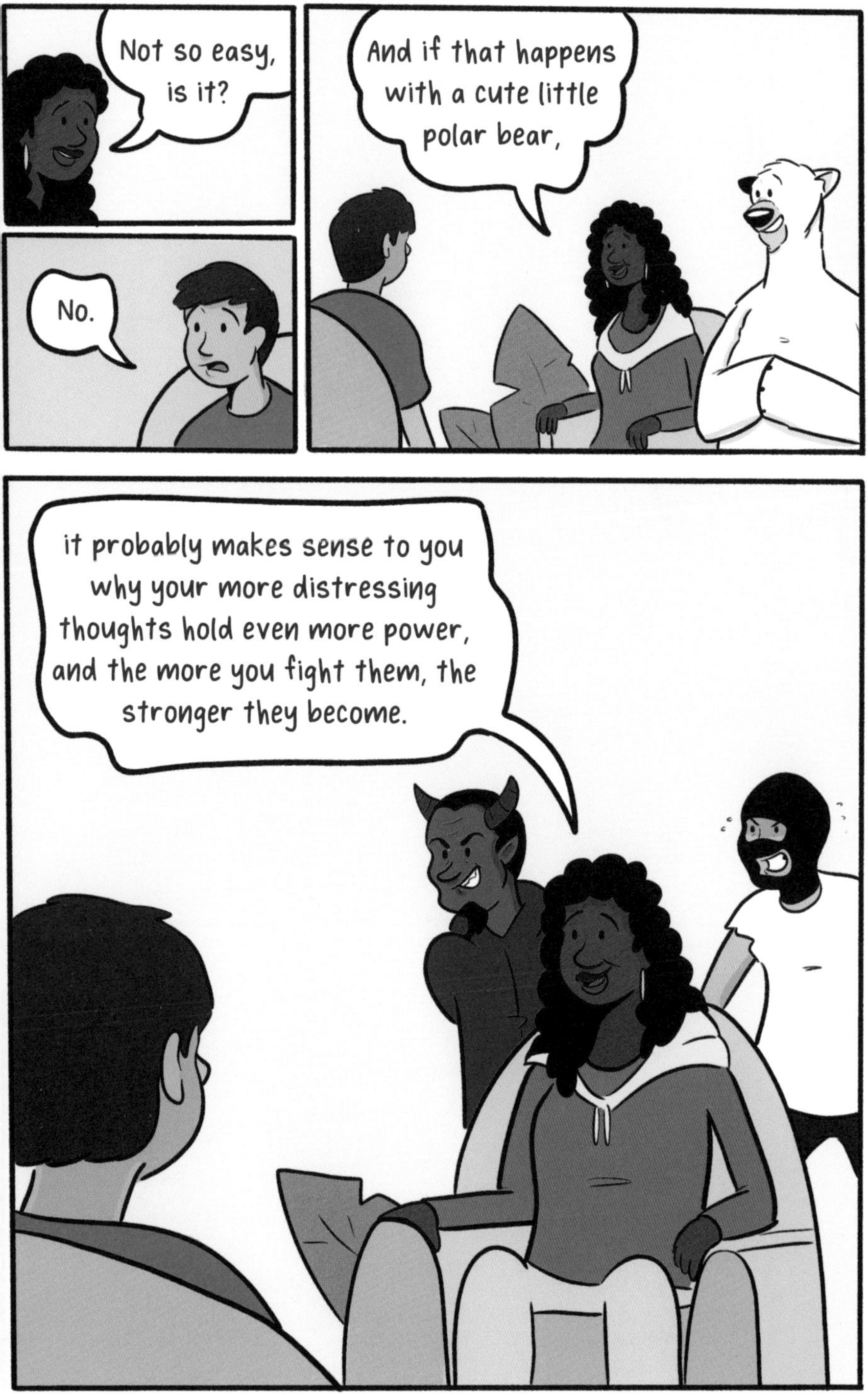
Not so easy, is it?
No.
And if that happens with a cute little polar bear,
it probably makes sense to you why your more distressing thoughts hold even more power, and the more you fight them, the stronger they become.

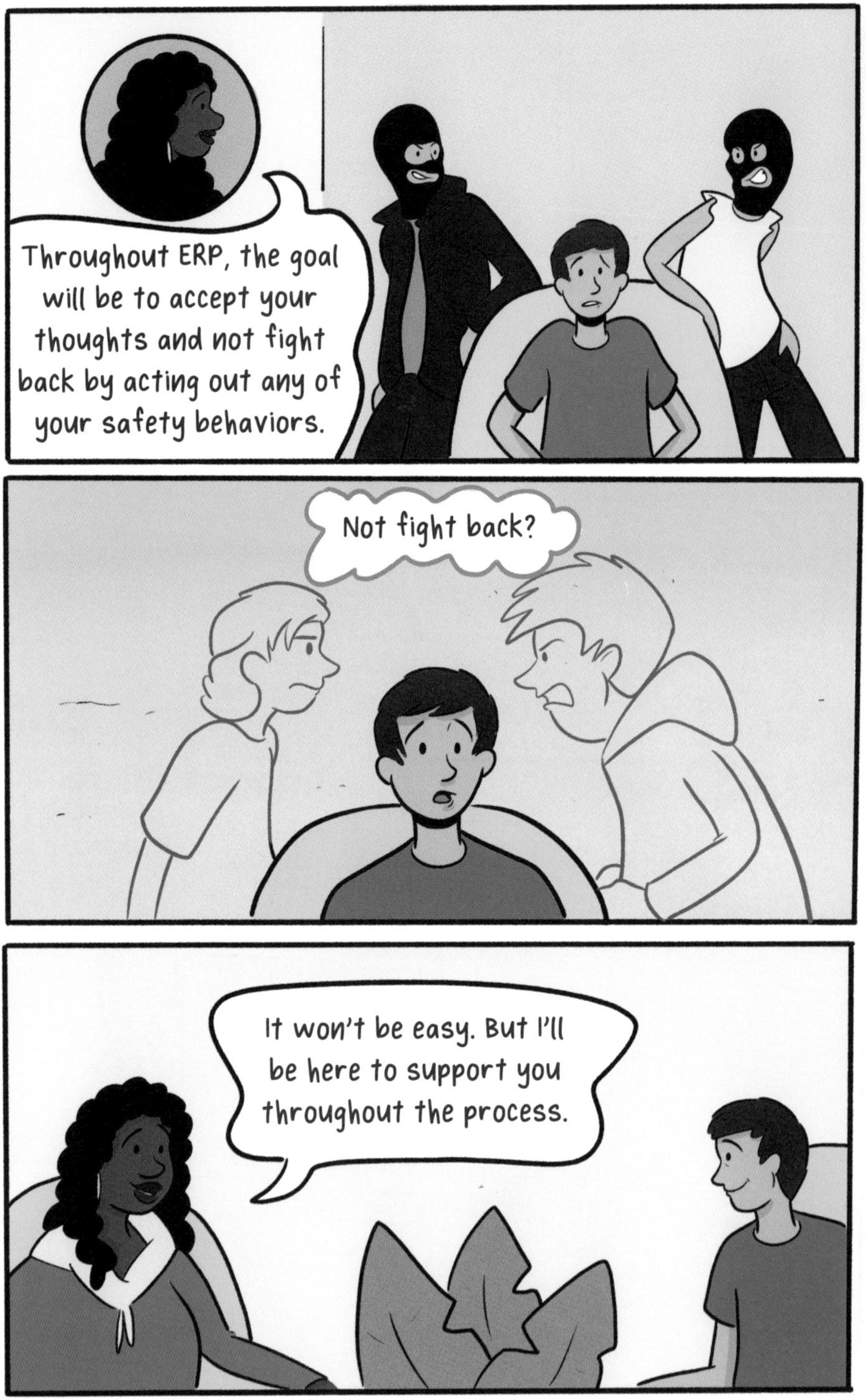
Throughout ERP, the goal will be to accept your thoughts and not fight back by acting out any of your safety behaviors.
Not fight back?
It won't be easy. But I'll be here to support you throughout the process.

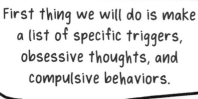

First thing we will do is make a list of specific triggers, obsessive thoughts, and compulsive behaviors.

Pan . . . ?

Sorry, yes?

What are you thinking?

Nothing. I'm just, well—

Thanks.

It's been a while, hasn't it?

Yeah.

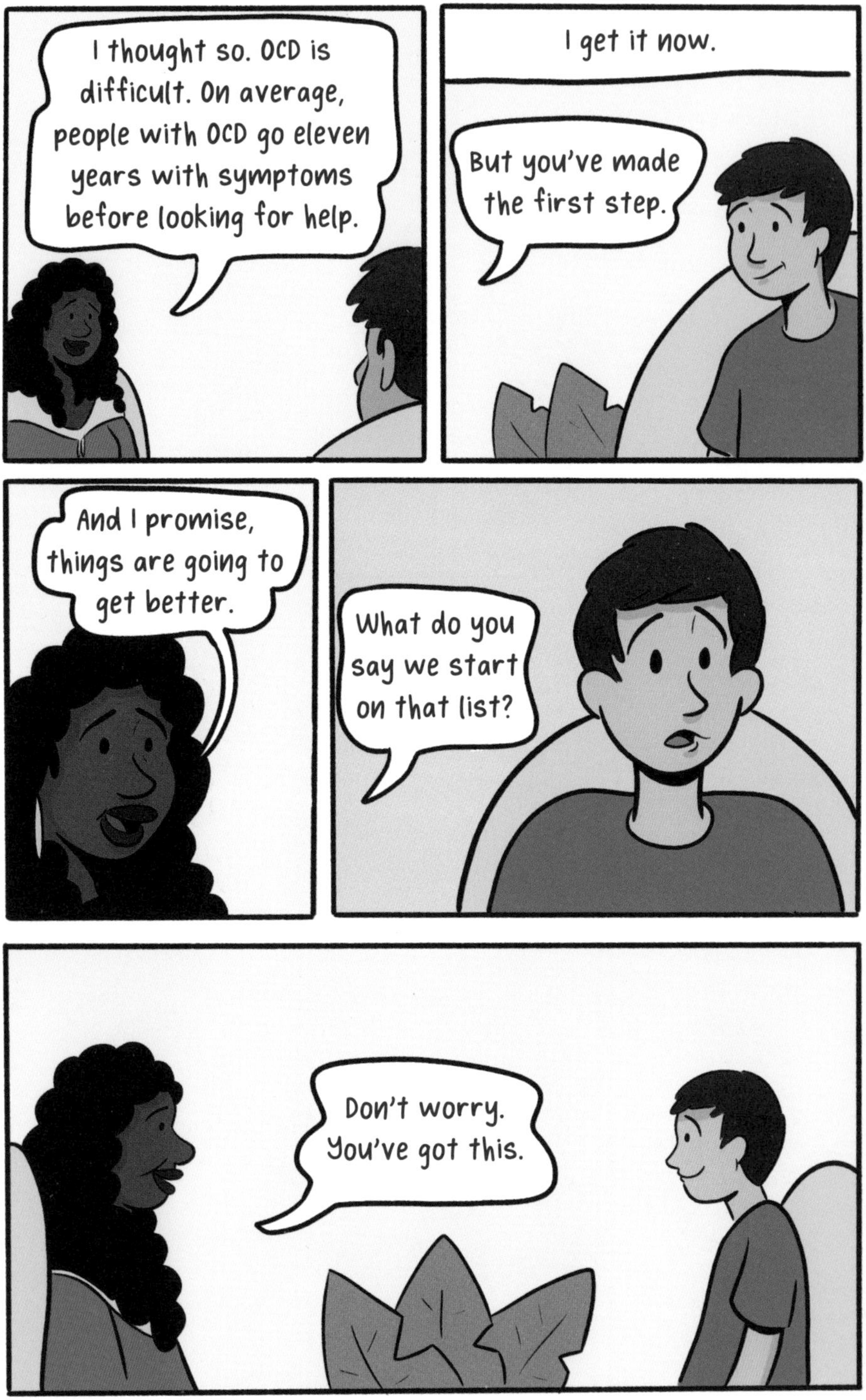
I thought so. OCD is difficult. On average, people with OCD go eleven years with symptoms before looking for help.
I get it now.
But you've made the first step.
And I promise, things are going to get better.
What do you say we start on that list?
Don't worry. You've got this.

I need to accept I'll never solve the Puzzle.

And do something else.

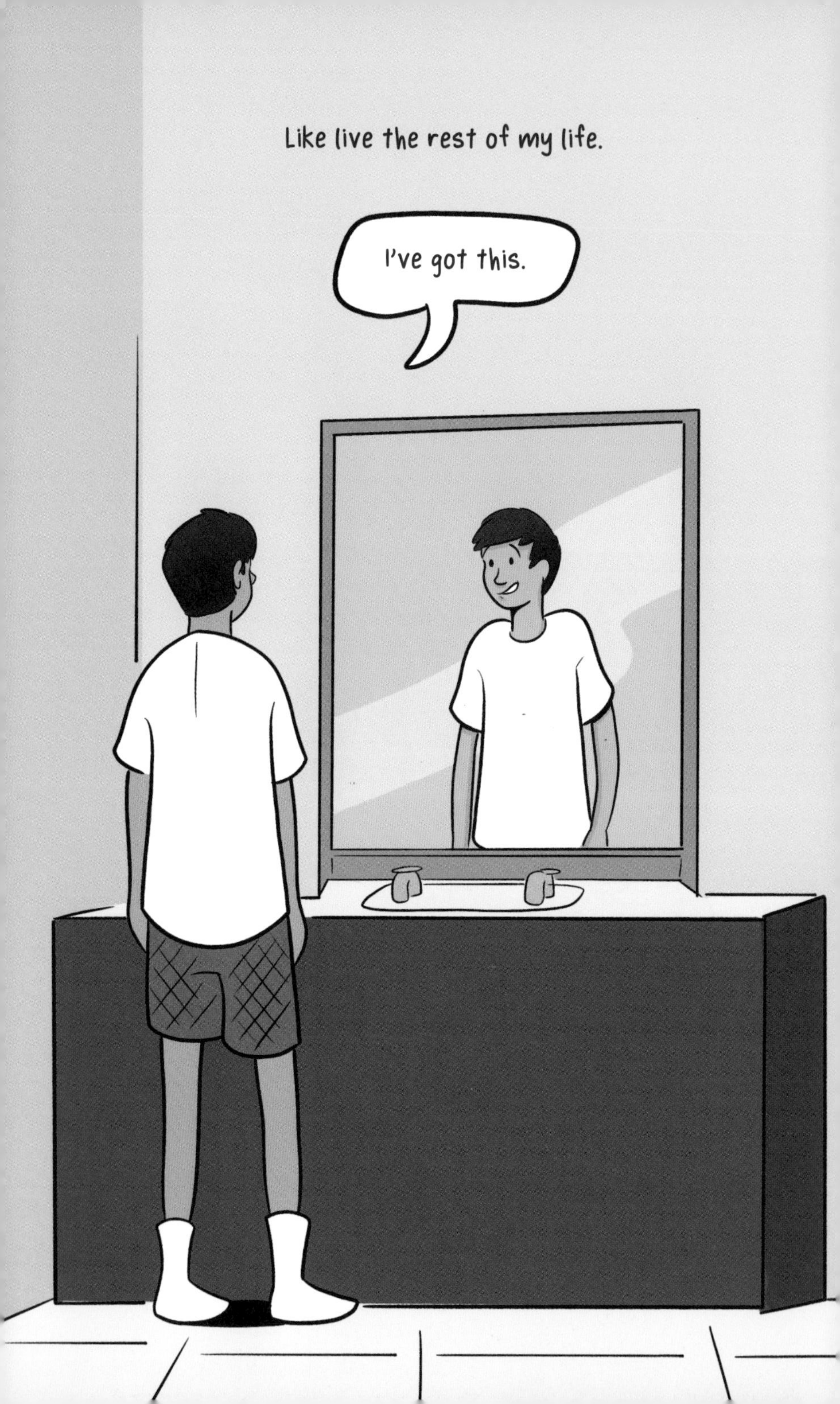
Like live the rest of my life.
I've got this.

Afterword

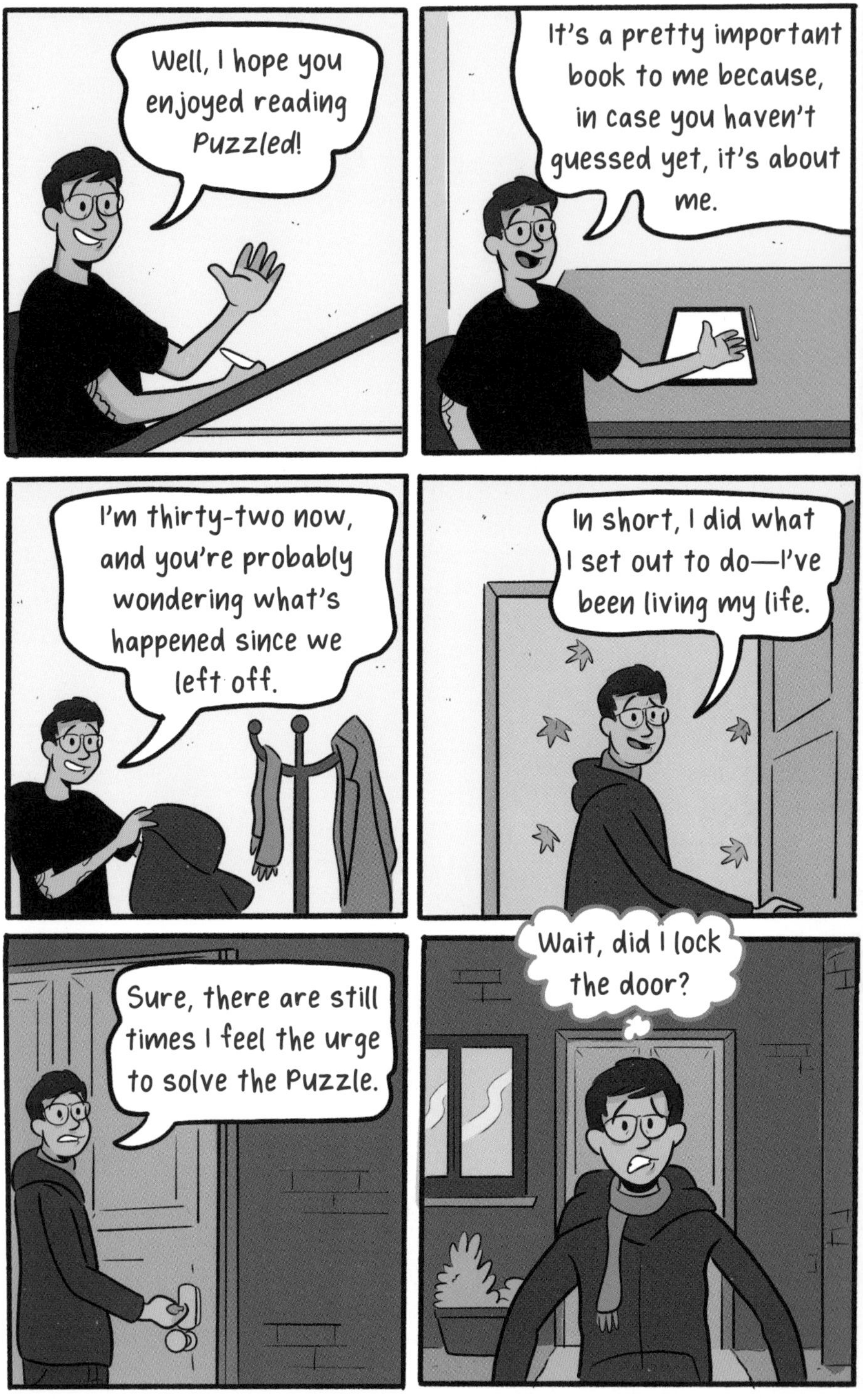
Well, I hope you enjoyed reading Puzzled!
It's a pretty important book to me because, in case you haven't guessed yet, it's about me.
I'm thirty-two now, and you're probably wondering what's happened since we left off.
In short, I did what I set out to do—I've been living my life.
Sure, there are still times I feel the urge to solve the Puzzle.
Wait, did I lock the door?

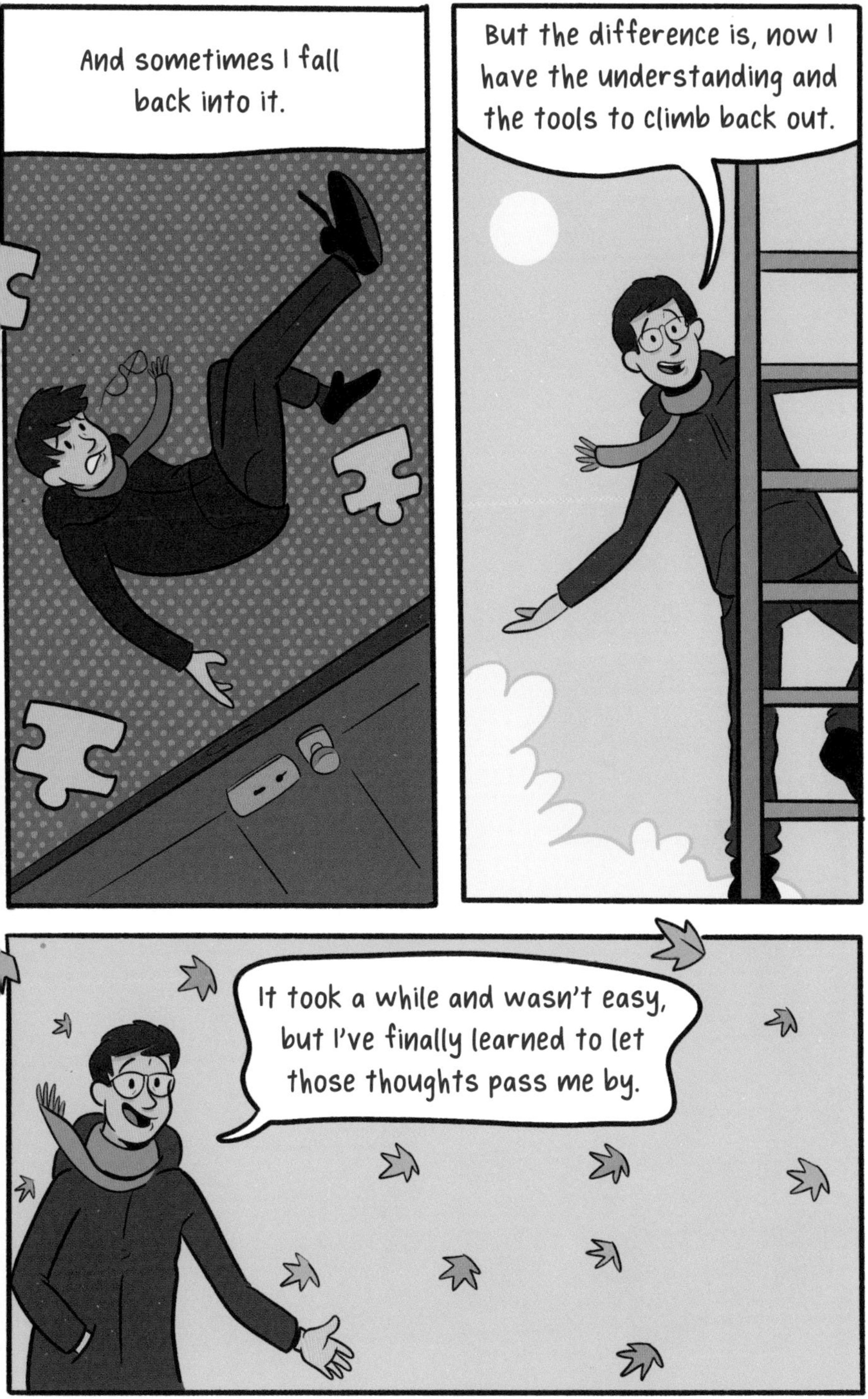
And sometimes I fall back into it.
But the difference is, now I have the understanding and the tools to climb back out.
It took a while and wasn't easy, but I've finally learned to let those thoughts pass me by.

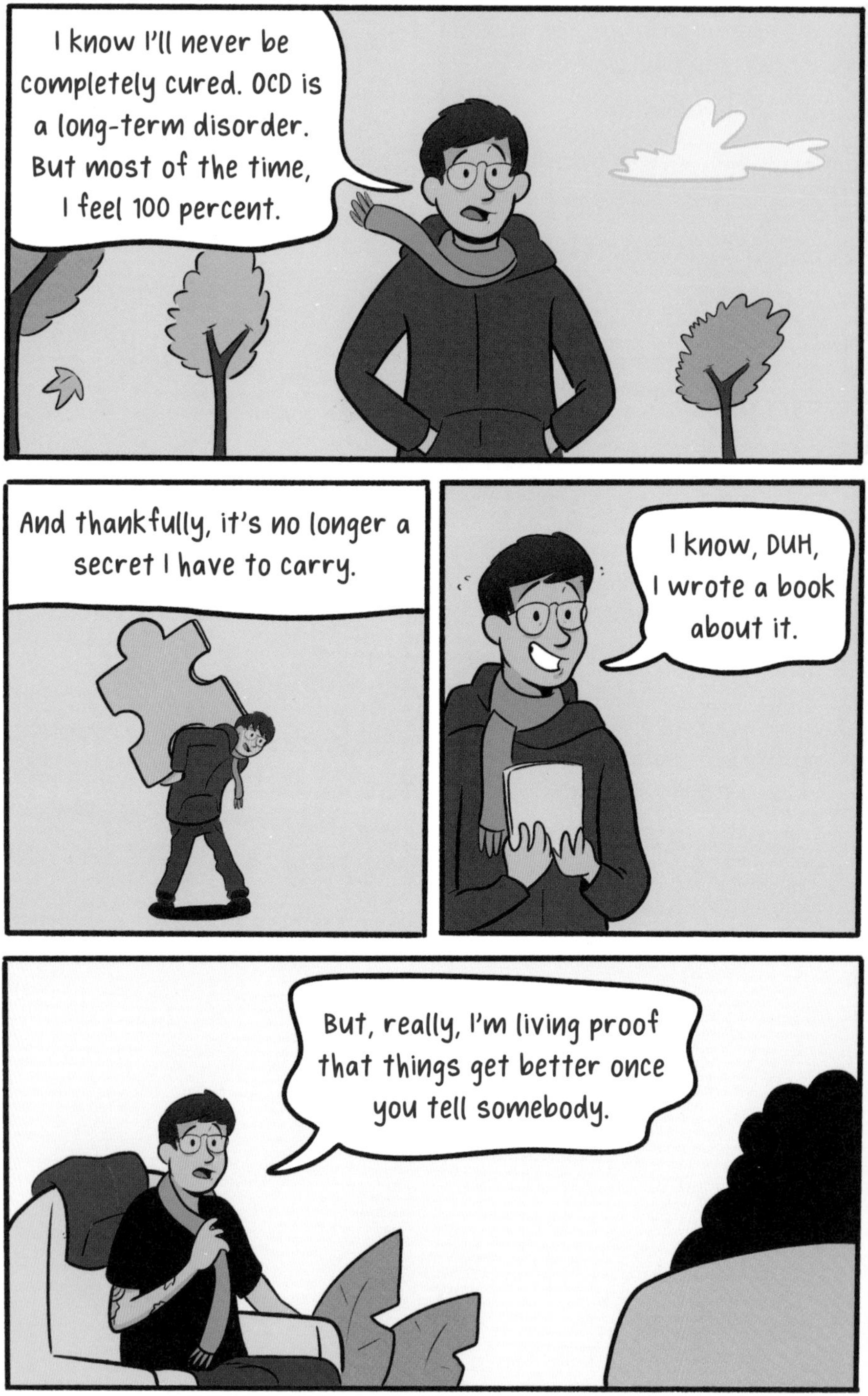
I know I'll never be completely cured. OCD is a long-term disorder. But most of the time, I feel 100 percent.
And thankfully, it's no longer a secret I have to carry.
I know, DUH, I wrote a book about it.
But, really, I'm living proof that things get better once you tell somebody.

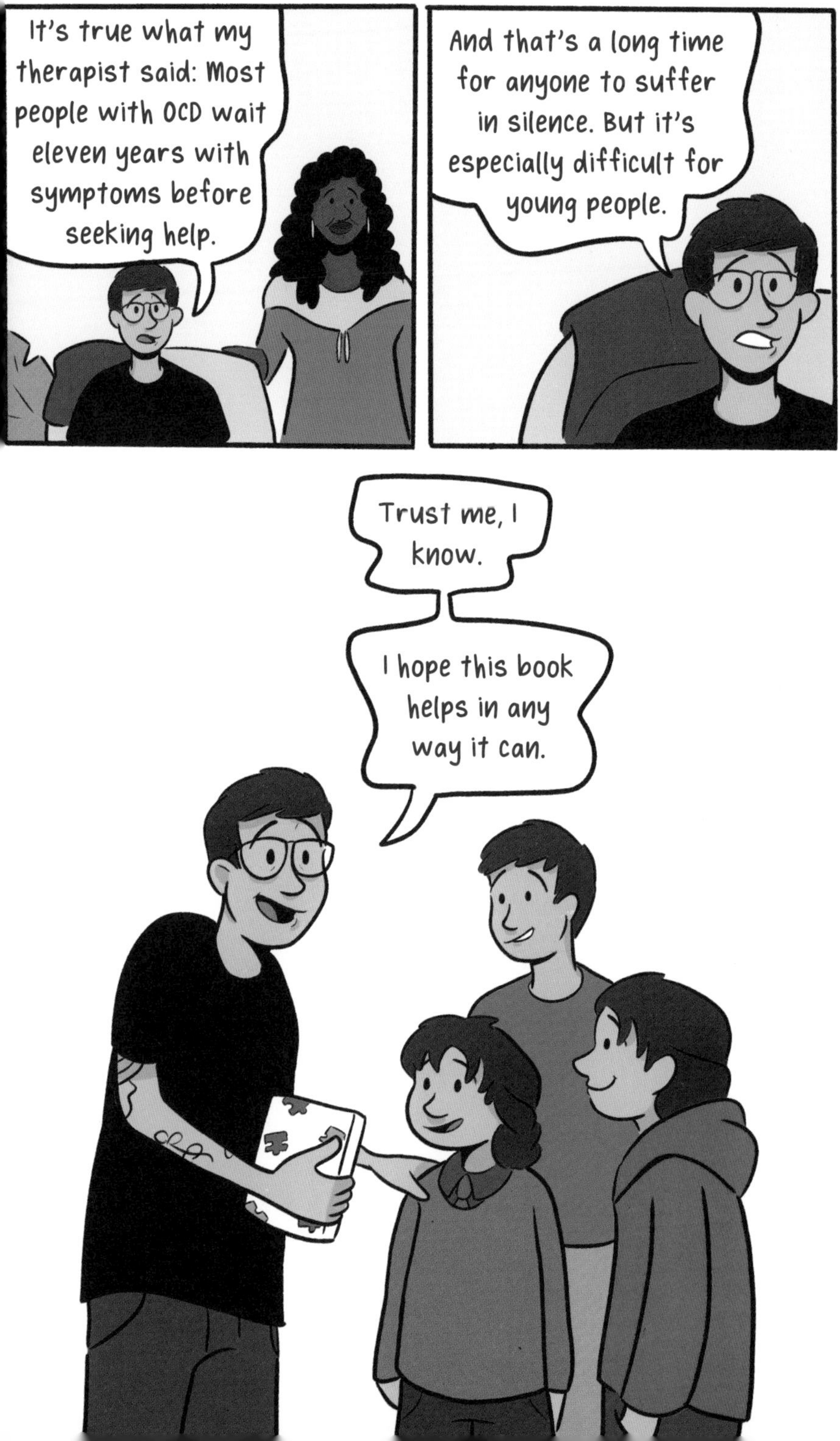
It's true what my therapist said: Most people with OCD wait eleven years with symptoms before seeking help.
And that's a long time for anyone to suffer in silence. But it's especially difficult for young people.
Trust me, I know.
I hope this book helps in any way it can.

Thanks to . . .

Firstly, Erica, for encouraging me when I needed encouragement and being my biggest fan. I can't believe how lucky I am.

Mum and Dad for believing in me.

Amy Schumer for her generosity and kindness. Without whom this book wouldn't exist.

My amazing agents, David Kuhn and Rick Richter, for their guidance and support during the early stages of *Puzzled*.

My brilliant editor, Lauri Hornik, for her insight and help every step of the way. Cerise Steel and Jennifer Kelly for their invaluable art direction, and everyone at Penguin for their belief and support.

All my readers, online and off, for supporting my work and enabling me to tell these stories. I don't take for granted how lucky I am I get to work on my passion every day.

Thank you.

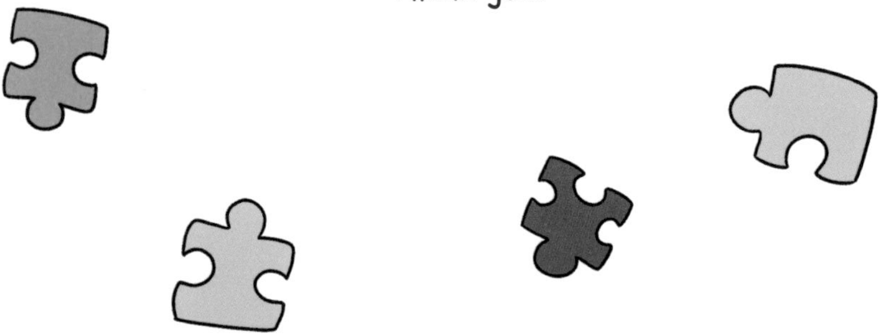

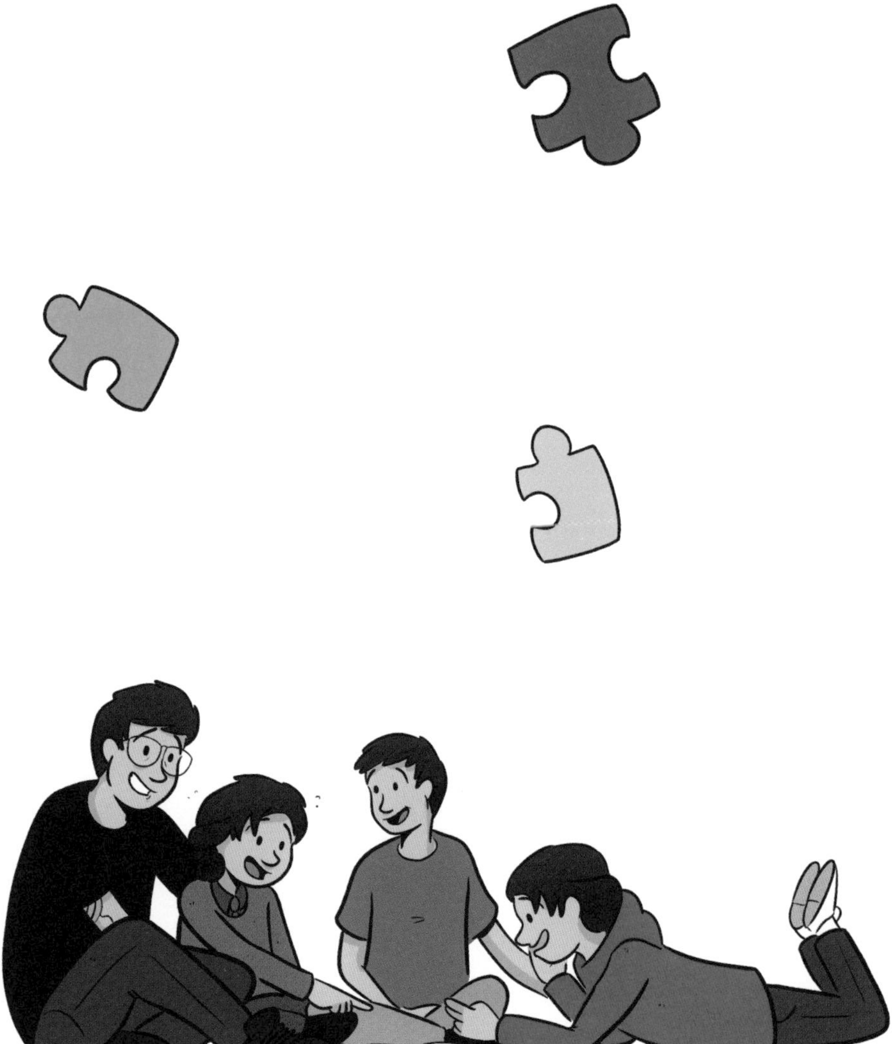

PAN COOKE is an Irish cartoonist and activist. His webcomics highlighting social justice and human rights issues are shared widely online. Collaborating with Amnesty International on several campaigns, he remains dedicated to advocating for causes he is passionate about. Pan lives in Dublin. To check out more of his work, visit his Instagram profile @thefakepan.

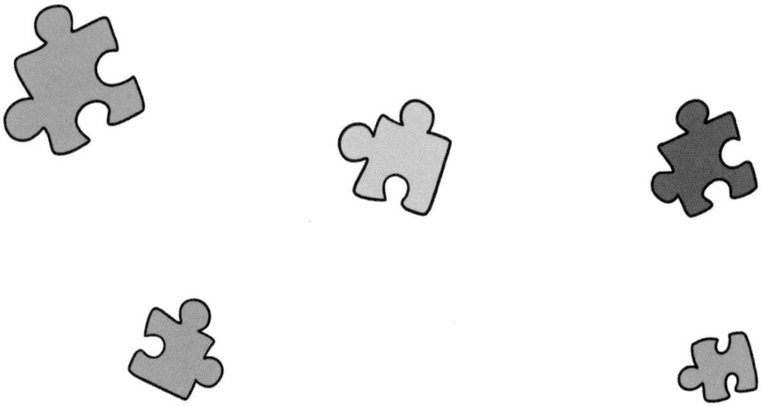